John Molony's b

GW01158299

Luther's Pine [2004]

'this beautiful book [is] about celebration, not just of the world of nature but of the triumph of the human spirit'

Ross Fitzgerald, *The Weekend Australian*, 4–5 September 2004

A Soul came into Ireland: Thomas Davis 1814–1845 [1995]

'a masterly biography of one of the most important Irishmen of the nineteenth century'

William Nolan, *Geography Publications*, 1995

The Native-Born: The First White Australians [2000]

'a work of passion and of professional seniority'

Nicholas Rothwell, *The Weekend Australian*, 7–8 October 2000

'a highly original and insightful look at Australian identity, written with great eloquence and style'

Rostrum, The History Institute of Victoria, September 2000

'the sense of belonging and longing evoked by the first generations of native-born remain relevant today'

Michael Sturma, *Australian Journal of Politics and History*, 2002

Ned Kelly [1980, 2001]

'As Professor Molony has shown, the echoes can reach out across a century and grab Australians by the throat. Who among us has stood out against oppression with the courage and flair of that boy from Greta?'

Overland, 1981

Eureka [1984, 2001]

'with controlled passion and powerful prose [Molony] has told a convincing tale about men deprived of human rights and human dignity'

Brian Dickey, *Adelaide Advertiser*, 16 February 1985

'a classic, scholarly work'

Nina Valentine, *Ballarat Courier*, 21 December 2001

The Penguin Bicentennial History of Australia [1987]

'it is the land that fascinates Molony … its fragility and beauty, its scope and contradictions and finally its mystery. This is Molony's Australia'

Kevin Peoples, Canberra Times, 13 February 1988

The Roman Mould of the Australian Catholic Church [1969]

'this scholarly volume is notable for the equilibrium with which it argues that the Catholic Church in Australia reflected the Roman structure. The faithful were seen as a support rather than an entity with their own autonomy'

Guiseppe Monsagrati, Rassegna Storica del Risorgimento, 1970

The Emergence of Political Catholicism in Italy 1919–1926 [1977]

'the first monographic history of the Partito Popolare Italiano to be published in the English language. Molony's study is more thoroughly researched than is [Richard] Webster's and he is more disinterested and impartial than [Gabriele] De Rosa, the acknowledged doyen of PPI scholarship'

Richard Camp, American Historical Review, February 1978

The Worker Question: a new historical perspective on Rerum Novarum [1991]

'an excellent original contribution to our knowledge of the encyclical'

Bruce Duncan, CsSR

AUSTRALIA,
OUR HERITAGE

John Molony

Australian Scholarly
Melbourne

© John Molony 2005

First published 2005
Australian Scholarly Publishing Pty Ltd
Suite 102, 282 Collins Street, Melbourne, Victoria 3000
Tel: 03 9654 0250 *Fax*: 03 9663 0161
Email: aspic@ozemail.com.au
www.scholarly.info

A Cataloguing-in-Publication entry for this title is
available from the National Library of Australia.

ISBN 1 74097 055 1

Page design and typesetting by Shawn Low
Printing and binding by Griffin Press
Cover design by Shaw@Neithercorp.com
Cover image by Fred Williams, by courtesy of Lyn Williams

CONTENTS

PREFACE

Some men and women turn their minds to the matter of the past of their people. They study it, think about it and then prove brave or impetuous enough to put what they have come to know into a book. The thing they have given to others is called a history and those who read it can take a step towards maturity. In so doing the readers have done well because to remain ignorant of our past is to be forever a child.

When they thought about the past some people concluded that it was a place in which the dead did things in other ways to those of the living. But it is the living who do things differently and the past is forever the same. It remains that way, a thing of the dead, until we embrace it with generosity and understanding. Then it takes on its own life: we call it our heritage.

The mistake we can easily slip into is to pick and choose the parts of our heritage that please us. By our act of selectivity we elide the dark passages of our pathways and we betray what we were. In the end we inherit a falsehood and thus we live in a delusion.

There is another path to take and we do so when we embrace all that we were; when we learn from the darkness of our past and commit ourselves to a future throbbing with hope. Racism and jingoism made us look down on, and reject, other human beings as mortals of lesser moment; ravaging the land and forgetting its frailty wounded the fibres of its being; judging progress in purely material terms created gulfs between the rich and the poor. Yet we need to pause and not go morbidly down that dark path lest we risk losing sight of the good. There is much good along the pathways we have journeyed.

Our task is to be the living link with our heritage, to be its carriers because we have been entrusted with its precious gifts. We must enrich it further and make it vital so that we can pass it on to the generations of the future.

These pages try to tell the story of the Australian past. They speak of the 2,800 generations of those who lived here in unity with the land before the coming of the whites and of the nine generations of those who have become part of this ancient land since 1788. This is a story of joy and sorrow, of birth and death, of glory and shame, of oneness and fracture. But it is our story; it will be ever thus.

We can read our story and then shelve it. We can make it part of our being and transform it. Above all we can treasure it. That way it becomes our heritage.

John Molony
Canberra, 2005

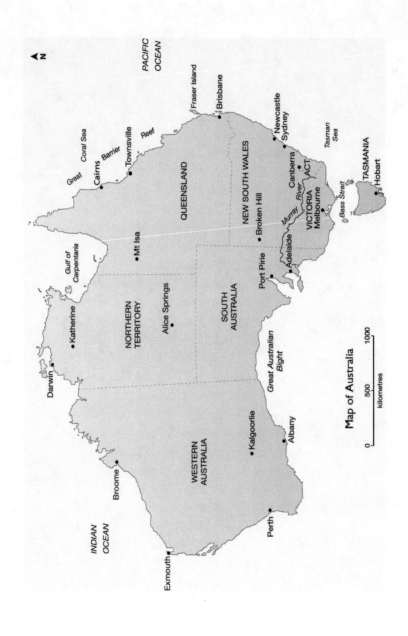

Map of Australia

1

Awakening the Dreamtime

For ages before the foundations of the Greco-Judaic world were laid, Aborigines had lived in the great land of the south. Throughout all of that time they had loved, married, mourned their dead and passed on their knowledge from generation to generation. By elaborate rituals of dance, music and song, cave and bark paintings, through rock engravings and carefully woven stories, they preserved their understanding of a past that stretched back to the dawning of the Dreamtime when all things had their origin. Their own being had no existence separate from the land, with which seashore and river, tree and shrub, rock and mountain, bird and mammal were entwined.

To these people, the question of when they came to the southland was meaningless because it presupposed a time when they were not. The sun, stars and moon had always been with them; the seasons followed each other in patterns which they understood and which they expected to recur endlessly. The mountains, rocks, rivers and plains were their landscape; life came from the land and was sustained by it, and by the community in which they lived. This continent was, and had ever been, their place; and the people of the land had always been their people. When death came it struck only at the body. The spirit returned home to its first ancestral world.

The Europeans knew exactly when they took up residence in the place they eventually named Australia and dated the event precisely, at 26 January 1788. They were slow to think about the previous arrival of the Aborigines and, when they began to do so, they made little progress. To the British settlers, one thing was clear and certain. Humans had descended through the ages as the children of Adam and Eve. If the Aborigines were part of the human race, a belonging that many whites refused to accept, they could not pre-date those Biblical parents. A literal interpretation of the Old Testament texts implied that Aborigines could not have lived in Australia for more than about 5,000 years B.C. To some scholars, this was a fanciful conclusion.

In the latter half of the Twentieth Century archaeologists studied the matter more closely and came up with astonishing results. They used a method called radiocarbon dating and applied it to remnants of organic matter to date the presence of humans. Gradually, these experts pushed the time of Aboriginal arrival back to beyond 30,000 years ago. This was remarkable enough but, recently, a new and more exact method, based on the emission of light, [thermoluminescence], had come into use by which earlier periods of up to 200,000 years can be dated. This method is accurate to within a ten per cent error and it now seems probable that the Aborigines have lived in Australia as long as 50,000 years, perhaps even 60,000 years. The experts are careful not to rule out an even longer period, but they have not yet found conclusive proof of it. The task of the archaeologists and prehistorians is to examine the evidence of the ages and explain its meaning to us. This precious work will continue long into the future.

There is still argument, however, about whether one or more distinct groups of Aborigines inhabited the continent. In 1969 and 1974 Jim Bowler of the Australian National University found skeletal remains at Lake Mungo in south western New South Wales which, at the time, were then dated from 25,000 to 30,000 years ago. The remains pointed to the conclusion that these Aborigines were essentially 'modern' people, despite the ancient time in which they lived. Almost simultaneously, at Kow Swamp, about 200 km distant from Lake Mungo, an earlier skeletal form was discovered and dated to some 13,000 years ago. Much ongoing debate has resulted from these discoveries.

There is another, related matter, on which scholars are also careful not to be dogmatic given that no conclusive proof can be adduced. Did the Aborigines, like the rest of the human race, come out of Africa where the oldest evidence of human habitation has been discovered? The 'Out of Africa' thesis holds that *Homo sapiens,* or humans as we know them today, migrated from Africa; some came as far as South-East Asia and eventually reached the islands that make up modern day Indonesia. From there they could not walk across dry land to Australia, which was isolated by oceans. However, the distance was not great and the passage was a moderately simple thing to accomplish in canoes or on rafts. Because there is now no reliable evidence available that establishes an Aboriginal presence in Australia of longer than about 50,000 years, to some experts it seems reasonable to suppose that the Aborigines came by crossing the seas. Another school of thought holds that *Homo sapiens* evolved at about the same time in various places and that the Aborigines need not have come 'Out of Africa' but directly from South-East Asia to Australia.

Little of this is acceptable to many of today's Aborigines who claim that they have always been here, despite the present lack of the evidence of primate ancestors in Australia. They point out that there is nothing in the material sources that substantiates their having come to Australia across the seas. The same applies to their communal memory that has passed down through more than 2000 generations before white contact and just over eight since. They do not deny that there has been intermingling with the peoples of Papua New Guinea because the two land masses were joined until about 8000 years ago. Nor do they deny that, in more recent times, people have joined them from Indonesia. For these matters there is proof. 'Macassans' is a word used to describe fishermen from South-East Asia, some of whom came in their praus (boats) to northern Australia from at least the 1700s to gather trepang (sea cucumbers). The Macassans had an effect on Aboriginal life during that period and left evidence of their vocabulary in Aboriginal languages; some customs were exchanged; art and ceremonies recorded their visits and children of mixed descent were born. During those years of contact some Aborigines returned home with the Macassans. Perhaps these reciprocal visits suggest a source for the incidence of venereal disease, leprosy and tuberculosis common among some Aborigines before 1788.

Tasmania, with its Aboriginal people, was once joined to the Australian mainland. From about 13,000 years ago the rising seas in Bass Strait gradually cut the island off until it became separate, and it has remained so for 8000 years. It is also thought that the dingo arrived in Australia about 3,500 years ago, and thus never reached Tasmania. This fact accounts for the survival of the Tasmanian tiger there until recently because the dingo quickly wiped out that mammal on the mainland.

Although it remains uncertain how many Aborigines there were in Australia in the first few thousand years of their migration, some claim that they took about 10,000 years to spread throughout a continent of 15 million square kilometres. Others contend that the occupation took place in only 3,000 years. In any case the continent has had an Aboriginal presence for at least 50,000 years compared with a white one for about .025 percent of that time. For many years in the Twentieth Century scholars tried to estimate the numbers of Aborigines present in Australia when the white settlers arrived in 1788. Were they few in number any guilt arising from knowledge of the ravages white invasion wreaked on the original inhabitants would be lessened. Furthermore, a small population would suggest that the Aborigines would soon become extinct which, given their alleged biological inferiority, seemed inevitable. The low figure of about 300,000 was once accepted as a reasonable estimate but more recent studies have increased that number to at least 500,000, possibly to about 750,000. How many died in the early years of white settlement, whether through disease, murder or the loss of their land and culture, can never be calculated exactly.

By 1858 there were an estimated 170,000 Aborigines in Australia. If the original population was only 300,000; over sixty years the loss was almost one-half. If there were 750,000 initially, three quarters were lost. This figure reveals a stark and tragic reality of human loss which the word decimation cannot encompass because it means only one in ten died. The figure was closer to 7.5 in every ten. The truth is even worse when it is remembered that by 1840, following the rapid occupation of pastoral land by the whites in the 1820s and 1830s, most of the damage had already been done to the Aborigines. At that time there were only 190,000 whites in Australia which means that the death of the greater part of the blacks had occurred when there were very relatively few whites in Australia. For many of those whites it was a case of seeing the Aborigines die before their own eyes.

Nonetheless, the worst killer of Aborigines during the first years of settlement was smallpox. Recent research, principally by Judith Campbell, has established that the First Fleet did not bring the disease in 1788; rather it came to Australia in the north through contact with Macassar fishermen. It then spread rapidly inland and south through the continent and, in his short term of office, (1788–1792), Governor Arthur Phillip estimated that 50 per cent of Sydney's blacks had died of smallpox. Many of them died from starvation after infection.

In 1788 the Aboriginal population in what became the Colony and State of Victoria was about 20,000. Only 774 remained in 1877 but, although some murders were probably concealed, only 500 deaths have been attributed to white atrocities. Diseases to which the Aborigines had no immunity caused most Aboriginal deaths. Besides small pox, which killed none of the whites, other infectious diseases were measles, tuberculosis, common colds, influenza, whooping cough and venereal diseases. They all contributed to the deaths across the continent that occurred with tragic rapidity, but a principal one was the loss of the will to live among many

Aborigines. The basis and structure of their existence, land and community, had been taken from them.

As this tragedy unfolded, some Aborigines asked themselves whether they had anything left to live for. For many there was no answer to that question while others carried the answer in their hearts. Derrimut, an adult male Aborigine, put the matter succinctly in Melbourne in the 1850s. After explaining how his people and his land had been taken from him, he said, 'Why me have lubra? Why me have piccanniny? Me tumble down and die very soon now.' Ironically, given the circumstances, grateful colonists later erected an inscribed tombstone over his grave in Melbourne, thanking him for his 'noble act' of saving them from a massacre allegedly planned in 1835 by 'up-country tribes of aborigines'.

The land in which the Aborigines lived throughout the last 50,000 was much as it is today. The Great Dividing Range ran down the east coast. Central Australia, known as the 'Dead Heart' by later generations of whites, was extremely dry. The marsupial animals and the birds, the eucalyptus trees, the acacias and other vegetation differed very little. However, one significant difference in the early millennia of Aboriginal occupation was the presence of some of the largest marsupials that ever existed, some weighing 2000 kilograms. There were animals called diprotodons that resembled huge cows, very large kangaroos, koalas and others, including one meat-eater about the size of a large dog. Fairly soon after the currently estimated date of arrival of the Aborigines (50,000 B.C.), the fauna began to diminish; by 10,000 years ago some forty mammals, six or so reptiles, and some birds were extinct, including all of the very large fauna. There is an understandable tendency to link the arrival of humans with that fact. The Aborigines had to survive from the land and if, to do so they were forced to burn the native vegetation and thus reduce the woodlands of the ancient animals, the result was an incidental consequence of firing rather than from deliberate intent. While no site proving slaughter as the cause of the extinction of the fauna has been unearthed, changes in vegetation took place in the period which may have been caused by burning off by Aborigines. If another event, such as cataclysmic changes in climate, caused the extermination it needs to be weighed as a causal agent together with human intervention. Nevertheless, it is difficult to explain why some animals such as the grey kangaroo and the wombat became much smaller. Perhaps, over thousands of years, they adapted as their customary food sources decreased. It is also possible that smaller animals were more able to evade hunters.

In at least one important respect the continent differed markedly from today. At its lowest ebb about 20,000 years ago, the sea level along Australia's coast line was roughly about 130 metres lower and the continent was 20 per cent larger. It cannot be established how many Aborigines lived in that larger Australia but, if the land in those coastal areas was more fertile than elsewhere, it is possible that there was a larger population than has been estimated which spread inland and through the continent. A greater rainfall than that of today is suggested by evidence of the presence of large lakes in the past, such as Lake Mungo, and of a considerably increased flow of the great river system around the Murray–Darling basin. The desert areas, with which we are now familiar, would have been less extensive as a consequence.

Over a period of about 45,000 years the climate became much colder. Fifteen thousand years ago the last glacial era had left conditions similar to those that prevail today. It is from this period that our knowledge of Aboriginal people before white settlement principally comes. This is especially so during the last 7,000 to 10,000 years when there was a change in technology in the making of smaller stone tools, food conservation and processing, seed-planting and canoe and water-bag making. The population grew larger and, in eighteen main regions, depending on climate and location, Aboriginal culture expressed itself in particular forms.

However, over a period of 50,000 years, embracing 2,000 human generations, an estimated one billion people lived on, and walked across, the Australian continent before any European had seen it. That fact needs to be stressed when so-called discoveries of Australia, as well as its exploration, are mentioned. The most remarkable thing is that, even taking into account the skilful use of burning-off, relatively little change occurred in that long period. In effect, the Aborigines lived in a state of harmony with their environment and the population was balanced with the capacity of the land to sustain it. It could even be said that Australia was one vast pastoral property managed with skill and knowledge by the Aborigines.

It is inconceivable that a billion people would not have left tangible evidence of their presence. The sources from which our knowledge of the Aborigines is drawn were not written because they did not communicate as we do. Nevertheless, reliable sources do exist from which we can establish a good deal. The material sources are often hidden beneath the layers of the ages, but they reveal their riches to the archaeologists. Digging down, they sift graves, bones (whether human or animal), remains of plants, shells and other food traces, tools and weapons. All these can and do provide evidence for archaeologists, scientists, anthropologists and pre-historians who study the ancient past. From such evidence, scanty though it may be, they can then tell us much about how people lived in those times, how they passed across the land, how they used it and even something of what happened to them in their passage through time.

Another rich source is art and the Aborigines have one of the longest art traditions in the world. Whether in caves or on rocks that are more exposed to the weather, the Aborigines painted or carved; including the remarkably delicate form called X-ray painting which shows the subjects' inner organs, whether human or animal. The earliest examples of painting possibly date back 20,000 years, but from more recent times there are paintings or carvings on bark and on artefacts, such as boomerangs and other weapons, that have also been preserved. From Aboriginal art we develop our understanding in a way that is not possible through excavation. In art we are dealing with the human spirit expressed by the creative imagination of the artists. They have translated their thought processes and their perception of reality into concrete forms. Through Aboriginal art we glimpse the emotions and the culture interwoven into those emotions. We begin to understand, even if only faintly, what it was to be an Aborigine who belonged and related to the land and the people of the times in which the art was executed.

Every people, including those lacking written means, preserve and pass on their culture. Language is the normal matrix in which communication between humans, and therefore culture, is embedded and few people have shown such a remarkable aptitude for its development as the Australian Aborigines. When 2,000 generations share their thoughts and convey them to succeeding generations over 50,000 years, a richness of language successively refined through time develops. When much of that sharing occurs among small groups situated in specific places where they must interact with other groups for peaceful relations and commerce, that richness and refinement will increase. Among the Aborigines over 250 separate and highly complex languages were spoken, each with its own subsets or dialects amounting to perhaps 650 in number. Most expert opinion holds that, apart from two Aboriginal languages, the others are related genetically and belong to a single family called Pama-Nyungan. Despite this relationship those languages can be as different from each other as French is from English. Furthermore, and especially among the women, there were also complex sign languages which permitted the Aborigines to communicate in ways peculiarly their own.

In one instance the richness of the spoken languages is exemplified by the four different words used for a newly born baby, a small baby of less than three weeks of age, a young child and a pre-pubescent child. Most Aboriginal nouns had a gender, which strictly differentiated the object referred to, so that the moon, husband of the feminine sun, was masculine. Verbs sometimes changed, dependent on the object. As an illustration, the verb to eat changed in relation to what was eaten, such as fruit, fish, or meat. To the Aborigines, water was especially important because over half the continent was arid or semi-arid, and rainfall was often low elsewhere. Thus, many of the names, which the Aborigines gave to places, were connected with the availability of water. Once engaged to be married, a ceremony sometimes took place when the bride-to-be was in her infancy; in some places an Aboriginal male thereafter addressed his future mother-in law in a different mode of language from that of the normal day-to-day. It was also common for such males to avert their eyes when in the presence of their mothers-in-law. This was one of the 'avoidance rules' practised according to kinship ties.

The Aborigines have been criticised for not having developed a form of writing. Even the Greeks, so admired for their culture, did not develop the alphabet until about 7000 B.C., and then only after long exposure to other cultures in which primitive steps in writing had been made. From the few contacts the Aborigines had with other people before 1788, little progress could be made, or expected, in a written language that stemmed from outside influences. Therefore language, in its spoken form, remained their unique tool of communication.

Of the 250 Aboriginal languages, 160 are now totally extinct, or are spoken only by so few elders that they will not survive. Of the rest, only 20 are spoken fluently and passed on to children. Thus the majority of the languages used by Aborigines in 1788 have been irrevocably lost largely through the agency of newcomers who claimed to possess a superior culture. To cause a people to lose their language is to deprive them of the essence of their culture, as well as their most vital connection with the past. It can also strip their sense of nationality from them, together with their self-respect and independence.

In the world of the Aborigines, culture was transmitted through story, ceremony and music with its structural forms and songs. Ceremony constituted a binding force that drew them together, turned their minds to the transcendental, underpinned ancestral 'law' and helped to control esoteric knowledge. It did this while also instructing, entertaining and bringing joy and pride alike to participants and to onlookers. From 1788, white society in Australia was largely secular in its origins and was imbued with elements of triumphal praise of individualism and progress. Aboriginal society, however, looked beyond itself and the term frequently used to describe that otherness, or beyondness, is 'the 'Dreaming'.

Dreaming is a word that can seriously hinder understanding because it implies the unreal. In the Aboriginal Dreaming, the past and the present, the infinite and the finite, the material and the spiritual are interwoven in a reality that is life itself. Among Aborigines there was a wide variety of beliefs about the Dreaming – from the sky-beings of the south-west of Australia to the terrestrial emphasis in the Western Desert where almost every rock embodied an ancestor. In the south-east, the first creators returned to the sky; in Gippsland, shamans did likewise to commune with the ghosts of the dead and to gain magical powers. With all its variations the essence of the Dreaming passed down through the ages through story, song, dance and music. Through belief in the Dreaming the Aborigines thought of the world in spiritual terms and, to them, life and culture were concomitant with a religious base. To them there could be no dichotomy between life and culture and to engage in a cultural act by simply looking at a painting or an engraving was meaningless. Life was culture and culture was life.

An Aboriginal map sketched in the sand or upon the soil, or drawn or painted on a bark surface, would be unintelligible to the outsider. To the Aborigines, it was a teaching instrument, a practical guide to a locality and a means of sustaining and passing on knowledge of a way of life. To the initiated Aborigine every part of that map was related to the other parts; taken as a whole, it delineated the contours of his existence. From it, he could learn the place of the water-holes, the grazing land of the kangaroo, the boundaries between his territory and that of his neighbours, the state of relationships with them, the sacred places that were never to be desecrated, the areas controlled by hostile spirits and the names, origin and meaning of the sacred spirits whose existence stemmed back to the dawn of creation. All of these things stood in relation to one another in a complex and multifaceted way. Were Uluru, for example, depicted on the map, it would be as the body of its creator, the Dreaming spirit, and it could only be understood as part of a totality. John Mulvaney has summed up the *Weltanschauung,* the conception of the world of the Aborigines; 'Expressed succinctly, their traditional world is a humanised landscape which is indivisible and immutable, and every natural feature has a name and a meaningful mythological ("Dreaming") association. Place and person are inseparable, while past and present form a unity of on-going creation.'

From his youth the Aborigine was carefully tutored in what he should do and what he should avoid, the spirit beings who would protect him and those who would harm him. He, in turn, was expected to pass on all this knowledge, this understanding of reality, to the next generation and a map would frequently help in that instruction. In many places a paramount character in Aboriginal knowledge was the rainbow, acknowledged as the great father or mother of all, and represented by a serpent. Rain was another significant ancestor, especially in the drier areas of the continent.

From the sources uncovered by archaeologists something can be learned of the day-to-day customs of the Aborigines before they came into contact with whites. Much can also be gained from reliable written sources based on detailed observations made in the years before 1800 when it was a case of Aborigines meeting whites for the first time. Their lives had not been radically changed by contact in those early years except about Sydney. In other places this generalization was applicable for longer periods where Aboriginal customs were not newly created or influenced by white contact but they had a background in antiquity. It is not possible to observe what was happening in one place and conclude that the customs and social circumstances seen there applied to other Aborigines throughout the whole continent.

Early observers, some of them acute-minded and well-balanced men like David Collins, took note of the Aborigines in the Sydney area, of their customs, language, numbers, frequency of movement and of the nature of their dwellings. Their homes were extremely modest and simple, frail bark constructions that provided little more than a form of temporary protection from the weather. Collins said: 'Their habitations are as rude as imagination can conceive.' The people who lived in them did not wander about aimlessly, but moved in the same area to find sources of food, fish and oysters, if they lived near the coast. They joined together in small groups and their total numbers in the same locality were low, with about thirty being the upper limit. Collins's and similar observations tended to become the norm so that Aborigines in general were thought of as few in number in any one place, as incapable of building permanent dwellings and as nomadic in their habits. That generalizations took hold in the minds of most whites and still persists.

To the first Europeans it seemed obvious that the Aborigines used the land only as a place in which to hunt and to gather foodstuffs. They then concluded that the Aborigines did not own the land and that the continent lay open for the taking – for agriculture and grazing. Yet, there were notable examples of whites who believed that the Aborigines had been robbed of their land and that the day would come when white society would pay dearly for its occupation by force.

On the islands off the Queensland coast and – as it was subsequently realized – throughout the continent itself, there was material evidence of human habitation that proved the existence of a people with a developed and intricate culture who had lived in possession of, and harmony with, the land and had done so for almost countless generations. Middens or large heaps of shells, carefully delineated tracks of passage, stone ovens, quarries and sites from which the material for tools was extracted, areas for ceremony and ritual, traps and dams to catch fish: all attested to a permanent and productive human presence. If it had been in the mind of the Aborigines that the land they lived on, and from, did not belong to them according to their sense of ownership, why then did so many of them resist, often unto death, the wresting of it from them by white invaders? They resisted by attempting to repel the white invader of their homeland and their resistance was judged to be a criminal offence.

Other false generalizations also took hold, including that of the profligacy of Aboriginal women. Nonetheless, it soon became apparent to unbiased observers that, generally and in favourable economic circumstances, the women did not freely consent to sexual relations with whites and that their own men often decisively repulsed any advances made by whites to their womenfolk. There was also a widespread concept that Aboriginal women generally lacked the accepted characteristics by which physical beauty was gauged. The surveyor general and explorer, John Oxley, referring to the Stradbroke Islanders, remarked, 'The women that I saw were far superior in personal beauty to the men, or indeed to any native of any country whom I have yet seen.' Others described Aboriginal men as masculine, tall, graceful and swift in movement.

There have also been accusations of cannibalism among the Aborigines. Yet, such cannibalism, to the extent that it did occur among the Aborigines, was of a ritual form and based upon respect, not savagery. It was a means of identifying with a deceased who had a direct kinship and spiritual relationship with the living or of proving mastery over a dead enemy by eating a portion of his thigh. Major Collins had reported of the Sydney blacks in the first years of settlement that 'On our speaking of cannibalism, they expressed great horror at the mention, and said it was wee-re [bad or wrong]'. In 1825 Major Edmund Lockyer said of the people of Stradbroke Island. 'Stories told of their cannibalism are fabulous and absurd'.

Stradbroke Island is 27,000 hectares in extent and lies off Brisbane. In 1803, Matthew Flinders visited the island, but little is learnt from his brief stay. Over the next twenty years other whites visited the island and among them was Peter Finnigan who spent some time there in 1823. He found there were numerous habitations belonging to a defined group who were 'occupying its own designated area' which indicated that some form of 'ownership', often passed on through the paternal line, was known. Furthermore, the Aborigines on the island lived in 'very large, well built huts … forming a village'; there were thousands of 'blacks' in the whole area and 'they were far more advanced in civilized life than the Aborigines about Sydney.' In 1824 Allan Cunningham stated that he entered one dwelling on the island by 'a low doorway, [which] presented a capacious area, nearly 50 [17 metres] across, amply sufficient to afford shelter and accommodation to 40 persons … ' It has been claimed that Aboriginal women took a major role in building such dwellings.

Some years later a visiting naturalist travelled to Bribie Island, 50 miles to the north, of Brisbane and wrote of dwellings there 'of great length, extending upward of eighty feet [26 metres] … One of them was in the form of a passage with two apartments at the end. The arches were beautifully turned, and executed with a degree of skill which would not have disgraced an European architect.' The roofs of these dwellings were made from tightly bound paper bark and were capable of withstanding the wildest storms. In 1861 Burke and Wills passed an Aboriginal camp a few miles inland on the Gulf of Carpentaria. They saw 'a fine hut' which was 'much larger and more complete' than those they had seen at Cooper Creek and they thought it could house a dozen people in comfort. They also noticed that the blacks had been digging yams and, having selected the best, they had left the others scattered about. Wills said, 'We were not so particular, but ate many of those that they had rejected, and found them very good.'

In 1799 Matthew Flinders, accompanied by the Sydney native, Bungaree, was sent to gain information of the coastal areas far to the north of Port Jackson. He arrived at Moreton Bay in August and concluded that technological developments among the Aborigines of the area surpassed those in use at Port Jackson. To Flinders, these innovations had resulted in a 'favourable change', in the 'manners and disposition' of the Aborigines of the area. In particular he noted that they made large canoes and nets, up to eighty feet in length, to catch fish. Other observers at the same place were surprised that the Aborigines knew the local dolphins by name, welcomed them when they came near the shore and used them to drive in shoals of mullet which were then easily caught. The same phenomenon was noted elsewhere on the Queensland coast.

Flinders also commented that the natives were introduced to him by name in a ceremonial manner and, 'being encouraged and requested by signs to sing, they began a song in concert, which actually was musical and pleasing, and not merely in the diatonic scale, descending by thirds, as at Port Jackson: the descent of this was waving, in rather a melancholy soothing strain.' Bungaree followed with a Sydney song that 'sounded barbarous and grating to the ear' which prompted the locals to again respond. They, 'having fallen to the low pitch of their voices, recommenced their song at the octave, which was accompanied by slow and not ungraceful motions of the body and limbs, their hands being held up in a supplicating posture, and the tone and manner of their song and gestures seemed to bespeak the goodwill and forbearance of their auditors'. More natives then arrived and 'a general song and dance was commenced. Their singing was not confined to one air: they gave three, but the first was the most pleasing.'

After the onslaught of small pox and other diseases, the Sydney blacks had been greatly reduced in number and in the cohesiveness of their society. Their sense of helplessness and dislocation had profound effects on them and especially on the males whose feeling of responsibility for the women and children was tested in the extreme. In that early period of white contact, David Collins, during his residency (1788 to 1797) as judge-advocate at Sydney, wrote at length about what he learned by personal observation of the local Aborigines. He also came into regular contact with Bennelong and Colbee, two Aborigines from whom he was able to glean information

The way in which Aboriginal men around Sydney generally treated their women was deplorable by any standards of acceptable human behaviour. That there was 'a delicacy visible in the manners of the females' served to worsen in Collins's mind their regular subjection to violence 'of the most brutal nature' which made them 'the unfortunate victims of lust and cruelty.' Bennelong, who had come into close and friendly contact with Governor Phillip and other whites, had 'severely beaten' his wife a few hours before she was delivered of a child, while Colbee murdered at least two young Aboriginal women. When a male treated his women violently, such behaviour was regarded as his business and it seems that no mechanism existed to punish him for it. Notwithstanding the above, it cannot be substantiated that, before and in the early stages of white settlement, violence to Aboriginal women among all groups was widespread and therefore deeply embedded in the culture. Yet it is certainly undeniable that, when violence occurred by the forced and violent abduction of women, the common response was to reply in kind rather than to prevent or deplore it.

Collins also remarked upon the practice of abortion – effected by 'pressing the body in such a way, as to destroy the infant in the womb' – often also causing the death of the mother. Abortion, and the practice of burying the live baby with its mother who had died in childbirth, added to the loss of Aboriginal life and resulted in a high death rate when joined to the numbers lost in what seemed to him an almost constant state of internecine warfare among the males. Collins connected the rapid fall in population of Aborigines in the Sydney area to these practices, but small pox and the effects of dislocation were more likely reasons. Nevertheless, abortion and infanticide seem to have been common methods of population control.

The Aboriginal system of 'pay back', by which injuries or other wrongs were settled by retaliation, banishment or spearing in the thigh, marked an attempt to bring reciprocal violence within the ambit of the 'Law' as the Aborigines understood it. Retaliation for sexual transgressions, homicide and injury was customary. In the case of a death, it was often seen as being caused by an enemy's sorcery. Given the sense of self-respect among Aborigines, an effective method of retaliation was 'shaming' which made the offender conscious of the gravity of the transgression. When punishment went to the extent of exclusion from the group, it virtually amounted to the death penalty because an the Aborigine lost part of his essence when cut off from a relationship with his kin.

The family was the basic unit of Aboriginal society, even though polygamy was widespread. Some men had several wives in northeast Arnhem Land but perhaps only two in Gippsland and in the Darling–Barwon River regions. The number of wives depended on kinship and environmental factors, but rich resources and a high population were necessary for high rates of polygamy. Given that older men were favoured in obtaining wives (who usually entered into marriage at puberty), it is not surprising that some young wives sought, or accepted, relationships with other men. Such behaviour did not necessarily cause resentment on the part of the elderly husband provided there was a bond of kinship with the interloper. Divorce and separation were acceptable, but there is no evidence of homosexuality or lesbianism being common in pre-contact Aboriginal society. Illegitimacy was unknown because new life came into the mother's womb as a spirit child and therefore lacked carnal paternity. None-the-less it was often believed that the conception spirit was 'found' by the mother's husband. Slavery was unknown among Aborigines.

By and large the whites convinced themselves of the Aborigines' intellectual inferiority. Such an idea fitted neatly into the prevailing ethos of eugenics, which held that the black races were inferior to the white in their intellectual development. Thus they were said to lack the ability to perform simple feats of arithmetic. In fact they were able to count, add and subtract in effective ways and the Aborigines of eastern Cape York Peninsula had a complex counting system related to the positions of the arms. Yet, this conviction of intellectual inferiority became the basis of a persistent prejudice against them. That it is mistaken is clear and evidence on the complex structures of Aboriginal society furnishes proof that they were at least intellectually equal to any other race on earth.

At the same time, Aborigines often expressed themselves in ways that were beyond the understanding of the whites, which merely served to strengthen the prevailing bias against them. A striking example was the basic element of kinship that regulated social relations among them. It was made up of numerous, intricate and highly developed networks governing such matters as the application of the 'Law', language, marriage and the sense and use of the concept of 'country'. That the concept of kinship was more deeply embedded in Aboriginal society than among Europeans only served to further hinder the development of mutual understanding between the two races.

The first concern of every race is survival, as individuals, and as a collective. In both senses Aborigines survived in Australia for 50, 000 years, which proves their ability to adapt to its conditions and to vary or modify them when necessity demanded. In like manner they attempted to control their inter-tribal conflicts so as to cause a minimal loss of life. While not imposing modern concepts of warfare on the Aborigines, it is clear that conflict often arose among them due to disputes about land, to the abduction of women and to revenge. A large number of weapons were made, including clubs, spears, boomerangs and shields and stones, the use of which was not confined to hunting native fauna. Collins noted that some Eora men used a type of walking stick made necessary by injuries received before the arrival of the whites and Watkin Tench was told by Gomberee, a Darug man of the Hawkesbury area, of the warfare engaged in by his people. The numbers engaged in such wars were small and the conflict limited. High death rates in conflict would have devastated Aboriginal society.

David Collins remarked on the eagerness with which local groups of Aboriginal males fought each other in Sydney. He was impressed by their skills when throwing and deflecting spears, and also noted that no deaths occurred on these occasions. What did not cross his mind was the probability that it was all a kind of pantomime staged for the benefit of the whites who gathered eagerly for the spectacle in much the same manner as crowds flocked to public executions in London. For their part the Aborigines deplored the savagery with which the white authorities punished convicts for breaking the law. The Aborigines were not above displaying their own savagery for the benefit of whites who sometimes rewarded them with food, grog and tobacco.

One striking fact is that the Aborigines alone have understood the land. The ravages caused by a lack of understanding among the white population are evident in salinity, polluted waterways, soil erosion and forests subjected to fierce and uncontrollable bushfires. Through 2,000 generations the land fed over a billon people. Periodic, but regular, burning off, served to purify the land and make it more productive of verdant grasses, thereby providing a source of food for the kangaroos and other fauna. By burning off the Aborigines created vast pastures that were crucial to later European expansion and that had a profound impact on the ecology for many centuries. Yet, it was the Aborigines who passed the land down unchanged in its essence. They were Australia's first pastoralists of Australia but the soft, padded feet of their 'flocks' did not break through the fragile surface of the land as the hard-hoofed flocks and herds of the whites did.

In their first settlement, and for decades afterwards, the whites hugged the coastal areas. What they called the 'bush' or the 'outback' was, and in great measure remained a dangerous unknown. To the Aborigines in those places it was their home, they were part of it, and it was entwined with them. Even in desert areas they were able to subsist on food and water in a way that the whites were unable to imitate as the unhappy fate of the explorers Burke and Wills later proved. In Torres Strait Aboriginal farming was common, especially of coconuts and bananas, but throughout the continent there were practices of land and resource management similar to those seen elsewhere. Great care was taken not to deplete a tree of its fruit, for example the bush berry tree, in such a way as to denude it. There were also systems of crop selectivity and new plants were introduced to suitable environments. Besides their skill in tracking game, Aborigines were able to find water in unexpected places, and to extract it from certain trees. In both instances they took care never to drain the precious resource to depletion.

When the Aborigines expressed their concept of land they used a word more akin to that of 'country'. Among them, the passing on of the concept of 'country', – the place to which one belonged and where one's own 'mob' was to be found – was a primary responsibility of the elders; it was also one in which Aboriginal mothers had a role. This perhaps stemmed from the realization that the sense of relationship between a mother and child best conveyed the meaning of 'country.' John Mulvaney has related the story of Jackey White who was pining away on a mission station in western Victoria. Jackey said, 'This country don't suit me I'm a stranger in this country I like to be in my own country.' His 'country' was only thirty miles away but that distance, for Jackey, was immense, involving as it did another world. He no longer sensed the bonds with his 'country' or his 'mob'.

A 'country' was the land on which individuals or groups of Aborigines had their dwellings and from which they drew their sustenance. The 'country' of any given group, or related number of groups, was carefully defined. Kinship ties, especially through the mother, meant that to conduct business, to obtain food and water or to attend and participate in ceremonies, or to visit sacred sites, they were able to enter or pass through another 'country' by right.

Other Aborigines without such ties were strictly bound to obtain permission to do so.

Movement over long distances was imperative for survival in desert areas when creek beds and water holes dried up, or the seasonal ranging of game occurred. In this way, the knowledge of languages and customs was enriched by exchange. Their maps, crisscrossed with the pathways of the spirits of the Dreaming, were dotted with places recalling the sacred hand of creation. All this was a landscape of the mind which, given substance in ritual and story, permeated Aboriginal memory and understanding and became a total world view. Salman Rushdie rightly observed that the Australian landscape is 'mapped by stories.'

When conflict occurred between people of different 'countries' there was no set system to provide a solution. In the event, the problem was often solved by consultation or by single combat, which generally resulted in no loss of life. No hierarchy of authority made up of kings or chieftains existed among the Aborigines. This did not preclude the old men and those in the groups who were regarded as the preservers of tradition and, in certain circumstances, the elderly women, being respected if not venerated. Medicine men, healers, the so-called 'clever men' and warriors also held places of importance, though not superiority.

Under such a system, there was no need for a centralized form of control. All authority stemmed from a higher source upon which an individual Aborigine, or a group, depended for guidance in all the circumstances of daily life. That source was religion and, whether in life or death, marriage or birth, hunting or digging, travelling or building a dwelling, it was always available to the Aborigines of the entire continent, albeit in different forms. Aboriginal religion was born with the Dreaming and it was kept alive through story, song, ceremony, dance and music. The spirits who gave meaning to the Dreaming were there at the beginning of time when all things had their origins, whether men or mountains. The 'Law' of the Dreaming regulated the unfolding of an ongoing reality in which everything had its place. That same ancestral 'Law', ancient and unchanging except by interpretation and the development of its essence over generations, had to be obeyed by man, woman and child, by bird and beast, by cloud and river, by all created things.

The Aborigines did not worship sacred objects and thus they were not totemic. They were not pantheistic because their concept of the sacred extended beyond the material world. Their religion required no sacrificial offerings of beasts, and much less of humans, by an angry god demanding to be placated. Every Aborigine wanted to do the will imprinted at the beginning on all things. Not to do so was to risk departing into a region of the fearful unknown.

It is common to imagine that the Aborigines lived in brutal hardship, with meagre and unvarying food supplies. There were obviously times of abundance and scarcity, there were localities in which food abounded and others where it had to be sought with constant diligence. Species varied from place to place, but there was an extraordinarily wide range of foodstuffs that supplied the main nutritional elements needed to sustain life. Men hunted singly or in pairs, except while using large nets or in a game-drive when they hunted in groups. They sometimes used tame dingoes to find game or to harass it until caught. It has been reported that men ground seed and also worked with women, as for example, on a grass dam erected to catch fish in Arnhem Land.

The men were skilful in their use of various throwing instruments including spears which, when aided by a throwing device, could accurately reach an object fifty metres distant in two seconds. They also used clubs and boomerangs to bring down kangaroos, possums, wallabies, snakes, goannas, lizards, scrub turkeys and a wide variety of birds. Knives were made for carving, needles for sewing, and spears, hooks, nets, traps, weirs and narcotics were used to catch fish and such marine creatures as turtles, eels, dugongs and water pythons, as well as ducks and other birds. Fish were sometimes mustered in water pens in anticipation of a ceremonial feast and, at Toolondo in Victoria, a three kilometre ditch was found joining two swamps that had been dug in order to help eels breed more prolifically. In the high country of the Australian Alps groups came from coastal and other areas annually to hold ceremonies, barter and feast on the much-appreciated bogong moths that summered there in millions.

There was some division of labour in that women did not hunt large animals, but they did provide the greater part of the food and spent much time in obtaining it. Equipped with a finely woven bag or a carrying dish called a coolamon (and perhaps carrying a baby in a basket), they gathered eggs, seeds, moths, nuts, fruit and berries, honey, leaves, yams, insects, witchetty grubs and lilies. That kind of work often entailed expert digging with sharpened sticks. The contribution of the women was especially valuable in the desert areas, but it was also time-consuming and arduous. Although there were 140 varieties of food plants available to the high number of Arabana people around Lake Eyre, 75 of them were in the form of seeds, which demanded attentive work in gathering. It was work that the men found unattractive. The women also spent many hours preparing food, including the use of cereals to make flour. Some plants or fruits containing poisonous substances required ingenious methods of preparation. For example, among the people of north eastern Queensland, the black bean (mirrany) provided a staple food which was inedible until steamed in a sand oven for up to 24 hours. The bean was then sliced and sprayed with a stream of water for a further two days. Any surplus left over from a meal of mirrany was buried, rendering it edible for about six months A highly toxic plant, macozamia, found in the central highlands of Queensland also demanded much labour to render it edible although it could be roasted easily or simply left to weather. Bush tomatoes, sometimes sun dried, were a favourite food as were bush oranges. The major elements of a meal were either roasted on coals or baked in an earthen oven. The main meal, eaten communally and shared according to ritual custom, was taken in the evening. Women shared the food they gathered with their immediate family or camp group, while the larger game brought down by the men was shared with a wider group of neighbours or passers-by, on the reasonable expectation that such hospitality would later be repaid.

In some places bush or native tobacco, a strong narcotic, was chewed and much valued, as a medium of exchange. The psychoactive drug, pituri, made from the leaves of a similar plant was also used, as were several other 'stupefying beverages', likewise made from plants. Otherwise, there is no convincing evidence that intoxicating drink was taken, though there are reports from a few areas of the brewing of fermented beverages from, for example, honey.

The dress worn by the Aborigines of necessity varied from place to place dependent on the climate. In the south it was customary to wear a kangaroo or possum cloak in winter, or a garment made from the skins of either. When the cold was severe, some people carried smouldering banksia cones under their garments for warmth. In the northern rainforests, cloaks were woven from fibre. Fringes to cover the pubic areas were sometimes fashioned, and waistbands were used to carry weapons and game. Wearing sandals woven from the bark of shrubs counteracted the heat of the sand in the central desert. Among the men, armbands and headbands were common. The women wore ornaments or jewellery, especially necklaces, pendants and beads, made from animal bones and teeth.

On reaching puberty, the males bore the symbols of their initiation in raised welts on the body, or in the removal of an upper incisor from among the front teeth. As yet, no explanation has been given why circumcision of boys spread elsewhere from the desert areas where it began except to the far north, the south-west or eastern Australia. As an important ceremony, its use served as a cultural differentiation between the Aborigines throughout the continent. Whether for mourning and decoration, or as a result of fighting, body scarring was common to all males. The practice, begun at puberty and continued through into adulthood, served to indicate status, skills, and individual and common identity. Women inflicted scars on their heads as signs of mourning. Red hair was regarded as a desirable attribute in some places where it was customary to attempt to dye it. This may partially explain why the strikingly red-headed explorer of south-eastern Australia, Hamilton Hume, was so favoured among the Aborigines in the 1820s.

In material terms, Aboriginal civilization was based more on an understanding and use of the environment than on technological developments. Nevertheless, at least 20,000 years ago, the Aborigines were capable of making highly refined tools from stone in a manner that was technologically advanced on those made at a contemporary stage of development by other stone-age people. The main material for making artefacts of all kinds was wood, of which at least 240 varieties were used. More durable tools were made from stone, some of which, over 40,000 years old, have been discovered. Adzes and hatchet heads for axes were of necessity made from especially hard stone which meant that it sometimes had to be carried long distances for exchange. Greenstone, used for sharper tools, was so prized that it has been found at a great distance from Mount William in Victoria where it was quarried. Thus, long before Australia became in part a quarry, the Aborigines had been miners and particularly for the much-prized ochre used for painting and body decoration. The most famous deposit of red ochre was at Pukardu Hill in South Australia's Flinders Ranges, to which ritual journeys following prescribed routes were undertaken annually. The ochre, shaped into cakes and baked, was used as far away as the Gulf of Carpentaria in northern Queensland.

Fire and its origins form a rich component of the Dreaming. Its importance to the Aborigines was paramount, as it was used to cook and heat, repel insects, fashion implements, hunt animals and smoke them from trees, to clean up vegetation and in burial and other ceremonies. Made by the rapid rotation of one stick in a notch on another, it was often carried from place to place, and even in canoes a small fire was sometimes kept to immediately cook the catch. For a reason never since ascertained, the technology of making fire in Tasmania was lost, so the Aborigines of that island were forced to carry fire in a smouldering bundle wherever they went.

The ceremonial and ritual gatherings could last from a single day to as long as a few months. Around Sydney, the word used for these events, 'corroboree', eventually became a term of derision among whites who did not understand their significance. Everywhere, great care was taken, according to long-established practice, to prepare for the ceremonies. Pipe clay, ochre, charcoal and feathers were used to paint and decorate the body in different patterns and hues. The patterns had a deep religious significance and much care was taken in their execution.

The main musical instruments were clap sticks, boomerangs, rattles, wooden rasps and drums, although the drum was used only in the Torres Strait, Arnhem Land and Cape York. In southern Australia hollow logs or similar objects were beaten to make drum-like sounds. The didjeridu, (the name is not of Aboriginal origin), was initially used only in northern Australia and there comparatively recently dating from the last 1,000 years. It was unknown until about 100 years ago in southern Australia. The sound depends on the length of the instruments; accomplished players normally have several instruments to add variety to their performance. The so-called 'bull-roarer', a sacred object, seems to have been used to incite fear in its hearers, rather than as a musical instrument. In Arnhem Land it is interpreted as the voice of an ancestor.

In ceremonies, at birth, initiation and death, all Aboriginal life was touched by song and there were also secret songs and love songs. All songs were connected with the travels of the ancestral beings and thus they always existed. The songs were only brought into the present by the singer and the actors who, in dance or mime, repeated the story in a representative way. Some songs were exceedingly long and they would be repeated so that, on important ceremonial occasions, the singing could go on all day and into the night with perhaps 400 people involved. The men took the major role in ceremonies; women had their own, but different, role. However, women also had their own ceremonies to which men, boys and uninitiated girls had no access. In that way, the women, especially in desert areas, had their own life of secret song, particularly in reference to the mystery of procreation. Until recently, women have been undervalued for their spiritual and domestic roles in Aboriginal society.

The country was mapped long before 1788 with the tracks used by the Aborigines, along which they passed for purposes of ceremony and barter. Men carrying message sticks with information of impending events travelled on those same tracks. One such track went south from the Gulf of Carpentaria to Spencer Gulf where pearl shells from the north have been found. At these gatherings gifts were exchanged and barter took place for objects that were unavailable locally. This system of barter in Australia, as elsewhere in the world, was also a means of exchanging ideas, customs, bonding rituals, words and languages, songs and dances, as well as genes thus enriching both the culture and the genetic composition of the participating groups. The children shared their games and toys, the males wrestled and in some places played forms of football and the women exchanged their stories of family and communal life. In all these ways, Aboriginal society lay open to a constant state of development based on factors operating throughout the whole continent. In a manner that Australians today are only beginning to comprehend in their own culture, the Aborigines in long ages past lived in a society where to be multilingual was common and where cultures were enriched by sharing with those of others.

For the birth of a baby the mother usually went off alone, or perhaps together with one or two older, experienced members of her sex. The mother usually recovered quickly and was able to resume her normal life within a few hours of the birth. With the exception of some forms of arthritis, there do not seem to have been common health problems among the Aborigines and there is no evidence of epidemic diseases before contact with the outside world. Dental decay was unknown, as distinct from the wearing down of teeth, but in skeletal remains there is evidence of broken bones and fractures caused by accident or violence. Head injuries are most evident on the skulls of women. The skill with which injuries were cared for indicates considerable medical knowledge, especially in the setting of bones. Medicine-men and healers regularly contributed to the health of their community using ointments; smoke from selected plants was inhaled. The older women prepared the various medicines. Sorcerers, in varying practices including that known as bone-pointing, sometimes used an aberrant form of medicine that implied a malevolent understanding of human psychology. Its purpose was to cause death or illness, but a healer, if brought in time, could intervene to lift the 'spell.'

There is clear evidence that the Tasmanian Aborigines were essentially part of the same race as those on the continent itself. The offshore islands of Tasmania do not seem to have been inhabited, although they were a source of food, including seals and sea birds. The mountain regions were never more than sparsely populated, and the principal segments of the population lived in the east and west. Rich sources of food were available and huts or wigwam-like structures were erected for housing of a lasting nature. There were nine major languages, giving rise to differing cultural groups although, granted the long period Tasmania's isolation, it is understandable that different developments took place there in language, material culture and in the economy from those on the mainland. The principal features common throughout the island were passed on from previous millennia and retained, but monogamy seems to have been the custom and, as on the mainland, there were many trade routes and places for ceremonial gatherings. For some unexplained reason, the people there stopped eating fish about 3,500 years ago.

Deaths, except for those of infants and the very elderly, were taken to be the result of some form of sorcery which often gave rise to accusations against others and consequent retaliation. The strong bonds of kinship that encompassed numerous families and groups meant that death was never a solitary act but one that reached out and profoundly touched those of the same kin. Following death, the name of the departed was not used because it expressed the essence of the person and was sacred to the deceased until, when due time had elapsed, it was given to another person. In death the spirit did not die, but returned to the ancestral world where it again found its rightful home. Beliefs about the ultimate destination of the dead varied widely. Some believed that, after a long journey, a form of reincarnation took place; others that the spirit went to a land of the dead in the setting sun and others again that the departed spirit went to meet Daramulan 'the all-father who took charge of the spirits of the dead' and who had once lived on earth and taught men. The ceremonies connected with death and burial were directed at assisting the spirit on its journey and consoling the loved ones in their grief. It was also important to reunite the body with the land and burial sometimes served to strengthen a form of title to a particular area of land. The skeletal remains found by Jim Bowler in 1969 at Lake Mungo in the Willandra Lakes area of New South Wales were those of a female known as Mungo Lady. Her body had been cremated, which is the earliest known cremation in the world. Aboriginal forms of burial signify essentially human values of life, an awareness of the significance of death and a capacity for abstract reasoning.

The Aborigines throughout the continent had varying and elaborate rituals of ceremonial burial. Among them were the careful laying out of the body, sprinkling it with red ochre, exposing the body on a raised platform, cremation and, sometimes, secondary burial. The population was both sedentary and dense along the middle and lower reaches of the Murray River because of the abundance of readily available food both in the river itself and throughout its hinterland. A large number of ancient cemeteries have been discovered in the area. Studies of bones and teeth perhaps indicate that close habitation resulted in disease. It seems also to have been common to leave selected items belonging to the deceased person in the grave, a practice, which has also been observed elsewhere in the world

Throughout the whole continent in the decades before 1788 the Aborigines were living much as their ancestors had done for untold generations even though there had been changes in that period of 50,000 years. There were families and homes, communities and social structures, artists, singers and storytellers. The Aborigines were neither savages nor primitive nobles, but a people who had developed a degree of civilization, which impressed many white observers and, in the judgement of Lieutenant James Cook, gave them a happiness and tranquillity unknown to Europeans. Among them, the contours of the Dreaming retained the form and spirit that had been passed down through the generations since ancestral times. Those contours were about to be shattered, as was Aboriginal society itself.

2

Sydney Cove

On 26 January, 1788, during high summer, a flotilla of eleven ships took up moorings at a small cove in a noble and extensive harbour on the eastern coastline of the southern continent. A few Aborigines, whose ancestral home that harbour and its beaches had been for age upon age, watched closely from nearby scrub. The British newcomers named the cove after an English politician, Lord Sydney. To the Eora people such things meant nothing. Their reaction to these monstrous, white-winged vessels with their unknown cargo was to stay quietly in the bush. The modern history of the world's oldest continent had commenced with the coming of a new people. The Aborigines and the land with which they formed a unity were – for good and for ill – the setting of one of the last significant developments of human expansion on earth.

That expansion had its remote origins in the ancient European dream of a great southland that was thought to balance the Northern Hemisphere. By the Sixteenth Century the dream was given more concrete form when combined with the lust for gold, spices and land itself all of which tempted the northerners to explore in the south beyond the Equator. In the beginning the Portuguese came and went without finding the fabled land. Bartolomeus Dias rounded the Cape of Good Hope at the tip of South Africa in 1487 and Vasco de Gama reached India in 1497–98. The Spaniard, Magellan, in 1520, made the first crossing of the Pacific via South America in the *Vittoria*. He came into Australian seas, but neither sighted nor touched the land.

In Spanish blood the longing for new adventures ran strong and they sent Pedro Quiros in quest of the 'Continent towards the South'. In 1606 Quiros came to a port, which he called Vera Cruz, possibly present-day Vanuatu; he named the land 'Australia of the Holy Spirit', but he had not reached his goal. Some have subsequently argued that both the Portuguese and Spaniards charted parts of the east coast of Australia in the Sixteenth Century. The arguments continue and a number of experts in such matters remain unconvinced. Of the coming of the Dutch, however, there can be no doubt. During the early 1600s the Dutch used a southerly route across the Indian

Ocean to reach the Spice Islands (Indonesia) and occasionally came in contact with the west coast of Australia. In 1606 the gracious, tiny, vessel named *Duyfken (Little Dove)* sailed into the Gulf of Carpentaria and along the west coast.

Abel Tasman, a Dutchman, touched on and charted part of the south east coast of Tasmania in 1642. He named it Van Diemen's Land, but he was unaware that it was an island cut off from the mainland by a strait. In 1644 he sailed down part of the west coast of the continent and New Holland was the proud name he gave to that vast segment of the land mass. Later, in 1699, an English adventurer with universal interests in all that pertained to man and nature, William Dampier, had landed on the north-west coast; he found it arid and barren with native inhabitants who seemed to him the most miserable beings on earth. He was unaware of the cup of misery they had yet to drink. In these varied and partly understood ways, successive waves of 'discovery' touched the shores of Australia almost by accident; without fanfare or triumph. This last corner of the earth, a continent that was alleged to belong to no one, lay open in its innocence to the embrace of European invaders.

A former farm labourer, stable boy and grocer turned sailor, James Cook, became one of the finest navigators of the ages. Cook, aware of the Dutch voyages, sailed westward from New Zealand in the *Endeavour* and, on 22 April, 1770, sighted the east coast of New Holland. The great mariner was aware that he was doing nothing new and would be surprised to find that he has since been called the discoverer of Australia. In passing up the coast he entered Botany Bay where he and his party received much the same resistance from the Aborigines as had the crews of the Dutch vessels, the *Dufyken* in 1606 and the *Pera* in 1623 in the Gulf of Carpentaria. Two Tharawal men, having sent their families into the bush, did their utmost to prevent Cook's landing even though he had small presents thrown ashore for them. They were forced to flee after Cook fired three musket shots at them. The second, 'loaded with small shot' struck one of them. Cook later said that 'all they seemed to want was for us to be gone'. Despite these unhappy encounters, there were others of a more friendly nature because about 60 Aboriginal words have been discovered, which Cook and his party collected during their visit to Botany Bay.

Cook, and his botanist, Joseph Banks, were impressed with the novel flora and fauna, the apparent fertility of the soil and the healthiness of the climate at Botany Bay although they saw little else of the continent except during the seven weeks spent repairing the *Endeavour* after it ran onto coral in the Great Barrier Reef. Cook named the land New South Wales, charted its coast to the farthest northern tip and, on 22 August 1770, landed at Cape York where he took possession of the country in the name of the British king. It was of consequence that he did so without 'the Consent of the Natives', which he had been expressly ordered to obtain. He had not judged this formality a necessity, as it seemed to him that those he encountered made no use of the land and therefore did not own it. Cook also informed his superiors that Norfolk Island, a thousand miles away in the Pacific, possessed pines and flax. They were commodities that the English, as a naval power, always needed for their vessels in the form of masts and sails.

The British decision to send Governor Arthur Phillip to found a penal settlement at Botany Bay, a few miles south of Sydney Cove, was made under the strain of finding a rapid solution to the pressing problem of British criminality. The men in the government offices in London were much concerned with the realization of practicalities and, to them, the ancient European dream of a great southland was of no moment. What counted was that Cook had made it British. The fact that the declaration of possession might also be an act of rapine had never seemed to trouble their minds since Cook's return in 1771, especially when they realized that land in vast abundance, and seemingly lying idle, was available in New South Wales. Furthermore, it was sufficiently remote from England to be a suitable location for an open-air prison from which escape would be virtually impossible.

The problem of what to do with English prisoners demanded action because the growth in the number of persons being sentenced had resulted in crowded and unhealthy gaols, particularly those in the old hulks of vessels moored on the Thames. As well as being expensive to maintain, these prisons posed serious consequences in the form of moral and physical contagion to the London populace. Moreover, since the American War of Independence in 1776, it was no longer possible to cast off the unwanted refuse of British society by sending convicts to America, and an experiment in 1775 in West Africa had resulted in the death or desertion of eighty per cent of the 746 sent there. Another destination to which convicts could be transported had to be found.

In 1779 Joseph Banks, who had been the botanist on Cook's expedition, suggested Botany Bay as a suitable site for a settlement, and in 1783 James Matra, also a member of the expedition, recommended it as a colony for those Americans who had remained loyal to Britain in the War of Independence. Matra stressed that the flax plant, used for making sails, could be grown at Botany Bay, that a trading post with China, Russia and Japan could be established there and that, in time, it could become a site for a naval base, while its very occupation would be of strategic use in keeping the French and Dutch at bay. The idea of settling American royalists was rejected, but the Pitt government chose Botany Bay as a site for a penal colony. The choice was made even though no one had visited the place for sixteen years and, on his return to England in 1771, Banks had admitted that, despite its botanical attractions, it was the most barren region he had ever seen.

Suggestions were put forward that Botany Bay be further investigated before committing a large group of men and women to exile there, but to no avail. The need to get on and quickly remove as many criminals as possible from London was further illustrated by the choice of Phillip as commander. Part-sailor, part-farmer, Phillip, though in the long term an admirable choice, was given a job no one else sought and it was not one those in control considered of any real significance. Indeed, the hasty nature of the whole venture was finally illustrated by Lord Sydney's wish that the First Fleet sail in December 1786. This would have allowed only a few months to get together the provisions for the voyage and the later settlement, but that seemed to be ample time to achieve the main objective of disposing of a body of troublesome wretches. If further good came in the form of a trading post or a strategic naval base, so much the better.

Over a period of seven months two naval and nine merchant vessels, that had been hastily converted to carry the convicts, assembled at Portsmouth in southern England. About 1080 persons came aboard and the vessels were loaded with provisions to last for two years. Meanwhile, Phillip found time to set down principles to guide his governorship. He would treat the Aborigines kindly and establish harmonious relations with them. He would discipline the convicts, but he would also try to reform them. To achieve those aims he was determined to introduce the laws of England into a free land rather than into a vast, open-air prison. He said, 'There can be no slavery in a free land, and consequently no slaves.'

Although hasty preparations were made for the voyage, the infant settlement was fortunate because Governor Phillip was a man of high integrity with a practical mind and, under his guidance, the venture had some small chance of success. No detail was too small to escape his close attention even to the extent of his suggesting the inclusion of saddles for explorers, grindstones to sharpen knives and small tin lamps to present to the native chieftains. Largely due to his initiative in making as thorough preparations as possible, the Fleet did not sail from Portsmouth till 13 May 1787. It left with scarcely a mention of its departure in the newspapers, but to the undoubted relief of the scheme's initiators. The two naval vessels, *Sirius* and *Supply*, together with the nine merchantmen converted to carry the convicts, called at Rio de Janeiro in August and Cape Town in October, procuring fresh supplies at both and, at the latter, 500 animals of various kinds were taken aboard.

It was some comfort for all to know that, given the vast distance of about fifteen thousand miles between Botany Bay and home, in a period of grave necessity some form of relief would be available from the Dutch at Batavia or at the Cape. The passage of 252 days was remarkably successful with only forty-eight deaths since embarkation and the vessels of the Fleet were never separated by accident from each other for even a single hour. From the quarterdeck of the armed sloop *Supply*, Phillip led his fleet with 1030 people aboard, of whom 736 were convicts, into Botany Bay on 18 January 1788. The 736 convicts included 188 women which indicated an ominous imbalance in the sexes that remained for many years. The rest were marines and civil officers, 27 with wives, and 37 children. As they had less than two years of basic supplies, the need to settle quickly and begin the cultivation of the land was apparent to the Governor and his subordinates.

The earlier, favourable opinions given on Botany Bay seemed fantastic to Phillip and his officers in the light of the reality they encountered. Apart from the apparent infertility of the soil, the most compelling, negative aspect of the location for a settlement was the lack of fresh water. In those circumstances there was no option but to move to a more suitable site. A few miles to the north of Botany Bay lay Port Jackson which Cook had named but not entered in 1770. Phillip investigated its possibilities as a site and returned with the good news that it had the 'finest harbour in the world, in which a thousand sail of the line may ride in the most perfect security'. More to the point was the fact that a stream provided fresh water at a cove so deep that the fleet could easily and safely unload its cargo there.

Botany Bay was quickly discarded, but its name became part of the historical legend as the first place chosen to accommodate the felon, the outcast and the casual offscourings of British society. To Phillip it had no value although he regularly sent back detachments there in the following months as if he were afraid to accept that Cook and Banks had been so mistaken in their judgement of the place. Meanwhile, men, women and children, the convicts and the free depended upon Phillip for their lives. Their confidence in the Governor was not misplaced. He had undertaken a high task for his monarch and he was not about to see it fail.

As preparations were being made to leave Botany Bay on 26 January, everyone's attention was diverted to the arrival of two frigates flying the golden lilies on a white field of the flag of France. Under the command of Jean-François de Galaup, Comte de la Pèrouse, they carried a French exploratory and scientific expedition. The subsequent, fleeting contact between the English and French was harmonious. Both bore with them the long traditions of their past and, in the case of the English, some vestiges of those traditions remained intact despite the fact that they had come to found a penal colony. The idea of parliamentary democracy, the role of the monarchy and traces of experiments in republicanism arrived, together with the Authorized Version of the Bible, the Book of Common Prayer, philosophical and political theories and the thought of Hobbes, Locke, Hume and Berkeley. The spirits of Shakespeare and Milton were also with them, as were those of Francis Bacon, Isaac Newton and Edward Gibbon. A few of the officers had some understanding of the first steps of modern science and technology and were aware of the high standards of the Royal Society.

In the persons of those British officers, as well as in the sailors and convicts, some of this past was subsumed and in various ways it was to pass on, filtered through the strands of a penal society, to the generations of the future. All rivalries between the French and English, whether economic or military were set aside in those first days of the presence of white races at this lonely outpost in the Pacific. Set aside also, even if only temporarily, was the division between Protestant and Catholic. The Protestant religion was represented in the person of Reverend Richard Johnson, Anglican chaplain to the First Fleet, while Father Louis le Receveur, Franciscan friar, man of letters and scientist with the French, personified the Catholic. Le Receveur died and was buried at Botany Bay three weeks later – almost symbolic of the early fragility of the Catholic faith in the new land. Johnson lived on to help affirm the predominance, by convention at least, of his own.

In the early afternoon of 26 January Phillip went ashore with a party of marines and convicts at the place he had named Sydney Cove. In the evening musket volleys were fired and toasts to the success of the new colony drunk when the British colours were raised and New South Wales was proclaimed a possession of the British Crown. Captain Arthur Phillip was appointed Captain-General and Governor-in-Chief in and over the Territory called New South Wales and its Dependencies. At nightfall the entire First Fleet lay at anchor within Sydney Cove. By 3 February it was time to turn to religion and Richard Johnson chose as the basis of his first sermon to the assembled community the words of the Psalmist 'What shall 1 render unto the Lord for all His benefits towards me?' To the preacher it was ordained by God that some should be in an exalted state and others subject to them. About Johnson stood the upholders of good order, resplendent and sweating in uniform; above him flew the flag of Great Britain, while the tones of 'God Save the King' had scarcely died away. The convicts who stood about listening to Johnson were possibly unclear on the nature of the benefits for which they were expected to be grateful, nor were they aware their sovereign, George III, was spasmodically insane and that, across the English Channel, the stirrings of a revolution of such magnitude were afoot in France that, given time, the values held sacred by their rulers in Great Britain would be questioned.

What meaning those values held for Phillip and his officers is uncertain. It is, nonetheless, certain that they had set afoot a process without parallel in the history of colonial expansion by Europeans. It was no easy matter to weave high or noble motives into the act of founding a prison and, when they came to set down their purpose on paper, the London authorities did not attempt to do so. The other great, colonial powers, Spain and Portugal and, to a lesser extent, France were conscious that they had a responsibility to God. Thus they undertook their expansionist drive by calling on His favour and, in their turn, they promised not to forget His bounty and to share their faith in Him with those whose rule and rights they displaced. Phillip suffered no such constraint. His commission was to found a prison and God's name was not found in either that commission or in any of the official documents relating to the settlement of New South Wales. There was, however, a good deal about the moral standards that were expected to apply to the inhabitants of the prison and, understandably, Anglican forms had to be observed in public services held in the name of religion. Notwithstanding such forms it came to pass on 26 January 1788 that the first, entirely secular, state in the world was born. New South Wales was secular and secular it would remain.

Much feverish activity connected with settling-in followed, highlighted by festivities approaching a sexual orgy when the 548 male convicts welcomed ashore the 188 women convicts during a violent thunderstorm on the evening of 6 February. Other celebrations took place when the British form of government in the shape of a military despotism was officially set up on the following day. The Act of Parliament founding the colony was read and Phillip made a speech exhorting the convicts to industry, decency and righteousness. All white persons, of whom more than two-thirds were in bondage, were assembled. The youngest convict was John Hudson, aged nine, who had been given seven years' transportation for stealing, and the oldest, a woman of eighty-two, Dorothy Handland, who had been convicted of housebreaking. She hanged herself from a gum tree a year later. Two-thirds of the convicts had been sentenced for minor theft and their average age was under thirty. Apart from the English and Scottish the main nationalities were black and white Americans, Germans and Norwegians, while the Jews were a minor but significant religious group.

In those first days at Sydney Cove a sense of strangeness overwhelmed the newcomers. They were at the end of the world, separated by immense distances and vast oceans from their homes and loved ones, neither of which the far greater part of them could never hope to see again. They had come to a land where winter came in the months of summer and the sounds and sights of the birds, animals and insects were unfamiliar and sometimes repelling. Above them the sun shone with unaccustomed ferocity in a sky so deeply blue that it seemed like a painted canopy. To the children nothing was strange because they knew no other place. Their suffering was of another kind and it was to last for generations. As they grew they came to know that their birthplace was the home of the felon, most of their parents were convicts and they would carry the stain of their origins throughout their lives.

The land on which they moved was unrelenting in its dryness and harshness. Try as they might it would prove almost impossible to wrest a living from the earth, but they knew that they had to tame it to survive. In the following week fourteen marriages were solemnized among the convicts, thus planting the seeds of a new, white society in assuredly unpromising soil because the motives of many of the contracting parties were based on the false notion that marriage would ensure better rations and other favours from Phillip. Nonetheless, following the birth of the first white child on 26 January, a male whose father was a marine and whose mother was a convict, twenty-seven more children were born in 1788 and another statistic was added to the annals of humanity. These children were the first native-born of a new nation and, if asked in adulthood to state their origins, each one could reply 'I am an Australian.'

Governor Phillip, by his example, determination and rigid command made survival possible through those first starving years. The unskilled, often unwilling, always hungry, convict workforce gradually built the humble dwellings, tilled the stony soil, laid out the winding streets and thus set down the first, fragile signs of white civilisation. In the beginning shelter was a paramount necessity, as well as fresh water, although fine weather was an advantage. There was the occasional torrential downpour but, as it was summer, the sun soon shone again and spirits lifted. Only a small group of carpenters could be found among the sailors and convicts, and Phillip himself had to lodge in a canvas structure that let in rain and wind. Most of the cattle, which survived the voyage, soon disappeared into the bush and, in September, the last remaining cow was slaughtered for food. The sheep, pigs and poultry fared better as they stayed about the settlement, but six months later none remained except for one sheep. No plough was available to till the soil and no one possessed satisfactory expertise in cultivating a place where even the seasons were unfamiliar.

Above all it was the land itself that daunted them for its soils were thin, sandy or rocky, which bent their picks and hoes, its vegetation strange, and its trees generally resistant to carpentry except for the abundance of cabbage-tree palms that were growing near the small creek upon which everyone depended for water. It became known as the Tank Stream after a large tank was cut out of sandstone in its centre to hold the water. There about the Cove, the little settlement could only achieve its primary objective of existing, with the occasional bird or fish to vary the diet of salt meat, while bread became so scarce that guests brought their own supply when they dined at an officer's table, including Phillip's. In July all but two of the convict ships sailed for home, and in November everyone watched with heavy hearts as the others, the *Golden Grove* and the *Fishburn*, slipped out of sight through the Heads. By the end of the year, most of the officials were convinced that the whole experiment had been a disaster and were hoping that common sense would prevail in London and that Sydney Cove would be closed and an end put to the settlement in New South Wales.

In those very early days, Phillip, acting according to his instructions and his own benevolent disposition, had insisted upon cordial relations being established with the Aboriginal inhabitants, commonly called natives or Indians, who numbered about 1,500 in the Sydney region. The Governor had been impressed by their behaviour. Indeed, the upright bearing of a group of them at a cove on the harbour had led him to give it the name 'Manly' and he took no retribution when an Aborigine later speared him at the same spot. Arabanoo was a Manly native whom Phillip befriended and who dined regularly at the Governor's table. He was the first Aborigine to teach the whites something of his language and the customs of his people. The marine officer Watkin Tench saw in Arabanoo the quality of independence of mind and the assurance of their own dignity that was common among the Aborigines.

As time went by, several things became apparent to the Aborigines. Most importantly, their visitors had come by sea and from that same sea others could follow them. Furthermore, they were clearly bent upon permanent residence and the hive and hum of activity that followed their arrival, with the cutting down of trees to build their shelters, testified to that fact. There were ominous portents also because the arrival of the whites was followed in April 1789 by a virulent outbreak of smallpox that decimated and eventually killed at least half of the local blacks. Although it is now certain that the disease had already taken its toll in other parts of the continent before white settlement, such a coincidence at Sydney could scarcely escape the notice of the Aborigines, whom most observers credited with considerable intelligence. Arabanoo immediately turned to nursing some of the victims, but contracted the disease himself and died on 19 May. Phillip's attachment to him was such that he had his remains buried in the garden of what passed as Government House.

To the great consternation and resentment of the Aborigines, there were those among the whites who did not scruple to take, by stealth or force, any of the natives' possessions which took their fancy including canoes, spears, shields and fishing lines. Phillip, who issued fruitless instructions forbidding the whites to appropriate them, accepted the fact that these objects were essential to the survival of the Aborigines. The Aborigines themselves retaliated by killing several convicts and stealing their shovels, spades and pick-axes.

Phillip had been told that his role was to govern the whole eastern portion of New Holland. No one knew for certain whether the east formed a whole with the west, because there was still the possibility that a sea divided the continent. It was nevertheless taken for granted that a vast tract of land was open and free for the taking and, in those first encounters, the Aborigines did not appear to dispute possession of the land except during one episode in which a party of convicts was driven away from a cove where they had attempted to land. Given the nature of the local Aboriginal economy it is possible that they were determined to protect their fishing rights rather than their use of the land. Nonetheless, the very nature of those initial, generally amiable encounters tended to make concrete in the white mentality the erroneous notion that the relationship of the Aborigines with the land did not matter to them. This happened despite the fact that several whites perished when, unarmed and singly or in pairs, they encountered Aborigines in the bush. Such reprisals surely indicated that, despite the apparent passivity of the Aborigines, their true appreciation of the white presence was given expression when possible. Among them there was a warrior who had no hesitation in making his opposition clear. Pemulwuy, unlike Arabanoo, Colbee and Bennelong, remained aloof from, and wary of, the whites. He organized guerrilla like attacks in and around Sydney, thus becoming the first patriot to offer concerted resistance to the white invasion of his country. He was ambushed in 1802 and his head, enclosed in a butt of spirits, was sent to Joseph Banks in England.

Phillip, and some few of his officers, realized that they had come among a people possessing their own unique culture. There was, however, little time to indulge in speculation on such matters because, like the blacks, the most pressing concern of the whites was to survive and long-term reliance on the supplies brought with the Fleet was not possible. A little agriculture was begun on small plots around the settlement, but stealing became so widespread among the whites that Phillip resorted to the use of the death penalty for the worst cases and flogging, sometimes up to 2,000 lashes, for the lesser. Scurvy soon became prevalent, and Phillip reported to the home authorities that it was raging 'in a most extraordinary manner.' The Aborigines did not suffer from it because of their abundant supply of fresh and green food taken from the land, which augmented their daily diet of fish. The whites soon began to take similar measures but with only a small measure of success.

When the French were at Botany Bay, La Pèrouse had said that, from his observations, Norfolk Island was so steep and desolate that it was a place fit only for angels and eagles to inhabit, but Phillip, obedient to his orders before leaving England, sent Lieutenant King there in February 1788 with a party of twenty-three, including fifteen convicts. His task was to found a settlement, obtain timber from the pines, cultivate the flax plant and forestall occupation by any other nation and, given the recent presence of the French, the Governor's alacrity in the matter was understandable. The actual settlement was moderately successful, although the timber proved to be unsuitable for shipbuilding while the flax was diseased.

By 1790, want, loneliness and general unhappiness at Sydney Cove caused many to despair so, in an attempt to alleviate the situation on the mainland, Phillip sent 183 convicts, twenty-eight children and eighty-one marines to Norfolk Island where, it was hoped, there was a better chance of survival. Despite the fewer numbers, by April the residents at Sydney were down to drastically reduced rations and in May an elderly convict, Joseph Owen, died of starvation. Those who suffered most were the women and their children. One convict woman wrote home to tell of their desperation 'in this solitary waste of creation' where they could not get a cup of tea. Some asked why they had been abandoned by England complaining that 'the mother country has entirely forsaken us' in 'the worst country' in the world. No one dared to conclude that neglect was part of the pattern of improvidence in which the origins of the settlement lay. To the English authorities in London, New South Wales was, after all, no more than another prison.

It was becoming increasingly clear that even existence itself was at stake, especially when Phillip's flagship, the *Sirius,* was wrecked at Norfolk Island. She had already returned successfully with provisions from the Cape after circumnavigating the globe under Captain Hunter's command and on this occasion was on her way to Canton for more supplies. A relief ship, the *Guardian,* sent out from England, was also lost after striking an iceberg near the Cape of Good Hope and the situation worsened at Sydney with consequent dismay and misery. By mid-1790 New South Wales was entirely cut off from any means of contact with the outside world except through the small vessel, *Supply,* which no one, including Phillip, wanted to risk losing on a further, and perhaps, final voyage.

Despite the difficulties, Phillip tried to buoy up hopes by keeping an air of optimism about him. The marines who had accompanied the First Fleet were disinclined to attend to other than military duties, which in effect were non-existent so the Governor had to turn to selected convicts as overseers and even as police. This step caused much resentment among the marines and especially from their commandant Major Robert Ross, who, chagrined at being forced to live at a place where 'Nature is reversed', became a constant thorn in Phillip's side. Phillip solved the problem of his irritating subordinate by sending him to take charge on Norfolk Island in March 1790; there he was at least out of sight.

A civil and a criminal court had been set up on 7 February 1788, and floggings and hangings became regular occurrences thereafter. The first person executed in the colony was Thomas Barrett, aged seventeen, for stealing, and on 26 March 1789 six marines were hanged for robbing the stores. The first woman to be executed in the colony, Anne Davis, was hanged on 23 November 1789 for theft. The convicts attempted to add another facet of civilization in 1789 by performing a comedy, 'The Recruiting Officer', which was well received. Sydney itself was laid out about the Cove, the first streets of 200 feet in width were planned, orange trees planted, bricks were made at Brickfield Hill and a bridge was built across the Tank Stream. Phillip himself issued strict orders forbidding the pollution of its water. Exploration took place and the Hawkesbury and Nepean rivers were discovered and partially mapped although it had been possible to penetrate only to within some twelve miles of the Blue Mountains to the west.

Sydney remained little more than an infant town situated on a splendid harbour where the soil was unsuitable for cultivation. The gradual realization of this fact had caused Phillip to make the most important decision of his governorship. About sixteen miles from Sydney there was a place, which the Aborigines called Parramatta. Surrounding it, the land seemed fertile and by November 1788 it was settled. Phillip had a town laid out there with a mile long main street, a residence for himself, a barracks and houses for the inhabitants. The town was set on country and, with trees, gentle grassed spaces and general luxuriance there was 'a very park-like and beautiful appearance.' The settlement was originally called Rose Hill and, nearby, some beautiful birds were noticed which, after the place of their discovery, were given the name 'rosella.'

Near Rose Hill, cultivation of the land by the white settlers began. Phillip's instructions were to try to persuade former convicts to remain in the colony and farm it rather than go home. He was empowered to grant them thirty acres of land with twenty more if married and ten for each child. At Rose Hill in 1791 an ex-convict, James Ruse, who began life as a Cornwall farmer, received the first land grant of thirty acres in New South Wales upon which he grew wheat and other crops and from which he proved to Phillip's satisfaction that he could support himself and his convict wife, Elizabeth.

The first sign of relief for the colony was seen on 3 June 1790 when the transport *Lady Juliana* with a cargo of 222 female convicts, provisions for those on board and mail and news from home sailed up the harbour. Men wept, women with babes in arms were distracted with joy and the settlement seemed saved at last. A fortnight later the store ship *Justinian* berthed with supplies of food, followed by the 'sick ships' of the Second Fleet with their cargo of ill and dying. Even though a dreadful toll had already been taken on the voyage out when a quarter of the 1,000 convicts had perished, another 150 died soon after landing. The Second Fleet was the most cruel and most inhumane episode of the whole epoch of transportation, and its origins lay in the utter neglect of the English authorities.

Despite all these new arrivals, who by their presence gave the clearest possible proof that the home authorities had remained mindful of the purpose for which the colony had been founded, it was not until December, when a ship arrived laden with provisions which Phillip had procured from Batavia, that the crisis was over. The point had been well, if unintentionally, made that in an emergency white civilization on the southern continent would have to make shift for itself.

In 1792, weakened in health, Phillip prepared to leave New South Wales forever. He looked back on five years of stoically borne hardship, criticism from subordinates both convict and free, much opposition, frustration and human misery all around him. Nevertheless, his purpose had been achieved for the settlements around Sydney and on Norfolk Island had survived with their populations of over 3,000 and 1,100 respectively. The convicts were in the proportion of five males to one female yet the birth rate was rising, 1,700 acres of land were under cultivation, 3,500 acres had been granted to seventy-three persons on the mainland, livestock were increasing in numbers and general hopes were buoyant. Before leaving England, Phillip had stated that he did not intend to lay the foundations of an Empire using convicts; but by 1793 only a handful of free settlers had arrived. This meant that the pattern was already shaped of a society dependent upon convict labour employed and fed by the government. Moreover, it was a workforce markedly ill-fitted and ill-disposed to work. Through the ages that has always been the case with forced labour.

Phillip sailed for home on 11 December 1792 with a few dingoes, four kangaroos and two favourite Aborigines. One of them was Bennelong who was later commemorated by the naming of Bennelong Point on Sydney Cove because he had lived in a hut built there for him. The other Aborigine, Yemmerrawanyea, had been taught to wait at Phillip's table in Sydney. Both left home readily enough, but their families were greatly distressed at their departure. In England, Yemmerrawanyea suffered from the climate and he died there in 1794. Several unsuccessful attempts were made to have his remains brought back to Australia. Bennelong was presented to the King and returned later to the colony with a weakness for alcohol. In subsequent years Phillip, now ageing but formerly absolute ruler of half a continent, became an admiral. He died in 1814 and there is a memorial to him in Bath Abbey. He was perhaps secure in knowing that he had served humanity well in his total devotion to the founding of the colony, although at times he had felt compelled to act harshly and especially in his use of the lash as the main form of deterrent.

As time passed and memories were muted, a mythology grew up around the First Fleet with its cargo of human jetsam washed up at Sydney Cove. Because they were the pioneers and in some measure the cornerstone of the new society, it was considered necessary to distort the reality of their origins and of those who followed them. The stain of the convict origins was another powerful factor, which led to either forgetting or whitewashing the past. Poverty, land enclosures and a brutal system of legal enactments in England tended to obscure the truth that a sizeable proportion of the convicts were professional thieves hardened by repeated criminality. In the main they were working class, unskilled, town dwellers to whom law breaking had become a way of life. In most instances their law breaking was engendered by environmental factors consequent upon the dislocation caused by the Napoleonic wars and the rapid growth in population.

Nevertheless, it became part of mythology to see the convicts as sturdy agricultural labourers or downtrodden city people who had poached a hare or stolen a handkerchief to buy bread for their suffering families. Unquestionably there were some such among the convicts but in too small a minority to matter; poachers, for example, made up less than one per cent. Crimes against property predominated with over eighty per cent of the convictions, while crimes against persons were less than three per cent. At the time of their transportation the majority were unmarried, aged fifteen to twenty-five and had been sentenced to seven years' transportation that, effectively in most instances, was a sentence of permanent colonial residence in the same way as a fourteen-year or life sentence. The females were almost all former domestics except for the thirteen per cent of them who had been prostitutes.

In September 1791 the first convict ship from Ireland, the *Queen,* arrived with 133 men, twenty-two women and a Dublin boy, David Fay, aged eleven, aboard. From that day the Irish became another source of myth making. No one could justly question the effect upon Ireland's population of England's long occupation, the subjugation of its people and the suppression of its dominant religion. Similarly, the centuries-old struggle, political and often violent, of the Irish for their freedom and their land, was part of history immortalized in symbol, song and memory. It was easy to see the Irish transportees as political prisoners tinged with the nobility of rebellion.

Yet of the 50,000 Irish transported up to 1852, at least two-thirds were convicted for theft. A higher proportion of them was drawn from rural areas than was the case with the British convicts and the religion of ninety per cent of them was Catholic. The small but constant trickle of political prisoners among them, to whom thievery was repugnant, made up about a fifth of the Irish convicts, although in the first fifteen years the proportion reached a third. While that minority was made up of men of high principle and integrity, the majority of the Irish did not vary significantly from the English in their background of criminality.

Other mythologies grew up around the convicts centred on the ideal of mateship, a quality they allegedly possessed in abundance. There is little evidence that they shared such virtuous necessity more than others who formed bonds to protect life or property. Certainly they were mates in their hatred of law enforcers, their distaste for work, their use of rhyming slang and flash language to disguise the meaning of their conversation and in their feeling of being the dregs of society. But several factors combined to produce the one significant result of transportation, despite all its indignity and misery – a turning away from criminal activity by most convicts to a life based on economic independence. Better food, a healthier climate, a sense of freedom rather than incarceration in a dingy prison, all helped to transform and reform the convicts. Above all there was the chance to make a living by other than criminal means. Upwards of ninety per cent of the convicts eventually turned to respectable ways of life because they were given the opportunity to become independent in a land where abundance was the norm.

A partial explanation for this reformation also lay in the methods of deterrence. Phillip had established the pattern in the earliest days when the lash and the gallows became the way of punishing wrongdoers and of terrifying those so inclined. Broken skin and exposed rib cages were common and 100 lashes by an experienced flogger became a normal penalty for even minor transgressions. Deterrence was accompanied by the constant hope that a noticeable practice of good behaviour would result in rewards, and freedom from servitude was the one goal to which all strove. Gradually a system was established based on a 'ticket of leave' granted by the Governor. Although freedom of movement was restricted, the 'ticket of leave' permitted the convict to become self-employed and to hold property rights. A conditional pardon gave freedom and all rights provided one did not return to the United Kingdom. Both a full pardon and the expiration of a sentence meant a convict became fully emancipated. An emancipist, whether by pardon or completion of servitude, was rarely permitted to forget that his or her original condition was that of a convict or 'a Government man or woman' as the local saying put it. The old stain of convict origins died slowly, whether for individuals or for society itself.

A subtler attempt at reformation was the manner in which the authorities, closely allied by the law and the Anglican Church, sought to inculcate submission, repentance, obedience and the desire to conform. The convicts knew that their one chance of earthly redemption lay in conformity and subservience and, given the incentives, it is scarcely surprising that so many of them took it. A few hardy souls, however, chose another path, and as early as July 1788 eleven men and one woman had absconded. Attempting to escape became a regular practice amongst the homesick and the desperate and the Irish in particular were prone to bolt into the bush. In November

1791 one group of them, made up of twenty men and one woman, set out for China, which they believed to be within six weeks walking time. Eighteen survived their ordeal and returned to the settlement even further dispirited. Some of the obdurate tried it a second time, but gradually the conviction was borne in upon all that New South Wales was a place from which escape was well nigh impossible.

Five years after settlement there was still much distress but the sense of isolation was breaking down. There were ships lying at anchor in the harbour. Trading vessels from India, the United States, China, Batavia and England, and whalers and sealers, were calling at Sydney regularly. Nevertheless, the colony was to continue as a gaol because in London the authorities remained convinced that the cheapest way to solve the problem of crime and its effect was transportation. Over 4,000 convicts had arrived in five years and the pattern for the next fifty years of white settlement of the continent was set with a penal colony as its essential basis.

3

Traces of Permanency

Forlorn, tiny, uncertain of its future, the settlement held a precarious foothold about Port Jackson in 1792. Thinking inhabitants, whether convict or free, realized their insignificance in the eyes of those who had sent them there. The sender of a letter, whether private or official, could not expect a reply within a year so that problems, sorrows, joys and plans all took on an element of the unreal as they faded into the past. New South Wales was another world, washed by seas of silence that stretched endlessly from one end of the globe to the other. Between the settlement and home there were lands peopled by strange and nameless races, while inland from Sydney Cove lay the vast, mysterious continent locked behind the mountains to the west. Life went on with new arrivals and departures, births and deaths, primitive manufacturing, commerce and social relationships. For the majority of the white inhabitants there could be no turning back: henceforward home was forever New South Wales.

In some senses the colony was rapidly becoming a virtual slave farm because the government increasingly used the assignment of convicts to landowners to decrease costs on the public purse and increase profits to private individuals by providing them with free labour. With considerable justification, a convict wrote to Governor King in 1805: 'By what authority do those in power at Home – by what right do you – make slaves of Britons in this distant quarter of the globe?' Maurice Margarot, (one of the 'Scottish Martyrs' transported in 1794 for fourteen years on charges of sedition) refused to work, claiming that he had been sentenced to transportation, not to slavery. Margarot was fortunate in being able to avoid forced labour, but most convicts had no choice either of their masters or of their mode of employment.

With their fishing grounds and hunting lands increasingly invaded the Aborigines were rarely seen except for those who came about the town. They had learned a lesson from the fire-power of the whites even though they could throw several spears while the whites had to reload their weapons. Although to go alone to solitary places was imprudent, the whites, when armed and grouped together, normally travelled without fear. A little knowledge was gathered about the local languages and even about the beliefs of the Aborigines, but the native people increasingly became mere objects of curiosity to whom food and other items were sometimes dispensed as if to a lower order of humanity. Unlike the settlers at the Cape of Good Hope, white society in New South Wales, given the supply of convicts, did not have to rely on black labour, which further lessened the white estimate of the Aborigines. Although quickly, and falsely, judged to hold no belief in a Superior Being, little real effort was made to bring the Aborigines to an acceptance of the Christian God. Furthermore, the rudimentary structure of Anglicanism was unable to undertake the task, given its many problems in dealing with a military and convict society in which the observance of religion was not regarded as a priority.

Initially, the Aborigines played very little direct role in the economy of the whites, but other relations occurred and it was soon noticed that venereal disease had spread among them. They quickly named it Goobahrong as if to imply its dreadful effects. Because some Aboriginal women seemed loose in regard to sexual relations, the idea strengthened among the British that marriage and fidelity were of no consequence to the Aborigines. All that logic could imply was that a proud people, once reduced to bewilderment and even to starvation, would barter for their survival. As for the convicts, the gross imbalance of the sexes meant that they knew needs of another kind and took every opportunity to satisfy them.

In England some critics thought that the settlement in New South Wales was absurd, impractical and grossly expensive. Half a million pounds had been spent on the penal colony by the end of 1792, but the prime minister, Pitt, felt convinced that no cheaper method could be devised of disposing of the kingdom's worst criminals who, it was thought, would tend to corrupt society further. It was, of course, a straightforward matter to set up the convict establishment, but it was another to police it. An alternative force was clearly required, given that the marines had shown reluctance to undertake a task, which was usually not their responsibility and, in any case, they left with Phillip in 1792. Replacements had to be found; the answer, devised in England in 1789, was to send out a special New South Wales Corps which some newspapers called 'The Botany Bay Rangers'. The Corps arrived in 1790 and its commander, Major Francis Grose, who had been appointed lieutenant-governor, assumed control when Phillip departed for

England in 1792. From the moment of its arrival, the Corps became an influential force in shaping the future of the colony.

The Corps consisted of about 500 officers and men and, as a garrison, it had little to do except to look after its own needs, which Grose was quick to foster. He gave land grants and the use of up to ten male and three female convicts to his officers. The combination of free land and virtually free labour proved to be a particularly useful device. The convicts remained dependent on the government for provisions which, as time went by, the military officers sold to the government from their landholdings. Because no thought had been given to the necessity of a currency, the most precious commodity, liquor – principally rum – became an important medium of exchange for goods and labour. It remained so until 1813 when Spanish dollars with the centre removed, called 'holey dollars', circulated widely, together with promissory notes. The Corps assumed control of the economy, chiefly through using rum as a major item of barter and for paying wages. The whole of economic, legal and social life quickly took on aspects peculiar to a despotic military regime.

In January 1793 the first free settlers arrived from England in the *Bellona* and they received land grants in February. This occasion could well have been seen as one of momentous proportions in the transition of a convict colony to a free society. It passed unnoticed because, with Grose in charge, civil authority had passed into the hands of the military, where it was both used and abused for years to come. The original Corps had drawn a sizeable proportion of its numbers from ex-criminal elements, as had often been the case with British regiments. In Sydney, ex-convicts were soon enlisted in its ranks, which did nothing to enhance its reputation. Captain Paterson, second-in-command of the Corps, succeeded Grose late in 1794 until a new governor, John Hunter, arrived in September 1795. Paterson merely accentuated the worst aspects of Grose's system by making further land grants to the Corps. Yet, in some respects the colony benefited because, with free land and convict labour readily available, economic development ensued and the opening of rich land in the Hawkesbury River district continued. The Corps also contributed to growth in the free population because, in those early days, it was almost impossible to induce free persons to migrate as settlers. Upon their discharge, many Corp's members settled in the colony where they had prospered.

The days of famine appeared to have ended by 1796. Livestock flourished, agriculture–with the production of corn and potatoes–went ahead, the first shipment of cedar logs was made to India, trading ships continued to arrive with stores, a handful of free settlers took up land, and most convicts whose terms had expired remained in New South Wales and felt that they belonged there. After eight years, the town of Sydney welcomed Hunter with traces of permanency, of which the building of the first Anglican church by Johnson in 1793 was a symbol, even though it was paid for in rum bought out of his own pocket at 4s 6d per gallon and, raised to 10s per gallons, it was distributed to the builders in place of wages.

It was quickly taken for granted that conflict with the Aborigines was part and parcel of development. In the Hawkesbury River district black-white relations soon deteriorated almost to the point of open warfare. Nonetheless, in the first few years until the end of 1791, relatively few whites and blacks died as a result of conflict between them and relations were generally peaceful. Eight convicts were certainly killed by Eora men who also may have killed a marine and a naval officer. The number of Eora who perished from violence done by whites is uncertain, but it was not large and the overall conflict gains perspective when it is remembered that Phillip, in the same period, hanged 17 convicts and 6 marines. No whites were punished in this period for killing Aborigines. British law was taken as being unintelligible to the Aborigines and their evidence was inadmissible in court because they were considered to have no belief in God. As a result they could not be tried for criminal acts. The only way left to deal with them was, 'to pursue and inflict such punishment as they may merit … when they deserve it'. In practice, this meant killing them. Nevertheless in theory, they were regarded as being under the king's protection and it was explicitly stated in the 'Port regulations' of 1810 that they were to be treated 'in every respect as Europeans; and any injury or violence done or offered to the men and women natives will be punished … as if done to any of His Majesty's subjects'.

Furthermore, in the earlier period of settlement, while the blacks thought of the whites as enemies who seemed bent on taking their land, they were prepared to come to some form of accommodation with them and satisfactory relationships were established. At that time, very little land had been given over to agriculture so that the blacks were not seriously hindered in their economic activities; they continued to fish the harbour and they could still hunt and gather food. They were long accustomed to barter among themselves and they readily traded fish for bread and salt pork. They helped the whites with fishing, for which they received payment in such welcome commodities as blankets. The Eora people became increasingly jealous of the special position they held with the British, and they did their best to prevent other groups from taking advantage of it. To cement the bond between him and the governor, Bennelong asked Phillip to allow his pregnant wife to give birth in Government House. Phillip suggested that the hospital would be a more appropriate place.

Although the Aborigines showed no interest in trying to acquire firearms, they did make use of glass on the tips of their spears (rather than shell, stone and bone). They also used axes to make their traditional weapons. They were anxious to receive watchdogs (in the form of spaniels and terriers) from the British, which they kept near their dwellings at night when raiding parties from other groups were most likely to attack them. Collins wrote, 'not a family was without one or more of these little watch-dogs, which they considered as invaluable as guardians during the night'. Despite the development of these relationships, after the Hawkesbury was more closely settled, trouble began to brew there which resulted in warlike activities on both sides.

The Hawkesbury river banks and it flats were chosen by the settlers as the most rewarding and convenient land on which to engage in agriculture. The land was fertile, and the river offered safety and transport. Farming, however, necessarily conflicted with the economic activity of the Aborigines, both in regard to fishing and digging for yams in the river's banks. In the five years to 1799, twenty-six settlers were killed, and many acres of crops and several farmhouses were burnt by the Aborigines. Raiding, burning and the slaughter of livestock became effective weapons in the hands of the Aborigines and, at times large numbers of them, as many as 150 of the Darug on one occasion, were engaged. The number of Aborigines killed is not known, but it was certainly higher than that of the whites. That the peaceful and secure existence of the Aborigines was at stake is unquestionable and that they resisted settlement with all the traditional means at their disposal is equally true. In the end the British, with their superior firepower and technology, were assured of victory. Only seven British soldiers were killed by Aborigines in the 43 years to 1831.

Hunter, aged 58 in 1795, had come out to Botany Bay with the First Fleet so he knew a good deal about the early days of the colony, but his life had been largely spent at sea. While he was fortunate in being able to build on Phillip's solid foundations, his years as governor were unhappy. He was quickly aware that his subordinates had a vested interest in the continuation of the rum trade, in their monopoly of commerce, in their use of convicts and in increasing the size of their landholdings. At that time, Captain John Macarthur, aged 28 in 1795, was both leader and exemplar to his fellow military officers in the Corps. He was one of its original members; he had fought a duel with a marine captain before embarking to New South Wales' he later quarrelled with Phillip, but prospered under Grose. In the four years following his arrival in 1790, Macarthur had extensive land under cultivation at Parramatta and was selling its produce to the government, of which, as Inspector of Public Works, he was a part. Seemingly insatiable in his lust for power and wealth, he rapidly made Hunter's life miserable by vigorously resisting any effort to curb his and the Corps's control of the economy.

The five years of Hunter's period in office were spent in a losing battle trying to wrest control from the military. The good done by the Corps for the economy was in part negated by the harm it did to small landholders, who could not compete with it when selling their produce to the government stores. Moreover, they were often reduced to poverty and bankrupt by the prices, sometimes reaching 500 per cent higher than cost, of the goods imported or bought on arrival by the Corps. Profit meant everything to the Corps' officers, whose devotion to duty and sacrifice for the common good, was minimal. Accordingly, they laid down the first stones of Australia's market economy which, perhaps emblematically, was based on rum. To curb high profits going into private hands Hunter tried, without success, to establish a public store. He also failed in his attempt to cut back the number of convicts working for the officers and, generally, expenses outlayed for government requirements rose. A drought occurred in 1798–99, the Hawkesbury flooded in 1800, and the Irish political prisoners proved troublesome. The governor's period of command was marked by disappointment.

Hunter took refuge in travelling and exploring, using his considerable talents as a naturalist to good stead, while Macarthur and other detractors denounced him, unjustly, to London so that he was eventually recalled. He was not a capable administrator, but his only fault was to have clashed with the Corps, which brought about his downfall. He left in October 1800, pleased that his name had been given to the proud river at Newcastle and that a fine herd of sixty cattle had been discovered beyond the Nepean River on an area known subsequently as the Cow Pastures. Since 1788, they had thrived in the wild after the disappearance of their progenitors –two bulls and four cows, and had increased in number to about 300 by 1800.

Hunter did not then realize that the most significant event during his governorship was the arrival of thirty-three Spanish merino ewes from the Cape of Good Hope on 16 May 1797. They were sold to Macarthur and other officials, who added them to their flocks made up from various strains, including Bengal sheep. The governor was mainly responsible for the 'discovery' of the lyrebird, koala, platypus and wombat; many of his original drawings of them were deemed worthy of preservation. He permitted the opening of the first brewery in Sydney by John Boston and gave licences to public houses selling beer in order to curb the rum trade. He also attempted to set rates of pay and made attendance at church services compulsory. The opening of a playhouse on 16 January 1796 had caused him some misgivings, but the recitation of a couplet on opening night summed up the ability of the early colonists, free and felon, to laugh at themselves: 'True patriots all, for be it understood, we left our country for our country's good'. Richard Johnson left the colony with the outgoing governor, and Samuel Marsden became senior Anglican chaplain. Johnson had served his Lord with honour, and humanity with love. The words of a grateful convict, who called him: 'physician both of soul and body', were his epitaph.

The years of Governor Philip Gidley King (1800–1806) saw remarkable progress. In 1788, King had arrived in the colony as a naval officer with the First Fleet and then served as lieutenant-governor of Norfolk Island until 1796. He draw on his personal and practical knowledge of those early years with Phillip, and his attachment to the colony was shown by the names he gave his first two sons, Norfolk and Sydney, both born at Norfolk Island to a convict mother, Ann Inett, without benefit of marriage. In 1800, he quickly settled into his governorship, but the penal colony's progress depended more on private than on public enterprise, despite his increasing use of convict labour on government buildings.

Like Hunter, King tried to control the rum trade by reducing imports, but the widespread use of illicit stills thwarted his purpose. Goods were sold through the public store at only a fifty per cent mark up; profits on imports induced more private speculators to enter trade, which weakened the monopoly of the Corps. With the increasing interest shown in wool by Samuel Marsden and John Macarthur, its quality began to improve, although sealing and whaling had already become the major exports. Coal was mined at Newcastle for local use, but some shipments were made to India and the Cape of Good Hope, while more vines and tobacco were planted in the colony. In 1803 King permitted the establishment of the first newspaper, the *Sydney Gazette*, edited by the convicted shoplifter George Howe and censored by the governor's secretary. As the founder of the press in New South Wales, Howe began a tradition of generally responsible, if often inflammatory and rowdy journalism.

King's treatment of, and dealings with, the Aborigines were humane and placatory. He considered them to be 'the real Proprietors of the Soil', but that did not prevent him from making a large number of land grants, including one, improperly made, to his successor. Despite his good intentions, King came no closer than others had to understanding the Aborigines, whose conduct he deplored as ungrateful and treacherous without stating what benefits they had received from the coming of the whites. The Cadigal people had been reduced from about 50 in 1788 to three in 1790, and other bands living in close proximity to Sydney had so dwindled in number that they were little more than an irritant. To his credit, King tried to protect them. The vaccinations he introduced against smallpox, which had killed at least half of the Aborigines by 1789, were too late to be of any consequence to those already ravaged by it.

As naval officers, both Hunter and King, encouraged exploration by sea. In 1798 the naval lieutenant, Matthew Flinders, and George Bass, a sailor and surgeon, found the strait between Van Diemen's Land and the mainland, which was named in Bass's honour because he had already deduced its existence. Its use on the passage to and from England reduced the voyage by two weeks because it was no longer necessary to go south around Van Diemen's Land. Flinders returned to England, where in January 1801 he was given command of the *Investigator*. In this ship he charted the southern coast of Australia before returning to Sydney Cove in May 1802. From July 1802 to June 1803 he circumnavigated the entire continent. This voyage in the leaking *Investigator* constituted one of the great feats of navigation and hydrography in modern times. Flinders was the first to give general use to the name Australia for the country to which he made such a significant contribution. On a voyage trip home to England, he was detained in December 1803 by a heartless French commandant on Mauritius. Longing for his beloved wife Ann during the seven years of detention on the island, he was broken in health and hope. Flinders died in England on 19 July 1814, only a day after his monumental book, *Voyage to Terra Australis*, was published.

The idea still prevailed that there was an inland sea in the centre of the continent, but it was at least certain, after the circumnavigation by Flinders, that eastern and western New Holland were both parts of the one vast land mass. Meanwhile, knowledge of the east coast had expanded with an exploratory voyage that resulted in the finding of 'a noble sheet of water' in 1802, which was first named after Governor King and later changed to Port Phillip. Fears that the French intended to occupy Van Diemen's Land, combined with a desire to get rid of some of the convicts from Sydney to convince King of the need to put a settlement there. Strategic motives were therefore foremost in the founding in September 1803 of what became Tasmania. Under Lieutenant John Bowen a party of twenty-four convicts settled near the mouth of a small stream flowing into the broad Derwent River. They called the place Risdon Cove, but it was a miserable, wind-swept and infertile place.

In that same year, 1803, David Collins, who had arrived originally with Phillip in 1788 as deputy judge-advocate, was sent out directly from England to set up a new dependency on the Australian mainland. Troops, 308 male convicts, 18 hopeful settlers, several married women, children and stores accompanied him. On 9 October 1803, the true birth date of the later colony of Victoria, Collins landed near Sorrento on Port Phillip Bay. The chosen spot was unsatisfactory given the hostility of the Aborigines, the sandy soil and scarcity of fresh water, although the Bay teemed with crayfish which were caught and consumed in thousands. The troops proved difficult to control and everyone was miserable in such a barren place, so Collins transferred his little settlement to the Derwent, which he and his party reached in early 1805. Five convicts were missing at the time of the departure from Port Phillip, and one of them, William Buckley, survived and lived with the Aborigines for the next thirty-two years.

At Risdon Cove, Collins was again dissatisfied, so he moved across the river to Sullivan's Cove, which became the site for Hobart Town. Founded much as Sydney Cove had been, with the same hardship, uncertainty and lack of interest by the home authorities, the new settlement was sustained by Collins's cheerful spirit and unfailing decency although everyone was forced to live on the local game, chiefly kangaroos, for the first two years. As lieutenant-governor, Collins suffered loneliness of mind and heart. He was separated for many years from his wife Maria, who could not come out with him in 1788 and refused to do so in 1803; he fathered four children in the colony, thus earning the disapproval of some of the upright who knew little of the human spirit, but much about the rules by which they judged it.

New South Wales continued to prosper, especially in children. The small number of convict women bore them in increasing numbers largely due to their improved health, which stemmed from a better climate, more wholesome food and greater freedom. Many women opted for marriage, even to scarcely acceptable partners, because to do so was preferable to becoming a domestic servant, which usually entailed prostitution and no permanency. In 1801, King founded an orphan school for females at Sydney in the hope of removing them from 'prostitution and iniquity', which he felt prevailed to an unacceptable degree. The Female Orphan School added to the handful of rudimentary establishments which were engaged in education and run by the Anglican Church or by private entrepreneurs.

The children born in the colony had already taken on some common characteristics, being in general fine-limbed and of fair complexion, with light hair and dark eyes. They were also said to have volatile dispositions and to be proverbial talkers. By 1800, after twelve years of settlement, one in six of the white population was born in–and knew–no other home than New South Wales. Their parents still longed for news from Britain and Ireland but, to the native-born, the world across the seas was already foreign. Their physical reality was the harbour with its township around Sydney Cove, the little settlement at Parramatta and the struggling farms on the Hawkesbury, the yet unpassed mountains to the west, the heat and humidity of summer, the familiar songs of the birds, the scents of the flora and the shapes of the fauna. To the native-born, none of that reality was strange: they accepted it as their own world. In many ways they were kindred to the Aborigines, for their sinews were moulded from the same earth which knew neither bond nor free, black nor white. Like the Aborigines, they were indigenes.

Hunter considered the Irish political prisoners very troublesome and King's greatest fear was of an expected Irish uprising. The Sydney garrison remained in 'a constant state of alarm' throughout the period and it seemed certain that an insurrection would occur. After an unsuccessful rebellion in Ireland in 1798, the presence in New South Wales of about 600 'United Irishmen', who were thought to be infected with seditious sentiments, gave focus to the fears. Unconfirmed rumours of an insurrection led King to have several Irish convicts cruelly flogged in 1800. They included one lad of 20 years, Paddy Galvin, who was sentenced to receive 300 lashes by the Reverend Mr Samuel Marsden. As the skin and blood fell from him, Paddy was asked where their pikes were hidden. He replied that he did not know, but added that he would not tell his tormentors, even if he did know. Paddy said that they could hang him before he would make music to the tune of which others would dance upon air.

Despite his unease, the governor was sufficiently liberal-minded to permit a convict priest, James Dixon, to celebrate a public Mass in Sydney on 15 May 1803 and thereafter monthly. Dixon was an innocent, though convicted, victim of the 1798 rebellion. That one quarter of the population, which was Catholic and grieved the loss of the Mass, was delighted by the governor's decision. King's indulgence seemed at first to have good effects, and yet by 4 March 1804 he regretted his decision. At Castle Hill, near Toongabbie, about 300 Irish convicts, with a sprinkling of English, rose in futile insurgency against their gaolers to the cry of 'Death or Liberty'. , Armed with a motley collection of muskets, revolvers, pikes and pitchforks, they were bent on an escape from the colony. All hope of conciliation was lost when Major George Johnston, at the head of the government troops, dishonourably tricked the leaders into capture and the slaughter commenced. There were fifteen killings, followed by nine hangings and nine floggings each of from 200 to 500 lashes; the remaining prisoners were sent to gaols and coal mines.

This ill-conceived episode had both an immediate and a lasting outcome. Some saw Irish Catholicism and insurrection as being synonymous, and by none more than Samuel Marsden who even envisaged the colony being lost to Britain unless stern measures were taken to restrain the Catholics. To him, the Irish were ignorant, uncivilized and savage, destitute of true religion and lacking all morality. Marsden was convinced that the Mass was nothing more than a depraved superstition, but that all would be well if the authorities imposed his form of Christianity on everyone. Marsden's logic led to Catholics being compelled to attend Anglican services after the withdrawal of Dixon's permission to celebrate Mass. More importantly, it gave impetus to the opinion that the Irish were second-rate human beings or worse. Nonetheless they were coerced to conform to Anglicanism, which itself held little sway over the hearts and minds of most, whether convict or free. Thus, in the long term, further point was given to the idea that Anglicanism was a mere handmaiden of the state in the preservation of good order.

A minor, but more disappointing, source of anxiety to King stemmed from the behaviour of John Macarthur whose inclination to rebel was no less than that of the turbulent Irish. The difference lay in Macarthur's background, position, persistence and artfulness. In 1801, William Paterson, commanding officer of the Corps, had refused to join Macarthur in refusing allegiance to the governor's authority and the two men had fought a duel. An enraged King lodged Macarthur in prison and sent him to England for court martial. There, after being censured for misconduct, Macarthur resigned from the army. He was promised a grant of 5,000 acres of the best land in the colony to foster his visionary scheme of providing the home market with the finest of wools. To that end he bought, at auction, eight prime Spanish sheep from the Royal flocks and returned to Sydney as a civilian in 1805. King had to admit, with some pretence at good grace, that the cunning mischief-maker had outfoxed him. Although he ironically called Macarthur the 'hero of the fleece', he was forced to grant him 5,000 acres of land at the Cow Pastures. King ended his relations with Macarthur and the Corps with much relief knowing that his own days in the colony were ebbing. In August 1806 he departed cheerfully, leaving the 'hero' to his lands, flocks and plots. In fact, King was entrusting New South Wales to hoodlums bent on power and wealth.

In 1805 a census of all the white population and its flocks and herds had been taken in New South Wales In round figures there were 7,000 people of whom 4,000 were men and 1,300 women; the rest were children of whom less than 100 had received any formal education. About 600 officials guarded some 2,000 convicts. The colony had at last become self-sufficient in grain; while the number of sheep had risen to 20,000 of which Macarthur owned at least one-quarter. King had always been determined to cut costs for the one thing that ultimately mattered in London was to reduce official expenditure. His reductions led to a stockpile of unsaleable imports in 1801–03, but the frontier of economic expansion had opened, though it was to the sea rather than the land.

Further commercial contact had been established with the Pacific Islands, China, India and South America. The seal fisheries of Bass Strait seemed an endless source of riches attracting vessels from all over the world. Some of their crews were villains who abducted black women and often treated them barbarously; over time their offspring had families, which preserved the blood of the Aborigines of Van Diemen's Land. Sydney merchants, many of them emancipists, grew rich on the trade in seal oil and furs, and whaling became firmly established as the colony's principal industry. Fleets of vessels from many nations came in and out of Sydney and Hobart as they searched for deep-sea sperm whales and female whales were hunted when they came into bays to give birth. From the whales oil for lamps and tallow for soap and candles were produced and their bones were used in corsets and in umbrellas.

Outraged that the Americans were building vessels on the islands of the Strait 'in violation of the Law of Nations', in 1804 Governor King encouraged shipbuilding; within a year the first locally made whaling vessel, the *King George,* was launched in Sydney. Although the East India Company had a monopoly on trade, a Sydney merchant, Robert Campbell, had £50,000 worth of goods in his warehouse by the end of 1804. He decided to break the Company's monopoly openly in 1805 by taking a cargo of oil and fur skins to England, which was done in technical contravention of the regulations against private trading. Campbell had taken an important step in the commercial history of the colony and his act of defiance opened up New South Wales as a regular trading post. In the following year vessels sailed via Sydney to English and Chinese ports with over 2,500 tons of sperm oil. In 1807 one vessel alone, the *Favourite,* owned in Nantucket, USA, sailed for Canton with 32,000 seal skins. The carnage could not last, however, and sealing was already in decline as the islands were worked out. Notwithstanding, for thirty years, whaling, rather than wool, remained the colony's major export-earner.

The main feature, which the colony lacked, was a free labour force. By 1806, after eighteen years of settlement, there were only 610 free settlers and the local labour was occupied mainly in sealing and whaling. The resumption of the Napoleonic Wars meant that fewer ships were available as transports and there was a greater need for convict labour in the British shipyards. As a result, only about 500 male convicts arrived in 1805–07 and the cry was soon heard for more workers to make the land prosper. For the time being at least, England's seemingly inexhaustible source of criminals was the only long-term hope, and no one looked to the local Aborigines as an alternative. It seemed to be taken for granted that the black people were disinterested in taking part in a common economy except in the few instances, such as in Phillip's household, when they became part of the domestic setting.

Since the time, about 8000 years ago, when the waters of Bass Strait cut off Van Diemen's Land from the mainland, the Aborigines had survived on the large island undisturbed. They probably numbered about 5,000 in 1803. On 3 May 1804 the New South Wales Corps were surprised when they came upon a Moomairrener hunting party at Risdon Cove. They killed and wounded some of them and, in November, they killed a Leterremairrener man at Port Dalrymple, where a new settlement had briefly existed before Launceston was chosen as the permanent site. The commandant, William Paterson, rightly judged that the encounter would ensure much mischief in the future. From such bloody clashes, there and on the mainland, some whites concluded that they were dealing with treacherous, bloodthirsty and vengeful savages, who would bide their time before retaliating for the real or imaginary wrongs done to them. One way to placate them, it was thought, was to give them liberal supplies of food and trinkets. To the blacks such gifts could never make up for the loss of their land.

While the settlement of Van Diemen's Land was confined to restricted coastal areas, peaceful relations with the Aborigines were maintained. This lasted for fifteen years until 'the extension of the grazing Grounds, and progressive occupation of the Country' resulted in further conflict. In those first years the blacks continued their traditional way of life, although they did barter such commodities as kangaroo meat for mutton or seal meat. To some degree, they regarded the whites as having a role to play in black society and groups tried to enlist their help in skirmishes with their traditional enemies.

Within Sydney and in its immediate neighbourhood, the Aborigines had ceased to pose any threat to white settlement. There was an air of festivity and expectation there on 20 April 1806 when Governor King decreed that God should be praised for the mercy shown to the sovereign and his realm by the providential defeat of the Spanish and French at Trafalgar in October, 1805. His words also served to remind some how far they were away from home because seven months had passed before they heard the news of victory. Although Nelson was dead, it was hoped that Napoleon would eventually reap his doom even with Nelson gone. Furthermore, even the local Irish seemed suppressed. The new Union Flag was flown to symbolize the shackling of Ireland to Britain with the Union of 1801 and Freemasonry had been forbidden in New South Wales as a dangerous sect. It was reasonable to suppose that in London more thought would now be given to the future of Sydney Cove with the danger of invasion of England by the French finally over. Thus a general air of well-being prevailed in high quarters, although Collins and his charges in Hobart were at risk of starving. Their main source of meat was pigs fed on whale oil, which made the pork taste like the oil used in lamps. Expectancy, however, served to heighten the hopes of all, including the convicts, for a new governor was in the offing and who could tell what the change would bring?

The arrival of William Bligh in August 1806 should have given pause for thought to those whose disposition led them to question the orders, or even the whims, of higher authority. John Macarthur, on behalf of the free citizens, and George Johnston, for the military, welcomed him with an address in which they expressed their confidence that their new commander-in-chief, 'by a just, moderate, firm and wise government', would promote the happiness of all the deserving inhabitants of New South Wales. The new governor was, above all, his own man who had survived a mutiny on the *Bounty,* an arduous voyage calling for magnificent seamanship and courage on a small, open boat from Tahiti to Timor, two courts martial and several naval campaigns. Foulmouthed, autocratic, hot-tempered and impatient with incompetence, he was, nonetheless, prompt to obey orders and eager to have his own obeyed without question or hesitation. One order he had received was to stamp out the trafficking in spirits, which still prevailed in the colony. Unwisely, instead of tackling his problems in order, he soon issued an intemperate tirade against Macarthur, thus drawing up a battle line from which only one victor could emerge. In Macarthur's eyes, New South Wales since Bligh's arrival soon became 'a perfect hell'.

The rum trade and a suspect currency based on promissory notes combined with a decline in the transport of supplies during the Napoleonic Wars to ensure a setback in the colony's economy. The Hawkesbury River flooded in 1806, made 1,200 people homeless and worsened the distress. Bligh acted humanely by organizing relief for the Hawkesbury settlers and in promising that the government would buy their next crops, but the Corps resented this undertaking because it interfered with their own ability to control trade. The governor was forthright in forbidding the use of rum as barter, in outlawing private stills, and in attempting to consolidate the currency by insisting that sterling be used. Those measures would probably have proved acceptable provided he refrained from directly attacking powerful vested interests, whether those of the Corps or of private individuals.

Governor Bligh could not help himself. Three influential persons, Simeon Lord, Henry Kable and Joseph Underwood were imprisoned for a month for insulting his office and its authority; Dr D'Arcy Wentworth was summarily suspended from his hospital superintendency for using the labour of convict patients; the Irish were outraged because Bligh dispersed the leaders of a rumoured plot, even though they had been acquitted; and moderate elements in society were disgusted at his tolerance of Judge-Advocate Richard Atkins. The judge was a sensitive man broken on the wheel of a harsh society that he found unbearable and from which he fled to the solace of drink. Conscientious but incompetent, Atkins was already a shambling wreck by the time of Bligh's arrival, which deprived the governor of the legal advice he sorely needed. Bligh was forced to face his adversaries virtually alone.

With his encouragement of agriculture rather than sheep breeding, and the fact that in eighteen months he granted only 2,180 acres compared with King's grants of 60,000 acres, Bligh further alienated the wealthy and the powerful. Marsden perceptively remarked that any governor who attempted to curb such elements, among them the minister of religion himself, would be resisted implacably. The only firm support which Bligh received came from the poorer farmers, especially those on the Hawkesbury, who were grateful for his attempt to break the monopolies, but they were without a voice, unorganised and distant from Sydney. On the other hand, the Corps was closely bonded, capable of any mischief, including insubordination, and possessed a strong and impetuous *de facto* leader in John Macarthur. By late January 1808, Macarthur had every reason to act against Bligh for he found himself in court properly charged with several 'misdemeanours and outrageous offences'. The six officers of the Corps who acted as the jury in the trial released him after he had refused to be judged by Atkins. Bligh regarded the behaviour of the officers as treasonable, which prompted their commanding officer, George Johnston, to demand the governor's resignation and have him arrested on the twentieth anniversary of the colony, 26 January 1808. Two weeks before, a vessel had arrived from the Cape of Good Hope bearing 8,000 gallons of spirits destined to be used as currency by the Corps. The deposition of Bligh became known as the 'Rum Rebellion'.

Although not without precedent in British colonial affairs, the arrest and deposition of Bligh was caused almost entirely by his attempts at reform in the colony. Had he been permitted to continue in office there would have been a wider distribution of wealth in favour of those less well off. Having been used as a 'catspaw' by Macarthur and his friends, Johnston was abandoned by them and was fortunate that he was merely cashiered when found guilty of mutiny by a court martial in London. He returned to the colony in 1813 to die in riches and respectability in 1823; his beautiful Jewish wife, Esther, who had come to the colony as a convict aged sixteen, had remained 'through evil and through good report the faithful wife and companion'.

Macarthur found it convenient to remain in exile until 1817, while his wife, Elizabeth, watched over his affairs; most notably his sheep for those nine long years, thereby laying her claim to be a founder of the Australia's wool industry. Their marriage had been happy from the start and John acknowledged that his 'best beloved Elizabeth' was a woman beyond compare, to whom he felt eternal gratitude. She welcomed him home joyously after their 'cruel separation', even though it was entirely his own fault that they had been so long apart; she observed that he had changed little except that gout bothered him more.

The administration of the colony changed little under the interregnum during which three acting-governors were all commanders of the Corps. Bligh left Sydney on 12 May 1810 after a farewell fete given in his honour by his successor. He lived in obscurity in England as a vice-admiral, undaunted by the fact that twice in his life men had mutinied against his rule. He was a superb navigator and a loyal lieutenant, to whom Nelson once said: 'Bligh, 1 thank you; you have supported me nobly!' His imprudent spirit, unbridled tongue and vile temper had marred the substance of the good he had courageously attempted to achieve.

Recognition was readily granted in England that New South Wales had achieved its purpose and remained a fit place to receive more convicts. Any intention by the French to settle had been thwarted, Van Diemen's Land was firmly established after twenty years, the population had grown to 12,000, some schools, a few churches and a post office had been erected. Sydney itself was beginning to look like a future city. All manner of fruit and vegetables grew profusely. Land exploration had taken place to the south-west up to a distance of over 100 miles. Horse-racing, cricket, primitive football, cockfighting and sundry other English sports were common, and the upper echelons of society held evenings of more refined entertainment.

Trading and dealing in imports were flourishing, even if they sometimes resembled gambling rather than commerce; and local manufacturing had commenced. Woolen, linen and leather goods were produced and several potteries, four breweries and eight windmills were in operation. Hops had been grown since 1806 by James Squire at Kissing Point, but scarcely any wine was produced because the vines were blighted annually. The pastoral industry was developing slowly because there were still too few sheep in the colony able to grow fleeces from which coarse hair had been totally bred out. In any event, sheep sold at £2 each after the Hawkesbury floods and there were very few settlers with the capital required to put a flock together. Local publishing had begun to develop; the *Sydney Gazette* continued, and the first book, with the formidable title *New South Wales General Standing Orders,* was published in 1802, followed by the *New South Wales Pocket Almanack* in 1806 and thereafter annually from 1808 until 1835.

Some of the names of those who came in bondage became bywords for commercial success. Mary Reiby owned vessels, shops, warehouses and farms, while Simeon Lord and Henry Kable were pillars of minor commercial empires. Those with capital and contacts in England started valuable enterprises with comparative ease: the Blaxland brothers were notable examples. Gregory arrived in 1806 followed later by John. They were able to buy 1,700 head of cattle from the government herds, to receive in perpetuity 4,000 acres of land of their own choice, and they had at their disposal forty convicts who were maintained for eighteen months at government expense. It was indeed a liberal arrangement and partly explained the rapid prosperity of some free settlers to whom similar avenues would never have been opened in their homeland. Enterprise and necessity were the twins that led to abundance and ease; decency and order were enjoined on all, and observed by many; while the rights of free individuals were respected, provided they did not conflict with the ambitions of the powerful.

The lot of convict women continued to be a shameful and cruel one. In countless instances they were forced into prostitution on the long voyage to Australia. They arrived in a brutal society; many found themselves dumped on landing because there was no shelter in Sydney provided for them until 1803. Their condition was sometimes worse than that of the Aborigines, who, at least, had the consolation of their families. Without doubt some convict women were depraved by choice. For most, necessity knew no virtue when it came to obtaining the means of subsistence for themselves and their children, of whom over one-half were born out of wedlock. Only one-quarter of the convict women were married. One observer thought that the colony was a burden on the Mother Country because licentiousness was rampant due to the tolerance of fornication. To such observers, the fornicators, unless checked, would inherit the earth. In reality, the earth seemed to be gathered into the hands of the Macarthurs, Blaxlands and others in whom moral uprighteousness was taken for granted.

Many, nameless to posterity, continued to suffer under the convict system and among them some were exiled to Norfolk Island. Most convicts were lonely and longed for loved ones, whose fading faces and voices were far away in England or Ireland. On the mainland the chain gang and convict garb were familiar sights, constantly reminding everyone of the purpose of the colony's foundation; floggings and hangings were common occurrences to which even the refined grew accustomed. The convicts separated themselves into their own classes and informed on one another, creating hatreds and bitterness. In prisons and lock-ups, young men grew old and worn in bondage, while the road gangs were abominations in which vice and misery abounded. On many a wrist and ankle the marks of the manacles remained for life. Although many convicts escaped the worst hardships of the system by service in government offices or by being assigned to private individuals, New South Wales remained a vile prison for those who came there under sentence.

Close to hand, there were other forgotten ones as the Aborigines about Sydney, reduced to a remnant, were regarded by some whites as superior to brutes only in their use of weapons and fire; means which proved powerless when confronting the techniques of Industrial Man. Some few survivors had fled back towards the mountains or to places little known to them in previous generations. There, to the mournful melody of their songs and the recitation of their ancient legends, they dreamt of happier times before the days of Botany Bay and Sydney Cove. Forces far beyond their control were shaping the future.

4

'The Land, Boys, We Live In'

By 1810 the fate of New South Wales was still in the balance. While playing a minor strategic role as an obstacle to French settlement, the colony could have remained useful as a dumping ground for English and Irish criminals, as well as being a whaling station. However, there was little about it that would have ensured its long-term survival, especially if the cost to the British government outweighed its economic returns and prospects. To ensure the survival of the penal colony, a governor was needed who combined common sense with vision, had a deep sense of humanity and was determined to exercise proper authority. Economic success required a staple product to attract capital and ensure profit. A governor of the required calibre was at hand and, on the land that stretched out from Sydney, sheep in increasing numbers and with ever-finer wool were providing that staple. When Lachlan Macquarie reached New South Wales late in 1809, he found it a vast prison and called it, a 'Convict Country'. He governed it as such. When he left in 1822 it had grown into a colony.

Lachlan Macquarie, a Scot, a soldier and a man with enlarged opinions of his own capabilities, was quick to smart under criticism, but he was of loyal heart and remarkable vision. He took office as governor of New South Wales on 1 January 1810. Essentially he acted as a benevolent autocrat to whom the idea of being curbed by advisors was an anathema. To him, New South Wales was a large, unwalled place of punishment and exile in which all– free or bond – had to accept the reality of their condition. His powers, like those of his predecessors were immense. To let the death penalty run its course or to exercise mercy, to grant freedom or to refuse it, to give land or withhold it, to assign convicts or keep them in government service – all this and much besides lay in his keeping.

The new governor, like Phillip before him, had fallen almost by chance into his office when a duly nominated official declined to accept the position. Macquarie received detailed instructions on the need to improve the morals of the colonists by encouraging marriage, to promote education and to prohibit the use of 'Spirituous Liquors'. He was also told to encourage an increase in agriculture and stock raising. He was fortunate in that he had his own regiment of 700 soldiers who replaced the New South Wales Corps. The Corps had contributed something to the colony's progress, together with a good deal in monopolistic economic activity and widespread strife. The colony was well rid of the Corps, while the absence of the principal actors in the uprising against Bligh also helped. Macquarie set some matters right by reinstating the officers who had been dismissed after Bligh's arrest and by reversing the decisions of government enacted in the intervening years. As a result, the general population, especially those who were firmly settled, free or emancipated, saw in Macquarie's person and office the promise of stability after the turbulence of the preceding few years. Economic depression, droughts, floods and caterpillar plagues could not be avoided and occurred variously in 1814, 1817 and 1819. Yet the population, especially the number of convicts, grew rapidly with the final cessation in 1815 of the Napoleonic Wars in which Britain had been spasmodically engaged for over twenty years. Three-quarters of the convicts transported to Australia arrived after the end of the Napoleonic Wars.

Without work, especially among a large convict population, discontent and misery would soon have become widespread. Macquarie, with great good sense, was ever ready to embark on public projects and especially when the economic situation or natural disasters combined with an abundant supply of convict labour to put at his disposal a workforce not readily employable in the private sector. He built roads, schools, barracks and general utilities, which helped to compensate for the neglect of the previous decade. In this work he had the support of Francis Greenway, cantankerous and querulous but an architect of genius, who had been transported for concealing his assets in bankruptcy. Greenway was able to blend the new landscape and the lines of the classical past into buildings that reached their apogee in his masterpiece, St Matthew's Anglican Church at Windsor. At the same time he led a life of disorder and unhappiness; even Macquarie's patronage did not save him from a flogging by an enraged army officer who felt that the architect had insulted him. Thus a division in society based on the refusal of many of the free to accept the human worth of those who had been convicts was already apparent.

Macquarie was determined to enhance the observance of morality by encouraging marriages. In cooperation with the ministers of the now several denominations, he also enforced the convicts to attend church services. At heart, he held that only the Anglicans had any legitimacy and, in 1818, he deported Jeremiah O'Flynn, the original claimant to the Catholic chaplaincy. With some justification, he considered the Catholic priest to be uneducated and deficient in sound constitutional principles, but he soon established a relationship of greater trust with O'Flynn's successor, Father John Therry. Macquarie laid the foundation stone of St Mary's Church near Hyde Park on 29 October 1821 as the last public act of his governorship: when the priest passed him the trowel to set the stone, Macquarie put him at ease by saying that, as an old mason, he would do the job well.

Education for the growing population of colonial born had become a pressing concern. The governor decided to establish new 'Macquarie' townships at Richmond, Windsor and Liverpool in each of which he set up a school, and at Parramatta he also opened an orphan school for girls. His principles did not deter him from using a variety of flexible means to obtain his ends. A hospital was erected in Sydney and at no cost to the government by giving its builders the right to import 45,000 gallons of spirits and thus to control trade in that commodity. This transaction gave rise to the name of Rum Hospital, although the gracious building deserved better. In 1817 the governor showed considerable courage by helping to establish the Bank of New South Wales without authorization from London. He named many towns or geographical features after English royalty or government officials, but the Lachlan and Macquarie Rivers perpetuate his name.

As the first army governor, Macquarie's interest in exploration by land was uppermost. The country between the sea and the Blue Mountains was rapidly filling up with settlers; in 1813 William Wentworth, Gregory Blaxland and William Lawson crossed the mountain barrier and found pastures 'sufficient to feed all the stock in the colony for thirty years'. A road was built, opening the plains beyond the mountains to grazing, and thus, subsequently, giving rise to the foundation of the town of Bathurst in 1815. The fine lands of the Hunter Valley near Newcastle were soon occupied and Port Macquarie was named by John Oxley in 1818. Macquarie visited it and decided to place a settlement for hardened convicts there. With its majestic headland looking out to the Pacific and over the mouth of the Hastings River, with long miles of glorious beaches to north and south, Port Macquarie soon became a place of human suffering and degradation for the convicts.

To the convicts in Sydney, only one place was worse in its isolation; removal to its shores was feared more than death. Norfolk Island, a lonely, windswept speck a thousand miles north-east out in the Pacific was a hell hole where men's spirits shrivelled up in misery, but its redeeming feature was its smallness so that few could live there. After proving useless for timber and flax, it was abandoned in 1814 and the inhabitants were transferred to Van Diemen's Land. Some of the free among them made their new residences at New Norfolk. They built inns and churches, farmed hops and grew prosperous.

Collins had died in 1810 and, in 1813, he was succeeded as lieutenant-governor of Van Diemen's Land by 'Mad' Tom Davey, whom Macquarie considered a low buffoon. 'Mad' Tom did what he could with the human material at his disposal, but the material proved difficult to mould. The first direct consignment of 200 male convicts arrived in Hobart in 1812, but an American privateer captured a vessel carrying female convicts. Allegedly, they were put down on an island in the Atlantic on 17 January 1813 and never heard of again.

Davey's humane disorganization gave way to a semblance of order in 1817 with the arrival of William Sorell. The new lieutenant-governor quickly turned his attention to a lawless regime made up of escaped convicts led by Michael Howe, who called himself 'Governor of the Woods'. Sorrell also gave shape to the administrative life of the island; supported the development of agriculture and pastoralism and ruled firmly over the convict establishments. He also tried to protect the Aborigines who, in some measure, had settled into trusting relations with the whites on whom they relied for much sought after commodities such as tea and flour, as well as for dogs, which they used to hunt kangaroos and to guard their dwellings at night.

Elements of social harmony were established in Van Diemen's Land when free settlers arrived in increasing numbers. In recognition of their needs Sorrell helped to set up the Bank of Van Diemen's Land. He also imported merinos from Macarthur's flock at Camden to form the base of a fine wool industry on the island. Respected and even loved by many who appreciated his essential decency and sense of justice, and despite Macquarie's tolerance of Sorrell's situation, he fell into official disfavour because he lived with another man's wife while his own wife remained in England with their seven children. His career was terminated by 1824 and Van Diemen's Land owed much of its early development to his generally wise administration.

The convicts to Macquarie were children of misfortune, although he had a low opinion of many of the women whom he regarded as 'very depraved'. Once a convict became free, the governor held firmly that he or she stood on an equal footing with the free inhabitants, and he thought no obstacle ought to be erected by society to prevent them from attaining such equality. In his judgement, most convicts, with proper encouragement, would regain their rightful place in the community and, to illustrate his policy, he gave responsible roles to those who proved their value. He mixed socially with some chosen few of them and named Michael Robinson as poet laureate despite his ex-convict status and the generally poor quality of his verse. There were immediate objections to this policy of social equality. Samuel Marsden had been nominated to the board of trustees of the Parramatta turnpike road, but the clergyman refused to associate publicly with two emancipists whom Macquarie had also nominated. Judge Jeffrey Bent would not permit ex-convict attorneys to plead in his court, which effectively kept it closed for eighteen months. On similar grounds, the officers of a new regiment, which arrived in 1814, refused to dine at the Governor's table.

Undeterred, the Governor always looked favourably upon the native-born who, together with the emancipists (ex-convicts), made up three-quarters of the population. Macquarie regarded the native-born as true citizens of New South Wales and he gave them small grants of land, averaging 20 to 30 acres each. To his superiors in Whitehall, he made it plain that he regarded free settlers, like the Blaxlands, as 'by far the most discontented Persons in the Colony'. They thought that the government owed them favours simply because they had deigned to come to Australia. He also pointed out that it cost more to settle them in comparison to the emancipists. To Macquarie the best settlers were the former convicts 'who cultivate the ground in Gratitude', while many free settlers either allowed it to lie idle or sold it as quickly as possible.

Macquarie does not seem to have long pondered on something that was happening around him daily with the birth of people who called themselves, and thought of themselves, as Australians. He was proud that his only son, Lachlan, was born an Australian but the governor never questioned what an understanding of birthplace meant to his son. Unlike young Lachlan, nine out of every ten of the native-born were the children of convicts, and they carried the stigma of their parents to the grave. They were popularly known as 'currency' because they were deemed to be of lesser value than the 'sterling', who had been born in the British Isles, and who knew no shame in their birth. Most convict mothers were fiercely proud of their children for whom they wanted the best, despite the obstacles they would met as they grew to adulthood. Perhaps deep in his being Macquarie sensed something of this development: on 21 December 1817, he formally adopted the name Australia, suggested by Matthew Flinders in 1814, in his official correspondence. This was a sincere and lasting act, but the ancient continent became, and long remained, a pale reflection of its British progenitor. By mere chronological chance it escaped being named Queensland or Victoria because the monarch of that name had not then commenced her reign.

The Aborigines came early to the benevolent, if paternalistic, attention of the Governor. After meeting with the remains of the Sydney Aborigines, he invited them to establish closer and more open relations, and he set up a school for their children whom he wanted to make 'useful to the Country'. In February 1815 he established an Aboriginal farm at George's Head and declared Bungaree to be chief of the Broken Bay Aborigines. Annually, at Parramatta, Macquarie engaged in a kind of festivity, handing out medals and uniforms to the Aborigines and generally behaving as if the Indian Raj could be duplicated in Australia, but it was all futile because the Aborigines refused to relinquish their own ways, nor did they adopt, corporally or spiritually, the trappings of another's.

An old black man put into words the dilemma which the relationship between the two races now presented. In response to a remonstrance that his fire threatened to burn down a haystack, with the dignity of immemorial security, he replied: 'You know that we must have our fire; the country is *ours, you* must take care of your corn'. In the end it was an issue of whose fire was the strongest. Despite his good will, Macquarie sent three British army detachments to the Hawkesbury-Nepean districts in 1816. The overall strength of the detachments – 6 officers and 68 other ranks– was the largest deployed to that time. The intention was to punish the Aborigines for their predatory habits, which often included killing and stealing livestock, and to offer them the chance to become settlers. Women and children were to be spared, but the men, if they refused to surrender, were to be shot. The military shot 14 of them dead and took 5 prisoners, all of whom were released within a month.

Despite Macquarie's efforts at moral reform, the estimate of the colony held by many in the British Isles was low and, in the House of Commons, William Wilberforce said that 'a nest of vipers' was fast being built there. Some British politicians were also alarmed at the cost of Macquarie's administration and at the rumours of his lenient treatment of the convicts. In 1819 they sent out John Thomas Bigge to ascertain the true state of affairs. Bigge, former chief justice of Trinidad, reached Sydney in September 1819. He was asked to report whether transportation was sufficiently severe as a form of punishment or whether Macquarie, with his 'ill considered compassion' was turning the place into a happy haven for criminals.

Bigge went to work with a will, ably abetted by John Blaxland and others whose antipathy to Macquarie was deep-seated. Given his advisors, it was easy for Bigge to conclude that the colony should become a vast sheep-walk, ruled by men possessing large estates and with a properly submissive convict workforce at their disposal. This was a proposition Macquarie partly agreed with, but he also had another vision of a penitentiary gradually evolving into a society in which men and women, reclaimed from crime by honest toil and the chance of a stake in the land, would throw off the stains of their past and become the masters of their own destiny. Bigge's was an acceptable political judgement because it fitted closely the developing economic reality. It would also cut the cost to the home country of the upkeep of the convict establishment, a matter which necessity made uppermost in the minds of the British civil servants and their political masters. Bigge's other strictures on Macquarie's rule, accusing him of overspending, of erecting ostentatious public buildings, of showing favour to emancipists and of mismanaging convicts, were unjust and ill-founded. The principal accusation, that the Governor had deprived free settlers of convict labour, was wide of the mark. Macquarie had certainly turned to a renewal of public works in 1817 that necessitated the increased use of convict labour. Yet, 1817 proved to be a year of disastrous floods during which the influx of convict labour could not readily be assigned.

Bigge's accusations were fed by the exclusive element in society who wanted to keep ex-convicts on the fringes and to control the economy by using convict labour to that end. In the midst of all the tension caused by Bigge's visit, it was with relief that Macquarie finally heard that his third attempt to resign had been accepted. He sailed from Australia in 1822 and eked out his days at home trying to salvage his reputation from the 'false, vindictive and malicious' reports of Commissioner Bigge. Macquarie left his mark on the land not merely with his name, which was revered by thousands, but through a legacy worthy of every generation because he had tried to judge human beings on their potential rather than on their past.

The population was approaching 25,000 of whom two-thirds were convicts or ex-convicts, so it was easy to brand them all with criminality. The remarkable fact, however, was that the criminals and former criminals generally behaved in a way far removed from that which had caused them to be transported in the first instance. Even more positive was the notable manner in which the children born from them rejected a tendency to crime. They were often slighted by the local appellation 'Currency' which implied that they were of lesser value than those of sterling character born of free parents in the old countries.

The native-born tended to marry amongst themselves, to avoid the 'higher orders' in society and to work industriously. Newcomers sometimes regarded them with humour because – out of the amalgam of accents ranging from cockney to Irish, from rural English to Scottish, and from the upper classes to the dwellers on the hulks – a new idiom was emerging spoken in a new accent which, in both tonality and content, seemed inferior and slightly foreign. Finally with their quiet assumption that Australia was their home by right, their easy manner and their familiarity with each other and the land itself, they seemed to imply that their's was a unique position. Governor Macquarie had accepted all this and indeed seemed to show pride in it while others, and notably the well-to-do, deplored it.

In London the question was finally asked whether New South Wales could continue to be ruled by an all-powerful governor in the manner of Macquarie or whether it was time to give the more respectable citizens a say in their own affairs. It was clearly inconceivable that any form of democracy based on a vote could be introduced into what was, in effect, a huge prison. Nevertheless, some of the more worthy citizens could be called upon to advise the Governor in an official way and in 1823 a Legislative Council for New South Wales was established.

Van Diemen's Land was given a Council in 1825 and it then began to enjoy a little independence from Sydney. Chief Justices were also appointed in Sydney and Hobart to preside over the courts and a legal system began to proliferate with quarter sessions, petty sessions, paid and unpaid magistrates and all the other trappings designed to ensure that law and good order prevailed, especially in the realm of the acquisition and retention of property. New South Wales was especially fortunate in that, with the appointment of Francis Forbes as first Chief Justice, it acquired a judge of probity, dignity, wisdom and honour. At the same time, the role of the Church of England was also strengthened symbolically by a regulation, which never became effective, issued in London in 1825 which set aside one-seventh of the land for the support of its clergy and schools, despite the fact that the Church was not by law established as in England.

John Macarthur was the principal representative of that portion of the community which saw itself as possessing both the right and duty to lead other less advantaged persons, and he was duly appointed to the Legislative Council. Since his return to Botany Bay in 1817, he had greatly prospered with enormous increases to his land and flocks. By 1822 he was winning gold medals for his wool from the Society of Arts in London and also receiving extraordinarily high prices for it. His days of wholeness in mind and body were drawing in, and by 1832, officially now a lunatic, he was removed from the Legislative Council to die in 1834 survived by Elizabeth, three sons and three daughters whose loyalty and hard work were much responsible for his reputation as a breeder of fine-wooled sheep. His remains were put to rest at Camden Park which had grown to over 60,000 acres of the finest land in the colony. Never one to curry favour with friends or to forgive an enemy, implacably opposed to those who wanted rights he saw as contrary to his own, he remains the unique publicist of the pastoral industry, without being its only founder.

While Macarthur was declining, others were on the rise and none more so than William Charles Wentworth. Son of D'Arcy Wentworth's union with a convict woman, Catherine Crowley, William was born at sea on the voyage to Norfolk Island in 1790. Always conscious of the 'sacred claims' that Australia had upon him, he was educated in England, and went to the bar there but devoted much of his life to winning a free constitution for his country, although his own concept of freedom was limited by his developing conviction that democracy had to be reined in by men whose intelligence and position gave them an obligation to rule.

When Wentworth realized that his father had been tried four times for highway robbery and that, having quarrelled with John Macarthur, he could not marry his daughter Elizabeth upon whom he had set his heart, he became the most vigorous crusader for the Australian-born and the arch enemy of the exclusive clique who declined to mix with emancipists or to see them restored to their full civil rights. After being called to the English bar, he wrote, at Cambridge, a poem which was full of pride in his beloved Australia while still seeing her as England's 'last born infant' and therefore 'A new Britannia in another world!'

Like so many provincials since empires first founded colonies, Wentworth always suffered from not belonging in either world. His heart, his struggles and his sufferings were all Australian while his spirit, mind and final hopes rested in England. They proved to be irreconcilables that never fused. On his return to New South Wales in 1824, he spent his energies attacking the government and the landed establishment in the *Australian* newspaper which he and Robert Wardell founded. He praised Macquarie's successor Brisbane for his liberal stance and attacked Ralph Darling (Governor 1824–31), who believed that upholding the King's authority was his foremost duty even when doing so aroused widespread displeasure. Darling was openly in favour of the large landholders, but he brought some benefit to the colony by creating an effective civil service.

During his early years of struggle for popular rights, Wentworth's most notable victory, for which he had long fought, was the introduction of trial by jury into the criminal courts which was achieved by 1833. Privately, however, he was becoming a mirror image of Macarthur and those whom he most despised. He bought a stately mansion at Vaucluse and adorned it with all the trappings of another world, he multiplied his sheep runs to at least fifteen and his legal activity helped to swell his wealth. The poor, the humble, the emancipists and the native-born still looked on him as their hero, especially when he and his friends, from the beach at Vaucluse, farewelled the departing vessel of the despised Darling with a blaze of bonfires and barbecues, gin and beer. How far he would lead them if their desire was genuine equality with their betters, was another matter, but, in the meantime, lion-hearted and lion-maned, Wentworth went his way scarcely noticing that New South Wales itself was changing.

The ways of change were steady but perceptible and they included the establishment of a Chamber of Commerce in Sydney in 1825, a subscription library under the direction of Thomas de la Condamine, Darling's secretary, which was opened in the following year, and in 1827 the Colonial (later Australian) Museum was founded. Gradually Australia was developing from a much despised and maligned prison to a place suitable for British capital and British free settlers. Wentworth himself wrote a book on the colony detailing its development which had helped produce this effect. The economic advantages to be derived from wool, the opening of new lands to the pastoral industry and the ready availability of a labour force, still based on transportation but gradually including free settlers, all helped development. It was still fashionable in some quarters throughout the 1820s to portray Botany Bay, with intentional use of the name, as a sink of iniquity into which the scum of humanity was thrown, although by the 1830s this misrepresentation was wearing thin in the eyes of those with any real knowledge of the colony.

After the crossing of the Blue Mountains, exploration went ahead apace. In 1818 the Surveyor-General, John Oxley, pushed further west past Bathurst and then north-east, naming the rivers, the Namoi, Peel, Apsley, Macleay and Hastings. His most important discovery was that of the Liverpool Plains where settlement soon followed. Phillip Parker King, who was a legitimate son of the former Governor, was born on Norfolk Island in 1791. From 1817 to 1822 he carried out four skilful surveys of the coast of northern Australia, thereby making a significant contribution to exploration. At an early age, King was made a fellow of the Royal Society, and in 1855 he was promoted to Rear Admiral. He was among the very few native-born in that period who become well-known outside their own country.

For the brave, the skilled or the mere adventurous, exploration demanded courage and perseverance because it was always hazardous and arduous. The navigators and explorers had to face uncharted seas, dense bush, flooded rivers, extensive marshes, trackless wastes, high slopes followed by deep valleys, and not infrequent attacks by Aborigines which were forcefully repulsed.

While further coastal surveying had not revealed land fit for pastoralism, the conviction was still strong that close to the coast or beyond the mountain range there would always be fertile land available. Such proved to be the case when, in the steps first of James Meehan and later Charles Throsby, settlement took place in a vast area beyond the Cow Pastures through to Bathurst in the north-west and then down through Goulburn, past Lake George, to the south-west. Throsby said with justification and foresight that he had covered ground 'where fine woolled sheep may be increased to any amount in a climate peculiarly congenial to them'.

Although the continuation of exploration south-west of Sydney was relatively simple as the terrain was not difficult, in the opening up of pastoral country, it was one of unparalleled importance. Hamilton Hume, born near Parramatta in 1797, and English-born William Hovell set out from Hume's station near Gunning in 1824 with a small party, including six convicts. They soon came to a gracious river which they left with the Aboriginal name Murrumbidgee and going further south they saw the Alps, which they named, to their east. The highest peak of the Alps was not named until 1840 when, the Pole, Paul Strzelecki, called it Kosciusko in honour of his nation's democratic patriot.

When Hume and Hovell arrived at another imposing river, with winding billabongs and great gums hugging its banks, they called it Hume. It was changed later to Murray in honour of an English public servant of minor consequence and never went back to any of its names, such as Millewa, from the tongues of the old people who had lived from its munificence for long ages. Hume and Hovell arrived, eleven weeks after setting out, at Corio Bay and they mistook it for Westernport which was their goal.

Hume and Hovell's journey was not followed up until 1836 when Major Thomas Mitchell also went south and west. He penetrated into country which caused him to prophesy that he was 'the harbinger of mighty changes' because men and animals would trace his path into land of undreamt fertility. Unmindful of the Aborigines who had long been there, or even of the help given by them to him in his journey, Mitchell proclaimed that at length a country had been found 'ready for the immediate reception of civilized men' and he called it 'Australia Felix' to contrast it with those wastes he had seen a few weeks before as he explored the desert about the Darling River.

When searching for a suitable site for another penal outpost at an appropriate distance from settlement, Oxley discovered in 1823 a river flowing to the coast about 600 miles north of Sydney. He called the river after Governor Brisbane and a settlement was established at Moreton Bay in 1824. Convicts who had been reconvicted since their arrival in the colony were sent to Moreton Bay and Captain Patrick Logan became commandant in the following year. Logan was later remembered by some as the founding father of the north because of his drive to establish the settlement and his exploratory work in the region. By the convicts, he was regarded as a depraved beast to whom cruelty was natural. In eight months in 1827 he ordered 200 floggings totalling over 11,000 lashes in a convict population of less than 700. When he was killed by the Aborigines the convicts 'manifested insane joy at the news of his murder, and sang and hoorayed all night'.

Despite the presence of the penal settlement, pastoral expansion went ahead in the north. Allan Cunningham, botanist and explorer, made his way from the Hunter Valley onto the Darling Downs in 1827 and he described the more than 5,000 square miles of the Downs as inexhaustible in pasture with an 'extraordinary luxuriance of growth' suitable to both sheep and cattle. Cunningham then found a pass which bears his name between the Downs and the coast, thus allowing the settlement of the Downs and with easy access to a port at Brisbane.

While these exploratory expeditions had almost immediate economic significance through the expansion of the pastoral industry, another development in settlement occurred in those years which, while merely symbolic of its stated objective, had the psychological effect of making British claims to the whole of the continent a reality. Over twenty years previously, a French expedition had named the whole south-east coastline Napoleon's Land with a gulf called after Bonaparte and another after Josephine. There were fears that the French intended to take some part of the mainland for their own, a mistaken but understandable reaction given the Napoleonic Wars. The long-term effect was a determination to get in first and in 1824 a military station was placed on Melville Island to the north-west of the continent and moved onto the mainland two years later. A settlement was also established at Westernport where Hume and Hovell thought they had been and another began at King Georges Sound in the extreme south-west of the continent. The first two were quickly relinquished but the last became Albany and, in time, flourished, especially as a whaling station and was thus the first white settlement in Australia's western half.

In this manner, the secure tenure of the whole land mass was ensured by the 1820s and the means of using those parts of it which were regarded as suitable were increasing rapidly. By a happy combination of careful breeding for the climatic conditions and the available grasses, the sheep fitted the new land as easily as the kangaroo had done. It was an ominous coincidence that, when he came to Australia, the white settler in some measure adopted the precise means of subsistence of the Aborigines. For food, and eventually for profit, he fished the seas and for the same purpose he used the land but the pastoral industry caused immediate and understandable conflict with the

Aborigines. Where the kangaroos had grazed the sheep did likewise, yet, while the Aborigines were content with a moderate sufficiency of land, no boundary could contain the whites.

Thus, the spread of the pastoral industry was the most decisive threat to the continued existence of black culture and, in some real measure, to the very race itself. That the Aborigines opposed white expansion with all the forces they could muster is undeniable. It is equally a fact that in the end in Australia, as elsewhere when a more technologically advanced civilization clashed with one not so advanced, the civilization of the white race triumphed. One result was that, although in 1821 a meagre 175,000 pounds of wool were exported to England, the clip increased to a million pounds in 1826 and to two million four years later, although Spain and Germany still accounted for the greater imports of wool there.

The basis of a permanent and expanding economy was thus laid, which served rather than competed with British interests, opened up possibilities for surplus capital and labour, and gave prospects of beneficial trade. As a consequence, Australia showed no signs of becoming other than a large scale consumer of British manufactured goods, and India and China played a minor role in imports. Most attention was rapidly fixed on the pastoral industry to the detriment of manufacturing, which had already shown promise. Items ranging from salt to ships, candles, leather goods, some tobacco and good quality cheese, cloth, hats, blankets and stockings were made and the wine industry was improving. There were also some developments in exports with flour to the Cape Colony in 1820, horses to Batavia and India, timber to England and wheat to the Cape and Rio de Janeiro. None of this ceased, but its importance diminished as wool became the dominant, staple component in the economy.

In 1828, a census was taken in New South Wales, just forty years after Phillip and his contingent had perched themselves precariously at Sydney Cove. The blacks, or what remained of them, were not counted, but the whites now numbered 36,598, of whom a third lived in Sydney. The ratio of one, who had come by their own choice, to three, who had not, still prevailed amongst the adults while only one child in five could look to parents without the convict stain. There were three males to every female so that it was a male dominated society, and 25,248 declared themselves Protestants to 11,236 Catholics, which left only 114 non-Christians. Those simple figures reveal more about New South Wales than any number of diatribes designed to denigrate it. The colony was home to the native-born, to the emancipists and to those who worked its soil and minded its flock. The rest, jailers and newcomers, were transients to be tested by time. Amongst those who passed the test was John Dunmore Lang.

Lang was an indomitable Scottish Presbyterian minister, writer and historian. He was also a man of large vision, financial ineptitude, narrow prejudices and almost unrelenting bigotry. His whole life was given point by an unsurpassed love for Australia, which seemed to start from the day of his arrival in 1823 and grow in intensity thereafter. Impressed with the need to uplift educational standards, he was concerned with the founding of a school and, for the general population, he started a newspaper. His greatest weakness was an insatiable urge for litigation, while his quickness to judge his fellow man was legendary. Lang was encouraged and never criticised by his wife, Wilhelmina, whom he married when he was thirty-one and she, eighteen. The couple shared with many other Australians the tragedy of infant mortality, as five of their ten children died very young. Of Australia, Lang wrote that she could never be 'a land of slaves', and his life's work was devoted to her uplifting.

As early as 1804, Maurice Margarot, one of the 'Scottish Martyrs' transported to Sydney for sedition, contemplated a future Australian republic and said that New South Wales would 'bid adieu to its fond parent as soon as it feels sufficiently strong'. Wentworth wrote in 1819 of the possibility of revolution in Australia on the American model, but he quickly changed into a loyal imperialist. In the words of the American Patrick Henry, John Fulton, native-born son of a minister of religion who had been transported for sedition, cried 'give us liberty or give us death'. In Lang, these small beginnings of a move towards an Australian republic suffered a mighty surge. Because he was a proclaimed loyalist who feared no earthly master, Lang could afford to be outspoken. His great aim in life was to achieve a free and independent 'great Australian nation' in which there would be 'government for and by the people'. Having visited America in 1840 he came home fired with republican ambitions and wanted a 'President of the United States of Australia'. His vision remained a dream.

By the late 1820s, there were 13,000 convicts put out to work for masters, mostly in the pastoral industry, and their labour was the key to economic development. Bigge's recommendations had been followed about the use of convict labour, which made for a harsh system of chance in which a convict enjoyed reasonable comfort and dignity under a humane master but degradation and suffering under another. British capitalists had also listened to Bigge and New South Wales was now seen as a place where capital could be safely invested; they had turned their attention to the benefits to be gained from a colony where physical coercion was the accepted means of controlling a labour force. The lash was used vigorously throughout the whole of society, and public hangings, to the order of forty to fifty a year, provided a form of sport, as well as a warning, to the populace. When the rights of property were violated the law normally showed no mercy. William Longhurst, aged twenty-three, was hanged in 1827 at Hobart for sheep stealing, which was the only charge levelled against him since his arrival a few years previously. Port Macquarie and Moreton Bay (Brisbane) had become places of exile and punishment, and then, in 1825, Norfolk Island was reopened. It quickly became a place where death was often chosen as a way of escape by those whom the system had broken beyond hope. Under the command of Lieutenant Colonel James Thomas Morrisset and his second-in-command Foster Fyans the island of 'soft beauty' became again the 'old Hell' where men were driven to suicide by lottery. Michael Burns, was given 2,000 lashes in less than three years and one of his transgressions, for which he received a flogging was 'Singing a Song', presumably a rebel Irish song. Norfolk Island was 'a place of sorrow and wailing' into which men entered without hope, but filled with horror.

While the regime, with every encouragement from London, perpetrated its brutalities on the outcasts a veil of normalcy was gradually draped over public society. Another small step towards self-government was taken in 1828 with the enlargement of the Legislative Councils to fifteen members, seven of whom were nominated by the Governor while the rest were government officials, so that authority continued to reside where it had always been, except that the Governor now ruled through legislation rather than simple fiat. In other ways, society was developing despite a severe drought in the late 1820s which was made worse by the unrestrained buying of sheep and cattle by anyone with capital. An Agricultural Society had been founded, of which Brisbane was the patron, with the express purpose of importing further pure merinos to improve the colony's flocks. The pastoral industry was boosted by the free granting of land to settlers to the extent of three million acres on the mainland in the 1820s and a further two million in Van Diemen's Land, where settlement was necessarily much more confined.

The two most notable examples of patronage and dealing in high places of the period were the foundation of the Australian Agricultural Company in 1824 and the Van Diemen's Land Company in 1825. The former had its origins in the efforts of Macarthur, and other wealthy landowners, who formed a company in London with a capital of one million pounds and were then granted a million acres in the Newcastle-Port Stephens district of New South Wales. The Company proposed to concentrate on fine wool and cattle, as well as to produce flax, olives and other items. It initially faltered under bad management, but, gradually, with convict servants, vast flocks and the coal leases granted at Newcastle by the government in 1828, the Company prospered and gave an example of successful expenditure of capital, which was not lost on British investors.

The Van Diemen's Land Company received 330,000 acres in the north-west of the island at 1s 6d per acre. It suffered huge losses due to ineptitude and was detested by the locals for its demands for convict labour and claims to government favours. Gradually the Company developed an area of prosperous country that took in the whole of the north-west of the island and was based on centres at Burnie, Stanley and Woolnorth. The first manager, Edward Curr, held that a treaty ought to have been made with the Aborigines, but eventually the conflict between them and the Company's servants became so intense that the virtual extermination of the local blacks, either by killing or deportation to government reserves, became inevitable. Both companies survived, although much reduced. In its dealings with the general public, the Van Diemen's Land Company continued to act in the imperious manner it had begun to use in the 1820s.

Culture, whether popular or high, was a frail growth in a society still struggling to implant itself. Nevertheless, Sydney, with increasing numbers of fine houses, owned by officers, merchants, professional men and landholders, with flowers, vegetables, fruit trees, English dogs, fine carriages and servants, bore testimony to stability and permanence. The twice-knighted physician and landowner John Jamison had a fine estate near Penrith where he built a famous home called Regentville. At his table it was possible to dine casually on 'mock turtle soup, boiled fowls, round of beef, delicious fish of three kinds, curried duck, goose and wildfowl' all washed down by madeira, burgundy, various liqueurs and English ale.

Conversation among the majority revolved less and less around the affairs of the mother countries, and a greater emphasis was placed on the social, political, economic and personal matters of daily life in New South Wales. Dinners and balls were held and hunting, horse and boat racing were popular. Cricket, introduced in 1803, was given permanency when the military formed a club in 1826 and prize fighting was enjoyed by the 'lower orders'. The people could depend on an ample supply of food, with mutton and beef much more readily available to everyone than had been the case in England and Ireland. Fruit grew in abundance – figs, strawberries, gooseberries, oranges, apples, pears, grapes, and peaches. In fact, every common fruit known in England and most of its vegetables adorned tables which in the past had not seen other than potatoes and an odd apple.

Van Diemen's Land, despite its much more restricted area and cut off by Bass Strait, took on, with its dominant convict sub-structure, similar characteristics to New South Wales. Indeed, its history since 1803 was that of the parent colony but written small except in violence. Half of the island's white population of 5,468 in 1820 was convict. Some of them were sent to the far west coast to Macquarie Harbour where they suffered such misery that many preferred death to life and there was one notable case of cannibalism during a failed escape bid in 1822. Commercially the island began to stand on its own feet. Wool was exported to England and soon afterwards wheat was sent to New South Wales. Van Diemen's Land was an island of huge forest areas, wild rivers and impenetrable mountains, especially in the south and south-west, but in its central parts and on the northern and eastern coasts lay fertile land, and its general beauty had taken the hearts of many who had come there.

In both places, much of life was brutal and coarse, with sports and recreation that included over-drinking and brawling, while there were the ever-present reminders that both were penal settlements still. Soldiers stood about or marched through the streets of every garrison town. A whole series of regulations governed personal movement, firearms were controlled, the law was strictly enforced, and general musters of the population and its livestock held; thereby recalling to everyone the purpose of foundation. Yet because the means of subsistence were at hand, with employment of some kind open to all except those who were regarded as incapable or incorrigible, hope was also present. Hope for the future spelt the difference between Australia and the Old World, although most people were conscious for several months of the year of another difference, in Sydney at least. One visitor to the city in the 1820s wrote, 'English shops – English faces – English everything – but the heat! the heat alas! that destroys the illusion'.

Some colonial children in the late 1820s were the sons and daughters of men and women born in the colony. The sons continued to show a sense of independence, while casual observers often noticed that the young women had a saucy spirit and fetching look and were not afraid of work, even of the non-genteel kind. From the very beginning the newly opened continent had been regarded with astonishment in the scientific circles of Europe. Botanists, geologists, zoologists and geographers pored over this 'reversal of Nature', full of freakish things like egg-laying mammals and flightless birds, trees that held their leaves and shed their bark, red blackberries and black swans. The Philosophical Society of Australasia was founded to awaken a spirit of research and excite a thirst for information about all these natural wonders, but few of the native-born and old hands took any interest in its proceedings.

The first and second generations of the native-born were fiercely proud of being Australians and of Australia itself, and that, for the time, seemed enough. Few of them were invited to the dinners Wentworth and his friends put on, but they could all have joined in the toast which was invariably proposed on such occasions 'The land, boys, we live in'. Had they done so, they would presumably have been unaware that the rejection of Macquarie's vision of Australia, in which they would inherit the land, had meant the acceptance of Bigge's vision, in which the wealthy would come to control it. The land in large measure was being given to those who came with wealth and patronage, and the pattern of large scale ownership was already set for the future.

5

Pastoral Australia

The 1830s were crucial in shaping Australian society. They were the years of pastoral expansion, free immigration and new ways of granting land. During the decade, an economic system based on imported capital was consolidated, the struggle between the exclusives and the emancipists spent itself, the assignment of convicts in New South Wales ceased and the stage was set for the cessation of convict transportation there. In the west the first settlement began to show signs of permanency, while South Australia, much vaunted child of brilliant ideas, had to tread the hard road of practicality. Settlers from Van Diemen's Land came across Bass Strait to Port Phillip and overlanders followed Major Mitchell's route to the south from New South Wales. In turn they helped found Melbourne and open up Port Phillip to sheep. The progress made in democratic developments centred on trial by jury, and a national ethos was in the process of being formed in the bush by convicts, ex-convicts and the native-born. Finally, during the 1830s attitudes to the Aborigines hardened, causing their virtual extermination in Van Diemen's Land and their decimation along the eastern seaboard.

In the previous decade, civil servants in London and their administrators in Australia were in charge of a prison, the regulation of which was comparatively simple although, with the coming of more free settlers the nature of the old penal society was changing. In the 1830s it became clearer to the civil servants that, as well as a vast goal, Australia might also be an attractive location for a greater infusion of British capital. Perhaps it may even satisfy the urge of some of the middle class to acquire land, which was no longer a possibility at home. If so, Australia would provide employment for deserving unfortunates lying idle in an over-supplied labour market in Britain.

All these were laudable objectives, but a plan was needed to achieve them and, at the same time, untangle the web of favouritism, speculation, absentee landlordism and sheer ineptitude, which already plagued the administration of land settlement in New South Wales. Under Governor Darling some headway had been made in sorting out these problems. An attempt at a different method of settlement, based on British capital and without a convict workforce, was tried in Western Australia, but, by the early 1830s, it had begun to crumble and gave point to the need for a new and workable method.

Captain James Stirling explored the Swan River area of Western Australia in 1827 and was impressed with its strategic value and economic potential as a site for a new colony. A settlement at the Swan would forestall any desire of the French to take hold of the West; provide a link with India, China and the islands to the north; and, eventually, become a stopping place between Britain and eastern Australia. Possessed of a fine climate, some promising soil and abundant water, it seemed ideal. Back in London, Stirling pressed the British government to establish a settlement at the Swan and, although initially reluctant because of the expense, the decision was finally made to go ahead. On 2 May 1829, at the mouth of the Swan, Captain Fremantle took possession of the western third of the Australian mainland and the continent was now officially British. Stirling arrived six weeks later as the first governor, accompanied by free settlers, public servants and soldiers. On 12 August, 1829, a tree was felled to mark the foundation of Perth.

A mania for the Swan River had commenced in England, fostered by Thomas Peel in secret partnership with Solomon Levey, a former convict who had become a millionaire in New South Wales. Levey put up £20,000 towards the venture, all of which he finally lost. Peel was prepared to provide the settlers if the government gave the land; a million acres was promised but only 250,000 were granted in the first instance. More importantly, no convicts were to be sent out, but that decision meant there would be no cheap labour available to the settlers. Despite the presence, by 1830, of over 4,000 persons on the land between the coast and the mountains, and in the two towns of Perth and Fremantle, Stirling was confident of the future and held a ball in Government House to commemorate the foundation of Western Australia. In the event, the colony rapidly languished and only 1,500 settlers remained in 1832.

The main reason for decline was that, by 1832, land could only be acquired at 5s per acre instead of freely and English interest fell away. Furthermore, it had become apparent that sufficient suitable land, available markets and a ready supply of labour were all lacking, and, had it not been for Stirling's persistence and Peel's great fortitude, the settlement would probably have been abandoned. Stirling went to England in August 1832 to ask for further financial help but he met a refusal. Western Australia, like Sydney Cove fifty years previously, seemed to be left to work out its own destiny. Nevertheless, because it had started on the basis of private English investment, and its early men of mark were drawn from the lower gentry,

Western Australia remained more heavily under English influence than the other colonies.

It this atmosphere of unsuccessful settlement the ideas of a skilled propagandist and entrepreneur won favour. Edward Gibbon Wakefield had never visited Australia yet, while serving three years in Newgate Prison for the abduction of a fifteen-year-old heiress, he thought about the fact that although England lacked land she had an abundance of capital and labour. In 1829, while still in prison, he decided that a new age would dawn if decent English stock could be enticed to Australia with the promise of land and labour. The linchpin of his plan was to set the price of land high enough to ensure that only the moderately affluent could buy it. The other settlers would be, at least temporarily, a labour force for the landowners. On the one hand a high price per acre for land would ensure the concentration of settlement, which, in Wakefield's view, should result in the growth of civilized communities. On the other hand a low price would mean the dispersal of settlers on large tracts of land where they would lack the softening effects of civilization. If necessary, the proceeds of land sales could be used by the government to bring in more and more labourers. They in turn would eventually buy land and a chain effect would thereby be initiated. The basic elements of British civilization would thereby be planted on the limitless wastes lying idle in Australia.

All this seemed eminently sensible and practical, but one problem escaped solution. How high was the price for land to be set? Wakefield knew that too high a price would result in too few buyers. Yet, were it too low the balance between worthy buyers and those who were judged to be undesirable as settlers may be upset. Perhaps 12s an acre may be too low but would 20s be too high? Who knew? Was it not better to leave the problem to time and experience to work it out.

To make matters worse, Wakefield's theory ignored the possibility of ineffective administration, greed, the effect of speculation, differing soil qualities and the small size of local markets for consumable products. In New South Wales the scheme bordered on the absurd because the problem of what to do about those who had simply gone inland and squatted would not be resolved. The squatters there were already occupying thousands of acres of Crown land and it was unlikely that they would pay any price for it, no matter how low. In Van Diemen's Land, Wakefield's plan meant nothing because most of the good land had already been occupied.

Nevertheless, the civil servants in London were sufficiently interested to give the plan a try, and a new system came into effect in 1831. There would be no more free grants in Australia and in New South Wales land was to be sold within the settled districts contained within the so-called Nineteen Counties. The Counties covered an area of about twenty million acres stretching west to the Lachlan River, north to the Manning River and south to the Moruya River. The price was set at a minimum of 5s per acre and Wakefield was alarmed because he thought it was far too low. In fact, the new arrangement of sale at 5s per acre meant very little because, before 1831, no settler without means to hold onto land even when he got it for nothing was sure of success. The whole history of failure among small settlers in New South Wales had already shown this to be the case. After 1831, land was even harder to acquire and the only alternative was squatting beyond the boundaries of the Nineteen Counties. Even there it was still a problem to hold onto land, once acquired, if further capital was lacking to improve it. Men of slender means rarely passed on land as an inheritance, and Wakefield need not have been alarmed at the low price set by the government.

Nevertheless, there were advantages to be gained by the use of the revenue from the sale of land if it was applied to forms of assisted migration. England, with its unemployment problem, and Australia with a shortage of labour would benefit. In consequence, some of the money raised by the sale of land was used to finance the transfer of British and Irish poor to Australia. There was some hope also that the government may be able, through selectivity, to redress the gross imbalance between the sexes which, by 1833 still stood at three males to one female. In the event, from the sale of 350,000 acres in 1832 to 1836, £125,000 was raised in New South Wales and 40,000 immigrants, as well as 35,000 convicts, arrived in the decade to 1840. By the end of the decade the immigrants in New South Wales (53,000) outnumbered the native-born for the first time. Largely penniless and inexperienced, most of the immigrants stayed in Sydney or in rural centres and the urbanization of eastern Australia began with the formation of a coastal-hugging people. Among an urban people the roots of the bush myth, known also as 'the up-country', grew apace, but it remained a mystery which they made real only in folklore, poetry and art.

Many convicts were assigned to workers in the pastoral industry, but rural labour remained scarce and wages were high, while farming, fundamental to Wakefield's scheme, did not prosper. Methods of farming were often primitive, drought and crop diseases were frequent, transport to markets was costly and the alternative of pastoralism attracted those with capital. Others who wanted a quick return on their money found farming unappealing. There was an added anomaly in that the new regulations on land sales could only be applied in settled areas, where there was some hope of surveying the land. Meanwhile, the squatters out in the unsettled districts could freely take up land without the need for a survey. As a result, an invidious, but understandable distinction arose between the unlawful squatter on his broad acres out beyond control, on the Monaro, the Murrumbidgee River or on the Liverpool Plains, and the farmer eking out a less profitable existence on his narrow ones closer to Sydney, for which, moreover, he had to pay at least 5s per acre.

There was, however, one virgin territory where the ideas of Wakefield could be applied without prejudice from existing arrangements. A voyage remarkable for courage and tenacity by Charles Sturt in 1830 traced the Murray to its mouth at Lake Alexandrina in South Australia. He proved that the west flowing rivers in New South Wales flowed into the Murray, and that the great river then took its course to the ocean rather than into an inland sea. He also opened up South Australia from the east, and the promise of a territory about the Murray basin seemed to invite settlement in a fertile and vacant area. When he heard of this development Wakefield felt that here was the ideal place for his schemes of colonization on a systematic basis, but the Colonial Office vacillated until 1834 when the colony of South Australia was established on paper. It would have remained no more than a scheme had not George Angas formed the South Australia Company to finance the venture, which got underway in 1836.

On 28 December 1836, Governor John Hindmarsh landed in the *Buffalo* at Holdfast Bay where Glenelg now stands. The province of South Australia was proclaimed, and several toasts were drunk to its success. A few days later, Surveyor-General William Light persuaded Hindmarsh that the perfect site for the settlement was a few miles inland across the plains. At that place Adelaide was laid out to a masterly plan, and the business of opening up the country began in earnest. Young, mostly Protestant, upright and thoroughly decent, the first settlers were expected to live closely together in and near Adelaide and the hope was that the virtues of the Mother Country would flourish among them. Time soon told its own story and Wakefield's scheme went astray for there was an immediate tendency to speculate in land rather than to work it. By 1841, only 2,500 acres out of 299,000, sold at 12s per acre, were under cultivation; 12,000 assisted migrants, many of whom were totally unsuited to the pioneering venture, had arrived, and the total population was 15,485. Among the arrivals there were no convicts because the Colonial Office had decided that, like Western Australia, the new colony was to remain free of the penal taint, which was seen as a curse.

Land, rather than its produce, quickly became the unique commodity in which the colonists dealt and the South Australia Company led the field as a large-scale speculator. Under such circumstances, the labour force had to be given some purpose, so George Gawler, who succeeded Hindmarsh as governor in 1838, decided to equip the colony with all the necessary public works generally found in a flourishing community with a solid economic base. While living in a primitive dwelling himself, Gawler saw to it that harbour works, public buildings, roads and bridges went ahead, and he even gave aid to those who remained unemployed. The question soon arose as to who would foot the bill as the local treasury was clearly incapable of doing so for any length of time. In London, the civil servants refused, credit collapsed and South Australia, which had promised so much, came to a temporary halt.

There were some who were prepared to stick it out, but they did so in a way that contradicted Wakefield's ideal of systematic colonization. Squatters, ignoring the land sales, began to settle beyond the 150 square miles of the province, thus breaking any theoretical connection between land and labour. At Klemzig and Hahndorf there were German settlers who had come to South Australia between 1838 and 1839 to practise their own kind of Lutheranism in peace. They began to flourish in their neat villages, but again, their success owed nothing directly to Wakefield's plan because they leased the land from Angas at a nominal rent and worked it with their own labour. Their wives and daughters were soon seen in Adelaide selling dairy produce and vegetables to the townsfolk, while their men planted grains and, later, vines as a happy portent of future times. Among the first sheep shearers in South Australia there were German women who, by 1843, were shearing a large proportion of the flocks. In the late 1840s, German Catholics followed the Lutherans to South Australia and, with their Jesuit chaplain, settled near Clare at Sevenhill where a college, an imposing church and a flourishing vineyard were established.

Although scant attention was paid to his ideas, Wakefield made a contribution to Australian development as lasting as that of Macarthur and the founders of the wool industry. While they wanted to cover the land with the finest of sheep, Wakefield wanted to plant it with the best of people. Not for him the convicts, but rather the sons and daughters of England's deserving classes. In his scheme the land was to be used primarily for production and secondarily, by its sale, for settling England's surplus population. With his theory even partially accepted, immigration to Australia, free or assisted, became fundamental to future development. Like

Macarthur, Wakefield was a superb publicist, and during the 1830s the population of free persons in New South Wales rose four-fold, largely due to the spread and acceptability of the idea of immigration, which he, Wakefield, had fostered.

Despite the unpromising beginnings of the two new colonies in the west and in South Australia, Botany Bay wool, so fine, soft and long stapled that English wool sorters could pick it by touch in a mixed bale, had become the major element in the economy although fishery products still contributed heavily to export earnings. Pastoralists demanded more and more land, British manufacturers more wool, and the planners pleaded in vain for concentrated settlement, rather than haphazard dispersal into the interior. In the final analysis, the squatters were destined to emerge victorious because capital, mostly British in origin, talked louder than theory. Nothing, but especially not lines drawn on a map, could stop the squatters. It was idle to attempt to do so in South Australia and it had already proved futile in New South Wales where, since the declaration of the Nineteen Counties in 1829, the sheep had been expected to stop their outward movement at an imaginary boundary. Pastoralism, by its very nature, opened up vast tracts of land, even though it implied unbridled lawlessness to the authorities who also felt that the use of Crown land, without precise regulations on tenure and cost, was intolerable.

The land itself posed some obstacles to the coming of the squatters but never in a permanent manner. Drought, flood and fire were brutal but passing phenomena, although the effect of a prolonged drought was drastic on wool quality as well as flock numbers. On the pastoral lands there was no prolonged cold or snow, no impassable mountain ranges or huge rivers, no dense forests or immense swamps. There were no indigenous creatures to prey on the sheep except the dingo, which could be controlled but never, it seemed, conquered. The land appeared to betray its original inhabitants when it proved to be a welcoming haven to the hard-hooved sheep, which adapted remarkably quickly to the new environment and the merino blended with the landscape and flourished. Pastoral expansion also turned a society previously dependent on the sea and coastal shipping into one which looked inwards to the land itself as the source of its commerce, wealth and culture. The sheep were subject to catarrh, footrot and fluke, but they quickly recovered or multiplied again because the breed was extraordinarily prolific in lambs as well as fleece. The pastoral industry initially appeared to require no particular aptitude in those who undertook it, although time would prove the contrary, and thousands who had never previously touched a sheep quickly became pastoralists. The industry did not require the same kind of concentrated workforce as did agriculture because it was not labour intensive, except for brief periods, such as shearing.

The only force perhaps capable of stemming the squatting movement was the government, but Richard Bourke, Governor of New South Wales between 1831 and 1838, was reluctant to do so. He saw the signs of prosperity, the inflow of capital, the increase in immigrants, the opening of the country, the dulling of the old animosities between emancipists and exclusives, and the greater recognition given to Australia with the waning of the Botany Bay slur. For all these benefits he was prepared to accept the dispersion of settlement and even the effective transfer of thousands of square miles of land into the hands of a few. Bourke governed wisely and with forbearance in times of great prosperity, but his liberality left its legacy.

George Gipps, Bourke's successor, was an asthmatic who worried through sleepless nights in Sydney about the dispersion of the population into the interior but even more about the threat to the primacy of the Crown, which proclaimed a right over the land. More than anything, Gipps was troubled with his vision of a future Australia where a rough, unlettered, unskilled and godless race would arise. He feared that no cleric, policeman, schoolmaster or genteel influence would penetrate those vast and almost trackless wildernesses, upon which he foresaw that a civilization based on the development of a mixed race of black and white would take shape.

Gipps was not aware that the elemental force of racism was at work shaping white Australia. With the rejection of the Aborigines as equals and their virtual exclusion from an economy based on the pastoral industry – a rejection the Aborigines partially dictated because participation in a workforce that threatened to destroy the very basis of their civilization was an anathema to them – a great gulf had opened between the races. White and black went separate paths and, unlike in Latin America where there was an acceptance of interbreeding between the races and the subsequent offspring, those paths lead inexorably to an exclusive and foreboding conclusion for the dominant section. In the end they called it white Australia.

All these worries about the future or the encroachment on Crown lands meant little to the prospective squatters – to the military and naval officers, lawyers, clergymen, merchants, government officials, sons of the English gentry, assorted immigrants and a sprinkling of the native-born. All these, provided they had sufficient initial capital or could raise a loan from one of the new banks, which fed on pastoral expansion, could aspire to become squatters. The first step was to obtain a few servants, purchase a flock from one of the inner properties and acquire stores for a year. They then set out inland with drays, bullocks, a horse or two and a cow. Imbued with hope, they pushed out further and further until suitable water and feed was found on unoccupied country. If it was extensive enough to pasture their flock they squatted on it and called it a run or a station.

The shepherds, mostly convicts, ex-convicts and native-born, proved to be generally faithful and efficient. They lived in huts, with two shepherds and a hut-keeper in each. The huts were rough constructions of slabs and bark, spaced a mile or more apart, and the shepherds were responsible for guarding a flock of 500 to 1,500 sheep, depending upon the feed and water available. At night the flock was enclosed within temporary fences, called hurdles, close to the hut and a constant watch was kept for dingoes. The loneliness of the lives of the shepherds and the harshness of their existence sometimes resulted in madness.

The lives of the squatters in the early days, with only the barest commodities available, differed little from those of the shepherds. They also learnt to rough it in the bush, where many lost count of the days and recognized Sundays perhaps by having a shave, although some read the Bible or gathered the shepherds for prayer. Very little was done to erect permanent buildings, because squatting remained illegal until the end of the 1830s. Squatting was a life which, in both masters and servants, bred qualities of trust and dependence of man upon man because there were scarcely any women in the bush. To survive, a man had to turn to his mate and, if alone, as was often the case, to his own ingenuity and ability to improvise with whatever was at hand. Authority meant little in a society removed by weeks or even months from its source, while the only escape from boredom was drink, when it could be had, telling yarns and reading for those who were capable of it.

In New South Wales, including the District of Port Phillip, by 1840 there were 718 squatting stations with 7,000 people, of whom 2,600 were convicts, while a million and a half sheep ran on over a million acres of Crown land. Among the convicts, emancipists and native born, the ethos of early Australia was forged in the bush. It was a harsh creed of mateship between men, and survival was its purpose. In time the women came, bringing with them the gentle touch of more civilized ways but always at the cost of hardship to themselves. To lighten the harshness they planted fruit trees, vegetables and flowers, ran fowl yards, nursed the sick, read aloud to their menfolk and children and often they played musical instruments. They brought their religion with them, and on many a station the Bible was read or the rosary said at night.

The bush children depended upon their mothers for their early education, which was finished at boarding schools for the successful. The children of the poorer squatters and of the servants remained children of the bush to repeat the ways of life of their parents. All their lives the women had to battle against the same odds as the men, with the added handicap of isolation from other women. Illness, childbirth or death emotionally drained brave spirits like Georgiana Molloy at Augusta, Western Australia. Three years after the death of her baby girl she wrote, 'language refuses to utter what 1 experienced when mine died in my arms in this dreary land, and no one but Molloy near me' and, later, when her little son drowned in the well by the house, her sorrow was so complete she hid it in her heart.

The main thrust of the squatting movement from New South Wales was west and south until the good land was taken. In the 1830s it spread deeper south into Mitchell's Australia Felix, which was officially called Port Phillip. That movement had, however, been anticipated. For some years, sealers, whalers and wattle-bark strippers had harvested the waters and islands of Bass Strait and its mainland coast and at least a dozen of them had camps on the mainland. The Mills brothers, John and Charles, born at Launceston in 1808 and 1810 respectively, had built makeshift residences along the coast and made what became Victoria their permanent home as early as the late 1820s. They and a few others, including William Dutton, also native-born, were there when Edward Henty landed at Portland on 19 November 1834. Henty's later statement that there were no whites in residence closer than King George Sound in the west and Twofold Bay in the east was incorrect because there had been continuous and permanent settlement at Portland since 1829. The Henty family had moved from Western Australia to Van Diemen's Land in 1831, but failed to obtain permission to occupy land across the Strait in Port Phillip. They came over in November 1834, nonetheless, and joined the other squatters at Portland Bay. In 1835 John Batman, Sydney-born of a convict father and now a grazier in Van Diemen's Land, also came across Bass Strait. He went up a pleasant river called the Yarra and saw a spot he judged would eventually be 'fit for a village'. He also saw land of which he had not seen the equal and he was determined to obtain some of it for himself and his fellow Vandemonians.

No amount of legal argument could ever prove that the Aborigines had no right to the land and thereby that they had no right to dispose of it. Some very few observers of the relations between blacks and whites had recognized this fact, and Captain F.C. Irwin of the 63rd Regiment, after the tragic 'Battle of Pinjarra' between blacks and whites in 1834 in Western Australia, suggested that 'a formal treaty' should be entered into between the two races 'as a measure of healing and pacification'. Batman knew nothing of Irwin's suggestion, but he had marked respect for the Aborigines whom he known since childhood. He called them 'that much injured and most unfortunate race' and regarded them as 'the real owners of the soil'. He gave the Aborigines he met about Port Phillip Bay an assortment of trinkets in exchange for 600,000 acres of land, and promised to pay them an annual tribute as evidence of his desire to protect them. All of this was drawn up in treaty form and duly signed according to the ability of each party, but the treaty was rapidly found to be null and void because it was against the rights of the Crown. As a result, the one attempt made to give some recognition to Aboriginal rights was set aside lest it interfere with the British government's determination to dispose of the land in the manner it considered lawful. At no time did it ever see fit to pay for the land.

Others quickly followed Batman's move to Port Phillip. John Pascoe Fawkner was one of the first, and within a year a small community was flourishing. The Mills brothers, William Dutton and the Hentys at Portland, Batman and other settlers from Van Diemen's Land who lived around Port Phillip Bay, were responsible for the early development of what became the colony of Victoria. They had all crossed Bass Strait to settle the new lands. Victoria was never the daughter of New South Wales, although it remained dependent upon it in all administrative matters until 1851, but much written history has obscured its Vandemonian origins. Batman himself became an object of ridicule by many, although he had, with some civility and no violence, tried to acquire Aboriginal land which others simply took without any reference to the original owners who had never surrendered their right to it.

In September of 1836 the officials in Sydney were forced to acknowledge that a settlement already existed at Port Phillip. Later in that year a squatter, in the space of a few weeks, saw 100,000 sheep, with their owners and shepherds, cross the Murrumbidgee at Gundagai on their way south. On arrival in March 1837 at the southern settlement, the Governor named Batman's site after a British Prime Minister, Melbourne. His surveyor, Robert Hoddle, laid out the future shape of the city by dissecting a square mile with narrow, lane-like alleys and fine wide streets which, running almost south to north ensured that Melbourne and its citizens would be swept by hot or cold winds dependent upon the season. Four years later, 20,000 people lived under the generally benign and reasonable guidance of Charles La Trobe, who had been appointed superintendent of Port Phillip in 1839. With him La Trobe brought out his Swiss wife, Sophie, a daughter and a prefabricated house. He left a legacy of upright behaviour, high moral standards and devotion to culture and learning.

The squatters soon ran over a million sheep on their runs which stretched almost to the limit of pastoral land in Port Phillip. Some of them were women, who, after the death of their husbands, took up, or were obliged to oversee, a run hoping thereby to provide for their children. Others were single women like Anne Drysdale and Caroline Newcombe who together held a successful run on the Barwon River near Geelong in the 1840s and another on Indented Head in the 1850s. The runs were relinquished after Anne's death in 1853 and Caroline's subsequent marriage in 1861. They were pioneers of a long line of women who, throughout the continent, ran pastoral properties successfully. They earned the respect of their employees and the local communities and no one saw any anomaly in the fact that women could equal men in the adventure named squatting.

Usury was the usual basis of the pastoral economy because no fixed interest rates were set on loans and the squatters were often in need of extra capital, particularly in times of drought. Their tendency to occupy runs much in excess of their needs caused Bourke to attempt some control over them in 1836 by appointing land commissioners to sort out the frequent disputes that arose between them. He put a charge of £10 annually on their runs, which many of them regarded as excessive. The responsibilities of the commissioners were immense and the territory they had to cover equally so. They were often accused of bias and favouritism in their decisions, but their role was a necessary one in places where other forms of law were almost totally absent. In the settled districts and in Melbourne, Bourke priced land at a minimum of £1 per acre and in town land there was rampant speculation. In August 1840 the government received £14,220 from the sale of forty-five lots in Melbourne at an average of £316 each and within four months the same lots were sold at double to five times their original cost. The government gained nothing from those subsequent transactions, and, unless the economy prospered, only speculators reaped profits while genuine purchasers faced possible ruin.

Meanwhile, George Arthur, Lieutenant-Governor of Van Diemen's Land since 1823 and exercising full power after the island was made a colony in its own right in 1825, had set ideas on the land question as well as on most other matters. He was a highly efficient administrator, determined and inflexible in his control of the convicts, whom he regarded as slaves, and he was constantly aware of, and vehemently opposed to, moral transgressions of any kind. His high ideals did not prevent his acquiring great wealth in land which he bought with foreknowledge of its rising value. When he became aware that the new regulations of 1831 were about to be proclaimed and that, henceforth, free grants would cease, he parcelled out 250,000 acres to anyone to whom even the whisper of a promise of land had been made by London.

The basis of the island's economy was the assignment system, which land sales and immigration threatened, but Arthur need not have worried. In England, Van Diemen's Land was regarded simply as a prison so that convict arrivals accounted for 20,000 new hands in the 1830s, almost twice the number of free persons settling in the same period. Arthur had closed the old penal establishment at Macquarie Harbour on the south-west of the island and set up a new one at Point Arthur in 1830. It was close to Hobart, isolated on a narrow peninsula and joined to the mainland by a thin strip, called Eaglehawk Neck, which was successfully guarded by ferocious dogs although one bold escapee eluded their jaws. The convicts did all they could not to be sent to Port Arthur, and those who survived a term there did their best never to return. Only about seven percent of the convicts were confined at Port Arthur. The others worked in chain gangs on public utilities, notably road building, but the majority was forced to take their luck with assignment.

Liberal in matters touching religion and education, both of which he fostered, Arthur gradually became hardhearted toward the Aborigines. Settlement had taken place with such rapidity that one Aborigine, Monpeliatta, complained that, when he and his people left any area to hunt elsewhere they found, on their return a week later, that a hut had been erected there by a white. The result was that raids by Aborigines, especially by the Big River People around Bothwell and Oatlands, rose from 11 in 1824 to 222 in 1830. In those conflicts about sixty settlers and 240 Aborigines lost their lives. By late 1830, Arthur decided that any chance of peaceful relations between the races was negligible. He and others, notably property owners, failed to comprehend that to the Aborigines, a people whose very existence was threatened, retaliation by taking human life or stealing animals was an act to which they could see no alternative. For his part Arthur concluded that segregation was the only solution, so he determined to drive the remaining Aborigines, now much less than a thousand, onto the Tasman Peninsula which, with Port Arthur already nullifying its natural beauty, was to be their home. In a kind of hapless beat down through the island, named Arthur's 'Black Line', he personally directed about 2,200 men, including 550 soldiers. It was the largest deployment by the British military in Australia, cost £30,000 and managed to bag two Aborigines. Even though their skills in bushcraft had enabled most of them to slip through the 'Line', the Aborigines, given the massive nature of the operation were dispirited and the Governor decided on a form of conciliation which entailed removing the remaining Aborigines to Flinders island in Bass Strait where their extinction was virtually ensured.

The Christian faith was part of the common cultural possessions of the general population, although indifference or rejection of religion was the attitude of many. Nevertheless, the churches, with their ministers, cult and structures, were regarded as a fundamental part of society, as much as the burgeoning banking system and the network of public utilities were accepted on other levels. The government was prepared to recognize this fact by granting aid to any Christian Church prepared to accept it. This decision, hailed by Bourke as the 'Magna Carta of the Religious Liberty of this infant Empire', excluded the small community of about 1,000 Jews. In 1837 they converted a private house in Bridge Street, Sydney into a synagogue. The Jews built their first formal synagogue at Hobart in 1843, established the oldest women's organization in Australia – The Hebrew Ladies Maternity Society – at Sydney in the same year and their first newspaper, *The Voice of Jacob*, was published in 1842. Meanwhile, the Christians progressed rapidly with the benefit of state aid, which helped to build churches and maintain clergy to the number of about one to a thousand of the population.

The optimistic idea that the perfectibility of man could be achieved through the vehicle of education was widespread, particularly among the well-to-do. To that purpose, private schools were founded, some of which had educational standing of value. The majority was second rate or worse. Throughout New South Wales, churches of all denominations attempted to support schools where, more often than not, ill-prepared masters taught ill-disposed pupils. Bourke was troubled at the proliferation of such establishments, so he suggested that the government should itself enter the field by erecting and controlling schools in which religion would be confined to scriptural readings and a weekly visit from the clergy who would instruct their own particular flock. In the beginning, the Protestants were against the proposal and the Catholics were for it, so that, in a welter of opposition, approval and some recrimination, Bourke's proposal lapsed, leaving an enduring legacy of inter-faith bigotry.

The future of transportation itself was closely linked to the question of responsible government and, consequently, formed a major debate of the period. On the one side, there were those to whom the system had to cease for strictly practical, religious or humanitarian reasons. John Dunmore Lang was adept at describing its worst characteristics and implying that transportation was merely a method of promoting rogues, both socially and financially, while William Ullathorne, a young and impetuous Catholic priest, was even more eloquent. He proclaimed that 'a vast portion of God's earth' had been turned into a 'cess-pool' where 60,000 souls were 'festering in bondage' and called for 'the removal of such a plague from the earth'. There were, however, much more powerful economic interests whose arguments would win the day for or against transportation.

Free immigrants, some emancipists and native-born feared that the continuation of transportation would mean that wages would always be depressed. The great majority of squatters and large landowners of New South Wales and Van Diemen's Land saw the retention of assignment as essential to their prosperity. The followers of Wakefield and the founders of South Australia had turned their faces sternly against transportation to their colony, but they knew that their own economy faced a threat while their neighbouring colonies continued to receive a cheap, convict workforce. The fact was that the two systems of transportation and free migration could not go hand in hand.

In the event, a committee of the House of Commons deliberated on the matter. Hidden in its workings was the conviction that there were disturbing elements at large in British society, including the Chartists and the unemployed, who would be better out of the country but who would never go willingly to a convict settlement. The committee recommended in 1838 that transportation to New South Wales and the settled parts of Van Diemen's Land be abolished. In 1839 assignment ceased, and on 18 November 1840 Sydney Cove saw the last batch of convicts disembark from the transport *Eden*. Fifty-two years of a penal society, 80,000 convicts, misery, criminality and reformation, death in bondage and success in freedom, marriage, children and homes had all laid the foundations of the future.

The tentative steps towards responsible government in New South Wales began to show promise of fruitful fulfilment. In 1835 John Jamison, 'the hospitable Knight of Regentsville', became the first President of the Australian Patriotic Association, which was inspired by Wentworth and founded to secure some form of representative government in the colony as

well as trial by jury. The Association also busied itself with defending the old
land system, upholding transportation and attempting to introduce Asiatic
labour. It clearly expressed the new harmony of interests between the old
enemies – exclusives and emancipists – who, based on their propertied and
business wealth, now saw their position threatened unless they could achieve
power over legislation. Wentworth's old paper, the *Australian*, began to
attack him as one who had taught the people 'what liberty was' but had now
betrayed them.

In South Australia freedom from transportation permitted the reality of a
minor form of responsible government to be achieved. Adelaide, by 1840,
was a small city of 2,000 with all the outward symbols of civic pride, together
with churches belonging to almost every known sect. On 31 October 1840
the first election in Australia for positions of public responsibility was held
there. It was for a mayor and town council, the ballot was not used, there
were property qualifications and former paupers and criminals could not
vote. The election itself went off with moderation, good order and a careful
choice of candidates, which were expected qualities in a colony determined
to stay free of the excesses allegedly so prevalent in places where convicts set
foot. In Western Australia, itself still free of convicts, jealous eyes were cast
upon their young, neighbouring, sister colony, and the *Perth Gazette*
reported that runaway convicts were already infecting South Australia while
the 'newfangled system of emigration, it would appear, is not working so well
as anticipated'.

While some struggled to assert their rights against a distant Crown, others
were more anxious to uphold theirs in the society about them. Despite the
increasing influx of free immigrants, archaic regulations, more consistent
with a feudal society, bound servants to their masters. Magistrates who were
themselves employers, regularly sentenced servants to imprisonment for
disobedience, insolence and absconding although servants sometimes sued
successfully for wages due or redress of wrongs done. By 1840 some slight
improvement in the regulations was achieved in New South Wales. Women
servants could no longer be sent to prison, while males could only be
sentenced to three months for breaches of the Master and Servants Act. To
the workers the net result remained little more than virtual slavery.

In such circumstances, the embryonic beginnings of trade unions and
benefit societies took place among skilled workers, including compositors
who formed the Australian Society of Compositors. In January 1840 the
compositors on the *Sydney Herald* (1831), which became the *Sydney Morning
Herald* in 1842 and survives to the present, struck for an improvement in

apprentice ratios. The competition for readers in New South Wales was fierce with the *Australian* (1824–48), the *Monitor* (1826–42), Lang's *Colonist* (1835–40) and the Catholic *Australasian Chronicle* (1839–48) all in the field so that no paper could afford to publish later than the others. The compositors were quickly reminded that any combination amongst them was illegal, any dictation to their employers was intolerable, and that British or Indian compositors could be brought in at short notice to replace the recalcitrant. In the event, convict labour was used to break the strike as was done later in the year when the Sydney bakers struck. The struggle between capital and labour was already conducted by rules drawn up to ensure that capital retained the ascendancy.

Until 1803 no special provisions were made for female convicts, but in that year a building at Parramatta had been designated as a factory. It was little more than a refuge where conditions were so intolerable that the women preferred to face all manner of hardship rather than be detained there. After 1821 the Female Factory held 1,500 inmates, who broke stones, made cloth and sawed wood. The women were divided into three classes – prospective assignees, mothers of illegitimate children and those undergoing punishment. There had been repeated outbreaks of violence in the Factory, but some improvement was shown after the arrival of the first nuns to come to Australia. Five Irish Sisters of Charity, including two nurses who pioneered their profession in Australia, arrived with Ullathorne in 1838, and their devotion to the women was remarkable. Nevertheless, the Factory remained a constant reminder of the degradation of being a convict, especially as its occupants were women. This was never more apparent than on those occasions when a kind of slave market took place at the Factory – the women were lined up and men took their pick of them as brides.

Among the convicts, one group stood out because their background was different to all the rest except for the Irish political prisoners. They were 149 Canadian rebels transported in 1839 and 1840 for attempting to overthrow British rule in their homeland. The rebels with an English or American background came from Ontario and were kept at Hobart. They led a miserable existence there and fifteen were sent to Port Arthur for attempting to escape. After the death of one of their number in Van Diemen's Land, the 59 French Canadians from Lower Canada spent their exile in Sydney where they cut stone for the new Parramatta road. They found the environment alien and harsh, but were comforted by John Bede Polding, an English Benedictine monk who was the first Catholic bishop in Australia. The exiles left little mark of their passing, whether at Hobart or Sydney, and, unlike the

English and Irish convicts, the great majority of them returned home as soon as they were pardoned.

In the larger centres of settlement – Sydney, Hobart, Melbourne, Adelaide and, to a greater extent, at distant Perth – life continued to reflect the parent civilization in the British Isles. The convict era for Brisbane was over by 1839, and by the next year the Darling Downs were open to settlement with the squatters pushing to the north and west, but Brisbane remained small and struggling. Elsewhere, regattas were held, cricket played, the first steam vessel was seen on Sydney Harbour in 1831 and the Mechanics' School of Arts, founded in 1833, proposed to assist the citizens to become 'fervent worshippers at the shrine of science' with carefully fostered 'habits of intellectual intercourse'.

In Melbourne, La Trobe was happy that British 'perseverance and industry' produced banks, newspapers, churches and other comfortable reminders of the home country although the sides of the streets were still lined with eucalyptus stumps and in Collins Street one was so huge that a building had to be skewed to go around it. In South Australia, overlanders from New South Wales were arriving with flocks and herds, which added to the stability of the settlement and strengthened the economy of Adelaide where Colonel Light's plan for the city was taking shape. The *South Australian Gazette* had commenced printing in Adelaide in 1837. In May 1838, when the colony was only seventeen months old, the Theatre Royal was opened and *Mountaineers, or Love and Madness* played before an enthusiastic audience.

Visitors, who also expressed some criticism, noted all these signs of development. In 1839 an exploratory expedition from the United States called at Sydney. The men were delighted to find themselves 'in a civilized country' and more especially to be in a place where their own language was spoken. Their leader, Captain Wilkes, remarked that the inhabitants seemed intent upon making money; that the press was unruly; drunkenness abounded in a city where 250 taverns, in a ratio of one for every 100 inhabitants, catered for the thirsty; and that everywhere the cicadas were deafening – although his overall impression was favourable. Charles Darwin arrived in Australia on the *Beagle in* 1836, but he was disappointed in 'the state of society' in Sydney. He visited Bathurst and gave an incorrect explanation for the canyons in the Blue Mountains. Finally he passed the most 'dull and uninteresting time' of his whole voyage when he called at King Georges Sound in the west. Nevertheless, the evidence he gathered from the flora and fauna, and on the Aborigines, helped with his later formulation of the theory of natural selection, and he always maintained a keen interest in Australia.

On the frontiers of expansion, in river valleys, on vast plains bounded by countless miles of bush, on the slopes of hills and mountains, civilization was being established which had many faces. Georgiana Molloy lived on through her sorrows in the west, and when she carved a garden out of the wilderness she thought that she had come to a Garden of Eden. At night she turned to prayer and to the piano and thus the bush gradually became home. Robert Campbell on the Limestone Plains, 190 miles south-west of Sydney, reigned over seventy workers and pastured thousands of sheep, and, on Sundays, worshipped at the nearby Anglican Church of St John. He built a home which became a gracious mansion and, later, formed the nucleus of the Royal Military College at Duntroon. At Entally House, near Launceston, Thomas Reiby, whose emancipist mother, Mary, had made a fortune, lived until 1842 in a kind of fortress with two towers slotted with musket holes as a precaution against bushrangers. The furniture of his home was in the Regency style and Australian cedar was used for the timberwork.

The white civilization taking shape, both in the towns and in the bush, was an amalgam of those which had grown in England, Scotland and, to some degree, Ireland in the preceding centuries. In the main it was solidly Protestant, virtuous, hard-working, courageous and persevering against great odds. The pioneers were prepared to suffer hardship in order to get a foothold in the Australia they were in the process of building. Many of them were pretentious and looked down on those whom they considered to be of 'the lower orders', yet everyone had to contend with physical difficulties and varying degrees of loneliness, isolation and heartbreak. In their determined quest to conquer and possess the land, to wrest out a living in commerce and minor industry, to build schools, churches, roads and court houses, Australians began again the work their ancestors had taken centuries to accomplish in their homelands. Within a half-century of settlement, the foundations of a British civilization had been laid down on a continent months removed by sea from its cultural origins. The fact that one aspect of this civilization was that of a penal colony did not stop the determined drive of many citizens to shape a free society.

In the bush, normally far removed from the influence of either the law or religion, there were barbarous aspects to white behaviour. In 1837 and early 1838 in the Gwyder and Namoi River districts several whites were killed by Aborigines who resented their intrusion onto their traditional hunting grounds. Subsequently, on the Myall Creek, 350 miles north-west of Sydney, the convict servants of Henry Dangar murdered about thirty Aborigines – men, women and children. Their deed followed closely the slaying of ten drovers by a party of blacks on the Broken River in the Port Phillip District. The British authorities suggested a protectorate system and Governor Gipps set it up. He appointed George Robinson as Chief Protector with the task of looking after the interests of the Aborigines. In that way a well meaning, but nonetheless authoritarian and paternalistic system began which spread to the other colonies. It meant, in effect, that whites controlled the lives of the Aborigines and restricted their freedom. The protectorates survived in various forms for the next 140 years but, in the main, they were inept and costly failures.

However, many whites were convinced that they were the ones who needed to be protected and that it was natural for advanced civilizations to exterminate those who were seen as savages. They requested Gipps to 'levy war against the Blacks' but the Governor refused and was strongly supported in his stand by the Attorney-General, John Hubert Plunkett. As a result, some of Dangar's men were brought to trial at Sydney for murder, and seven of them were hanged. Many squatters saw Plunkett as the real murderer, and he was detested and feared thereafter. Both Gipps and Plunkett were helpless when the poisoning of waterholes and of flour became a more favoured method of extermination than shooting – white attitudes towards the blacks were hardening and an anonymous grazier on the Murrumbidgee summed them up. To him the Aborigines were 'a scoff and a jest on humanity' and he thought that their extinction was virtually ensured. His view was one which some segments of the press, notably the *Sydney Herald*, defended and propagated, thereby heightening adverse public opinion and helping to justify murder. As for the Aborigines, death, dispersal and the loss of their hunting grounds continued to take an awful toll as the past and its Dreamtime changed to a reality with which they could not cope.

There were other Australians who had begun to feel they were different. Hamilton Hume summed up the position of the new people born in Australia when he pleaded that, 'Altho' I am Australian', he deserved to be recompensed for the financial losses he suffered during his exploratory journey into Port Phillip. In a language with which many of them were familiar, that of the racecourse, they had suspect bloodlines and they were born in the wrong paddock. They were even beginning to take on an unfamiliar accent blended from Cockney, Glasgow and Dublin with its tonality softened by the mildness of the climate and of their own reticent nature. Its softness was such that newcomers only noticed that it tended to be nasal. They grew quickly and were thus called Cornstalks because corn also grew quickly in this country. Their eyes were often blue and their hair began as blonde but then darkened. Quick and agile in their movements they could swim in the harbour like fish and they took to the horse as if they had been born astride it. Every visitor noticed the charm, the grace, the gentility and physical attractiveness of the young women.

Their mothers, the fountain of the new nation, taught them to turn from crime and drink and those of them who broke the law were less than among those who came freely to the colony. The old lands of their parents meant little to them because this land was their motherland. Their most precious quality was to know their bond with the Aborigines based on birth and many of them, including Hamilton Hume, learnt their language and knew their ways.

Above all the native-born differed in their spirit. They rejected social ranks and titles; they placed no trust in the military and the police who so frequently ill-treated them because of their parents. They wanted to make a go of life in their own way; and they stuck by their mates and defended their women fiercely. The sea called them and they crossed it gladly because their land was sea-bound. The same land of their birth was closed to them and they were forced to stand aside while ninety-five percent of it was given to those who came with money and connections.

In the midst of the native-born society, English structures were shaped daily. Courts and councils, governors and parsons, place names, rules and regulations, titles and all the paraphernalia of an alien society began to grip the ancient continent as it was divided into parishes, counties and other minutiae of a small island in the north Atlantic. The Aborigines decided to take little notice of all this and rejected much of what they understood. The native-born dimly grasped their destiny as lowly citizens, placed one rung above the Aborigines in their own native land. They, like the Aborigines, could resist but they, too, were powerless. What lasted into the future was the spirit of endurance and independence that flowed strongly in both the native races.

Remote from all that was happening in her distant realm, an eighteen-year-old girl was crowned as Queen Victoria in London in 1837. When they heard the news in Perth the inhabitants gathered, as they did in all the centres of her vast Empire, to pledge their loyalty to the new monarch. Hopes were expressed that her reign would prove fruitful and memorable, but even the optimistic little dreamt how decisive it would be in binding Australia in all its parts to the distant Crown. Statue followed statue, colonies, buildings and landmarks were named after her and countless loyal toasts were drunk to an ever-absent Queen. The enthusiasm engendered for royalty among young and old served to soften and disguise the reality of cultural, economic and military dependence that permeated colonial life. When she died, over sixty years later, Australia was tied effectively to apron strings that girded the world.

6

New Peopling of the Land

To the Aborigines it was pointless to ask how many generations must pass before a land and its people become one. To them there had never been a time in which their unity with the land was lacking. For the whites, unity grew from long residence and involvement with the land and its people although it differed in meaning, and quality, from that possessed by the Aborigines. Nevertheless, in its own way, a kind of belonging did come about for many, although for some it never happened.

As an old man in Melbourne in the late 1860s, John Pascoe Fawkner could look back to 1803 and remember it vividly. In that year, as a boy of eleven, he had landed at Port Phillip with his convict father, his mother and sister. They were on their way to Van Diemen's Land with Lieutenant-Governor Collins where, in young manhood, Fawkner saw Lachlan Macquarie on the Governor's visit to Hobart in 1811. Three years later Fawkner was given 500 strokes for aiding a party of convicts in an unsuccessful bid to escape, and he then served two years hard labour as a cedar cutter on the Hunter River in New South Wales. Having married a convict, Eliza Cobb, at Launceston in 1822, he went on to lay the foundations of a fortune at Port Phillip where he established the *Port Phillip Patriot and Melbourne Advertiser* in 1839. He later became 'the tribune of the people' during his eighteen years as a member of the Legislative Council in the place to which he had come as a boy fifty years before when no white man lived there. Although the sounds and sights of his London childhood remained with him to the end, Fawkner knew no other home than Australia.

In 1835, at Leicester in England, Charles Glover, aged eighteen, was sentenced to fourteen years' transportation for theft. Two years later he was convicted at Sydney for stealing from a dwelling and putting its occupant in fear of his life. This time he received a life sentence to Norfolk Island which, for a lad of twenty, was little short of death and probably less acceptable. Throughout the following six years, he was in constant trouble with the authorities for minor offences ranging from refusing to work, being insolent, fishing without permission and not having his shirt on at a muster. Glover was fortunate in that his years on the island mostly coincided with the five years of Alexander Maconachie's superintendency.

Maconochie was an enlightened penal reformer, who did much to mitigate the vindictive barbarisms perpetrated on convicts at Norfolk Island, but he was removed from office in 1843 when it was decided in London that his regime was too lenient. Glover certainly benefited from Maconochie's decency and humanity, and he was removed from Norfolk Island before the reigns of Joseph Childs and John Price, two succeeding monsters of cruelty who deliberately fostered hatred and fear as they flogged and tortured the prisoners. In August 1844 Glover arrived at Hobart, and for the next ten years he was an irritant to the authorities, whether as a member of a chain gang or, later, as a ticket-of-leave holder. He was given 100 lashes in 1845 for striking a watchman, was in and out of solitary confinement, doing hard labour or having his ticket revoked. After nearly twenty years of servitude and now in his late thirties, Glover was given a conditional pardon, which meant that he could not go back to Leicester. Married and settled at Sidmouth, north of Launceston, he worked as a farmer and carter, had a family of nine children and died as a respectable member of society in 1869. Penal servitude and the passing years had made Charles Glover an Australian. His story was not atypical of the convicts.

Horatio Wills also had memories, but they were entirely Australian for he was born, the son of a convict father, on the Sydney waterfront in 1811 where the nearby Rocks area was a haunt of pickpockets and whores amidst a general scene of destitution and misery. In his youth, he probably spent time at sea as a sealer, but later settled to an apprenticeship as a printer and in 1832 published his own weekly journal, *Currency Lad,* to which he gave the motto 'Rise Australia'. Yet the old culture of lands he had never visited and people of whom he had only read remained entwined with his being although he loved the land of his birth. In 1840, on his way into the Port Phillip District with wife and child, shepherds and flocks, to find a suitable squatting run, he camped overnight near a hill to which, mindful of Noah and the patriarchs, he gave the name Ararat after the mountain on which the Ark came to rest. The native-born always carried the stories of other lands with them but coming to peace with Australia came easily. They were its sons and daughters, and keen observers noted that, in their knowledge of the bush, they were nearly the equal of the Aborigines.

A family with an indomitable mother was that of the Glasgow merchants of Huguenot descent, Forlonge. Eliza and John decided to send their two sons, William and Andrew, to Australia after the loss of several children to tuberculosis. In 1826 Eliza and the boys went to Leipzig to study the wool industry at first hand. When John joined them in 1828, Eliza set out on foot to visit the sheep studs and select ninety-eight Saxon sheep, which she and her sons drove from Leipzig to Hamburg and later from Hull to Liverpool. By 1831 Eliza and John had arrived in Van Diemen's Land in the wake of the boys and settled near Campbell Town. John died in England in 1834 on a trip with Eliza, but she returned to see her sons go insolvent in the depression of the 1840s. Andrew went to America, while William remained to become a wealthy pastoralist in Victoria and a member of Parliament.

There were some who tried to understand that Australia was not alien but only different from England. Annie Baxter arrived in Launceston as a young bride of seventeen in the early 1830s. Within a few years she was lonely, unhappily married and struggling to survive on a run north-west of Port Macquarie on the Macleay River. At first the bush, with its strange, huge trees seemed forbidding but in time she grew to love it. Its immense silence, broken only by rare bird calls and the wind rustling the bark and leaves, soothed her spirit and the profusion of spring wild flowers enchanted her senses. Gradually the wildness of the new land seemed tamed, and often, when out riding alone, Annie would remember the last line of a poem of her childhood, 'Man is distant, but God is near!'

Louise Clifton came out to Western Australia with the founders of the new settlement called Australind. It was a venture in systematic colonization based on Wakefield's theories and the founders laid out a town on the Leschenault Estuary with areas set aside for fine parks and public buildings. On her arrival, Louise found the original township of tents picturesque in its setting under spreading trees with hills as a backdrop and birds singing everywhere. Yet when a storm came and lashed the settlement that very first night she was terrified. The family tent became a scene of watery desolation, mosquitoes never ceased to flagellate her and the cry of the wild dog in the distance brought a fear of the unknown. The next day, Monday 7 June 1841, dawned fine and calm and the distant hills and valleys reminded her of the French countryside. Louise felt instantly at peace and, as the years passed, she came to terms with Australia, married, bore children and lived out her life in the west. Thousands like her, who left no written record, did the same throughout the Australian continent.

The fall of the mighty in the West was sharp and, for a time, definitive. The failure of schemes such as Australind, the attraction of the eastern colonies, the thinness of much of the soil, the reluctance of settlers to buy land at the now established minimum price of £1 per acre, and the consequent break in the cycle of land sales that had enabled free immigration caused, by the late 1840s, a change of heart in Western Australia. It seemed evident that the prosperity of the east had been built on convict labour, so the westerners petitioned London for the privilege of receiving felons into their colony although such a solution to their problems had churned their stomachs a decade earlier. With New South Wales now closed to convicts, and the source of same at home still far from exhausted, the British government found no difficulty in agreeing. From 1850 to 1868 ten thousand male convicts were shipped to Western Australia, after which the whole system was completely abandoned.

Throughout the penal colonies, the basis of the economy had gradually shifted to free labour, while the upkeep of the convict establishment, with its military and civilian personnel, became a burden on British government coffers. A sense of moral outrage added to financial considerations so that the convict was dispensed with and his and her memory erased as quickly as possible. Yet without convicts and that haphazard but largely successful system called transportation, Australia, had it been founded at all and then managed to survive, would have been a vastly different place by the middle of the century. Rather than a handful of stable colonies, it would probably have become nothing other than scattered and minuscule settlements serving the needs of a few, large, sheep runs. Essentially, transportation gave a purpose to settlement, while convict labour made the experiment in colonization possible. In the very early days, Australia as a white civilization existed because of the convicts. Sixty years later it could do without them and, where possible, even the physical remains of their passing were abandoned and fell into ruins. Instead of pride in generally useful and fruitful lives, shame was the lasting legacy of the convict era.

Transportation had helped solve the problem posed by the criminal element in Britain, and it was inevitable that the authorities there would turn their minds to using the new colonies as a receptacle for the poor. There were at least 100,000 on poor relief and, like the criminals, they were a seeming threat to both the economy and morality. In the twenty years from 1830 to 1850 over 200,000 immigrants arrived in Australia of whom 70,000 were assisted to come to New South Wales. Many lacked skills, but most wanted to better themselves, and the majority were under thirty, could read and write and their very presence helped change the face of convict Australia.

In the early 1840s the optimism of the pastoral industry was eroding. By 1839 George Gipps had become concerned that capital was flowing in at too fast a rate for its absorption and that speculation had dulled the wits of the colonists. Imports were more than double exports in value; much of the former in luxury goods – carriages, jewellery, wines and spirits – and the anxious governor contemplated with distaste the champagne bottles with which he asserted the Melbourne countryside was littered. The banks were overflowing with cash which made loans easily obtainable at rates from ten to twenty-five percent depending upon the security offered. Land sales, both rural and urban, rose daily. The newcomers knew nothing of the lesson of hardship learnt by the old hands. Five years of severe drought from 1837 to 1841, though causing further imports including wheat for flour, mattered to few because wool prices temporarily remained high until they began to fall in 1841.

In London, word of the drought caused alarm and investors began withdrawing their colonial funds, especially as there were good profits to be made at the time in British railway development. Merchants in Australia had a glut of imports, and graziers, to whom they had made loans or given credit, were asked to pay their accounts. There was a chain reaction of increasing withdrawals of cash from the banks, and four major colonial banks, including the Bank of Van Diemen's Land, failed. Credit became very hard to get.

The recession coincided with a labour shortage in the pastoral industry. Convicts, in New South Wales at least, were no longer available and new immigrants stayed in Sydney, causing further competition on a shrinking labour market and resentment among the local labour force. Large landowners, including Wentworth, wanted to import cheap labour from China, India and the South Sea Islands, which greatly concerned Attorney-General Plunkett who thought that the labourers would be treated like slaves. At the same time several hundred colonials left for Chile, in the hope of finding better times there.

Immigrants, however, continued to pour into New South Wales, largely financed by the land sales of the late thirties. In 1841 over 20,000 assisted immigrants arrived but by 1843 the number had dropped to a mere eleven. From 1837 to 1839 almost a million acres of land were sold. In 1843 and 1845 the total scarcely reached 10,000 which, in addition to revealing the weakness in the economy, proved the absurdity of Wakefield's theory based on an artificial price for land. The great days were gone and there were bankruptcies among all classes. Sheep, which sold at 35s a head in 1839, brought 6d a head with the station thrown in by 1843. There was widespread unemployment in Sydney, with 700 men registering at Gipps' newly opened unemployment office. Wentworth, himself a sufferer from the economic slump, told the Legislative Council that he knew a man with 10,000 sheep who could not get credit for a bag of sugar.

Gipps was unjustly blamed in London for the overuse of the land fund in bringing too many immigrants to the colony. In an attempt to remedy matters, he tried to curb interest rates, and, perhaps influenced by the fact that there was a lack of space for debtors in the prisons, he abolished imprisonment for debt and allowed Wentworth's bill of a lien on wool and stock to become law which meant that sheep owners could borrow on future wool and stock sales. Some survived on their future prospects. Others kept going by boiling down sheep carcasses for tallow, which was of considerable financial benefit and also helped to cull the flocks and thereby improve their quality.

The economy slowly recovered and by 1845, when the price of wool rose to 14d per pound in London, there were increasing demands for labour in the country districts, a slight revival in land sales and a greater air of optimism prevalent. An old resident with some insight said that 'the wool trade stopped grass growing in Sydney streets.' Despite all that had happened, there was little thought given to the main lesson: foreign capital in the Australian economy could be relied upon to the extent that profits were assured but would be quickly withdrawn if better profits were offered elsewhere. Another lesson, better learnt, was the folly of attracting immigrants without capital and then having little or no work to enable them to establish themselves. Assisted immigrants by their very circumstances were without the means to settle on the land, and the depression of the early 1840s meant that many joined the ranks of Sydney's unemployed.

Caroline Chisholm arrived at Sydney in 1838 from India with her husband Archibald who worked for the East India Company. She had neither means nor training but was a woman of immense courage, inflexible integrity and possessed of a great love for suffering humanity. She decided to go to the aid of the immigrants when, as depression and drought struck, she observed that single girls were being dumped on the wharves with nowhere to go. Finding a group of sixty-four girls sheltering in the Rocks area with only 14s 3d to share among them, she set up a Female Immigrants Home with the support of the clergy, the Governor's wife and, after some initial wariness, of Gipps himself. There she gave protection and shelter to hundreds of young women, some of whom she accompanied into the country districts where, having established depots at various points as far south as Gundagai and as far north as Armidale, she found employment for them, which was often followed by marriage. By 1842 she was also concerned about families who, having migrated in the hope of better things, found themselves destitute.

Caroline returned to England in 1846 and became a publicist for Australia. She formed a society to send out groups of families, which in five years dispatched some 3,000 persons, and she agitated for, and achieved, better conditions on the vessels carrying the immigrants. Her plans for families to immigrate, most of whom hoped to settle on the land eventually, alarmed some squatters and landholders who feared competition from successful farmers. Her Catholic faith and the possibility that her exertions would bring a surfeit of Irish Catholics to Australia stirred John Dunmore Lang to fury as he contemplated the possibility of his beloved New South Wales becoming a province of popery. Lang, for his part, helped many Scottish Presbyterians to immigrate, who, being of high moral character and of industrious habits, contributed to the growth of the colony and helped to balance the influx of paupers. Caroline continued her work, and in six years assisted 11,000 people to settle as servants, wives and farmers in New South Wales while her criticism, energy and experience contributed to changes in the selection of migrants, their treatment on the voyage out and their reception in the colony.

In South Australia, experience was the great teacher as the dream faded of eager farmers growing miraculous crops and finding prosperity in the course of a single season. The realization soon dawned that only the southern portion, or about a quarter of the colony, was suitable for agriculture while the rest was practically desert. The account of Sturt's journey into the Centre in 1845, where he discovered Cooper Creek and passed over land which made man and beast quail at its barrenness, had convinced the colonists that their future lay close to the coast. With increasing experience of local weather and soils, by the mid-1840s, 900 farmers had 27,000 acres under wheat, and were producing more than the colony could use. By the end of the decade there were exports to the other colonies and to ports on the Indian Ocean. In 1843 John Ridley perfected a machine that reaped, threshed and winnowed wheat, which helped reduce labour costs. Initially only the wealthy could afford the harvester, but its use gradually became widespread throughout the colonies. Within a few years, South Australia had become the granary of the whole continent and the pastoral industry also contributed to its economy with high returns from wool sold to Britain.

The rule of George Grey (Governor 1841–46) also helped South Australia climb to prosperity. He suffered demonstrations and abuse, a good deal of it warranted, because under him the days of plenty based on government spending were over and there were retrenchments and all manner of cuts in public finance. The colony was given a nominated Legislative Council, but

Grey largely ignored its requests for democratic reform and he ruled with much caprice and some wisdom. The discovery of minerals, first silver and lead, and then copper at Kapunda and Burra, meant that his governorship was eventually marked by economic developments of great importance to the future of the colony.

At the Burra, immense deposits of copper were found and mined by Cornish and Welsh miners, who flocked to its six small towns bringing with them the techniques they had learnt at home. They lived in three roomed, attached houses built for them by the mining companies which, lined up around a square, were perfect replicas of the villages from which they came. A hospital, churches, shops, a library and two Oddfellows Lodges were erected, and mail came five times a week from Adelaide, ninety miles away. By the late 1840s, there were 5,000 people at Burra with some 2,000 of them opting to live in dwellings excavated into the sides of a creek, where they endured damp and disease. Burra produced three-fifths of the copper exported from South Australia. Thirty-seven mining companies were listed on the Adelaide Stock Exchange and the colony was the principal exporter in Australia of minerals worth over two million pounds sterling from 1845 to 1851. The mines closed in 1877 but open-cut mining started up again in 1971, and the homes of the Welsh and Cornish survived largely intact, to the benefit of those in later generations who visited there to think about the past and the pioneers who made it.

At the very height of the depression, London decided to give a further measure of self government to New South Wales, though not to Van Diemen's Land because democracy was considered incompatible with the continuation of transportation. Henceforth, the Legislative Council in New South Wales was to comprise twelve members nominated by the Crown and twenty-four elected by that one-third of the adult males who possessed sufficient means to be considered capable of voting. Six of the members were to be elected to represent the District of Port Phillip, which had been fruitlessly petitioning for separation from New South Wales since 1840. The local press in Melbourne, as well as Geelong where the *Geelong Advertiser*, which was started in 1840 as the District's first rural and morning newspaper, vociferously supported the move for separation. Gipps reported that election day in Sydney, 15 June 1843, had gone off well although there had been mild riots among the contending parties with the loss of one life.

At the time, Wentworth was at daggers drawn with the Governor because Gipps was determined to regulate the extent of squatting runs and make the squatters pay higher fees for their occupancy of them. The two men were also in conflict over Wentworth's intention to extend his domain into New Zealand. For the period between 1839 and 1841 New Zealand was officially an extension of New South Wales, so that Gipps had jurisdiction there. Wentworth and a few friends had attempted to acquire twenty million acres in New Zealand at a cost of a farthing per 1,000 acres, but the bid was blocked by Gipps who thereby earned the sworn enmity of Wentworth. Gipps was dismayed when William Charles was duly elected to the Council, and the fact that Wentworth wanted to be called 'Honourable' possibly indicated how far he had come from the days of his liberalism. James Macarthur, son of old John, stood for and was defeated in Cumberland, but Lang won a seat for Port Phillip, which meant that the old colonists were sure to have a voice in government.

The new Council met with neither parties nor plans, but it contained a group in opposition to the Governor, drawn largely from the squatting and business establishment. The opposition was conservative and represented those of the wealthy classes who survived the depression. The Council had no control over the land fund, other revenue or government spending, but it was in some measure a sounding board for grievances. It could pass legislation on other matters provided neither London nor the Governor rejected its bills. From a sense of frustration in the Council, a system of Select Committees arose which investigated many important facets of life in the colony and their reports eventually formed the basis of much useful legislation.

The major issue facing the government was that of the tenure of the squatters of whom fewer than 200 held seventy-three million acres of land, running 5,500,000 sheep by the end of the 1840s. Gipps was determined to make them pay some form of adequate licence fee but their resistance was such that he was anxious lest they rise in revolt and he hoped that in such an eventuality the army would be able to control them. The squatters combined and employed a London agent to persuade the British government to nullify Gipps, so that, by 1847, they were granted fourteen-year leases with the right to buy their land. The large squatters had thus won the battle and, secure in their tenure, they had consolidated their position once again, after the drought and depression. No amount of legislation but only bad luck, bad seasons, falling prices or ill management could ever make them relinquish their hold on the land. Their main contribution to public life in the period was a concerted effort to have transportation revived to New South Wales.

By 1846 there was only one remaining convict to every sixteen free persons in the colony and the majority of the population, particularly the townspeople and the workers, were implacably opposed to a revival of transportation. With good cause, they were fearful for their jobs and they remained mindful of the animosities of the past when emancipists and exclusives struggled for position. Nevertheless, a Council committee chaired by Wentworth and made up largely of squatters recommended revival on the grounds that it would build New South Wales into 'a mighty colony'. There was sufficient agreement in London to make it possible for a transport, the *Hashemy,* to arrive in Sydney in 1849 with 236 convicts aboard. Public meetings of protest were immediately organized, and the general outcry was such as to make it plain, even to Wentworth, that the days of transportation were over forever in New South Wales. It was also plain to the Sydney workers and their leaders that, provided they were united, they could win concessions from the government.

Port Phillip up to this time prided itself on being free from the convict taint, despite the numbers who had come across the Murray or Bass Strait with their masters and the 543 more who arrived from Van Diemen's Land with conditional pardons. The local squatters, ever seeking cheap labour, were convinced that an influx of convicts would be an economically sound move. London again acquiesced, and, starting in 1844, Port Phillip received allegedly reformed felons directly onto its own shore from the model Pentonville Prison in Britain. Many residents referred to them as Penton-villains. To soften the criminal connotations, the British government called them exiles, and 1,727 of them arrived up until 1849, which made lame the later claim of freedom from convictism in Victoria's past.

The coming of the exiles, in which the generality of citizens had no voice, served to strengthen the argument by the Port Phillip District for separation from the rest of New South Wales. Separation remained a recurrent theme of the 1840s and revolved largely around the proceeds from the sale of land, most of which, though raised in Port Phillip, were used in the older parts of the colony. Separation, it was claimed, would give the residents of Port Phillip a much-needed, direct voice in their own affairs. In protest, they elected only one member to the Legislative Council in 1848 out of their available six. To make the point even more firmly, they voted in the distant Earl Grey, secretary of the Colonial Office in London, to represent them on a body which they considered to be a farce. Such buffoonery was a legitimate attempt to force the British authorities to act. When people in Melbourne heard on 11 November 1850 that separation was on the way, they lit bonfires on the hills to spread the word to the interior and the celebrations went on for a week. On 1 July 1851 Charles La Trobe became Lieutenant-

1847 his *Don John of Austria,* the first opera composed, written and performed in Australia, was produced at the Victoria Theatre in Sydney. Lepanto and the battle of Don John against the Turk was little known in Sydney and the opera evoked little response.

Charles Thomson was the first native-born poet of quality and he spoke of Australia as the 'Refuge of all the oppressed of all the world', but he was little read or noticed by his contemporaries. William Wentworth tried to say something of his homeland with the poem he submitted for a prize at Cambridge in 1822. He ran second to the pretty effusions of Winthrop Praed who, having never seen Australia, relied on his own fervent imagination. Wentworth's poem was a song full of triumph and undisguised love for the land of his birth, which he called 'Mother Earth', while England seemed foreign to him at the time. He spoke of the Aborigines as the 'lords of this old domain', but, forgetful or unmindful of their culture, he asked the goddess of the Warragamba mountains:

> To wake to life my country's unknown lyre
> That from creation's date has slumbering lain.

He concluded with the promise that, in her decline, Britain would be able to look 'with parent eyes' to the south where she could then relive her old glories in the new land. This possibly gave the English judges pause for thought and even more so when it was clear that, unlike Praed, Wentworth did not see the Christian religion as the carrier of the culture that would make his country great. In the footsteps of Arthur Phillip, he began, probably unconsciously, a tradition that endured.

Charles Harpur was born on the Hawkesbury River in 1813, received a wide but informal education, never set foot out of Australia, became a gold commissioner at Araluen in New South Wales and, though a currency lad, was determined to become the 'Muse of Australia'. Living in an age in which beauty was equated with classical forms, Harpur remained stilted and guarded in his poetry, but in his landscape and narrative poems he came to grips with the reality of his native-land and they are of true merit. He drew around him others, Daniel Deniehy, Henry Kendall, N. D. Stenhouse, and John Le Gay Brereton who understood and admired his work, and he made them realize that, in the shaping of an essentially Australian culture, poetry was fundamental. He loved the bush where 'a mighty stillness broods' and he cried, 'My country! I am sore at heart for thee!' as he watched the 'lawless Squatters and their 'Hacks' claiming it for their own.

Generally, by the end of the 1840s, an air of optimism had begun to prevail with the weathering of the depression. In Western Australia, the colonists eagerly awaited the arrival of the first convicts but in the meantime they had to get by with a handful of Chinese who had arrived in November 1847, while on many properties flocks were shepherded by Aborigines. However, non-white labour was regarded as a temporary expedient, and wages of £50 to £60 per year with rations were offered for white shepherds. The first batch of seventy-five convicts disembarked from the *Scindian* on the twenty-second anniversary of the foundation of the colony in June 1850 which was regarded by the *Perth Gazette* as 'a very fit day for the commencement of the new order of things.' The newspaper immediately demanded that the convicts be put to work building a goal for the local Aboriginal prisoners, who were incarcerated in such a confined space that one of them had died from suffocation.

Education and state aid to religion were still burning questions, especially in South Australia with its vaunted role as a haven for religious dissidents. Immigrants were now flocking there and, with its promise in wool, wheat, metals and commerce, the colony was determined to apply the principles of religious and civil freedom dear to many of its founders. In 1851 state aid was abolished in South Australia, which put the churches of all denominations on an equal footing. Meanwhile, New South Wales had started to fund both public and denominational schools in the fond hope that peace would be assured between the churches and educational standards improved. Almost everyone agreed that Christianity was basic to education, but what was Christian, as distinct from purely denominational, was the issue at stake. Those few who thought that the matter was of no moment could afford to bide their time until the protagonists wearied themselves, at which juncture the secularists would have their day.

Moral enlightenment was part of the creed of the day and was expressed in savings banks, temperance societies, the building of private schools, and the setting up of charitable organizations. Sydney had a Benevolent Society; an asylum for the destitute in Pitt Street; and a number of hospitals, though they were generally of a very low standard. The Christian ethic of loving one's neighbour was evident in some aspects of public and private life, and everywhere there was a sense of striving to build the Australian colonies on the pattern of the home societies.

Secure in their own particular belief in a supreme being and convinced that it was both unique and exclusive, it was easy for the whites to conclude that the Aborigines had no such belief at all. One practical result of this arrogance was that the blacks were judged incompetent to give evidence in court under oath. The Aborigines' Protection Society stated bluntly that the rejection of black evidence, 'renders them virtually outlaws in their Native Land which they have never alienated or forfeited.' Plunkett, as Attorney-General, had long held the view that it was monstrous to deny the blacks a right to give evidence, yet he was ineffective in shaking the law makers in either Sydney or London.

Indeed, Robert Lowe, an outspoken champion of the rights of the underdog and of so much else in the slow process of democratic development in Australia, refused to support Plunkett because admitting Aboriginal evidence would put whites at the mercy 'not of man [but] of savage and blood thirsty cannibals.' There may have been instances of ritualistic cannibalism practised in New South Wales although no one came forward to assert having witnessed such an event. Aborigines sometimes told whites what they knew their interrogators wanted to hear, rather than what they themselves knew to be true. That the Aborigines were cannibals in any true sense of the word was a gross misrepresentation.

In 1849, the matter of Aboriginal evidence came to a head after Edmund Kennedy, on an exploratory journey on the Cape York Peninsula, was speared to death in the presence of his Aboriginal companion, Jacky Jacky, who had shown great courage and loyalty throughout the whole episode. It was clear Jacky Jacky knew the Aborigines who were responsible for the slaying, but Plunkett was powerless to act in bringing them to trial, as the only witness, Jacky Jacky, could not give evidence. Plunkett had another try at putting a bill through the Legislative Council, and he used the argument that, as the Aborigines were being poisoned and shot, the only remedy was to accept their evidence in the hope of convicting the white killers. His remarks alarmed the squatters and their allies in the Council, and Plunkett was again accused of showing favouritism to the blacks. In forlorn anger, as he saw the majority line up to defeat his bill, Plunkett said that as every Aborigine 'had stamped on him the image of his Creator, he could not but believe that the treatment that had been visited on these blacks was sufficient to call down the vengeance of Heaven'. Aboriginal evidence was finally admitted in the New South Wales courts in 1876.

7

Golden Land

The great southern continent and its white inhabitants lay at peace in 1851. Sixty-three years had changed much of its more verdant land where sheep now walked in millions, while the cultivation of crops and the rearing of stock for food had taken some hold on the coastal fringes. The white settlers had barely touched the vast heart of the continent, to whom it was a distant back country of desert dunes, forbidding heat and unknown dangers. The whites had come to terms with the ancient fauna, although the wild dog, like themselves a newcomer, remained a menace. No one realized that some of the birds, unlike the dog which had arrived in the previous 5,000 years, were so native to the land that they had no origin apart from it. Was this the cradle of all that grew and walked? What other mysteries did it hold in its keeping? These questions remained unasked because the business of the day was to acquire and retain the means of sustenance, and about that men and women, and many children also, went by force and habit.

Already Australians were showing an inclination to become urban dwellers in cities that hugged the coast and they looked back to the bush as an unknown land. The needs of administration and the facilities of ports helped the growth of the cities and created a demand for labour, but it was clear that immigrants in particular preferred to live in an urban environment. In Sydney, over a quarter of the 186,000 citizens of New South Wales lived in a city which had its gentry and its slum dwellers, its offices and factories, and banks and shops of all varieties. Melbourne held about the same proportion of the 80,000 who lived in Port Phillip as did Hobart of the 70,000 in Van Diemen's Land. The tanneries, foundries and breweries were almost all in the cities, but of the 500 industrial enterprises in operation by 1850 a half were flour mills, which were constructed where convenience dictated.

In Melbourne, the tradesmen were found about the central areas and the professional men had moved onto Eastern Hill, while some workers and others of the better-off had taken up residence in the suburban land beyond the township. Richmond and Collingwood were already dotted with villas and cottages, and Toorak and Prahran, south of the Yarra, had seen the same process. In both Sydney and Melbourne, the suburban sprawl had already begun. There seemed to be limitless land and, as yet, only the sheep were there to occupy it.

There was little variation in day-to-day life over the vast areas where pastoralists had expanded. Out beyond Bathurst in New South Wales and in that land, so often wet with creeks and swamps beyond Mount Buninyong in Victoria, little stirred except the sheep, followed by their lonely shepherds. It had frequently happened in previous years that one of their kind, idly kicking at the soil or scratching at a rocky outcrop, had seen something gleaming which had proved to be gold. Gold, however, was a treasure it was unwise to talk about in a convict colony, and silence was kept as to its whereabouts because all gold was supposed to belong to the Crown.

Other mineral deposits had already been found as well as coal. Mining was already fundamental to the South Australian economy and since 1848 iron ore had been smelted to pig iron near Mittagong in New South Wales. In such circumstances, it was not strange that some men should begin to think of the probable existence of gold and other precious metals in useful quantities, but an event elsewhere was needed to cause the next step to be taken. By 1849 the rich goldfields of California had drawn some Australians to go prospecting there and they learnt the prevailing methods of separating gold from mud and dirt. Among them was English-born Edward Hargraves, who returned to New South Wales convinced that the gold he had come across in meagre amounts in California lay in abundance under Australian soil. He was proved right in a measure that even Hargraves, much given to self-importance and exaggeration, never dreamt possible.

Hargraves taught four young Australians how to use the Californian techniques of panning and cradling, and they soon found rich deposits of gold in the Wellington district in early 1851. Hargraves publicized the finds in the press, named the area Ophir and claimed, and eventually received, £10,000 as a reward from the government. There was an immediate rush across the Blue Mountains to the fields situated beyond Bathurst, and by 15 May, 300 diggers were on the Ophir fields. Australia's first gold rush had commenced. This prompted an old soldier to ask for the importation of a regiment to keep order as he feared that 'all the horrors of California' with murders, riots, lynchings and general unrest, would follow in the wake of the diggers.

Sanity prevailed in Sydney and the government decided to maintain the even tenor of society: to exact in a humane way a licence fee of 30s a month from the diggers to finance the administration of the fields, and generally assist rather than impede them in their search for gold. Prices of all commodities rose astronomically as diggers came in from the other colonies, labour in the towns and pastoral districts became scarce and the news of prodigious finds prompted the London *Times* to state, 'this is the Arabian nights over again.' In the main, the early days of gold in New South Wales, though marked with some unrest and resentment at the licence fee, saw all the romance and hardship which the lottery of gold digging entailed, together with stability and a quick return to normalcy when the early rushes were over.

Gold mining continued in New South Wales especially on the Turon River where the diggings were very rich. The golden period in the colony reached its symbolic apogee in 1871 when the world's largest reef-gold specimen was found in the Hill End area. It weighed 630 pounds and was brought up almost intact. One of the owners of the claim was Bernard Holtermann, born in Hamburg in 1838, who later built himself a home in Sydney with a tower in which a stained-glass window depicted him standing beside the huge specimen. By his patronage and enthusiasm, Holtermann became the father of Australian photography, and the reconstruction of the historical period of gold about Hill End and Gulgong was possible from the photographs of those fields at their peak. The photographs, which were used abroad to publicize the colonies of New South Wales and Victoria and encourage immigrants to come out to them, were also made possible by his sponsorship.

While the first discoveries of gold were being made in New South Wales, Port Phillip was still reeling from the catastrophic bush fires of Thursday 6 February 1851, named Black Thursday because ashes fell in the Melbourne streets in 120'F heat. From Westernport in the east to across the border with South Australia in the west, in a vast swathe of country stretching beyond Mount Macedon, the awesome fire destroyed all in its path when, swept by high winds, it raced beyond control, but there was little loss of human life. Soon the rains fell and the earth became green with a refreshed and increased luxuriousness.

The news from New South Wales had drawn many workers from Victoria to the goldfields there, and Charles La Trobe waited anxiously for word of discoveries in his own domain. Wisdom should have indicated patience. New South Wales with its settled population, its established system of law and order, its seasoned administrators and its healthy treasury was able to handle a gold rush. Born on 1 July 1851, Victoria was but an infant. Nine days later, at Clunes, ninety miles northwest of Melbourne, gold in payable quantities was found. The rushes did not begin in earnest until late August when rich deposits were discovered at Ballarat. Within three months, the richest goldfields the world had ever seen were opened, especially at Mount Alexander where the diggings spread over an area of fifteen square miles and made Victoria the mecca for thousands from Europe.

The cold statistics tell little of what life was like in those golden days, but they reveal much of how gold affected Australia, and particularly Victoria. In the decade of the 1850s over 1000 tons of gold worth £110,000,000 came out of Victoria. New South Wales produced about 140 tons valued at £15,000,000 and Australian gold accounted for forty per cent of the world's total production in the 1850s. It remained a more valuable export than wool until the 1870s. But it was in the numbers of people that the big change took place, thereby laying to rest Governor George Gipps's fear that Australia would remain a vast sheep walk.

In the ten years of the golden decade, Victoria's population grew from 80,000 to half a million, while that of New South Wales rose from 186,000 to 350,000. Of the 600,000 who came to Victoria in this decade, over half stayed, but of those 86,000 who crossed from New South Wales almost all went home. This indicated where their long lasting emotional and economic roots were. Although the United Kingdom was the major source of the new population, the goldfields attracted 40,000 Chinese. Many of them were debtors who came to work, save their money and then return home. Their passing created a legacy of racism, which over a century later still showed its mark. As an indication of how money will be spent when available, the value of exports never exceeded imports into Victoria in the decade, and indeed in 1854 goods to the value of £18,000,000 came in while £12,000,000 worth went out. This caused a glut of unsaleable commodities, high rates of unemployment in Melbourne and the failure of many business houses.

Among the first on the goldfields were the ex-convicts and native-born, many of whom had been shepherds. Their presence initially alarmed the squatters, who foretold doom for themselves and anarchy for all, neither of which proved true. In fact, the squatters doubled their cattle numbers and did very well supplying mutton and beef to the fields and breeding horses for transport. In the wake of the early comers, bankers, tradesmen, parsons, lawyers, doctors, clerks, sailors, farmers, government employees, policemen and prostitutes followed. Alfred Tennyson would have come had his wife permitted him, and Henrik Ibsen wrote, romantically but absurdly, of 'Ballarat beyond the desert sands.' So many policemen left the ranks to become diggers that there were only two left out of a normal force of forty in

Melbourne by the New Year of 1852. Ex-convicts and scoundrels soon took their places.

The past life of the gold digger was of no consequence to anyone except himself. All that mattered was his ability to wield a shovel, to withstand heat and cold, water and mud, flies and fleas, dysentery and eye disease – meanwhile fortified by meat, damper and tea, with an odd glass of doctored grog because the government was too obstinate to permit licensed premises on the fields in the early years. The diggers were sustained by the search for gold, which rewarded a minority handsomely, kept others in moderate comfort and sent away about a third empty-handed. As a group, the diggers were young, unmarried, adventurous, of some slender means, better educated than the norm and Anglo-Saxon or Irish in origins. Equally, they were, in the main, law abiding, God-fearing, hardworking and upright. Amongst them, however, there were some who possessed little of those qualities, and the goldfield population, which was never more than a third of the total Victorian population, was often judged harshly because of the behaviour of a rowdy or criminal minority.

In the beginning, the diggers merely scratched at the surface, taking what gold was readily available by panning in the creek beds and rivers. They then rushed to another place when word came of new finds. Millions of years earlier in the Tertiary period, volcanoes had erupted, twisting and turning the rivers and burying them, with their golden deposits, sixty, a hundred or more feet below the surface of the earth. By the end of 1852, at Ballarat, the diggers were going down and down through timber-lined holes searching for the deep lead. The holes quickly filled with water and the work was hard, unsafe and costly so they banded together in groups of eight to twelve, often of the same nationality, British, Irish or American, to work a common claim. Each claim was limited to 576 square feet. If they bottomed out on a lead they could win riches, even great riches, especially if they hit a spot where old riverbeds ran together. One such place was called the Jewellers Shops. It was on Canadian Gully at Ballarat where nuggets of 84, 93 and 136 pounds were found in January 1853. Alternatively the diggers could miss the lead or find it unproductive, so the heartbreaking work of shaft digging had to begin all over again.

With deep-lead mining a change came over the fields, for the diggers had to raise capital for equipment and daily necessities because they were forced to settle in the one place for months. As a consequence, the fields gradually took on the aspect of a stable community. Ballarat, by late 1854, was a thriving township with banks, shops, stores, hotels, theatres, libraries, churches, lawyers, doctors, a newspaper and a hospital under construction. More importantly, there were women and children, 15,000 of them in a total population of 50,000. Charles Hotham had recently replaced La Trobe as Governor of Victoria, and it was not a mob of uneducated vagabonds and assorted criminals that he had to deal with on the fields. On the contrary, they were mostly men who were literate, respectable and determined to be treated with dignity as upright citizens, and in many cases fathers of families.

The diggers had neither land nor votes, and they paid for their right to dig for gold by an extremely high tax of 30s per month. The tax was brutally enforced by a government bent on wresting every possible penny from them, while offering little in the form of services in return, especially in roads, bridges, transport and postal facilities or police protection from thieves. Increasingly the diggers began to agitate for their rights and at Ballarat, Castlemaine, in the Ovens River district and on the largest field, Bendigo, crowds of up to 12,000 met to protest and to refuse to pay for a licence to dig. The government compromised and reduced the fee in November 1853.

The event, called Eureka, of Sunday 3 December 1854, did not happen by accident. Goaded for three years by a repressive and corrupt administration at Ballarat, the diggers formed the Ballarat Reform League on 11 November. It demanded full civic rights together with abolition of the licence fee and proclaimed the doctrine that 'the people are the only legitimate source of all political power'. The editor of the local *Ballarat Times* called the League, 'the germ of Australian independence', and, to the extent that the movement was a decisive step towards a future republic, he was right. In London, Karl Marx, when he heard of the goings on at Ballarat, prophesied that the movement there would be quickly suppressed. Marx was also right.

On 1 December, a group of about 200 diggers gathered within a flimsy and hastily erected stockade of logs near the Eureka lead. They were determined to resist, if necessary by arms, any further arrests for the non-possession of a licence, but they made no plans to launch an attack on anyone. Hotham and his Ballarat subordinates were equally determined to break the resistance of the diggers by the use of superior arms. They were convinced that seditious foreigners organized the diggers' movement. In fact the diggers were not in revolt and, to the degree that they engaged in armed resistance, they were deliberately goaded to do so because it was the express wish of the authorities to 'catch them with arms in their hands so as to crush this democratic movement at one blow.'

Essentially the diggers demanded the fundamental right to be treated with justice and respect. They were repeatedly dragged from their damp holes and ordered to produce their licences and their failure to do so resulted in being forcibly carted off into custody where they were fined. Apart from the question of taxation without representation, which the licence fee virtually imposed, and the fact that it was a tax on labour rather than on products, the diggers wanted a chance to settle on the land, most of which was still held by the squatters. Regiments of the British army supported the law enforcement agencies on the fields. To the many diggers who had participated in, or witnessed, resistance against the presence of a standing army in the midst of a civilian population in their homelands, this was an affront of immense proportions.

Over thirty diggers died on that Sunday morning, when, outnumbered by more than two-to-one, they were attacked at dawn by police and troops, four of whom also lost their lives. In the heady aftermath of the affair, the police engaged in a senseless orgy of killing among innocent civilians and over 100 arrests were made. It was later said that the diggers died in vain because the freedoms and the rights for which they sacrificed their lives would have been eventually granted in any case. Partial reform did come about in 1855 when the licence fee was abolished and replaced by an annual miner's right. The right also gave an entitlement to stand for parliament and to vote in elections. The diggers' leader, Peter Lalor, bewailed the fact that the English so often found it necessary to baptise in blood the rights they granted. Public opinion in Victoria was clearly on the side of the diggers.

The men of Eureka left behind a legacy carried on in prose, poetry and painting and in the powerful symbol of their flag. A newspaperman who suddenly discovered he was a friend of law and order, H. R. Nicholls, scorned the diggers as Irish drunkards, but Raffaello Carboni, the chronicler of those events of late 1854, saw it differently and he was able to plumb the symbolism of Eureka. To him, the flag, with its white cross and five stars on a blue background denoting the Southern Cross, was a thing of beauty under which free people could stand upright and proud. The Southern Cross flew briefly for those few days at Eureka but long and purposefully enough to win its place in the loyalty of many Australians. To them the stand taken by those who had fought beneath it was a promise of lasting democracy. With the passage of time, Eureka passed into mythology and its flag was seized by restless elements of the political and industrial left, which temporarily put paid to its claim to be a universal symbol. But the legend remained to proclaim that, in the new land called Australia, the right to oppose tyranny and to be treated with respect, to have hope in and to work for a better future, was inalienable.

The already established society of the eastern colonies proved resilient to the coming of so many thousands in the 1850s because it was firmly shaped as white, male-dominated, hierarchical, dependent on Britain, closely governed and highly urbanized. The freedoms, inherited from Britain, of religion, press and association were upheld and treasured by many. Law and order on the English model was accepted and, unlike California, the rule of the mob never took hold on the goldfields. The older popular movement that had helped stop transportation and was deeply involved in the demand for self-government was indigenous to Australia. The small elements of Chartism that came with the diggers refined it but did not change it. The diggers helped to strengthen the ethos that had become peculiarly Australian in a positive way. They had to support each other and find ways of confronting the problems thrown up on the goldfields. Their experience of the government officials on the fields, who so often acted without compassion or ordinary decency, caused many of them to become anti-authority. The repeated acts of brutality and corruption of the police enhanced a hatred that had its origins in chain gangs and convict hellholes.

The Australian characteristics of a fondness for strong drink, a readiness to take a risk and a general air of independence were reinforced on the goldfields as was racism, which, beginning with the blacks, now included the Chinese and had developed from contempt to loathing. The proportion of three males to one female had not changed much by the end of the 1850s but there were seven times as many females as before 1851. This made a difference to the whole fabric of society, as did the greatly increased attendance at schools and churches. Gold, with its ability to make the poor rich, to delude even the astute and to turn the sober into drunkards was a unique leveller. Servants left their masters; mistresses had to cook, clean and open doors. Men of no substance yesterday now rode in splendid carriages and drank fine wines. The hierarchical orders of old England, based on birth or distinction in the martial arts, found no role on the goldfields and little more in the society that grew around them.

Gold brought changes of enormous consequence to Victoria and New South Wales. With the threefold increase in population from 1851 to 1861, the influence of squatterdom was threatened, though the squatters remained. The cry of the diggers to unlock the lands in Victoria was partially heard so that there were 13,000 farmers and market gardeners in 1861, mostly ex-diggers, compared to 3,000 a decade before. Gold built or made prosperous numerous country towns, which was more important than its contribution to the development of the cities. The towns brought to the bush those elements of civilization without which life can be brutish, and for which a week's holiday in the city for the races or an agricultural show never sufficed.

Some of the towns thrived to become cities like Bathurst, Ballarat, Bendigo and Ararat, the only Australian city to owe its origins to the Chinese diggers who found gold there in 1857. Bendigo and Ballarat founded first-rate Schools of Mines and the technologies developed in them spread throughout Australia and into the Pacific. Everywhere settlements took root which were named by such simple expressions as the distance from the previous resting place – Five Mile, Ten Mile and Fifteen Mile and similar names were given to creeks and other watering places. Towns now forgotten sprang up overnight and had populations of 20,000 or more with numerous pubs and other amenities. They prospered while the gold lasted. In the end they became mere names – Hill End, Sofala, Mount Alexander, and others who had their fleeting moment in history. Out of them, and places like them, came the romance and hardship of gold. In and about them, and especially in Victoria's Golden Triangle, the great nuggets were found and often their names were enough to sum it all up – Welcome Stranger and Welcome Nugget of 2,284 and 2,217 ounces respectively – for there were many diggers who never saw a nugget.

The rise of new towns created a demand for new means of transport. The state of the roads was a guarantee of intense discomfort for travellers and heavy costs for goods. In 1853 a young American, Freeman Cobb, with his partners, founded a coaching firm in Melbourne called Cobb & Co., which provided speedy and reliable transport to the goldfields and eventually to towns right throughout Victoria, New South Wales and Queensland. The early drivers, called Yankee whips, were Americans, and the coaches were Concord jacks of the thorough-brace type, imported initially from America. Only the best of horses were used, and the change stations were spaced about ten miles apart to provide fresh horses. Some of them, such as the bluestone stage at Buangor on the run west from Ballarat were imposing structures, while others left no trace. Cobb sold out at a large profit in 1856, but the name of his firm remained to be cheered by thousands, in the next eighty years, whose moderate comfort and speedy delivery at their destination was made possible by his enterprise.

Developments on land were paralleled at sea when steam was introduced onto the England to Australia route in 1852. The *Chusan* made the run to Sydney in eighty days carrying mails and passengers. The ship so delighted the citizens on her arrival that they created a new dance tune called the 'Chusan Waltz'. In 1854 the most important of all modern technical revolutions in communications arrived when the first electric telegraph line was installed between Melbourne and Williamstown. The telegraph quickly spread throughout the colonies. It annihilated distance, making joy and grief only moments away, but as the Melbourne *Argus* observed, its use was especially important to 'those engaged in commerce.'

The gold discoveries ended transportation to Van Diemen's Land and the possibility of it being resumed in any of the eastern colonies. In Van Diemen's Land opinion was still divided between those who wanted the labour of convicts and those whose morals or pockets were threatened by their presence. Victoria had taken the drastic step of refusing entry to anyone from the island unless the newcomer could offer proof of his or her civil freedom. In England John Pakington, Secretary of State, decided it was time to act. On 14 December 1852 he wrote to William Denison, Lieutenant-Governor of Van Diemen's Land, to tell him that no more British refuse would pollute Tasman's fair isle, partly because of the undesirable impression English criminals could gain by seeing their companions transported to 'an island in the immediate neighbourhood of the gold colonies of Australia.' On 26 May 1853 a final batch of convicts sent to Van Diemen's Land landed from the *St Vincent* at Hobart to end that dark chapter in the history of the island. The last convicts to eastern Australia arrived at Norfolk Island in 1855. In the following year, 194 descendants of the mutineers against Bligh on the *Bounty* were taken from Pitcairn Island for resettlement on Norfolk Island where their own descendants flourish into the present although a remnant remain at Pitcairn Island.

Pakington was not one to deal in half measures. Gold freed Van Diemen's Land of convicts and so moved its citizens to reject the past that they changed its name to Tasmania in 1855. Gold also induced Pakington to take the other long awaited step and grant political freedom to the eastern colonies. He wrote to Charles Fitzroy, Gipps's successor in New South Wales, to tell him that the decision to grant self government was prompted, not merely by listening to requests from the colonists but also, because of the 'extraordinary discoveries of gold.' The colonists could now go ahead and draw up constitutions for the approval of the Queen.

In his letter, Pakington said that there had to be provision for two houses of parliament written into the constitutions. The lower would be elected by the people and the upper one, preferably, nominated by the Crown. The colonists would be given control over land and finances. This was the crux of the matter as without such powers responsible government would be a sham. Pakington fondly hoped that such generosity would result in further cementing and perpetuating 'the ties of kindred affection and mutual confidence' between the colonists and the United Kingdom. It was a shrewd assessment for, although the colonists would bicker long and loud amongst themselves about the shape of their emerging freedom, they would never be permitted to forget its source. In vain did John Dunmore Lang, Daniel Deniehy, Charles Harpur and others cry for full independence from the Crown even if blood had to be shed to obtain it. The British statesmen had learnt how to give the needed inch. In any case, a golden age was not one in which to cry revolution. Most people had more pressing matters at hand than dreams of a republic and the pursuit of wealth had ever proved to be the handmaiden of conservatism.

Much argument followed in New South Wales about the exact shape of the new form of government, although little of it mattered. Wentworth generated a great deal of heat and comedy when he suggested that the members of the upper house, called the Legislative Council, should be given tides with hereditary rights to pass on to their successors. In itself the suggestion was a piece of nonsense, although it had been mooted earlier in Canada. Deniehy, brilliant lawyer and son of convict parents, quickly burlesqued it in a speech of wit and invective and dismissed the idea of a 'bunyip aristocracy' with contempt thus bringing the whole idea into public ridicule. Wentworth, by now a proclaimed conservative, remained unperturbed. He had failed to get his aristocrats, but few noticed that he got the nominated Legislative Council, which he, not wishing 'to sow the seeds of a future democracy' was determined to have as he hoped it would be a bulwark against the tide of radical change. Furthermore, the squatters, whose hold on rural electorates was secure, were ensured of retaining considerable weight in the new government. This was an assurance that change would never come about suddenly.

By the end of 1856, New South Wales, Victoria, Tasmania and South Australia all had self-government. The Victorians had decided to elect the members to their Legislative Council but, because its members and electors had to have wealth or education and preferably both, it remained particularly impervious to change and became a bastion of entrenched privilege. The secret, or Australian, ballot was used for the first time in the Victorian elections in March 1856 and progressively in the other colonies. Western Australia adopted the method in 1877. The South Australians also used the ballot box in their elections in April 1856. Furthermore, they gave the vote to every adult male, which was an unprecedented stride to full democracy.

The ensuing elections in the four colonies went off with little fuss because the differences between the candidates generally amounted to little. There were no real leaders and policy formulation was unclear so that parties did not exist. When the new, nominated Legislative Council and elected Legislative Assembly met for the first time in Sydney on 22 May 1856, it was not remarked upon that a change had come about in the development of the colony of far greater significance than the much vaunted existence of parliament and parliamentarians: there were now more females than males in Sydney's population of 53,118 persons for the first time in 68 years.

John Dunmore Lang's political career was temporarily in abeyance as the Reverend Doctor had been lodged in Darlinghurst Gaol for six months convicted of libel, but there was one person of some stature elected to the Assembly. Henry Parkes was an English immigrant whose colonial career began in 1839 as a labourer in the employ of John Jamison. His talents soon stamped him as a man of the future, and his patriotism was shown when he supported England in the Crimean War against Russia. His enthusiasm for the war was shared generally, and a spate of place naming occurred, particularly around Ballarat, with battles and personages such as those of Sebastopol, Inkerman, Raglan and Redan being commemorated. Parkes had moved through various business and journalistic ventures, joined the radical elements of the reform movement striving for universal suffrage and land reform, flirted briefly with republicanism and finished as a liberal with his own paper, the *Empire*, founded in 1850 as the chief voice of the movement.

Vain, bigoted and blustering, there was also in Parkes a touch of greatness which made him stand above the crowd. His opposition to the old guard of colonial society, with its entrenched interests based on land, gave him entry onto the political stage. There he remained devoted to change, even when to conform may have served his own interests better because he was constantly in debt. Above all, Parkes embodied some of the finest elements of early Australian democracy, which grew from the middle classes, was stamped with their values and remained far removed from that supposed nightmare which Wentworth dreamt it could become. Colonial democracy posed no threat to Wentworth and his kind because the same, generally favourable, economic forces sustained them both.

In Britain, the Australian gold discoveries were a source of astonishment and, to some, profit. Fortunes were made in shipping and in supplying anything manufacturers deemed appropriate to fill the needs and fancies of the diggers. Overseas, Australia was on everyone's lips for a time and Ballarat and Bendigo became the chosen destination of thousands who wanted to go to the fields. Others came to the colonies because labour was short in the Australian cities and in the bush and the government was prepared to assist them to migrate by subsidising fares. The effects of the potato famine, which had reduced the Irish to 'a rag of a nation', were still being felt, and the large numbers coming from Ireland in the late 1840s kept up in the 1850s. Half of those who came in the 1850s were assisted and, in the main, they settled in the cities and towns, becoming labourers, craftsmen and servant maids, although the males perhaps spent an intervening stint on the goldfields.

In England, Caroline Chisholm had maintained her work of assisting migrants. She was not impressed by the news of the gold discoveries as she feared that they would cause instability in society. Her husband came to Australia in 1851 to work as her colonial agent, while Caroline kept sending families and girls from the British Isles, including a party of Jewish girls. Now famous and supported by such powerful figures as Charles Dickens, she decided to return to Australia in 1854. She was imbued with the optimistic but never proven idea that the health of a society lay in the settling of many, small farmers and she worked for the unlocking of the land. She died in poverty and obscurity in England in 1877. The inscription on her grave at Northampton reads 'The emigrant's friend' without recording the fact that her husband, whose bones rested with Caroline's, had shared in making her work possible by his faith, love and, above all, unlimited patience.

On another level, Caroline's work was aided by that of the Melbourne born Mary McKillop. She was of Scots parentage and, with all the determination and grit of her forebears, she founded the Sisters of St Joseph in 1866, with the encouragement and guidance of a remarkable English priest–scientist, Father E. Tenison-Woods. After the Bishop of Adelaide lifted the excommunication he had put on her for alleged disobedience, she worked tirelessly for the education of the children of the poor, especially in the bush. She founded numerous schools and charitable institutions to that end up until her death in Sydney in 1908. In 1973, Mother Mary, as she became known, was the first Australian to be formally proposed in Rome as a candidate for canonization. When she was beatified in 1995 few seemed to have noticed that one of her outstanding virtues, a readiness to stand up for justice rather than bow to authority, was notably Australian.

Some immigrants joined the native-born and old hands in concluding that both the system of land tenure and the policy of assisted immigration needed revision. A change to mining by companies was taking place on the goldfields from the mid-1850s and the consequent arrival of diggers in Sydney and Melbourne caused unemployment. The constant influx of newcomers from the ships stirred up resentment against the government, employers, squatters, immigrants and Chinese. The *Operative,* a Sydney paper founded in 1854, struck a loud note calling for the cessation of any government assistance to immigration as well as the protection of the workers from the depreciation of the labour market by the 'introduction of inferior races', meaning the Chinese. On the goldfields the Chinese were often ill treated, at times barbarously. In 1857, on the Buchland River in north-eastern Victoria, a mob of diggers drove the Chinese down the valley, destroying and burning their property and their joss house. They were seen as economic competitors although opposition to them was often clothed in quasi-cultural terminology on the grounds that they threatened to dilute the British nature of society. By late 1861, Victoria, South Australia and New South Wales had passed laws restricting their entry.

The early years of the gold rushes inspired ballads, poetry, art and some literature. Samuel Gill, an artist of great delicacy of line, left a lasting monument with his carefully drawn sketches, full of vitality, of life on the Victorian fields. Catherine Spence, preacher, reformer and feminist, published anonymously in 1854 her *Clara Morrison,* which dealt with South Australia in the days when gold lured many thousands away from the colony. A contemporary critic judged it the best work of literature yet written with Australia as its setting and even better than Alexander Harris's *The Emigrant Family* or the earlier *Tales of the Colonies* by Charles Rowcroft. The most important contribution to the gold period, however, was William Howitt's *Land, Labour and Gold* published in London in 1855. Howitt spent only two years in Australia but his gift for narrative and his incisive judgements on the bumbling ineptitude of Hotham's administration made his work a gold mine in itself for those who, later, wanted to know what life on the goldfields was like in the days of the great rushes.

The most formative element in the lives of literate Australians was the newspaper. Indeed, the editor of the newly founded Melbourne *Age* said, with some truth on 17 October 1854, that 'The Newspaper has become the great teacher of the age' with more influence than either pulpit or school. It was opportune in the days of Eureka, and during the ordeal of the thirteen men put on trial for their lives after the event, that the *Age* held to a 'strong sense of popular rights' together with the conviction that, unless closely watched by the defenders of freedom, all governments would naturally tend 'to corruption and tyranny'. All the men of Eureka were acquitted. In Sydney, John West was appointed in 1854 as the first official editor of the *Herald.* Since the publication of David Collins's An *Account of the English*

Colony in New South Wales in 1798, little worthwhile Australian history was written until West's excellent *History of Tasmania* was published in two volumes in 1852. He was also the father of the anti-transportation movement as well as a firm believer that 'Australia was one' and thus an early federationist. West brought his strong convictions as a Congregational minister to the editor's desk, together with a blend of liberal-conservative attitudes and moral stances and a rigid adhesion to principles.

In the early days of Sydney Cove, Phillip had noticed that there were numerous and admirable rock carvings about the harbour, some of which, he thought, were executed in a superior style. In white Australia, sculpture, before all other art forms, began badly. Lacking patronage, whether by state or church, sculptors could only deal in busts of the would-be famous, although Melbourne in the 1840s had two 'Madonna and Child' groups by Emil Todt. Todt, later, did a remarkable work depicting the gold diggers. In Tasmania, Benjamin Law sculptured two Aboriginal busts, one being of Truganini wearing the doomed look of a woman conscious that her people were dying. Teresa Snell Walker, Australia's first woman sculptor, also worked on the island. Thomas Woolner, an original of the Pre-Raphaelite brotherhood, sailed for Australia in 1852 and Ford Madox Brown painted the departing vessel in his *The Last of England.* Woolner remained only briefly, so the early palm goes to Charles Summers who first exhibited in Melbourne in 1854. To show his true worth, Summers had to await a later tragedy when the story of Burke and Wills gripped the imagination of all Australians.

The most notable events of the period on an intellectual level were the founding of the University of Sydney in 1850 and that of Melbourne in 1853. Ironically, the very step of founding a university, and thereby proclaiming a commitment to liberal principles, almost caused Sydney's opening to be postponed. William Bland's was among the names put forward as original senators. He was a scholar, a surgeon of high repute and a pioneer who had made a great contribution to the colony. He was also an emancipist, having been transported in 1814 for killing his opponent in a duel in Bombay. Robert Lowe publicly refused to sit on the Senate were Bland appointed, although Plunkett shared no such inhibition. It was a bitter affair with all the odour of the past about it. Bland's subsequent omission from the Senate indicated that old passions still ran deep.

Sydney's university, like some powerful elements in the society from which it sprang, was secular largely because its founding fathers were not prepared to allow sectarian conflicts to mar the beginning of their University.

Its teachers and governing body were all laymen and, overall, its foundation indicated that the powerful and the wealthy would no longer tolerate the 'frightful dearth of Colonial education' that had persisted for over 60 years. Down in Melbourne, the already existing rivalry between the southern city and Sydney would not permit any delay in founding a university, although some Victorians thought it an act of insane extravagance. Nonetheless, the price was not considered too high to give a colony not yet fifteen years of age an institution of prestige.

At a river crossing on the Murrumbidgee called Gundagai, the few hundred inhabitants were witnessing the growth of a flourishing community with moderate prosperity by 1852. Despite the warnings of local Aborigines, the township had been laid out on the river flats, which were clearly exposed to danger from flooding. On 25 June the river rose rapidly overnight, six families and a total of 77 persons were drowned, homes and businesses were washed away and the community all but destroyed. It was noticed that very few turned to God to give gratitude for their survival. On the other hand, they were certainly mindful of the role played by an Aborigine who paddled out in a frail canoe on perilous trip after trip to rescue scores of them as they clung to roofs and trees. In a later time they erected a monument to commemorate Yarrie and his deeds of valour. On the plaque of honour they spoke of him as 'one of Australia's greatest heroes'. In one place at least, the black man, in the person of Yarrie, during the darkness of a night of swirling waters, became acceptable to the white community.

8

Change and Development

On 17 April 1861, at a desolate place in Central Australia, three men paused to bury the body of their dead companion, Charles Gray, in a shallow grave. It was an act of great courtesy because the survivors, Robert O'Hara Burke, William John Wills and John King, all stood unsteadily in their exhaustion. Emaciated, bewildered and despondent, they now tasted bitterness after the jubilation of a few weeks previously. On Sunday morning, 9 February 1861, Burke and Wills had left their companions and set out on foot until they came to 'a channel through which the sea-water enters.' Although unable to pass further through the swampy ground, they knew their goal was reached. Burke and Wills were the first white men to cross the continent from Melbourne in the south to the Gulf of Carpentaria in the north. After the burial, they pressed on to their depot at Cooper Creek, but they found it deserted when they arrived on 21 April. The party which would have brought them safely back to Melbourne had left seven hours previously. Burke, the leader – brave, impetuous, unskilled and obstinate – and his loyal and honourable lieutenant, Wills, were dead from starvation by the end of June, while King, young and strong, lived on with the help of the Aborigines.

The remains of Burke and Wills were buried with much solemnity in Melbourne in 1863. Charles Summers sculptured a magnificent statue in their honour and the Royal Society of Victoria gave a title to that successful but largely useless tragedy – 'The Burke and Wills Expedition.' The Society did so knowing that economic interests, hoping for pastoral and business expansion, had engineered the whole affair. Burke and Wills walked upon the vast continent, as did Sturt, Eyre, Oxley, Leichhardt, McDouall Stuart, Giles, the Forrests, Grey and the Gregorys. Yet the land remained largely unconquered and the foolhardy perished as they ventured forth to seek respite from the wilderness in their spirits. The names of Burke and Wills live on in legend as testimony to the supremacy of the land.

Burke and Wills also symbolized the passing of the early colonial period. The period's pre-eminent representative William Charles Wentworth finally retired to England in 1862 and died there ten years later. Brought back for later burial, Wentworth's remains were interred near his home, and he was spoken of as Australia's 'greatest son'. Time had softened much, and even

Parkes was contrite for his rejection of the eldest statesman, but Wentworth's legacy was permanent.

William Charles's mighty heart had been broken on a triangle of conflicting emotions, England, Australia and his own overpowering ambition. Each in their way had brought him undone. He had fought for a whole range of causes: responsible government, freedom of the press, trial by jury and much else. Despite all his reforming work, the one thing that stood out was his struggle for the illegitimate rights of the squatters, which gave them a hold over their lands in effective perpetuity. In time the squatters changed, much as Wentworth had done from the days of his rebellious youth to patriarch and consul and finally to committed defender of the conservative values based on wealth and privilege.

Gone were the times of the rude dwellings, flimsy yards and makeshift shearing sheds. The squatters became graziers, and built fine houses with long drives of pines, elms, oaks and other exotic trees leading to well laid out gardens. Their shearing sheds of corrugated iron or bluestone became symbols of the squatters' permanence for they signalled that on these vast acres the sheep would run in thousands and that each year the ritual of shearing the golden fleece would take place under the watchful eye of the master. But the squatters also had to struggle unceasingly with the land for it could be full of caprice. Fine seasons were followed by others in which the clouds passed overhead to pour their abundance on distant mountains and seas, the earth cracked, the creeks dried up, the skeletons of stock whitened in the dust and crows cawed a requiem for hope.

The new forms of government in the east had helped to entrench the hold of the squatters, because it was clearly in the best interest of those with property to ensure the stability of the economy, and wool promised security while gold, to the astute, was a transient commodity. In vain, conventions of delegates drawn from the landless met in Melbourne and Sydney in 1857, both to protest and to plan a suitable form of legislation for the future sale of land. One major obstacle to reform was that, although the best land had been taken up, there was still so much more yet to be occupied on the mainland. It was available to anyone with the will and means to push further out onto it but, until it was surveyed, who could tell who was master and of how much?

Furthermore, it was apparent that with the entry of the colonies into a boom period in the aftermath of the gold rushes, most people were comfortably placed, although there were still pockets of unemployment in the cities. By the 1860s per-capita income and consumption was 50 per cent higher than in America and 100 per cent higher than in Britain while the external signs of prosperity were apparent with developments in business and the erection of imposing buildings. In short, it was not a favourable time for a reform movement. Yet, unlock the lands became a catch cry upon which unity was achieved among the land hungry, or the merely discontented, and the politicians were quick to jump on the bandwagon.

It seemed, however, that little could be done about the squatters given their standing in a society which they had dominated for years. Their almost complete grasp over grazing land which they held on long leases, their political base in the parliaments, their favoured position in the eyes of British capitalists and their own industry, which allowed the most successful to double their capital every two to three years, made them the supposed enemy of the workers and excited jealousy in those city dwellers who were financially less well-endowed.

Some of the resentment against the squatters was wrongly based. Although their hold on land allegedly prevented the spread of agriculture, the nature of the pastoral industry was such that only the first comers who occupied the land without paying for it, or, later, the wealthy who could afford to pay, were successful. Economic viability required large holdings and, the less fertile the land, the larger they had to be. In western and northern New South Wales, in parts of Victoria and South Australia and even in eastern and central Tasmania, the pastoral runs resembled principalities.

To the extent that dreamers or malcontents envisaged the breaking up of the pastoral runs into farms for a yeomanry, they were deluded at best and unhinged at worst. A square mile, 640 acres, was a block scarcely sufficient under wheat or other cereals to provide even frugal comfort for a man and his family, while blocks of a lesser size invariably led to ruin and misery. In short, no one, except the squatters, knew what the land further out could support, while by the 1860s land closer in to the main centres was already taken up. Under such circumstances, the growth of the cities was inevitable because the gradual use of wire fencing, the scooping out of dams or tanks and the breeding of better sheep-dogs lessened still further the labour required to run the pastoral industry, while the running down of the goldfields added more to the number of those who saw no future outside an urban setting.

There were some powerful men prepared to attempt to break the monopoly of the squatters and the foremost was John Robertson. Since his arrival in 1822, as a child of six, Robertson had become as one with the native-born although London was his birthplace. As he grew to prosperity, he too became a squatter and defended his peers although he wanted to share the land with others. In 1861, he resigned as Premier of New South Wales to devote his energies to the cause. Dan Deniehy worked with him on drafting a suitable bill and in essence their proposal was simple but radical. Anyone with £80 could select a block of 320 acres in that half of the colony with a ten inch or better rainfall. He could then get a title to it after three years provided he had his residence on it, improved it and paid the residue of £240 at the overall price of £1 per acre.

Two years previously, a Land Act had been passed in Victoria which proved a failure as land could not be selected until it was surveyed, and any form of effective survey would have taken several years to complete. The radical element in the New South Wales proposal was that the land could be selected before it had been surveyed, which meant that selectors could go practically anywhere onto unoccupied land and stake a claim to land. Robertson got the legislation through Parliament and, on 1 January 1862, a period began in which unbridled rapacity was widespread. Selectors scrambled for land and squatters defended themselves by buying up the finest lots on their runs through dummies or by 'peacocking' the best land. Squatters enlisted the inmates of the old men's home at Parramatta to act as dummies. By 'peacocking', many squatters got titles to river or creek fronts, thus effectively excluding others. To achieve their aims, loans were sought by selectors and squatters alike and ruin was the outcome for many in both groups, but principally among the selectors.

It seemed that the insatiable thirst to possess land – born out of ancient slaveries and feudal serfdoms, nurtured further by enclosure in England and dispossession of land in Scotland and Ireland – could not be curbed by an honest man's legislation. If anything the thirst was sharpened, putting men at each other's throats and defeating the admirable purpose the reformers, Robertson and Deniehy, had in mind. In the end less than 100 men bought eight million acres and pastoralism remained triumphant.

Pressure for further reform in Victoria was strong as there was an increasing population and a temporary turndown in the economy. In 1862, the Lands Minister, Charles Gavan Duffy, agreed to reserve ten million acres for relocation as agricultural blocks of forty to 640 acres to be sold at £1 per acre. High-minded, like Robertson, Duffy had the additional encouragement of ensuring that Victorian diggers who were leaving the goldfields remained contented members of society. Later, Duffy lamented the shameless manner in which the squatters had defeated the purposes of the law by perfecting the techniques their fellows had used in New South Wales. The upshot was that within two years about 100 individuals had bought two-thirds of all the land sold. Thus the original Selection Acts, to the extent that they were intended to release land for cultivation, were largely unsuccessful although some settlement was achieved and some small landholders were able to expand once they had become established and financially viable. With the introduction of the Grant Act in Victoria in 1869 matters improved. In the following decade about eleven million acres were selected, while in South Australia, by the 1880s, most of the agricultural land had been taken from the squatters.

The story of the selectors was generally one of constant hardship and frequent failure and it often came about that even the most determined and experienced among them were unable to prosper. At the heart of their problem lay the inadequacy of the area of land they took up, but lack of finance or heavy borrowing, bad seasons, distant markets, ravages by pests and stock disease made the lot of even the most thrifty and industrious a burdensome one.

In the early 1880s some 200 Italians fled from the ill-fated venture of colonization initiated by the Marquis de Rays on New Ireland in the Bismarck Archipelago. Henry Parkes welcomed them to New South Wales, where they went onto small selections south of the Richmond River. The Italians, as a group, were capable, hard-working, thrifty and co-operative, and gradually they formed a happy community called New Italy. The government provided a school and they grew most of their own necessities, built homes and a church, made their own wine and blended well with the local community to the extent that, within a few years, they were the backbone of the district cricket team. Nevertheless, they could not survive on the produce of their selections. The men had to go away for long periods to increase their income by cutting cane and felling timber. Gradually other selectors left and the Italians were able to enlarge their selections and turn to dairying. It was all to no avail as necessity required that the land holdings got bigger and bigger and within fifty years the community had dwindled to nothing. It was an experience repeated constantly throughout the colonies by other selectors.

All reforming land legislation was part and parcel of the fundamental flaw which caused men to regard land as a mere commodity to be exploited. In the beginning, this meant that the Aborigines were denied any right to that which they had been part of since their origin. The next step was to give the land away freely to a favoured minority or permit it to be occupied by the squatters without their even seeking permission to do so. Finally, the attempt was made to parcel it out to the needy in meagre lots, almost irrespective of climate and fertility. Through the whole process of its alienation the land remained, though ravaged by the ringbarking of trees which turned millions of acres into ghostly forests; the destruction of stands of timber around the headwaters of rivers and creeks; the consequent erosion which scarred and gullied countless acres and the exhaustion of soil through too frequent cropping. The land was ever eager to repair itself, but in some measure it was changed beyond reclaim.

Arable and pastoral land in the south, and particularly in Tasmania, was becoming scarce, but in the north of New South Wales there was still a vast area of unoccupied territory. Starting 200 miles north of Brisbane and stretching for another 2,000 miles to the Cape York Peninsula, it comprised 670,000 square miles. Running inland from the coast there was a thousand miles of pastoral country, fit for sheep and cattle, which was finally swallowed up in a forbidding desert, so that the area north and northwest of Rockhampton became known as 'The Never Never'. Nearly as large as France, Germany, Spain and Italy combined, the north was that part of the continent where contradictions abounded. Rainfall of stupendous proportions fell in tropical areas while there were years of drought throughout the interior. In the Channel Country the whole earth was laced with streams in wet seasons that were followed by periods when all things, even the air, remained dry. Lush vegetation with all manner of exotic flora gave way to great plains further out where the eucalyptus, emu and kangaroo flourished.

After the departure of the convicts, the settlement at Brisbane declined until 1849 when John Dunmore Lang decided to send out 600 God-fearing and hardworking Scottish Presbyterians. They were intended to found the cotton industry, which Lang believed would help to absorb many immigrants. Although the government refused to give them land freely, as Lang had assured them would be done, their arrival did give an impetus to the district but the cotton industry still had a slow start. Brisbane depended in all official matters on Sydney, where Lang represented the territory in the Legislative Council, and from there he agitated for separation of the north from New South Wales.

Meanwhile, from the 1840s, the pastoral occupation of the Darling Downs pushed west and north. Leichhardt's journey in 1845 as far north as Port Essington on the Arafura Sea had opened up more country, and the squatting movement went on and on, but not without resistance. In those parts, the blacks had decided to make a firm stand for what they held.

Shepherds were killed, homesteads attacked, black and white alike died, and black, native police were used to hunt down and kill their own people. In October 1861 Horatio Wills arrived as the new owner at Cullinlaringo station of 100 square miles (640,000 acres) on the Nogoa River in northeast Queensland. A few days later Wills and 18 of his party; men, women and children, were dead. The previous owners, the Gayiri, were a proud people among whom the women wore 'fringed' skirts and shell necklaces while the men carried delicately carved and ochred shields and wore necklaces of eagle claws. The Gayiri had been outraged by previous parties who had ill-treated them and taken their land. The massacre was followed by a massacre of the blacks and from that time on the Gayiri buried their dead strewn among the rocks rather than facing the sun at dawn or sunset. The sun had truly set for the Gayiri.

Despite the black resistance, nothing could stop the penetration of the country by the whites with their sheep and cattle. Ancient names with a pleasing lilt, Maranoa, Barcoo, Diamantina and Warrego were mixed with the absurd or merely pretentious, Comet, Charleville and Roma. The foundations of fine towns were laid because the distances were so great to Brisbane and Sydney that the scattered population had to rely on centres of commerce closer to their homes. Along or near the coast, Bundaberg, Gladstone, Rockhampton, Mackay, Townsville and Cairns were among the places to which the people of the north eventually looked for the comforts of civilization. In 1858, 15,000 diggers rushed to the valley of the Fitzroy River near Gladstone, but the gold was worked out in a few weeks, and the men, mostly from Victoria, went away downhearted and impoverished because the 'golden days' had not yet come to the north. Nevertheless, the abortive gold rush gave rise to Rockhampton in 1859, which took its place with the other towns as urban centres in the north.

In Sydney, the Governor and his Council gave no serious consideration to separation but, in response to petitions, London decided in 1855 to cut the north off and make it a colony. In December 1859, the colony was proclaimed and the sovereign, whose appetite had apparently been whetted rather than satisfied by the naming of Victoria, suggested Queensland as the name of the new territory. Parliament sat for the first time in May 1860, fittingly in the old convict barracks as unconscious recognition that this part of the continent was also opened by convict labour. The Governor, thirty-eight year old George Bowen, was advised by the London authorities never to permit his thoughts to stray from finance, a matter firmly impressed upon him as the true basis of a prosperous state. With a mere seven-and-a-half pence in the treasury when Bowen arrived, it was good advice, and his twenty-eight-year-old Treasurer, Robert Herbert, needed a cool head to give the colony a good start. Implicit in that start was the power of the local squattocracy which, with its rough and ready style of conservative politics, indelibly etched the image and set, in part, the reality of public life in Queensland for the next century.

Right across the occupied areas of the continent a grid pattern was formed according to the size of the holdings and throughout the grids ran roads or tracks because the pastoral industry and, later, the selectors relied heavily on transport. The squatters needed efficient means to shift their wool from the sheds to the wharf from where it was shipped to England for auction. In the early days bullock teams were the main means, taking stores out to the stations and returning with a back-load of wool. Ex-convicts and the native-born proved the most reliable bullock drivers as they knew the country and seemed to have the knack of controlling the large teams of sixteen or eighteen bullocks yoked in pairs.

After the explorers, squatters and drovers, the teamsters or bullockies helped to open up the continent. Their tracks became roads. Their stopping places, at about fifteen mile intervals were the beginnings of towns and hamlets, while many a landmark, creek or resting place was named where the teams halted, breakfasted, lost a bullock or merely recorded the distance from the previous settlement. Their colourful language, their clothing of red shirts with moleskin trousers and cabbage-tree hats, and their long-handled whips became the stuff of many a legend.

Gradually horses replaced bullocks on the long tracks in the outback, although the bullockies held their own for many years in the mountainous coastal regions. There were places where neither bullocks nor horses were useful and other means had to be sought for transportation. Thomas Elder and his brother-in-law, Robert Barr Smith, owned or leased more land in South Australia than the whole extent of their native Scotland, and Thomas concluded that the vast distances of the dry inland would be well served by camels. In the mid-1860s, he imported over a hundred of them and within a few years his original herd had grown to thousands. In the wake of the camels, Afghans came to manage and drive the camel trains, which became a familiar sight in the outback with up to eighty camels per train. The camel was used successfully in exploration and in the building of the Overland Telegraph line from Port Augusta in the south to Port Darwin in the north that was completed in 1872. The first cablegram from Britain was transmitted on 22 October in that year. For eighty years, the camel and the

Afghans were an essential segment of the transportation system in areas impassable to other means and the gentility and honesty of the Afghans remained in the memory of the outback long after the last of them had died or returned to their homeland. When it became possible to run a railway over the route the Afghans had pioneered through to Alice Springs, the train was named the Ghan in their honour. It retained the name when the line was extended further north to Darwin in 2003.

The river boat trade on the Mississippi inspired the undertaking of a similar venture on the Murray and its connected river system. Melbourne in the 1840s had become the port to which wool was sent by wagon from the vast area around the Murray, Darling and Murrumbidgee Rivers. In South Australia the idea dawned slowly that if rivers could be served by steamboats, the natural overseas and inter colonial outlet for wool and for trade into the interior would be Adelaide. The opening of the Victorian goldfields made this even clearer as it was cheaper to transport goods by river to them than by other means over Victoria's atrocious roads.

Francis Cadell and William Randell were the first masters of steam driven vessels capable of negotiating the snags, the sand bars and the long periods of low-water level of the rivers. From the 1850s the new form of transport burgeoned and ports sprang up from Wentworth to Albury on the Murray with Echuca and Wahgunyah as the main ones. On the Murrumbidgee the major centres were Balranald and Gundagai and on the Darling they were Menindee, Wilcannia and Bourke. Pacific Island labour and the Chinese were often employed on the paddle steamers, which grew in length and often towed large barges.

The steamers carried all manner of supplies for delivery to the stations and the goldfields, including fruit, vegetables, beer, lobsters, saddlery, doors, windows, farm machinery and equipment, clothing and books. After the introduction of fencing, some large stations shore half a million sheep by the late 1870s and produced 1,000 to 2,000 bales of wool, which were carted to the river ports by camel train or horse-drawn wagons. At its peak the Murray system had 300 steamers operating with the largest of them carrying 300 bales. About 100,000 bales passed through Echuca in 1880 with the whole river trade worth over half a million pounds. In 1883 a severe drought combined with the expansion of the railways to affect river shipping adversely, and with their cargoes of iron rails and wooden sleepers, the river vessels carried the seeds of their own destruction. Gradually the steamers fell in numbers, the skippers retired and died, and the voice of the Darling was rarely broken by the splash of the paddles. The welcoming sound of a steamer's whistle was seldom heard again as only a handful of steamers survived into the twentieth century. By the end of the century they had returned to the Murray, transporting happy tourists in place of wool.

Until the gold rush period and the consequent growth of inland centres, railway construction was negligible. A line from Sydney to Granville junction, near Parramatta, was opened in 1855 and one to Newcastle in 1858 with all construction in the hands of the government. Victoria had put through a line from Melbourne to Port Melbourne in 1854 and then to Geelong in 1857. The development of the gold towns, Ballarat, Castlemaine and Bendigo, and the need to compete with the river trade, saw lines opened to those places, as well as to Echuca, by 1864. Lines from Sydney through to Wagga Wagga (1879), Albury (1881), and Bourke (1885) meant that New South Wales was linked in its main parts, and from that time progress was rapid.

Links were made between the New South Wales and the Victorian systems through Albury in 1883 and with Queensland at Wallangarra five years later, so that a traveller could pass from Melbourne into Queensland on the railways, but not without changing trains. The difficulty of having rival colonial administrations was apparent in the choice of railway gauges, although their reasons for selecting differing gauges, given the variation in terrain, the purpose for which the lines were built and the availability of finance bore some weight. The New South Wales government, after much dithering and obstruction, decided on a 4ft 8 1/2in gauge, Victoria 5ft 3in and Queensland 3ft 6in, but South Australia showed its eclecticism by having all three major gauges with three others for small, private lines.

The development of the railways in all the colonies was closely bound up with politics and the pressures that vested interests exerted to ensure that lines ran through places where benefit could accrue to such interests. Nevertheless, the opening of a line – with the attendant construction of stations, many of which were imposing edifices and some indeed works of true architecture – filled the locals with pride and gave employment to an ever-increasing workforce in which mere numbers were, too often, no proof of efficiency. To those who saw romance and power in the trains with their mighty engines, who enjoyed the passing fragrance of coal smoke, who watched from afar the approaching light of a train at night and looked with interest at passengers as they alighted at the end of journeys, the railways remained a source of pleasure.

Nevertheless, the railways never inspired a significant literature or art form, which was also true with the transition from sail to steam at sea. Yet, the social transformation brought about by the railways was immense. People who had previously lacked the money to take private means of transport were now able to go from place to place for work, leisure or schooling. The 'Refreshment Rooms' at railway stations, where tea and other hot beverages, sandwiches and, eventually, hot pies could be consumed, became places familiar to generations of Australians as they awaited the signal to board the train again for destinations throughout the land.

Little progress was made with shipbuilding in Australia in the nineteenth century but, as a continent with a vast seaboard, transport across the oceans or on the coastal waters was always necessary. The Americans were the first to build the fast, softwood clippers, which were soon rivalled by British-made vessels. Some of the wool clippers and migrant ships on the England to Australia run became famous. In 1869 the *Themopylae* left The Lizard in England, and arrived at Port Phillip sixty-two days later and that record under sail stood through the ensuing years. Other famous sailing ships were the *Marco Polo* and the *Cutty Sark*. But the great days of sail gave way to steam which provided efficiency and safety but little romance except, perhaps, among the passengers.

Everything that the white settlers brought to Australia came across the oceans but not all of it was brought intentionally and some of it had undesirable effects that were long lasting or permanent. Vast numbers of sheep and cattle, with their hard hooves, tore at the frail surface of the ancient soil and unbalanced its vegetation. Birds, trees and flowers often added beauty, but native grasses gave way to imported ones, while pests like the Capeweed, Bathurst burr and Scotch thistle proved impossible to eradicate. Fauna was also introduced – dogs, cats, foxes, ferrets, hares and buffalo – all of which competed with the native fauna, while camels, donkeys and horses often multiplied to pest proportions in inaccessible areas. Trout and redfin were let loose in rivers, lakes and streams and the blackfish, the Macquarie perch and the Murray cod declined in numbers as they tried to compete with the voracious or cannibalistic new varieties including the European carp in a later period.

The worst of all pests, the rabbit, arrived with the First Fleet and then successively with other vessels. It prospered so abundantly in some places that by 1842 an island in Bass Strait was named after it. The first arrivals had been domesticated rabbits, but Thomas Austin imported twenty-four wild ones for sporting purposes to his property at Barwon Park near Geelong in 1859 and the tide turned for the rabbit. Within six years their numbers had reached such proportions that, having destroyed 20,000 rabbits, Austin calculated that 10,000 remained on his land. By 1880 the rabbits had crossed into New South Wales and South Australia, infesting agricultural and pastoral lands. In vain they were declared noxious and war was waged against them. They consumed the grasses, ringbarked young trees, ate seeds and left a desert in their wake throughout large areas. The females bred up to six litters annually in good seasons. The use of dogs, ferrets, fences, poisoning, trapping, fumigating and warren destruction saw the spread of devastated pastures as testimony to their ineffectiveness.

Before the 1880s the greatest threat to the pastoral industry was a disease caused by a parasite in sheep called scab. The very word was whispered for its presence in a flock could mean ruin. Annually, it killed hundreds of thousands of sheep. In Victoria alone, it caused millions of pounds in losses, despite the successful use of a dip with a tobacco and sulphur mix as its base. Scab, together with fluke and footrot, drought and fire, cold and wet, crows and dingoes combined to make the life of the pastoralist difficult. Nonetheless, the industry, still mainly based on the Spanish merino, continued to flourish so that from the stunted, hairy prototypes of fifty years previously over forty million fine-fleeced and well-bodied sheep walked the continent by 1870. It was among the most successful pastoral achievements of all ages which reached its annual climax when, across the sheds, vast and small, to the quiet click of the shears, the golden fleece fell from those millions. Out on the stations, women in increasing numbers accepted the land and its people while a minority rejected it bitterly. Sheep, wool prices, the seasons and shearing were always on the lips of the men. One English governess, employed on a station near Glenorchy in Victoria, found a great grossness of spirit and weakness of intellect among Australians, whom, together with the land, she professed to hate.

In the outback and in the cities, a generally dedicated band of pastors helped their flocks fill the void in the human spirit, caused in part by the attainment as well as the lack of material success. The pastors – known as priest, parson, minister or simply reverend – often performed their duties discordantly because vast valleys scooped out by the rivers of the Reformation lay between them. Yet, the days had passed since religion was seen as little more than the handmaiden of a coercive state, although in some measure the same state was still clothed in Christian garments. Admittedly, state aid to religion was abandoned by the 1870s in the eastern colonies. But in matters of morality, such as divorce (which was avoided by having legal separation instead, until each colony passed its own divorce act, which they had all done by 1873) the state gave little offence to the churches. Queen, parliament, chapel and cathedral all seemed devoted to the one purpose of mankind's betterment.

Here and there an odd Irishman muttered unkindly about the Queen, but there were Irish Catholics such as Judge Roger Therry and Premier Gavan Duffy who were proud to be her knights. Equally, there were a few, even in high places, who professed themselves free from the chains of religion and proclaimed that, unaided, mankind could rise to unsurpassed heights of harmony, enlightenment and general well-being. Lacking cohesion or structure, the secular creed had little appeal and, for the thousands who invoked the name of Christ, only a handful knew of Voltaire or Rousseau.

Among the better off there was a widespread conviction of the usefulness of something called a ' liberal education' which it seemed good to ensure for the male children if possible. Institutions of a superior type such as The King's School at Parramatta and Geelong Grammar on Corio Bay in Victoria were founded, as preparatory schools for higher education, social attainment and to avoid the need to send the boys to Eton and Harrow. Within their walls, it was reasonable to hope that, together with a 'liberal education', students would be given a sound basis in loyalty and Anglicanism. At the other end of the scale stood the state and the denominational primary schools, which were still state-assisted throughout the 1860s. They all fought for funding and it was increasingly clear that even the strongest denominations could not meet the demand for places. Yet in the 1860s they educated twice as many children as the state system and they thought that their position was secure, despite the fact that, throughout the colonies, half the children under twelve could neither read nor write.

Whatever else Christianity and education managed to achieve, they failed to convince many of their beneficiaries that all human beings possessed equal rights. The Chinese, in particular, remained the butt of much odium, especially on the goldfields where their coming was likened to an influx of barbarians. Civilized people considered their habits unmentionable and their very presence was feared, because they were regarded as alien, degraded and heathen. Paradoxically, the Chinese thought exactly the same of those who were not Chinese. The argument was put forward by some whites that, as they had discovered and settled Australia, no Chinese had any rights in it, and all manner of restrictive, fiscal legislation was passed to keep them out. This kind of thinking reached its climax at a locality called Lambing Flat in New South Wales in June 1861. The gold there had run thin and the European diggers resented the alleged success of the industrious Chinese. The diggers rioted and attacked them ferociously, cutting off pigtails, destroying property, beating and terrifying them as they fled from the field. Troops were sent from Sydney to restore order and, later, a government commissioner arrived who said that he regarded the Chinese as deceivers. Inexplicably, he awarded claims to 706 individuals. But no pecuniary measure could heal the outrage done or received.

By 1858 there were one million white Australians. By 1863 some of them thought it proper to participate in the suppression of another people outside Australian territory. By the end of that year, 1,475 volunteers had sailed from Sydney, Melbourne and Hobart for New Zealand to participate in the Maori Wars that had been waged intermittently since 1845. In 1863 and 1864 the Waikato War, which threatened Auckland, saw almost 20,000 troops, including the Australians, engaged against a confederation of Waikato tribes numbering less than 3,000. As was the case in Australia with the Aborigines, the main cause of the conflict in New Zealand was justifiable Maori fear that all their land would be taken by the whites. In 1864 at least another 1,200 Australians, with their wives and children, sailed for New Zealand to act as military settlers on land taken from the Maoris. In due course the conflict was resolved in favour of the dominant power and the Maoris had no choice but to accept a settlement. Many of the Australian volunteers subsequently left the land to work in the towns or to go to the Thames goldfields, which were opened in late 1866. The Maori Wars had indicated that colonial Australians would take up the call to arms willingly were Queen and Empire alleged to be threatened and a volunteer from North Melbourne summed up the prevailing sentiment by signing himself, in a letter to the *Age,* as one, 'Who will shed his last drop of blood for his Queen'.

A more positive face of colonial Australia was shown by the gains made in social legislation. The right to strike, bitterly resented by employers, was recognized by law and a traditionally exploited sector, shop assistants, benefited from early closing. By the mid-fifties, the creed 'eight hours labour, eight hours recreation, eight hours rest' had become widespread. Annual festivities in Victoria acclaimed its partial achievement amongst stonemasons and others after 1856. The workers were now heard through the use of the ballot box and the introduction of triennial parliaments and no government could afford to ignore them. Some great institutions, such as the Melbourne Public Library, and lesser ones, such as the Mechanics Institutes, catered for the leisure of the workers, while a few informed voices spoke on their behalf At the opening of the Melbourne Trades Hall in 1859, a speaker urged that, as well as reading and thinking, workers also needed to learn from and associate with each other and achieve their rightful place in society.

Unions, Guilds or Benefit Societies which had existed in most trades before the gold-rushes had been broken up by the consequent dislocation of the labour force, but they soon began to regroup and the gains they won, especially in reducing working hours, convinced them that they led Britain and Europe in achieving satisfying living standards. They probably did not realize that the wealth of the country and the need for labour had rendered the employers powerless, temporarily at least. In Victoria their efforts were symbolically crowned in 1859 when Charles Jardine Don was elected to the Legislative Assembly for the seat of Collingwood as the representative of the Political and Social Labour League. He claimed, probably correctly, that he was the first worker to represent his class in any legislature in the British Empire.

Don was a stonemason, who worked at his trade on Parliament House by day and sat in it as a member at night. The city in which he worked embodied in stone the motif of the age of progress. Buildings of the most pretentious and ornate design, that had their origins in the golden days of the 1850s, were gracing the city. The magnificent Treasury Building with its Italian Renaissance style climaxed the Museum, Houses of Parliament and the National Gallery. Nevertheless, Parliament House was not far distant from 'radical and riotous' Collingwood with its terraces, which dwindled away into blocks of decrepit weatherboard cottages and smelly tenements. Already the fierce civic pride of the residents and their rivalry with neighbouring Fitzroy was evident. On one important level it expressed itself with the founding of the Britannia Football Club in the late 1870s, which became the famous Collingwood Football Club in 1889.

The houses of the upper-class spread south of the Yarra to St Kilda, which, by the end of the 1860s, had become the most attractive place to live where the wealthy, the merchants and the professional men built their imposing homes. The dwellings of the workers in the Melbourne suburbs were much more humble, but the land still had to be bought, the houses constructed and services provided, all of which required massive capital. Manufacturing industry provided little investment capital as its exports were minimal, so the whole financial edifice rested on gold, wool and British loans.

The times of 'jam and honey' for the workers had commenced, and no one could foresee their ending. Colonial beer was threepence a glass and the workers drank it in great quantities. There was a gay and independent spirit everywhere and, even in Melbourne, the streets were thronged at night in summer with men dressed in shirtsleeves and women in light dresses. It was not unusual for singing and music to go on until far into the night. An

English visitor in 1869 thought that he was in another world where the citizens considered themselves as good as any other. He had no difficulty in believing that, once Australians 'become acclimatized, they scarcely ever leave the country, and, if they do, they often return'.

In both Melbourne and Sydney, there was another face to progress. A report on the condition of Sydney's working class in 1860 was damning in its condemnation of the conditions under which the urban workers lived. The older tenements were 'unfit for the occupation of human beings', and high rents caused over-crowding: seventy people were found in one lodging-house of six rooms and 315 Chinese were found in another. Neglected and vagrant children roamed the streets. For some of them, their condition was another legacy of the breakdown in family life caused by the gold rushes. Some parts of the city saw the erection of a better class of house for the worker with 'indoor sinks, fitted pantries, suitable stoves and clothes' closets' but the slums in Woolloomooloo, for example, showed all the worst aspects of the older cities of Europe. The report concluded that, despite their living conditions, the generality of Sydney's workers were 'a credit to the country' for their 'honesty, intelligence and sobriety'.

Colonial governments were loath to involve themselves in relief measures for the poor, believing that social provisions by the state undermined self-reliance and fostered pauperism. Governments, instead, encouraged charitable organisations to assist the hungry, the homeless and the sick aged. The Melbourne Ladies Benevolent Society virtually controlled all non-denominational outdoor relief in the greater Melbourne Area. The Benevolent Society of New South Wales, founded in 1813, cared for the chronically ill, the blind, the paralytic and the mentally-ill. By 1862 the New South Wales government took full responsibility for the aged and destitute who required residential facilities, but the Benevolent Society continued to function with government subsidies. The mentally-ill were a group which suffered from neglect until the arrival of F. N. Manning, an English medical practitioner, who initiated reforms that were finally reflected in the New South Wales Lunacy Act of 1878. Manning encouraged visitors to the Tarban Creek hospital for the mentally ill and ignorance and prejudice were slowly broken down.

Henry Parkes was especially concerned about the state of the Sydney Infirmary and Dispensary. He appealed for help to Florence Nightingale for trained nurses, and in 1868, a remarkable woman, Lucy Osburn, arrived as superintendent of the Infirmary accompanied by five other nurses. Pretty, slim and with a 'bright ingenuous manner', Lucy won Parkes's complete trust and she threw herself into the almost impossible task of cleaning up the crumbling, foul-smelling, vermin-infested buildings. She met opposition from the doctors and the Board, and she was lonely and often dispirited. But she stuck to her task and by 1874 she had partially succeeded. By the time the institution's name was changed to the Sydney Hospital in 1880, Lucy had achieved her objectives and she returned to England, where she died in 1891.

The 1860s were a period of consolidation and progress brought about by the increase in population due to the gold-rushes. The Scottish-born William Arnott found he made more money selling his own pies and bread on the Turon than by panning for gold. He and his brother David later opened a factory in Newcastle, and soon they were shipping tons of biscuits weekly to Sydney. Arnott had his own dairy farm where 200 cows produced the milk for his popular milk arrowroot biscuits, but he died before his sons put his most famous biscuit, the Sao, on the market in 1906. Maria Ann Smith grew apples from Tasmanian seeds in Sydney in 1868 and from them produced a new strain called the 'Granny Smith', which was eventually exported, as was canned meat, to England. On 23 December 1861 two horse-drawn tramcars started to carry passengers along Pitt Street in Sydney. They excited much attention from the passers-by, not surprisingly, because they were painted bright yellow and named 'Old England' and 'Young Australia' respectively.

Sport and communications were other aspects of progress. Regular cricket matches between New South Wales and Victoria began in 1856 and attracted much interest and mild inter-colonial rivalry. Horse racing had fast become a favourite pastime of both the high and the lowly and towns of even a modest size had their own racecourse. In November 1861 the Melbourne Cup was run for the first time. A horse called Archer, which had been walked down from near Nowra in New South Wales for the event, won it. In the same week Brisbane was linked by telegraph to the other eastern capitals. Hobart could be included in the link as there was a submarine cable running from Melbourne. Among the items carried by the telegraph to Brisbane was news of the largely victorious visit of an All-English cricket team, which had given much pleasure to the sport-minded citizens of Sydney and Melbourne. Tom Wills, son of Horatio who had escaped the massacre in Queensland, spoke the language of the Aborigines with whom he had grown up out of Ararat and, excelling as a cricketer for the Melbourne Club and Victoria, he was appointed captain, coach and mentor of an Aboriginal cricket team in the 1860s. Despite his remarkable ease and success with the Aborigines, he was not appointed to lead the team when it toured England in 1868. An Englishman, Charles Lawrence, was given the position.

Of these and other matters the inhabitants of Western Australia, cut off by a distance of more than 1,500 miles by land or by the waters of the Australian Bight from the nearest colonial capital, remained largely oblivious, but they too were making progress. The last of the convict colonies had benefited by transportation to a marked degree. The convicts blended well with the assisted free migrants who came with them. Convict labour on public works, roads, bridges and other public amenities was so valuable that many citizens preferred to see hardened criminals brought in. They would be forced to spend long periods constructing public utilities but lesser criminals would quickly be released on tickets of leave to work for themselves. The British government maintained the large convict establishment and as a consequence paid for public buildings such as the large Fremantle jail. The town prospered to such an extent that its free citizens were encouraged in 1854 to request, unsuccessfully, that the seat of government be transferred there from Perth. The convicts remained at Fremantle where the old, barbarous discipline of floggings and solitary confinement on bread and water in dark cells for periods up to fifty days still persisted into the 1860s.

While the convicts in the West toiled on the public works, the free grew wool, bred horses for the Indian army, cut timber, went whaling, explored the inland, and found lead and copper deposits. It was increasingly clear in Britain that free immigration and transportation could not continue together for long. The colony would soon want some form of responsible government and in 1865 the decision to stop transportation was made. Among the last transportees was a group of sixty Fenians of the Irish Republican Brotherhood, who arrived in 1868 and, as political prisoners, faced long terms in maximum security doing hard labour. By 1876 only a handful of them remained in custody at Fremantle and on Perth Regatta Day, 17 April, six of them made a daring bid to join an American whaler, the *Catalpa,* which had been purchased in the United States in order to aid their escape. After a skirmish with the government vessel *Georgette,* sent to intercept her, the *Catalpa* sailed for home and the Irish to freedom in New York where they were given a 'heroes' welcome.

About 10,000 convicts had come to Western Australia and in 1867 just over a half of the 20,000 inhabitants had been, or were, still in bondage. One English visitor in that year described Western Australia as a vast English prison rather than a colony. He berated the whole system of transportation as vile and corrupting, a judgement in which he was partially right. Yet his view was that of a passer-by who had no concept of the contribution of convict labour to the settlement and development of Australia. If transportation brought a stain, it was not one of moral infamy in the society that grew from it because, in general, the emancipists were indistinguishable from those who arrived free. The stain was red in blood from the floggings, dark-hued from the misery, despair and shame meted out to those 160,000 who from 1788 to 1868 were sent to Australia. The people responsible for the whole bloody system were the truly stained.

9

Making Australians

Before the opening of the Suez Canal in 1869, Australians made the journey 'home' to the British Isles by the Great Circle route below South Africa. Even with the advent of steam, they still had to face much tedium and some danger as they crossed the oceans. The sea provided a sense of security by throwing a barrier around the continent. It cut off Tasmania though, which felt isolated and neglected by the other eastern colonies. In contrast to the sea, the bush remained changeless, remote and full of mystery. From the earliest days, the bush became part of legend and literature. Stories with titles like Henry Kingsley's 'The Lost Child', Marcus Clarke's 'Pretty Dick' (who was found after six days dead in the bush 'lying on his face, with his head on his arm') and Barcroft Boake's 'Where the Dead Men Lie' all spoke of the relentless harshness of the bush and of 'the wastes of the Never-Never'. Nonetheless, there were some few who sang of its peace and beauty.

The bush was simply that part of the country where settlement was sparse or non-existent. It ranged from thick forest to eucalyptus scrub and further on to almost treeless plains; from the Barrington Tops and the Atherton Tableland to the Pilliga scrub and the Gibson Desert; from Geraldton to the Kimberley Ranges in Western Australia. But it was always called the bush. Out there, free of parson, priest or police, and, in large measure, of women, the old hands, who had come as convicts, did odd jobs about the stations – shearing, fencing, clearing scrub and, with horses and scoops, making dams and tanks. They stuck close to their mates because they had no one else. As their years were numbered, their places were taken by new chums who, filled with hope, had come to the land of opportunity and ended up in the bush. Unwilling, or unable, to settle on the goldfields working for wages as miners, they had drifted further out, where they became indistinguishable from the old hands. Some of the native-born, almost all of convict stock, also took to the bush where they were more adept than others in the ways of the land and especially those of the pastoral industry. They shared with the others a rejection of authority, an inability to settle long in the one place and a tendency to earn just enough money with the least trouble. This, in a practice known as 'knocking down the cheque', they spent in a bush shanty on a drunken carouse.

White civilization crept tentatively into the bush with the development, in the 1870s, of better means of communication. It brought with it elements of commerce and culture associated with the settled life of the inner districts and the cities. Religion and education, bankers and doctors, streets and stores, the post office and the telegraph, newspapers and books – all these, together with women and children, became part of life in the bush. Before this wave the old hands disappeared into obscurity. Some of the brave, when word came of new goldfields in Queensland and Western Australia, joined the rush. Others went on the tramp carrying their few belongings: a pair of blankets rolled in a swag, a billy to make tea, a few ounces of flour for a damper, perhaps a trap to catch rabbits, but little else. From station to station, the 'swaggies' went; avoiding the towns and the law when possible; begging a meal, often fruitlessly, from a station owner or manager; doing a little work here and there; but never settling until, in some lonely place, they finally met with destiny. They were the last of their tribe, and in them the legend of the bush was born and metamorphosed. It became a legend that rarely spoke of endless scrub; chains of dry waterholes called rivers; stunted mountains; desolate and derelict station buildings; the harshness, frequent brutality and servility of life in the shearing sheds; the ignorance and prejudice of many bush workers and the hopelessness of the life of the swaggies.

The inhospitable land moulded the white, restless tribe and, with the years, they became part of it. With their lack of concern for tomorrow, their inability to hoard, their constant movement over the land, partly living from it while refusing to possess it, and their intimate knowledge of it, they became as much Australians as the Aborigines had always been. The tragedy for both races was that, in the early days, no creole race was born, which, elsewhere, was the source of a new and vital people. In the end, the white nomads became the basis of a legend woven from a longing for what might have been, a lost sense of identity with the land, a guilt for its raping and a passionate urge to be different from the old European societies. The legend was a tribute to the land and those born from it.

The rising waters of a distant past had cut off Tasmania and its people from contact with the mainland. When the whites arrived in the early part of the century, the Tasmanian Aborigines were isolated on their island and there could be no escape. On the islands of Bass Strait a new race was born from the union of sealers, whalers and Aboriginal women. Also out there, onto Flinders Island, a remnant of the mainland blacks was taken, where they survived briefly. Originally 300 in number, they dwindled to a handful as, ravaged by pulmonary disease and demoralized by the loss of their past, they eked out a miserable existence at a place called Wybalena which some said meant 'last resting place'. In 1842 a fruitless attempt was made to save the race by transferring a handful to Port Phillip. In that same year their leader in the person of proud Woorraddy was lost. He had remained Aboriginal in all things and thousands of years of tradition perished with his passing.

The government chose Oyster Cove, on the mainland south of Hobart, in 1847 as the last resting place of the forty-seven individuals who had survived the years of exile at Wybalena. They came back home to die out slowly, painfully and shamefully of disease and drink. Of that forty-seven, by July 1871, only Truganini remained. Surviving her husband, Woorraddy, by thirty-four years, she died in 1876. With her passing, it was thought that the problem of the Aborigines of Tasmania was solved. Sole survivor of a people who had numbered perhaps 5,000 less than seventy years previously, the last 'full blood' died later on Kangaroo Island in 1888. The whites had not deliberately engaged in genocide, but they achieved it nonetheless. European diseases and cruel, wanton slaughter coalesced with the inability of most whites to understand that the Aborigines possessed their own culture and had a sense of fierce independence and a determination to live according to their own traditions. The Aborigines were deprived of a purpose for existence once their land was lost. For a time, few cared to remember that there were still those on the islands of the Strait in whom the blood of their ancestors flowed.

As its old inhabitants passed, the white man consolidated his hold on Tasmania. In a manner comprehensible to those who had shared the nostalgia of the exile or the shame of the felon, Tasmanian society took on, where possible, the shape of its parent societies. Place names, the architecture of the homes, the hedgerows, the gorse bush (which itself became an ineradicable pest) and the forms of government, all combined to give the outward appearance of another England, with some Scottish and Irish tones. Yet with the beauty of its coastal regions, the untamed wilderness of its south-west, the islands of its bays and the huge timbers of its bush, Tasmania was a unique jewel and its inhabitants, jealous in their own internal rivalries, were as one in their attachment to the island. In homes such as 'Panshanger' and 'Entally', the gentry entertained graciously, while at 'Gala' on the east coast, where hospitality was warm and generous, the hardy Scots survived with dignity on country which made the narrow strip of fertile land of the north-west appear a paradise. At Ross and throughout the midlands, the squatters lived on big estates of 10,000 or more acres, refining their wool and stud flocks year by year. 'Tasmanian blood' was highly prized by the flock masters on the mainland. The great squatters became haughty, entertaining one another in their gracious homes and turning their backs on the local towns. In the north the *Examiner* was their favoured newspaper while in the south they read the *Mercury*.

Tasmanians argued about their first railways, but the discovery of mineral deposits settled the question as to their need. After 1871, when the richest tin mine in the world was discovered at Mt Bischoff in the north-west, and gold, coal and silver deposits were found at Waterhouse and Fingal, the railways were rapidly developed. The economy fell into disarray when Tasmania did not share the gold boom of the mainland, but it recovered when people realized the extent of the mineral wealth of the island. New arrivals, no longer in convict garb, began to exceed departures and females rose to equal proportions with males, which changed entirely the composition of the old society of the 1840s. Nevertheless, the past was not forgotten and literature helped to keep it vivid. Marcus Clarke, a young English writer living in Melbourne, spent a month's research in Tasmania in 1870. The result, initially published in serial form, became the classic of the convict era with its story of pain, degradation, inhumanity and sorrow, intertwined with love and hope. Clarke's monumental *For the Term of his Natural Life* opened for thousands a mental gateway to the grim past of Van Diemen's Land, although it was taken for granted that Clarke's convict hero, Rufus Dawes, had to be innocent of any crime. In those days, it was not possible to make a hero of a former criminal.

Marcus Clarke, who wrote about the event with wit and impertinence, refused to join the thousands of Victorians who went wild with delirium when Prince Alfred, Duke of Edinburgh, visited Melbourne in November 1867. The occasion was such that electric light lit up the outside of Parliament House, apologies were made that the Australian accent may seem offensive to the royal ears, and throats were drowned in loyal toasts to the young gentleman and his mother, Victoria. In the following March, Alfred attended a public picnic at Clontarf, Sydney, which gave a mentally deranged Irishman, Henry O'Farrell, the opportunity to shoot and wound him. Despite the Duke's efforts to have his life spared, O'Farrell was hanged and Henry Parkes used the affair to raise a groundless and absurd scare of revolution by Irish republicans and Catholic Fenians. Hysteria reached such proportions that the New South Wales legislature, known locally as the 'Bear Garden' given its notoriety for dirty play, passed an Act which made it a crime to refuse to drink a loyal toast or to use insulting language of Her Majesty, while other zealots wanted to change the name of New South Wales to Alfredland. Soon afterwards, in the wake of the imperial hysteria and perhaps as a warning that henceforth Australia would have to stand on its own feet, the last of the British troops left for home.

Parkes's Fenian scare, deliberately engineered and falsely concocted, was all part and parcel of a wider conflict in society about the role of religion in education. In 1862 state aid to religion was abolished in New South Wales and, by 1866, Parkes managed to have his Public School Act passed which set up a Council of Education to control both the state and denominational systems and limit funding denominational schools. The Act heightened tensions and pushed many Catholics, hitherto practising their religion as a private affair, to take their convictions into the public arena and to accept the idea, proposed by Marsden in the early 1800s, that Catholics were different from the rest of the community – a concept that the members of Orange Lodges and many anti-Catholics had never found any difficulty in both believing and propagating. In the long run, a colonial community divided on a central issue was the fruit.

By the 1870s, it had become clear to all the colonial governments that their purses could no longer afford to support two systems of education. Parallel with and justifying such a conviction was the development of the notion that religion was divisive and obscurantist in the face of modern thought. The argument was put forward that a solid education needed to be based on a liberal and scientific foundation which had to be available to all children who, for their own and for society's good, ought to be submitted to it. Such ideas were easily put into a slogan and 'secular, compulsory and free education' at the primary level became the catchcry of the reformers.

The embodiment of the slogan in a system meant that the state entirely stopped funding denominational schools, which happened in Victoria in 1872 and in all the colonies by 1895. Catholics were prepared to follow the lead of their pastors in this matter at least, although very considerable personal sacrifice was entailed. They supported a separate system staffed by the free labour of men and women of religious congregations. In New South Wales the debate was heightened by the response of the Catholic bishops, led by the English Benedictine monk, Roger Vaughan, Archbishop of Sydney, who prophesied that the new secular schools would breed 'future immorality, infidelity and lawlessness.' To the extent that truth lay in such an assertion, Catholics, but more especially the bishops, carried some share of responsibility, because the absence of a large portion of practising Christians, including teachers and pupils, from the public system helped push it down the long road to indifference and then to aggressive secularism.

Most of the Irish were at the bottom of the social scale except in Queensland, where, first in the cotton and then in the sugar industry, it had been found necessary to acquire a source of coloured labour suited to climatic conditions which were alleged to be too trying for the white worker. Sugar was first grown, for a brief period only, at Port Macquarie in the 1820s, but the industry did not develop until the late 1860s, by which time there were eight mills near Brisbane. Later, cane was grown extensively in the north of the colony. As early as 1847, Benjamin Boyd, who controlled 2,500,000 acres of land on the Monaro and in the Riverina, imported 200 Pacific Islanders to work his properties, but most of them were sent back before the year was out when humanitarians and workers combined to reject their presence. Ironically, on a visit to the Solomons in 1851, the inhabitants of those islands he had intended to exploit for his own use are said to have eaten Boyd himself, but his early example in the employment of islanders was not forgotten in colonial Australia.

By the 1860s the labour shortage was acute, and the owners of cotton and sugar plantations imported natives from Java, Ceylon and the Pacific Islands. The unmarried, well-behaved, hard-working islanders, known as Kanakas, were mostly induced or duped into leaving their home islands, to work in Queensland for ten shillings per month, plus keep, although some left willingly and did not want to return. Some right-minded individuals judged their use as slave labour and there was certain proof of 'blackbirding', as the kidnapping of islanders was called. Amongst the blackbirders was the former medical practitioner James Murray, who had searched for Burke and Wills and spent time with the Leichhardt Ladies Expedition in search of the explorer before turning to blackbirding. As a blackbirder he was involved in the massacre of a group of Polynesians in the late 1870s.

The use of the Kanakas was seen by many as an underhand measure designed to bring in coloured labour to the detriment of the European workers at a time when assisted immigration had, between 1875 and 1890, reached 213,000. The number of Kanakas was initially small, with fewer than 2,000 arriving over five years, but the opposition, especially from missionaries, was intense. The numbers grew rapidly, however, and 50,000 had come in by 1895 and they died at a rate three times faster than other Queenslanders. The whole episode of Kanaka labour was sordid and it fostered a brand of racism in the workers' movement which was based on fear of cheap competition. It also strengthened the determination of the southern colonies to keep Australia free from all Asiatic or coloured races.

Racist sentiment was one aspect of a new but rapidly developing nationalism that had its visible expression in bodies such as the Australian Natives Association, which restricted its membership to the Australian born. It was fonded in 1871 as a mutual-aid society to promote the welfare of Australia and to oppose non-white immigration. Nationalism also developed on the goldfields, which knew no colonial boundaries. The goldfields extended from western New South Wales to Queensland, where Charters Towers and the Palmer River flourished in the 1870s and where Mt Morgan became the country's richest goldmine. In northern Australia, workers on the Overland Telegraph found gold; in the Kimberley region in the north of Western Australia, gold was mined in the mid-eighties, and at Kalgoorlie in the nineties. In Victoria, at Bendigo and Ballarat, Walhalla and other places, the great quartz crushers pounded on and on throughout the whole period.

All the fields attracted an itinerant workforce, largely made up of men who felt that their single allegiance was to Australia rather than to any of the colonies from which they sprang. The same happened with the development of other mineral deposits. In South Australia the copper mines gave work to 20,000 people. Sapphires and diamonds were dug for in many places. Tin was mined at Inverell, Glen Innes and Tenterfield in New South Wales, at Stanthorpe and Herberton in Queensland and at Mt Bischoff in Tasmania, making Australia the world's largest producer of tin from 1873 to 1882. In 1883, a German-born boundary rider with an interest in minerals, Charles Rasp, stumbled across an immense outcrop of ironstone on a broken hill in desolate, arid country 800 miles from Sydney. The Broken Hill Proprietary Company was founded and in a century the 'Hill' produced 120 million tons of silver, lead and zinc ore. Meanwhile the Tasmanian silver and gold, copper and tin fields continued in production.

The men who worked the mines increasingly brought their wives and children with them and they settled where prosperity, old age or mere contentment beckoned. The divisions of the past between exclusives and emancipists, the native-born and the new chums were of small moment to them. What mattered was the land that gave them an opportunity. Transformed rapidly from Cornishmen, Irishmen, Scots or Cockneys, they wanted to know no other place and they joined those others – urban dwellers, squatters, land selectors, farm workers and nomads – to whom Australia was already home. The miners carried with them traditions of unionism, mateship, a fair-go for the underdog and a sense of the family as the heart of society, and so, with time, they became similar to the other colonials in accent, vocabulary, and likes and dislikes in food, drink and dress.

In the cities an increasingly industrialized workforce settled to urban life. They made goods ranging from clothing, textiles, machinery, furniture, building supplies and saddlery to food and drink, and used products marked 'Australian made'. Among them many rejoiced in a standard of living which they ranked as the best in the world while others, especially in the factories, were exploited and made to endure physical hardship, much in the manner of their counterparts in Britain. Nevertheless, out of all this amalgam of miners, bushmen and city dwellers a form of nationalism grew which expressed itself by calls for the building of a defence force, especially after the withdrawal of the British regiments in the 1870s coupled with the proliferation of scares of a Russian threat and demands by the Australian Natives Association that New Guinea and the New Hebrides be annexed to Australia. Indeed, some New South Welsh politicians were so taken with the idea that a new nation was in process of formation that they wanted to assert their rights over it by calling their colony 'Australia.'

The Industrial Revolution, although it caused widespread and complex changes in societies, tended also to produce uniformity of thought. This meant that little room was left for people to choose consciously a way of life that was distinctive. Developments in technology caused the same phenomena to be repeated across societies. Steam brought powered ships and railways, electricity produced the telegraph and street lighting spread rapidly after the Edison method of incandescent lighting was first used to illuminate the Sydney General Post Office and Circular Quay in 1880. That same year the Melbourne telephone exchange was opened connecting forty-four subscribers and the new means of communication was soon widely accepted. Refrigerated meat was first shipped to London in 1879, causing the *Times* to hope that a normal meal for an English family would soon be Australian fresh meat. Education and the press, with newspapers now readily available to those even of slender means, produced common ways of thinking.

Partly as a consequence of its formation as a society in the nineteenth century, Australia was unlike others in which millennia had permitted, and geographic and climactic conditions encouraged, wide forms of diversity. In Australia there were scarcely any regional developments in language in the form of varying dialects and accents, little variation in clothing and food which, in other places, depended upon climate and locally available commodities. Perhaps more importantly there was no growth of high and popular culture with regionally distinct forms of song, literature, art and social relations. Even sport took on the forms developed in Britain except for Australian football. Finally, the new Australian race was homogeneous and white. Apart from a few Italians and Germans the rest were drawn almost totally from the one British society with variations for the Scottish and Irish. The Chinese and Kanakas were regarded as complete outsiders from whom nothing could be gained and with whom little could be shared, while many still judged the Aborigines as scarcely belonging to the human race. Inevitably the society that developed in the nineteenth century had an element, perhaps a grey element, of sameness about it.

By 1880 the United Kingdom was the birthplace of less than one in three Australians so that the population was markedly and increasingly indigenous. In general, they spoke the same language with the same accent, ate essentially the same food and drank similar beverages – tea and beer. Their clothes only differed in minor ways with the changes in climate. With some surprise, it was noticed in Brisbane that the men discarded their coats and displayed their shirts to the world. While some visitors to Australia were struck by the differences between the old societies and the new one, especially in the alleged lessening of tensions between the social classes, they rarely remarked on differences within Australian society itself. Indeed to Australians themselves, differences that did exist scarcely mattered and it was possible to travel within the country and not be affected by them. Rivalry between Sydney and Melbourne and between Hobart and Launceston, varying railway widths, border posts between the colonies and other minor variations did exist but they were either curiosities or irritants and not significant in themselves.

If anything it was the land itself that was capable of shaping a new society because it was so old, brooding, mysterious, threatening and embracing. Interminable in its distances, washed with the same blueness of sea and sky, covered with the strength of its flora, the puzzling quaintness of its fauna, passing from the richness of its coastal regions with their wild and beautiful coasts and their mountain chain called the Great Divide, to the seemingly limitless deserts; the land gave at once a sense of sameness and wonderment. The land had to be won by the white settlers, who used it, abused it, and made it productive in the things that were precious to them. In its use the changes they wrought sometimes brought about a transformation in that barren places were clothed in new grasses and trees, many of which were beneficial. In other ways the settlers wounded the land and time would reveal the gravity and depth of those wounds. Gradually, however, they came to know the land and an interaction took place so that those who had been newcomers from the early days of settlement had become, in life and in death, part of the land a century later.

In 1877 a poet, James Brunton Stephens, wrote, 'She is not yet' when expressing a yearning for a form of national unity that would result in 'the girdling seas alone" becoming the boundaries of all Australia. With this expression of hope no element of jingoism was mixed, but Stephens did not realize that, by the time he wrote, Australians had already forged a unity among themselves that later political measures would merely sanction but not strengthen. A year later, Peter Dodds McCormick wrote 'Advance, Australia Fair' thereby accepting the unity between the people themselves and with the land they inhabited.

The attempt by some urban Australians to define their distinct identity revealed itself clearly in sport. Australian cricket had its origins and most of its later development in Sydney, where it was played from the earliest days and where the long summer made it a particularly acceptable game. In 1832 the native-born in Sydney formed their own club, first called the Australian Cricket Club and then the Currency Lads Club. By 1835 their supremacy over teams made up of the 'sterling' who had come as free settlers was so decisive that matches between them were abandoned. In 1868 cricket became an international phenomenon with the despatch of the Victorian Aboriginal team to England under its new coach and manager Charles Lawrence. The team went through a strenuous tour winning and losing fourteen matches alike and English critics proclaimed its champion, Mullagh, as a batsman of high merit.

Two England elevens came to Australia in the 1860s, including a tour in 1873–74 captained by W.G. Grace who combined the trip with his honeymoon. The Australians had developed their skills considerably in the previous decade and Grace's team was beaten three times. At Melbourne in March 1877, a combined Australian team from New South Wales and Victoria played England in the first ever Test Match. The locals won by forty-five runs. In the following year, a win at the Oval in London caused the team to receive a national welcome on its return home, while the names of Spofforth, Bannerman, Blackham and Gregory became immediately famous. In 1882 the 'Ashes' of English cricket were symbolically created when Australia won a Test at the Oval by seven runs. The 'Ashes' became thenceforward the coveted prize between the two cricketing nations.

The Victorian goldfields in the 1850s gave rise to a unique code of football based partly on the Irish game, already codified in Ireland, called hurling. In its primitive form the new game was given a set of rules in Melbourne in 1858 and Thomas Wills was one of those who drew them up. Called 'Australian Football', the game made use of open space and freedom of movement and developed its own terminology drawn from the goldfields, with expressions such as 'lead', 'shepherding' and 'pockets'. Carried by the diggers and miners to South Australia, Tasmania and Western Australia, the game failed to become international although played in New Zealand. Identification with it was purely local, but the first intercolonial game was played between Victoria and South Australia in 1879. Nevertheless, its popularity, the fierce suburban and country-town loyalties engendered, the increasingly large crowds in attendance and its rapid spread through the southern colonies gave the Australian game a form of national prominence. Despite the native origins of 'Australian Rules', it has never displaced Rugby Union or, since 1907, Rugby League in New South Wales and Queensland. In those parts of Australia, both games retained their dominance and their proud following with overseas touring teams called the Wallabies for Rugby Union and the Kangaroos for Rugby League.

Rowing, sailing, sculling and swimming rapidly became favourite sports of a maritime people. When Edward Trickett returned to Sydney from England in 1876 as the world champion sculler, and Australia's first world champion in any sport, there were scenes of unbounded enthusiasm. Such sporting heroes as William Beach and Henry Searle quickly followed Trickett's footsteps so that, gradually, Australians began to realize that on the field and in the water they could match the best, and a particular pride in beating the English at their own games was widespread throughout the colonies.

Apart from the episode of the Maori wars, none of this sporting expertise was translated onto the field of the martial arts until a contingent of 552 New South Welsh infantry and 212 mounted men sailed from Sydney in March 1885 to take part in the Sudan Campaign in North Africa. By the time of their arrival, the conflict was almost over and they saw little action although three were wounded and six died of other causes. The experiment proved, ominously, that, when the glory of England and the defence of the Empire were invoked, Australians would be among the first to exchange their bats and oars for guns and bayonets.

In a society struggling for permanence, and where the wealthy were mainly concerned with the pursuit of more wealth, the fine arts were paid little attention before mid-century. There were no great personages, no ancient buildings, no scenes or battlefields deemed to be sufficiently pregnant with history as to cause their commemoration and the landscape was so unfamiliar initially that it defeated those who wanted to draw or paint it. Conrad Martens arrived in Sydney in 1835 and for the following thirty years his constant theme was the Harbour and its surroundings. His water-colours were of a high order, but he saw the landscape in unreal colours and shapes which resembled those of Europe.

A change took place with the arrival of Abram Louis Buvelot in 1865, because the Swiss-born painter had an instinctive sense of light and tone that allowed him to touch the reality he saw and, in particular, the plains of Victoria's Western District. Those who followed him in the 1880s recognized him as the father of Australian landscape painters. Buvelot left an unchallenged legacy, which flowered after his death in 1888. Eugene von Guerard was given the honour of becoming the first instructor at Victoria's National Gallery instead of Buvelot, but the latter's *Waterpool at Coleraine* remains, with other paintings, as testimony to his artistry and vision.

Thomas Henry Kendall, whaler, clerk, horseman, swimmer, derelict, bankrupt, dipsomaniac and poet was the sweetest voice of colonial Australia. He was born at Ulladulla on the beautiful south coast of New South Wales in 1839 and lived his entire life in Australia until his death at the age of forty-three. He loved the bush, sang a delicate song and possessed deep emotional forces, which were never more evident than in the lament for his dead infant daughter entitled 'Araluen'. As a lyricist, whose poems rang gently with the sounds of the bush, Kendall is a unique witness that in less than eighty years the land had produced a testimony to itself. With the balladist Adam Lindsay Gordon, whose span was even briefer (1833–70), Kendall needs no comparison as a poet. Gordon, supreme horseman, temporary politician and one hurt in his being by injury and despair, always remained an Englishman and an alien who loved Australia without helping to mould her. 'The Sick Stockrider', 'How We Beat the Favourite' and other ballads, the flamboyancy and physical courage of his life and its tragic end at his own hand won the hearts of many Australians, but his bust is in Westminster Abbey where it is at home.

Marcus Clarke thought that Henry Kingsley's novel, *The Recollections of Geoffry Hamlyn* (1859), was the best Australian novel ever written. It dealt with squatting in the pre-gold period and its assumption was that the true leaders of colonial society were the pretentious English gentry, which was the precise element in it that caused Joseph Furphy to dismiss the novel as trash. Thomas Browne also thought that Kingsley's work was "immortal' but Browne, Kingsley and Clarke were all English-born. Browne himself, under the pseudonym Rolf Boldrewood, wrote a work of far greater merit, *Robbery*

Under Arms. Browne was only five when he arrived in Australia. He eventually took up a run in Victoria until drought forced him to become a police magistrate at various places in the bush in New South Wales. He drew on his experiences to write a masterpiece of superb storytelling with characters that are Australian who use a bush vernacular. Serialized weekly in the *Sydney Mail* newspaper in 1882 and 1883, *Robbery Under Arms* was eagerly read by Australians, in both the bush and the city.

There were developments of importance in the study of the various branches of science. Government astronomers – H.C. Russell in New South Wales, R. L. Ellery in Victoria and Charles Todd in South Australia continued the systematic study of the southern skies begun by Governor Brisbane in Sydney. They provided the colonial time services, assisted the land surveyors and made important contributions to the study of meteorology. In 1877, using information provided by the telegraph, and after consulting with Ellery and Todd, Russell began issuing daily weather charts to the press, which later served as a rudimentary guide both to city and bush dwellers. Throughout the nineteenth century until 1896 local time, taken from the overhead position of the sun at noon, was observed. In 1896, three Standard Time Zones were introduced for legal, social and railway timetable purposes. In the eastern colonies, which based their time on the 150th meridian east of Greenwich, there was uniformity and South Australia and Western Australia were respectively one and two hours behind Eastern Standard Time. In 1899 South Australia and the Northern Territory decided to settle for being only half an hour behind Eastern Standard Time.

George Bentham who, assisted by Ferdinand von Mueller, published the monumental *Flora Australiensis* between 1863 and 1878, systematized the botanical work begun by Joseph Banks and Daniel Solander and continued by Robert Brown, Allan Cunningham and other explorer scientists. Von Mueller's work in botany greatly helped Australian science gain international recognition, but he is locally more often remembered as the foundation planner of Melbourne's botanical gardens. The geologist, Rev. W. B. Clarke, and zoologist Gerard Krefft of the Australian Museum both corresponded with Charles Darwin and supplied him with evidence to support his theory of evolution, but in Australia Darwin's theory was either fiercely opposed or regarded at best with great suspicion. Many distinguished scientists, including Father J. E. Tenison Woods, A.R.C. Selwyn, Robert Etheridge jnr, and T.W. Edgeworth David who, in 1886, discovered the important Greta (New South Wales) coal measures, continued Clarke's great pioneering geological work. When a visiting Cambridge zoologist cabled a terse message in 1884 to the delegates at a meeting in Canada of the British Association of Science that the platypus and the echidna were egg-laying mammals, he caused a mild sensation and an eighty-year-old mystery was solved.

Scientific effort was strengthened by the foundation of societies which had their model in the Royal Society of London (founded 1662). By the 1860s Royal Societies had been formed in New South Wales, Tasmania, Victoria and South Australia; 1874 saw the Linnean Society of New South Wales established for 'the cultivation and study of the science of natural history in all its branches'; the Royal Geographical Society of Australasia was founded in 1883; and the peak of nineteenth century scientific organisation was reached in 1888 with the holding of the inaugural conference of the Australasian Association for the Advancement of Science (now ANZAAS) in Sydney.

In the earliest days of settlement convicts frequently absconded into the bush, where, unable to live off the land, they turned to robbery to support themselves. By 1805 they were called bushrangers and they became known as bolters in Van Diemen's Land where their violence and daring were unsurpassed. The most famous bolters on the island were Michael Howe, Matthew Brady and Martin Cash. Cash was one of the very few who managed to cross the neck of land at Port Arthur, with its ferocious guard dogs, and escape. He went bushranging later but died a respectable man in 1877. On the mainland the early bushrangers were also runaway convicts. Bold Jack Donohoe was made famous in the ballad named after him, and Governor George Gipps forbad it being sung in taverns lest others be led to emulate his deeds. Jackey Jackey Westwood, Davis the 'Jew Boy' and Yankee Jack Ellis were others long remembered in New South Wales. They all lived in the pre-gold period when bushranging had become almost a profession among those who put little store on their own or others' lives.

In the gold-rush period, a few of the native-born began to turn to bushranging. Apart from the excitement and the bravado, it was a handy trade for young men who found living off the produce of the goldfields without actually doing the labour an attractive way of life. There was always a stagecoach or defenceless travellers on the roads who were easy prey and, at anytime, a foray could be made into the towns or to homesteads. At the latter, good and fast horses, and sometimes racehorses, were often taken because the bushrangers relied heavily on the reliability and speed of their transport to evade the law. In general they were ensured protection, shelter and food among their own families and friends. The 'bush telegraph', a quickly relayed word of mouth message, brought notice of police movements, while their daring won admiration from those who stood to loose nothing from the depredations of the bushrangers.

In central-western New South Wales, the Weddin mountains were a favourite refuge for small gangs of bushrangers who raided the towns, roads and homesteads and then were able to retreat into the mountains with impunity. A particularly audacious act was the holding up of the township of Canowindra for three days by a gang led by Ben Hall in 1863. Little of consequence was taken, but the bushrangers entertained the locals to free food and drink and left without hindrance. Two years later, Hall, then aged twenty-eight, was betrayed, ambushed and shot down by the police. For the main part, an early death by shooting or hanging was the lot of the bushrangers.

One notable exception was Frank Gardiner who, after a series of hold ups and robberies not involving the loss of anyone's life, was sentenced to thirty-two years hard labour in 1864. Released in 1874 on the condition that he go into exile, Gardiner lived until 1903, having run the Twilight Saloon in San Francisco for some years. His release, however, had caused the downfall of a government in Sydney when the Parkes ministry had to resign over the handling of the affair. The general behaviour of the bushrangers did not entirely alienate the people of the bush, although among them there were a few murderous madmen. By the late 1860s bushranging was largely over, and the killing of Frederick Ward, known as Captain Thunderbolt, on 25 May 1870, closed a chapter of colonial history apart from a few isolated phenomena of the seventies.

Australia's most famous rebel was Ned Kelly, son of an Irish, emancipist father. After his father's death in 1866, the family moved to a small selection at Greta in the northeast of Victoria, where young Kelly soon fell foul of the law. By 1873, he was on a hulk at Williamstown serving three years. He emerged to find the old bush days gone, with the electric telegraph and the railway linking the northeast to Melbourne. The home selection was too small to support the family so Ned found work for a time locally and then turned to horse and cattle stealing. Such activity was not simple criminality, but also a protest by the landless and the unsuccessful against the large squatters who had increased their land holdings despite the Land Acts of the previous decades.

Kelly may have faded into obscurity had the police not shown their determination to bring him and his companions to heel. High ranking police officers had become alarmed when the Premier, Graham Berry, sacked some 300 judges, police magistrates, coroners and other public servants on Black

Wednesday, 9 January 1878. The sackings had been brought on by the refusal of the Legislative Council, bastion of landed and merchant power, to grant supply. The purpose was to stop the payment of members of Parliament, a measure recently passed by the lower house as part of a reform package. Captain Standish, who incompetently ran the police force from the comfort of the Melbourne Club, decided it was time to prove his own value to society and what better way to do so than by picking off the Kellys.

A false accusation of the attempted murder by Ned of a constable led to the arrest of Ned's mother, her son-in-law and another innocent man, and rewards were put out for Ned and his younger brother, Dan. In an ambush, three police refused to surrender and were killed by Ned. Outlawed, the brothers with two mates, Joe Byrne and Steve Hart, took to the bush for twenty months emerging on two occasions to hold up banks at Euroa in Victoria and Jerilderie in New South Wales. In June 1880 they made a stand at Glenrowan near the old Greta homestead, where, in the ensuing battle with the police, all but Ned were killed. Sentenced to death, Ned was hanged in Melbourne on 11 November 1880.

Kelly, clad in the iron armour he wore at Glenrowan, became in time the archetypal legend of Australia's folklore with the expression 'as game as Ned Kelly' the byword of indomitable courage. Those whose values sanctified property, authority and the law and who accepted the police version of Ned as a terrorist and cold-blooded murderer, abhorred the legend. Others saluted Ned's identification with the land of his birth, his rejection of despotism clothed in law and his thirst for freedom from tyranny. In him they saw the first of a new Australian breed. Ned's monument was his legend, kept alive in ballads, prose, poetry, films and paintings.

10

Prosperity and Depression

One hundred years of settlement had bred a basic conviction in the minds of white Australians that marked them off from their forebears and many of their contemporaries in other lands. They grew up with the expectation that, with moderate effort, life could be sustained, families raised, fed and clothed in some degree of ease, and the cycle repeated. The subjection experienced by a European workforce and peasantry to factory owners and landlords, who could make or break individuals and families, was simply unacceptable to most Australians. In the natural course of events some Australians were not survivors, whether as small selectors or factory hands, but it was not the norm to go under when work of some kind was available to the willing. In particular the workers' movement was convinced that, with proper organization and unity, a balance could be achieved between capital and labour to the benefit of all concerned.

A labour movement embracing both bush and urban workers was already a necessity, because the rural dream, in which a high percentage of the population would live comfortably on smallholdings, had turned sour. The squatters maintained their dominance and, although there was an itinerant workforce especially of shearers, large properties employed permanent and settled workers, almost all of whom were males. On very large stations it was not unusual to find eighty or more employees. Over seventy per cent of the population was on wages or salaries while more than a third of the people of New South Wales lived in Sydney and approaching half Victorians were Melbournians. The trade union movement was formed to represent these Australians.

If worker representation was necessary for the males, it was imperative for the females and children. By the mid-eighties, twenty per cent of the workforce was female. In shops or factories women and girls worked in industries many of which previously had their base in the home – food, drink, textiles and clothing. The first Act regulating hours of work and conditions for females was passed in Victoria on 11 November 1873. Despite that Act, female workers in Victoria and elsewhere often worked for sixty to seventy hours a week, and in factories their wages were normally less than half the male rate. Sanitation and ventilation were ignored, as were health and safety issues. In the clothing industry the women often took work home at night which meant that, after nine hours in the factory, they did three more at home. Women who were unable to leave the home because of commitments to the children took work in, and, under the process known as 'sweating', they worked as long for less pay making it difficult for the factory women to claim higher rates.

Children were similarly exploited with cases of youngsters aged ten and eleven working sixty hours for 6s per week – about one-sixth of the adult male rate. Often children fainted from exhaustion and the apprentice system was little relief being no more than exploitation as apprentices in many trades were not paid at all in their first four years. With compulsory education far from realizable, many youngsters became 'street Arabs' begging, selling matches and trinkets, wandering the alleyways or gathered as 'larrikins' in pushes. They were mostly a nuisance but sometimes a terror as they marauded through the city and suburbs.

No clearly structured political parties had emerged, partly because the concept was strong that a member of parliament was responsible primarily to his electors rather than to a party. The main, divisive, issue in politics was whether free trade or protection of local products was preferable as a policy. Victoria became the stronghold of protection because the decline in revenue from taxes on gold inclined the government to listen to the voices of the farmers, who wanted to protect their wheat from imports, and to the founders of new industries who had to compete with products made elsewhere. By the late 1870s, a twenty to twenty-five per cent duty had been placed on imports into Victoria.

Protection caused no marked growth in industry, but a large domestic market was created on account of the population rise and in the thirty years from 1861 to 1891, the number of factories in Victoria grew from 400 to 3,300, and the growth rate of the urban sector was higher than that of the rural. In New South Wales, three times the size of Victoria, the continued revenue from the sale of Crown Lands meant that protection was not as badly needed, so free trade was espoused. Nonetheless, protection appealed not merely to pockets but also to emotions as it gave a sense of security from competition, initially economic and eventually racial, and it was adopted in the other colonies. The fact that free trade took hold and survived in New South Wales was a tribute to its exponents because it was based on belief in an ideal rather than on practicalities, and Australians had never shown much faith in political dogmas.

With politics largely confined to the intricacies of the free trade versus protection debate, the workforce, whether rural or urban, could not look to party representation for help, as no distinct groups existed with a defined policy on industrial or rural sector matters. Furthermore, the old form of the state, with its origins in the penal period, still prevailed, making it the key factor in all enterprises wherever large capital was required, such as railway construction, education and immigration. State policy, especially in regard to assisted immigration, necessarily had an effect on the workforce and there was a hardening of attitudes against immigrants among the leaders of the workers.

Although there were pockets of unemployment, especially in the mid eighties, the seventies and eighties were periods of general prosperity and there seemed no need for a theoretical blueprint upon which to construct social policies for the future. Trade union activity was based on crafts and directed at wages and factory conditions. In 1882 a strike on wages and piecework occurred among the 4,000 women employed as tailoresses in Victoria and they received widespread union and community support. The tailoresses formed their own union, the first union among females in Australia, and the employers capitulated. The voices of the unionists were joined by those of reformers, a few of whom were manufacturers although the majority were opposed to reform. The Melbourne *Age* added its voice so that Factory Acts regulating conditions were passed in Victoria in 1885 and 1896 with the other colonies following suit in the 1890s. The struggle for reform was long and slow however. Inadequacies were everywhere apparent because, without factory inspectors only the good will of owners, often markedly lacking, could be relied upon to ensure that reform took place.

In the same period the formation of trade unions went ahead, and, more importantly, central bodies were set up to assist in the coordination of their activities. By 1885 there were Trades and Labour Councils in Victoria, New South Wales and Queensland and inter-colonial congresses had been held since the first in Sydney in 1879. At Coolgardie, Western Australia, a congress was held in 1889 at which compulsory arbitration was put on the agenda and thought was given to a political programme. Finally, when the Australian Labour Federation was formed in Queensland in 1889, it clearly indicated that organised labour realized the need for unity to perfect its development.

The most significant step towards one strong union covering a whole industry was the formation of the Amalgamated Shearers' Union of Australasia (A.S.U.) at Ballarat in 1886 under the presidency of the indefatigable organiser and populist, William Spence. He had previously formed the Amalgamated Miners' Association of Australasia and, turning his attention to the pastoral industry, Spence managed to unionise shearers in the eastern colonies. By 1894 the A.S.U. had combined with the Amalgamated Workers' Union of Queensland and a shed hands' union to form the Australian Workers' Union (A.W.U.), which eventually became the most powerful workers' organization in the whole of the continent.

While the workers sought to organize, a symbol of those years of prosperity was rising with the building of 'Marvellous Melbourne', where the population increased, in the decade before 1891, from 268,000 to 473,000. Tramways, railways, bridges, schools, hospitals, offices, factories and homes, all rose as the suburbs spread out from the centre. The people went to the races, cricket and football, gambled and drank and, on Sundays, they worshipped God in the churches they so proudly built. Great edifices based on administration and commerce – Parliament House, the General Post Office, the Treasury building, St Patrick's cathedral and the Rialto – all added to the lustre of the Exhibition Building which was opened in 1880. Called by a visitor 'The Metropolis of Australia', the city abounded with libraries, parks, galleries, theatres and bookshops, including the famous Coles Book Arcade. In 1888 two million people visited the Centennial Exhibition. The city also abounded with slums, which were evil-smelling and ill-lit with unpaved streets and makeshift dwellings.

As it grew Melbourne also became an octopus. Ballarat's and Bendigo's mining exchanges, manufacturing concerns from foundries to breweries in the country towns, bush people with ambition – all were affected by the growth of Melbourne, which became the centre of economic and commercial activity and the place to seek work or skills. Above all, the city became the heart of the financial activity of the whole continent, and indeed beyond into the Pacific, so that a network of bankers, managers, clerks and civil servants grew apace.

The peopling of the city meant land development with housing and shops, gas and water, and the linking of the suburban centres by railway. The inner city was served by a cable tram system after 1885. By May 1888 there were 112 new land and investment companies registered in Victoria, and one of them declared a dividend of 66.6 percent before selling any land. Within eight months land sales totalled more than £13,000,000 and the building industry had begun to use seven-tenths of business profit, which resulted in a boom. Millions of pounds were lent, thousands of acres developed, prices rocketed and capital in seemingly limitless amounts flowed in, especially from Britain, as if it were another gold rush. Greed had overcome sense, speculation replaced wisdom and unbridled optimism dimmed well-founded hope. The land boom burst in a few short months, and by the early 1890s thousands were left with valueless allotments and shares worth less than the carefully inscrolled paper upon which they were recorded. Just as Melbourne's growth was a symbol of prosperity based on the catch-cry of progress and on imported capital, its collapse and stagnation served as the yardstick for the widespread economic downturn of the 1890s that had an effect on all Australians.

In the twenty years from 1871 to 1891, Australian governments had borrowed £126,000,000, but by the end of 1891 British capital was almost unprocurable because of a series of events which originated in Argentina and caused the leading financial institution in London, Barings, to fail. Colonial governments could no longer borrow and it became the case of the country riding out the storm alone as the eastern colonies witnessed failure after failure of respectable financial concerns. Corruption on a large scale was revealed, even among leading politicians in Victoria, and the confidence of the public was shattered. Next hit was the pastoral industry, which by 1890 had doubled all other exports in value. Over-production brought on a partial slump in wool prices, and the desire of the squatters to turn their runs into freehold properties entailed fencing and other improvements that combined with the high cost of labour to cause many squatters to mortgage their properties. Furthermore, large sums of capital had been outlaid on marginal lands, especially in western New South Wales, which proved expensive in artesian water schemes and unprofitable as fleece quality fell. Droughts, rabbits and new land legislation all helped to increase costs and speculation in pastoral properties had meant greatly inflated values. After 1891 a continuing fall in wool prices worsened an already critical situation.

The long-established backbone of the economy, pastoralism, went into decline and sheep numbers dropped by a half from the late 1890s due mainly to the onset of a great drought which began in 1895 and lasted for seven years. Agriculture, principally wheat production, was based chiefly in Victoria and South Australia, which supplied most of the needs of the whole country. In the 1870s farmers in South Australia had moved out beyond the line set down by the Surveyor-General George Goyder, which approximately marked the twelve inch rainfall boundary. Goyder was proved right in his estimate that productivity could not be sustained beyond his line and with falling wheat prices many farmers went broke. Too often they had overworked the land in vain on country with insufficient rain to grow regular crops. They left crumbling dwellings, shifting sand and arid, wind-swept clay pans as evidence that nature's limits could not be pushed with impunity.

The economy could probably have survived had the financial institutions, with government backing, remained firm. But the long period of prosperity had led Australian banks and other lending institutions to over-lend. This contributed to the slump as business could borrow too freely but then could not repay the loans. The business would then fail, productivity would be lost and people put out of work. The diverse and uncontrolled practices of the banks meant that they could not save themselves, nor could government intervention once the productive basis of the economy was shaken. Panic set in after the Commercial Bank of Australia suspended operations in April 1893 and a run on the banks commenced. By May only three large banks, the Union, the Australasia and the Bank of New South Wales, and six lesser ones, were able to operate.

Commercial life and the community itself were in chaos as the distressed banks converted savings into shares, accounts were frozen, wages and bills were not paid, and many of the retired or unemployed lost overnight any savings they had accumulated. Sensible government intervention with co-operation from the banks could have reduced the effects of the collapse but, although the banks passed into a period of so-called reconstruction, the damage was done and the country was gripped by depression. Workmen's wages fell by over a quarter, some of the unemployed roamed the country looking for work, evictions became common and people slept in the streets or in public gardens such as Sydney's Domain.

Australia's period of prosperity in the aftermath of the gold rushes was over. The economic structures were in tatters, capital had ceased to flow in, labour relations were strained or non-existent and the claim that here was 'a good place for a steady man' had become hollow. In three years, 50,000 people left Melbourne and in some suburbs the streets were deserted. Some of those who had previously been wealthy and many more of the poor starved. Thirty per cent of the workforce was unemployed. As no direct government assistance of any kind was available, the spectre of misery and hunger overshadowed thousands of homes, although some charitable organizations struggled to help ward off starvation. A few schemes of piecemeal work were initiated and co-operative settlements were founded in Victoria and New South Wales. Victoria lost 100,000 citizens in the decade, mostly to the West Australian goldfields to which they took their spirit of independence and their love of Australian Rules Football. Finally, nature added its own measure of flagellation to a society already on its knees as the great drought showed no sign of lifting.

Western Australia in the 1860s had seen the development of the vast areas of pastoral country in the north-west beyond Geraldton with about six million acres running 40,000 sheep. At the same time the east and south-east were further opened and about nine million acres were under lease by 1870. Concurrently the end of the convict period in 1868 saw in office a governor of some foresight, Frederick Weld. He directed the development of the telegraph and the construction of roads and, in 1874, the first public railway was commenced. However, it was not until 1879 that the railways began to expand in a measure commensurate with the needs of the colony. Pearling, timber, especially the splendid jarrah and karri woods, sandalwood and wool were the basis of the economy and the pastoral industry was given further impetus with the leasing, by 1883, of about forty-eight million acres of country in the Kimberley region. The colony was enormous in extent, one-third the area of continental Australia and larger by far than Western Europe, but the centres of long established political, social and economic power were still in the east. The opening of the Golden West was another element in the swing away from the coastal emphasis of the cities towards the inland and its goldfields and bush.

Consequent upon these developments, it was finally decided to give responsible government to Western Australia and, on 30 December 1890, the first Parliament was sworn in. It had an upper and a lower house as the colonists had resisted the single chamber parliament, which the Colonial Office had wanted to give to them. The opening of the 'Golden Mile' at nearby Boulder followed the discovery of immense deposits of gold at Coolgardie, and then by Paddy Hannan in June 1892 at Kalgoorlie. Gold transformed the colony economically and socially. Thousands flocked to Western Australia thereby quadrupling its population in a few years, otherwise the mass of unemployed could have caused chaos in the eastern cities. Lured by profits British capital was abundantly available for Western Australia and some of it was transferred to the east. The net result of the gold discoveries was that the eastern colonies were helped to get through the depression, while Western Australia itself went through a period of catching up and then mild transformation.

During the depression labour and capital in the eastern colonies engaged in a protracted and hard-fought struggle. The labour movement emerged chastened and defeated, but with the need for unity and political representation more clearly established. In August 1890 a maritime strike took out 50,000 workers in transport and mining for a period of two months. The shearers in New South Wales went out for a week as a defensive measure. The strike began over claims by marine officers for better accommodation and increased pay, which the shipowners refused to discuss until the officers were prepared to disband their own union. Meanwhile wool shorn by non-union labour was arriving at the wharves and in a matter of days, marine officers, seamen, wharf labourers and coal lumpers all had gone on strike both to support the marine officers and to prevent the loading of 'black' wool. The Pastoralists' Federal Council and the Steamship Owners' Association fought on the right of capital to organize a workforce as it saw fit and, in the case of the former, to break Spence's already loosening hold on an industry in which they regarded the 'closed shop' principle as an affront.

The unions quickly ran out of funds, men saw their jobs taken by non union labour and it appeared as if the employers, with strong support from government and the law, had won. In fact the workers' movement had been pushed so far that no alternative remained but to organize direct political action. In May 1891 three labour candidates won seats in the South Australian Parliament and in the June elections of 1891 thirty five nominees of the New South Wales Labour Electoral Leagues, which were the true founders of the Labor Party, were returned to Parliament and a party was formed in New South Wales. The Party differed in New South Wales from that in Victoria where liberal minded members of Parliament could be relied upon to pass reforming measures; it suffered internal discord, and only gradually formulated clear policies except on the exclusion of coloured labour. In 1890 Henry George, American writer, lecturer and visionary economist, whose book *Progress and Poverty* (1879) had been read by many thousands in the colonies, visited Australia and seeded some of his ideas on a tax on land into the movement. Old Chartist ideals and the concept of mateship had survived the golden days and they blended with faint traces of socialism popularised in the newly founded papers of the labour movement, the *Radical* (1887), the *Worker* (1890) and the *Hummer* (1891).

Nonetheless, the Labor Party lacked any blueprint for society, and therefore relied upon practical achievements to win and hold support. Its pragmatism made it a suitable vehicle to represent the society that gave it birth and the workers and small farmers rapidly looked to it as their party. Catholics, most of whom were working class, became the party's backbone because they saw its concern for the poor and oppressed as an indicator of hope in their own depressed economic and social conditions.

Most Australians shared the conviction that conditions for all could become increasingly better provided the state settled for the correct legislative measures. It was an innocent conviction resting upon a belief in progress and perfectibility. Men of principle from the workers' movement combined with liberal progressives to achieve a three year duration for parliaments and the abolition both of plural voting, by which property owners could vote in more than one electorate, and property qualifications for either candidates or voters. Payment of members of parliament was also introduced, and women were given the vote in South Australia in 1894 and Western Australia in 1899, followed later by the other colonies.

Some of the old guard politicians passed from the scene unable or unwilling to work with powerful Labor minorities. George Reid in New South Wales found no such difficulty and he was able to pass social reforms, aided by the Labor leaders Watson and Hughes, whose careers were shaped in the hardy days when Labor was forced to compromise in order to exist. In Victoria the liberals were so powerful, held views so close to those of the Laborites and contained such talent as Alfred Deakin and Isaac Isaacs that the fledgling Party could only give them quiet and effective support.

On 1 December 1899 the Labor Party in Queensland formed the famous 'first Labor government in the world' under the leadership of Andrew Dawson. His minority ministry did not receive the support it expected from the liberals, and the government lasted less than a week. Tasmania, lacking trade unions of any consequence, left the field to the liberals and conservatives and no Labor Party existed there until 1903 nor was there one in Western Australia until 1900. In South Australia a group of business and pastoral interests forced genuine liberals to coalesce under the leadership of John Downes, who worked with the Labor members to legislate in a markedly radical way. Independents were practically gone from the political arenas and factions no longer existed anywhere except under the label of parties. With the advent of the Labor Party, politics had taken on aspects of organization and discipline unrecognisable to the more relaxed but nonetheless devoted figures of the 1850s who had laid the foundations of Australian democracy.

In this atmosphere, Factory Acts became widespread, sweating of labour done in private premises was attacked but not stopped, and the first steps were taken towards compulsory arbitration, although the depressed economy put the owners in a strong position. Taxes on land and incomes, and the introduction of non-contributory old-age pensions in Victoria and New South Wales seemed to give the Australian colonies the right to be called a 'social laboratory' where progressive ideals were translated into legislation for the good of the poor and the powerless. In reality, the truth lay in a widespread recognition that all sections of society, including the owners of capital, benefited when the sources of discontent were alleviated.

There were some idealists who proclaimed in mildly socialist publications that socialism would make all men mates, which, for most of their readers, was only a pious hope. In 1890 William Lane stated his faith in a youthful Australia, which was also wise with the wisdom of the generations and therefore had a right to be foremost among the nations. He soon became convinced that he would never see his utopia in Australia and, in 1893, he led a party of ardent followers to the wilds of Paraguay to found the perfect settlement. Instead he discovered that greed and envy also held sway in the jungle. His community broke up in discord and Lane left it in 1899 for New Zealand where he became a conservative imperialist.

While there was abundant proof that Australians were prepared to experiment with the shape of their society, there was little proof that they wanted to tamper with its loyalties and allegiances. Despite some public unease at royal appointments, titles and courtesy titles such as 'Sir' and 'Lady' and the other assorted regalia of Empire, republicanism was always a fragile if not exotic plant in Australia. The distant but overwhelming presence of majesty in England's Queen, whose life had been dignified and imperial and to whom increasingly numerous statues were erected in 1887 and 1897 to mark her anniversaries, made loyalty a prerequisite of public sanity among colonial Australians. Little proof was needed that all were loyal children of the British mother but, when loyalty was called for with the outbreak of the Boer War in 1899, it was forthcoming with spontaneity and pride. The response puzzled only that vocal minority who, knowing the Empire was in no danger and suspecting that the retention of British mining interests was relevant, condemned the way in which 16,000 young Australians departed to fight for England in distant Africa under banners such as 'For Queen and Country' and 'The Empire Right or Wrong'. In any event it was no time to promote republicanism.

Henry Lawson, already widely accepted as a writer of stature, proclaimed himself ashamed of his fellow Australians and William Morris Hughes and others in the Labor Party called the war immoral, needless and unjust. Their voices were scarcely heeded. It seemed that the chance had come to prove that male Australians were really men and that the country had come of age. Up to the peace treaty of 31 May 1902, the Australian volunteers numbered 16,175 men, the dead, 518, the wounded, 882 and six Victoria Crosses had been won for valour. The other face to valour was seen in the concentration camps where Boer families were held while the British forces burnt their homes and farm buildings. Harry 'Breaker' Morant, who had been a bushman and horse breaker in Queensland and had later tried his hand at poetry, found peace for his 'soul world-weary' when he and his friend Peter Handcock were court-martialled and executed for shooting Boer prisoners. Their deaths helped to soothe the conscience of the British high command, which had begun to agonize over the whole dirty business it was involved in.

Meanwhile the opening of the land in Australia had gone ahead despite the depression and drought. Wool and gold had tended to obscure the contribution of agriculture to the economy as well as to the development of the country itself. Wheat was the principal grain both for home consumption and export especially when, with the repeal of the Corn Laws in Britain in 1846, which lifted tariffs on imported grain, Britain became the largest importer of wheat in the world. In South Australia; the Riverina; on the Darling Downs; south of Perth; in a large area of South Australia and Victoria called the Mallee and south of it again on rich soils called the Wimmera; wheat cultivation became intense from the 1890s.

Technological progress in the wheat industry was impressive. Farmers cleared the land with the Mullenizer, which pushed over the scrub with a roller and they prepared the soil with the stump jump plough that had been invented in South Australia in 1876. The better-off farmers harvested with the newly released McKay 'Sunshine' harvester. Most farmers began to understand the soils better, they improved fallowing, controlled weeds, varied their wheat strains, began to use superphosphates and worked hard. The farmers in New South Wales laughed at Victoria as a cabbage garden where small farmers called 'cockies' ate treacle on their bread and grew wheat on miniscule plots. Nonetheless, it was not until the 1890s that New South Wales began to feed itself for the first time and trebled its acreage under wheat. The very size of the contribution of the golden grain to the economy made farming respectable. The land selectors who went into the Wimmera and Mallee, including Germans from South Australia who settled around Horsham and the sons of Wimmera farmers who selected in the Victorian Mallee around Sea Lake, gave solidity and permanence to townships, which helped Victoria survive the depression of the nineties.

The grape, with so much else, had come with the First Fleet, but despite the pioneering work of the Macarthur family, it was not until James Busby imported many varieties from Spain and France in 1831–32 that an industry was firmly established at Kirkton near Singleton and Dalwood near

Maitland. Hunter River wines quickly began to gain a reputation for their lightness, fragrance and taste. By 1895 over 7,000 acres were under cultivation in New South Wales, but in South Australia the area was almost double that and its wines were praised at the Paris Exhibition as early as 1854. Victoria had rapidly become the leading wine colony after William Ryrie began a commercial establishment at Yering, near Geelong, in 1840.

Development continued in the wine industry even after the appearance of the dreaded vine disease, phylloxera, in Victoria in 1877. It was brought in on a vessel to the port of Geelong and, carried by the wind, the disease spread rapidly. In South Australia, where phylloxera had a lesser effect, the industry began to flourish under the direction of families like the Lindemans, Penfolds and Seppelts in the Barossa and Clare valleys, near Adelaide, and the future greatness of the South Australian industry was thereby laid. Although recovery in some parts of Victoria was rapid where 30,000 acres were under vines by 1895, further outbreaks of phylloxera caused a gradual decrease in production. Nevertheless the colony still led the industry at the end of the nineteenth century and names like St Hubert became famous. At Mildura and Renmark on the Murray, the beginnings of viticulture were connected with two Canadians of Californian experience, George and William Chaffey, who pioneered irrigation in the area and made vine and fruit-tree growing possible. Their contribution, together with the discovery from 1879 onwards of vast artesian deposits covering over a third of the continent, made agriculture and pastoralism possible in places where the lack of water resulted in 'hissing deserts' and uninhabited wastes.

There was an outbreak of foot and mouth disease among cattle as early as 1804 and later ravaging by pleuro-pneumonia in the 1860s. The cattle tick was an added hazard to the industry after its introduction, probably with Braham cattle in the 1870s, and it killed up to ninety per cent of some herds and helped to reduce stock numbers in Queensland from seven million to four million in the decade after about 1890. Nevertheless, cattle herds for meat and milk grew immensely and by the 1890s there were an added four million head in New South Wales and Victoria; most were derived from the English Hereford shorthorn and polled Angus breeds. In Gippsland and the Western District of Victoria dairy herds rapidly became common although in Gippsland, where huge forests had to be cleared and few good roads or other forms of communication existed, derelict farms testified to the general hardship experienced by selectors.

Queensland, after the opening of the Condamine and McIntyre river districts, became the home of the cattle industry. The industry spread to the

Northern Territory in the 1870s, giving life again to its small settlements and opening up a short-lived trade with East Asia between 1892 and 1897. The Durack family overlanded cattle from Queensland to the Kimberley in Western Australia in 1883–85, settled Argyle Downs and eventually controlled 6,000 square miles of property. They helped pioneer an industry and establish a legend of endurance and of urbanity as well as of civilized relations with the Aborigines. As skilled horsemen and stockmen the Aborigines became a versatile and dedicated workforce throughout northern Australia generally and their contribution was fundamental to the development of a prosperous cattle industry.

In those same years Aboriginal resistance continued in some parts and one leader, Jandamarra, carried on a tradition that went back to William Dampier's landing at Shark Bay in 1699. Dampier was alarmed when he was confronted by 'Prince or Captain' an 'active and courageous' young man who led a group of warriors in determined resistance. They disappeared into the bush only after he had shot one of them. In 1894 Jandamarra commanded a force of 50 warriors in a battle against the police in Windjana Gorge, Western Australia. For two years he evaded his harassers, taunting them from cliff tops, but was wounded so often that his people thought of him as immortal. He met his end in 1897 when he was killed trying to set free a group of his men who had been captured and chained by the police.

The long boom of the 1860–90 period and the subsequent depression had contributed to the birth of the Labor Party as a distinctive political expression of the Australian experience. In literature and the arts there was a similar attempt to create a spirit, centred both upon the land and its people, which would be equally distinctive. In literature this spirit fostered elements of insecurity and arrogance that helped breed a sentiment of intolerance, which was particularly ardent in the Labor Party. This intolerance was not merely towards the 'coloured' races, the Chinese and the Japanese, but also towards European, and more particularly, English immigration. In the 1890s, given Australian economic circumstances, immigration had dropped to a mere trickle.

The Sydney-based *Bulletin* was founded in 1880 by John Haynes and Jules François Archibald who were shortly afterwards joined by William Traill. It rapidly became the literary embodiment of Australian jingoism and chauvinism, expressed by 'Australia for the Australians' and, from 1908 to 1960, by its banner 'Australia for the White Man'. The *Bulletin's* forays into racism, radicalism, anti-imperialism, republicanism and thinly-disguised larrikinism served to delight many, confuse others and enrage some.

Archibald was a rare soul who, as well as being an insufferable autocrat, had the great gift of fostering the talents of others. As a consequence, under his direction and then that of Alfred Stephens and, later, James Edmond, the *Bulletin* became 'The Bushman's Bible' read by people in the outback all over the continent, although the *Sydney Mail, the Australasian* and the *Worker*, together with the *Town and Country Journal*, were more widely read by the workers in New South Wales, while the sporting novels of Nat Gould were read throughout the colonies.

The *Bulletin* was also appreciated by thousands in the cities to whom the bush had already become the symbol of a nostalgic yearning for a pioneering past. The black-and-white artists, Hopkins, May, Norman Lindsay and Souter, enlivened its pages with graphic wit and invective, while verse and prose offerings from readers, many of which were printed on the famous Red Page, poured in. Their reflections on their experience of life in Australia literally kept the *Bulletin* going as most of the contributors were never paid. However, there was enough revenue in 1892 for Archibald to send Henry Lawson to the bush with £5 in his pocket. It was the best used 'fiver' in Australia's literary history, for the Joe Wilson stories, 'The Union Buries its Dead' and other enduring masterpieces of Lawson's genius as a story teller came from those few months in the bush, when the drought which was gripping the country heightened Lawson's own tendency to gloom.

Other writers made their contribution, both in the *Bulletin* and elsewhere, notably the master balladist and poet of the horse, 'Banjo' Paterson. His *The Man from Snowy River and Other Verses* (1895) became an instant best seller and gave Paterson the right to be regarded as the composer of the national song 'Waltzing Matilda', which was first sung publicly in an hotel in Winton, Queensland, in that same year although the song was probably written in the Blue Heeler pub at Kynuna. Ethel Turner published her *Seven Little Australians* in 1894 and Joseph Furphy wrote his novel *Such is Life* (1903), which was set in the Riverina and northern Victoria. In Furphy's words, the novel had a 'democratic' temper and an 'offensively Australian' bias. Steele Rudd (Arthur Hoey Davis) began his 'On Our Selection' in the *Bulletin* in 1895. His figures of Dad, Dave, Joe, Mother and Kate became immortals of Australian literature and made the struggles of the poor selectors part of the national heritage.

In those same years, several artists began to assert their understanding of the native land when they attempted to paint Australian scenes. One of them, Arthur Streeton, said that an enduring theme was to be 'the quiet, beautiful wealth of the "Bush" that we must still endeavour to work'. On 17

August 1889, Streeton, Charles Conder, Tom Roberts and Frederick McCubbin held an 'Exhibition of Impressions' in Melbourne at which they showed their paintings, done mostly on the lids of cigar boxes. Leading, conservative critics roundly condemned the paintings and their creators were a neglected little band whose work sold for a pittance. The Sydney Gallery bought George Lambert's 'Across the Blacksoil Plains' for £105 and Streetons' 'Still Glides the Stream' for £70. On his return from Europe in 1885, Tom Roberts had formed a group around him named after the outer Melbourne suburb of Heidelberg. With McCubbin, Streeton and Conder, the 'Heidelberg School' began to acquire cohesion, vision and increasing fame. Pioneering life, the pastoral industry and the bush were their particular subjects and their intuitive grasp, bred in them from infancy, of Australian light, colour and form gave their work a quality which has rarely been equalled. Their paintings also helped to reinforce the legend of an innocent age, which the people of the cities could look back to and treasure. They avoided the turmoil of the cities, they were scarcely aware of any social conflict and neither the Aborigines nor the convicts had any role in their vision of the past.

Prior to the 1850s Australian music was practically non-existent, but the gold discoveries provided a market for the theatrical impresario, the piano importer and a flourishing sheet-music industry. Music of local or topical interest was often produced like Charles E. Horsley's setting to music of a Henry Kendall poem in 1870. The European musical tradition in Australia was pioneered by various regimental bandmasters and composers, among them Vincent Wallace, John Phillip Deane and Isaac Nathan. Their work was enhanced by the development of philharmonic societies and the Liedertafel movement. In the 1860s and 1870s choral music was very popular. George S. Coppin remained a major figure of the Australian stage, bringing many performers to the country and there was widespread support for W. S. Lyster's opera seasons in the eastern colonies. After Lyster's death, J. C. Williamson became the foremost stage and musical entrepreneur and his 'Firm' dominated the Australian stage for several decades. In 1888 two works were commissioned for the Melbourne Centennial Exhibition, Leon Caron's *Australian National Cantata* and John A. Delaney's *Captain Cook*. Henry Tate, Percy Grainger and Alfred Hill vigorously championed this latent musical nationalism. Hill's music was influenced by Maori and Australian Aboriginal musical folklore.

The writers and painters of the nineties sought a distinctively Australian ethos in things that they thought would endure and, for them, the bush stood for virtue, mateship, hardship and spirit of place. But the nineties marked the end of old, white Australia. Her poets, story-tellers and artists cried out to her to become again an Australia which, neither then nor later, could ever be recreated. In 1896 Joseph Furphy admitted the hopelessness of the task when he wrote 'there is no up the Country for us now'. The *Bulletin* was itself an ending rather than a beginning because the economic forces evident during the 1890s were already effectively changing the isolated continent and her people. Those forces were making Australians part of a wider world, but it was a world that remained within the spiritual, social and economic ambit of Victorian England.

To some extent that wider world was also aware of Australia because from the 1830s visitors had been attracted from overseas. They departed with their varied impressions and, at times, left something behind of value. In an age when the spoken word was still the principal means of communication, the lecture was much in vogue both as entertainment and education. Visitors of note went on widely attended lecture tours throughout the colonies and were given good press coverage. Annie Besant (theosophist), George Augustus Sala (war correspondent), H.M. Stanley (African explorer), Sidney and Beatrice Webb (Fabians), 'Arthur Sketchley' and 'Max O'Rell' (lecturers), Ben Tillett (labour leader), General William Booth (Salvation Army founder), and the novelists and poets Anthony Trollope, David Murray, Gerald Massey and Mark Twain – all passed through the colonies. Robert William Dale, the Congregational theologian, was joined by the musicians Frederick Cowen and Charles Halle; actresses Mrs Scott Siddons and Sarah Bernhardt; and entertainers, G.F. Blondin and Lola Montez who performed her famous 'Spider Dance' at Ballarat in 1855 and publicly horsewhipped the editor of the *Ballarat Times* for having the audacity to question her moral standards. Joseph Conrad, R. L. Stevenson and Rudyard Kipling made brief visits, as did Samuel Plimsoll, 'the sailors' friend'. Captain Joshua Slocum called in 1896 on his way to becoming the first solo yachtsman to circumnavigate the globe. The world had begun to embrace the ancient continent.

11

White Australia

By the end of the nineteenth century, the signs of white occupation of the Australian continent were everywhere apparent, except in that third of it where the deserts made settlement unprofitable. In the coastal regions there were cities and large towns, green pastures, gardens and other signs of a civilization brought from afar. Roads and tracks crisscrossed the countryside, although their condition was deplorable and became even worse with the coming of the railway. Fences now separated properties, trees had been ring-barked in millions and stood like grey ghosts of the past, gullies were eroded, the red cedar forests remained mainly in furniture and dust blew on pastures which overstocking and rabbits had thinned back to the clay. With imported trees, shrubs, flowers, weeds, animals and birds, with sign posts, railway stations, bush schools, churches and post offices, the evidence of white settlement was clear. In the cities some people lived and died without ever having seen a kangaroo, wallaby, koala or Aborigine.

Many changes were not for the worse. Sheep and cattle roamed in millions, thousands of square miles were under cultivation, the coasts were opened to shipping and there was regular contact with Europe. Colonial governments generally functioned smoothly, public services operated to the benefit of many, some form of education, although often rudimentary, was available to most whites and the civilizing effects of Christianity restrained many of the greedy and wilful. Social life had been transformed by the telegraph and railway, and the imprint of the latter was enormous. Journeys, which had taken days and even weeks, were reduced in time and immeasurably increased in comfort. People could move from one colony to the other, as well as within a colony, for business, pleasure or family reunions. City newspapers arrived in country districts on the day of printing, luxuries like ice as well as necessities were delivered to remote railway sidings and the days of bush lawlessness were over.

There was little attempt to innovate on the ideas and forms that the settlers had brought with them to Australia, whether of the mind or in material things. This was especially evident in the buildings, public and private, although the homes of the workers and the poor showed some distinctive variations from those in the old countries. In the first decades of settlement necessity had also forced some variation from preconceived forms. Trees were plentiful so homes were built with timber footings and exteriors, bark roofs and earthen floors; the slab hut became the first symbol of the penetration of the continent. A roofed veranda was introduced, which proved effective in combating the heat of summer, provided a place of respite and entertainment in the evenings and a ready-made beginning to additions when another room or sleep-out was needed.

Bark for roofs, being porous, was unsatisfactory, so bark gave way to wooden shingles and they, in turn, to galvanized iron. By the end of the nineteenth century iron began to fall from favour to be replaced by terracotta tiles. The iron roof had proved a useful catchment area for water, which was collected in tanks, both above and underground. The low rainfall and meagre creeks in many inland areas made tanks vital to even reasonable domestic comfort. By mid-century weatherboards had replaced slabs for walls and clay had given way to floorboards so that the construction of the Australian home was settled. It varied from its English counterpart in the materials used and in the addition of the veranda, while the widespread use of galvanized iron, even for walls, introduced a harshness that only time and rust could soften.

The interior of most homes was simplicity itself with a centrally placed passageway from which, normally, four rooms ran off although two were often as many as the poor could manage. The kitchen had become part of the house by the 1890s and, in the sewered areas of the cities, the lavatory had moved into or adjacent to the bathroom. In the suburbs each house had a backyard with a clothesline held up by a clothes-prop, a few fruit trees and a patch for vegetables. In the front of the house, if space permitted, exotic flowers, shrubs and trees were grown, often with the addition of a patch of lawn.

The older, inner suburbs had their rows of terraces, where life was often enhanced due to proximity to markets and places of entertainment. The rough but efficient furniture of earlier times was being replaced with imitations of English styles, while prints of scenes familiar only to those born in, or who had visited, the British Isles and Europe adorned walls. In the homes of the more affluent there was a piano around which entertainment of a genteel kind prevailed while in others they made do with a fiddle. At Christmas, families groaned and sweated before roast turkey or chicken followed by plum pudding. The heat was mocked by holly, strewn on a tree branch in the corner.

The main variation from the houses of the British Isles was seen in the tendency to build lightly-framed, semi-permanent structures in wood although the first brick veneer structure in the world was built at Swan Hill, Victoria, in 1850. Covering the studs with hessian over which paper was pasted to keep out the draughts and to give some semblance of comfort and decorum often made the inner walls of houses. Such houses were built as cheaply as possible and they could be abandoned if unsaleable. It was not uncommon to move them from one place to another, as happened when goldfields ran down. The vastness of the country, combined with the readiness of its inhabitants to pack up and move on, contributed a sense of impermanence to dwelling places and to aspects of life itself. Immigrants from countries where there was solidity in the construction of houses, even if gathered together in little more than slums, often found the Australian experience both different and daunting.

In some instances homes and public buildings of genuine beauty were constructed in sandstone, bluestone and other materials of a lasting nature that were locally available. The earliest building of merit, Old Government House at Parramatta, was begun under Hunter in 1799 and completed by Macquarie in 1816. It was a colonial replica of the country mansions of eighteenth century England, and, with chaste lines, classic portico and standing on a magnificent domain, Old Government House was a reminder of imperial authority in the days of penal servitude. Although Charles Joseph La Trobe, first superintendent and later lieutenant- governor of Victoria, brought a prefabricated house with him from England in 1839, later governors in the colonies built stately mansions but none surpassed that at Parramatta for its quiet dignity.

The wealthy, who had become so from commerce or squatting, built imposing residences in town or country – Como in Melbourne, Carthona in Sydney, Ralahyne in Brisbane and, perhaps the finest of all, Booloominbah at Armidale in New South Wales. They all could have stood their own with the homes of the lesser gentry in England. In the cities, along Macquarie Street in Sydney, North Terrace in Adelaide and Collins Street in Melbourne, commerce and government constructed buildings of impressive grandeur, while the buildings of provincial towns, especially Bendigo and Ballarat rivalled, and in some measure surpassed, those of the capitals. Built on the wealth that had accrued from gold, the buildings along Lydiard Street in Ballarat were striking for their dignity and restrained opulence. In Tasmania the simple Georgian houses of St John Street, Launceston, were a tribute to the restraint and good sense of their owners. Nevertheless, nothing of all this said as much about the Australian experience as did the humble, flimsy bush home.

Church architecture soon developed into rudimentary Gothic as is still evident in the ruins of the Anglican church at Port Arthur. St John's Catholic Church at Richmond, Tasmania, began as a gem of colonial simplicity but was gothicised in the late 1850s by alterations and an added tower. The Gothic Revival was given considerable impetus through the influence exercised by the master English architect and designer Augustus Pugin on Catholic churches in Tasmania, which gradually spread across the continent. Some fine cathedrals were built in the capital cities, while the country towns rivalled each other with their smaller versions of the same. The Anglican cathedral in Goulburn was an outstanding example while, in Bendigo, the Catholics were able to draw on the financial legacy of a remarkable Prussian-born priest, George Backhaus, to construct a cathedral which can fairly claim to be the finest ecclesiastical building in the land and stands with some of the glories of Europe.

The familiar, the venerable and the proven had won in architecture. In only one type of building, the hotel, did the purely functional achieve a distinctive form before the end of the century. It was immediately recognizable to whoever was seeking refreshment, a meal, a bed or all three, as was often the case in a land where distances counted little and so many were on the move. The larger hotels were generally of two storeys with the upper having a balcony, often encased in cast-iron lace painted black or white. On the ground floor there were one or more bars, a private parlour for guests, a ladies lounge, billiards room, dining room and kitchen with the pervasively sweet odour of alcoholic drinks greeting the thirsty everywhere. Out the back stood the stables and perhaps a row of rooms for lodgers and for the display of wares by commercial travellers. Upstairs the rooms were let, with shared bathrooms and lavatories in the middle of the corridor.

Some hotels were monuments to the affluence of a period, like Craigs in Ballarat and the Shamrock at Bendigo, which were built in the great days of gold. They were fit to lodge royalty or Australia's world famous singer Nellie Melba whose sensibilities, and imperious nature, were such that she demanded that the chimes of the clock on the nearby Bendigo Town Hall be silenced throughout the night when she slept at the Shamrock. In the smaller towns, the pubs, like the School of Arts Hotel, at Roma in Queensland, were a mecca to farmers and their wives on a Friday after shopping; to Catholics for a 'Holy Hour' after Sunday Mass; to all for wedding receptions, club activities, electioneering and the exchange of news on the weather, wheat and wool prices, and the general woes and joys of life.

The Australian pub also enshrined the ethos of a society that, outside the home, revolved around the male and his need for companionship with his own kind, which had had its origins in the early pastoral period. Shouting by buying rounds of drinks in turn was everywhere prevalent and was regarded by some as the foundation stone of drunkenness and alcoholism. Marcus Clarke called Australia 'a nation of drunkards' and became one himself, while a steady stream of overseas visitors, so many of whom put their repetitious reminiscences in print, went out of their way to deplore the demon drink. Priests prayed, parsons railed and ladies ran temperance tea-and-cake parties to wean their men onto less potent beverages. Meanwhile cordial factories and breweries abounded with every town of any consequence boasting one at least. Refinements in the brewing process and the use of refrigeration, which began in Victoria, gradually spread and beer replaced spirits as the staple drink, causing less harmful effects to the health and sanity of its devotees.

Three-quarters of the total population of 3,750,000 at the turn of the century were Australian-born. With two-thirds of that total living in New South Wales or Victoria and only one in three of its inhabitants residing outside a city or town, Australians, in the main, were urbanites and easterners. Whatever minor differences arose among them, they generally shared a dual allegiance to Australia and Britain. Australia, to most, was the land of their birth but Britain was still called 'Home', even by many who had never visited there. Few local traditions had been created and, in the schools, the teaching was necessarily British in content. The Union Jack was run up on flagpoles outside schools on Monday mornings while the children gathered around to express a loyalty most of them were unable to fathom. Maps of the world, at school or in the homes, were splashed with a vast swathe of red to denote an Empire encircling the globe, with the high seas controlled by a 'Glorious Navy'. British symbols from bulldogs to Kipling, from Shakespeare to Dickens, war heroes from Drake to Wellington and the great universities of Oxford and Cambridge were treasured as part of the

Australian heritage. The Irish did not stand aloof from all of this, especially in country areas where they normally attended government-run schools. Although they still heard stories of Ireland's woes, such things counted for little in a society where time, distance and some affluence had blurred memory, love and hatred.

The one thing that seemed to be lacking as Australia moved towards the new century was the administrative and political unity it had enjoyed in the days when the Governor of New South Wales was also governor of the whole. An attempt to revive this unity was made in 1851 when Charles Fitzroy was appointed Governor-General of all Queen Victoria's Australian possessions. The position had lapsed by 1856, but the idea of unity was taken up subsequently by some to whom colonies were unwholesome divisions. Gavan Duffy, an Irish patriot and former editor of Ireland's leading nationalist paper, *The Nation*, settled in Victoria and served as premier in the 1870s. He first introduced the idea of a conference to discuss federation in 1857 and claimed in 1890, when Henry Parkes had captured the limelight, that he was the principal agent in the early federation movement, as well as its unwearied organizer. He told Parkes that, for him, 'The flowers gathered from so much seed make such a scanty bouquet.'

The differing fiscal policies created friction, especially between New South Wales, South Australia and Victoria, and local jealousies based on political factors negated any steps towards bringing the colonies under one government. Nevertheless, interest in union was revived in the early 1880s, because external pressures engendered the fear that Germany had its eyes on New Guinea and that France had designs on the New Hebrides. France's intention to make New Caledonia a convict base was regarded with suspicion and fear lest escaped convicts settle in Australia and seep the stain into another generation. Internal developments also helped – the railways linked the eastern, mainland colonies, many manufacturing ventures had an inter-colonial market and some newspapers and journals had a continental reading public. The trade unions were no longer local institutions but had become powerful inter-colonial bodies, which saw themselves as representing workers throughout Australia. The lesson of the depression had pushed the middle classes into a realization that economic management needed inter-colonial co-operation rather than the rivalry, which had been increasingly evident in tariff barriers and sterile competition.

The first definite step towards federation was taken with the formation of a Federal Council in 1883 which anticipated having legislative powers over Australian relations with the Pacific and over the influx of criminals from New Caledonia. New South Wales, suspicious of the other colonies, stood aloof so that the existence of the Council was inconsequential and it last met in Melbourne in 1889. In that year the need for adequate defences was pressed home by a British military advisor who feared that the continent would be vulnerable were it attacked, although he left it unclear by what power. On 24 October 1889, Henry Parkes seized the opportune moment to propose a conference to discuss a federation although neither he, nor anyone else, including the vast majority of the inhabitants who already thought of themselves as Australians, had any firm ideas on what it all meant.

Nevertheless, the Australian Natives Association in Victoria, some recently formed bodies in New South Wales called Federal Leagues and organizations with commercial interests gave the movement impetus. Over all the deliberations that followed hovered the shadow of depression, bank crashes and drought, which made the economic motive of making Australia a safe place for investment strong. Any sense of sharing a common nationality had little to do with the whole development.

A conference was held in Melbourne in February 1890 attended by political leaders from all the colonies, including New Zealand, and it was agreed that tariffs were the main obstacle to federation. Parkes, with a fine turn of phrase about 'a crimson thread of kinship' running through them all, boosted hopes and a convention to work out the exact nature of the proposed federal body was proposed. In March 1891 the convention met in Sydney, with Parkes in the chair, and a draft constitution, largely the work of Samuel Griffith, Premier of Queensland, was accepted. Griffith's draft was substantially adhered to throughout all the debates of the ensuing decade.

The central concept, which governed all the deliberations, was the desire to retain autonomy for the colonies once they became states. The federal body was only required to co-ordinate such vital matters as customs and defence, postal and telegraph services, currency, immigration and foreign affairs. Lawyer-politicians dominated the proceedings. In 1897–8, a bill based on Griffith's original of 1891 was drafted to constitute the Commonwealth of Australia. Parkes, who died in 1896, never saw his work come to fruition, but he had firmly held that 'Australia ought to be Mistress of the Southern Seas'. With personal wealth per head considerably higher than in America it was safe to assume that his hope was well founded, temporarily at least.

The workers were not so sure of the future and spokesmen of their movement warned that federation would cause the Labor Party to be overwhelmed unless the proposed constitution was thoroughly democratic in electoral divisions. Unsurprisingly, business interests saw much benefit from federation with one of their number arguing, convincingly, that it would provide him and his fellows with 'a market as large as the whole of Australia'. A 'simple farmer' in Tasmania expressed both a grandiose and self-interested hope. He looked to the day when, with federation, they would 'found a great and glorious nation under the Southern Cross, and meat will be cheaper'. Imperial statesmen in Britain, realizing that there was no longer a possibility of bringing the whole Empire into an imperial federation, settled for less and gave cautious assent to its little brother in the form of an Australian federation.

In the midst of all this manoeuvring an Australian cricket team proved, in 1898, that a united Australian side was better than anything the 'old country' could throw at her. Five Tests were played in Sydney, Melbourne and Adelaide and, watched by a total of 332,000 spectators, Australia won four Tests to England's one. Australia went on to win the Ashes in England in 1899. To many of those spectators at the home Tests it was surely the case that federation could only improve, but not lessen, the combined strength on the playing field and elsewhere if needed, of a united Australia. Perhaps conscious of the expressions of colonial superiority Lord Beauchamp, the newly appointed governor of New South Wales, decided to remind Australians of their convict past on his arrival in May 1899. He surpassed the bounds of obtuseness generally accepted as prevailing among aristocrats by quoting a couplet from Kipling,

Greeting! Your birthstain have you turned to good,
Forcing strong wills perverse to steadfastness.

After two referenda, five colonies voted in favour of the Constitution Bill with Western Australia waiting to see the outcome of the vote in the east. The Bill then passed through both Houses at Westminster between May and July 1900. Western Australia, led by its cautious Premier John Forrest, who had been one of the country's greatest explorers, joined at a referendum on

31 July. There was an overwhelming 'Yes' vote from the goldfields, where a petition had been got up for separation if the Western Australians did not vote for federation. Drawn from all six colonies, most of the diggers were unaware that hitherto they had been anything but Australians. In England, Victoria, secure after sixty years on her regal throne, nonetheless had some misgivings about the use of the word 'Commonwealth' given its connection with the spectre of Cromwellian days. She preferred 'Dominion' instead, but bowed to the inevitable and consented to an entity called the Commonwealth of Australia coming into being on 1 January 1901.

The Constitution, on one level, was a triumph for common sense and it was partially modelled on the Canadian and United States experiments. On the other hand, recognition that Commonwealth meant a unity of separate colonies, now called states but retaining their own sovereignty in internal matters, was crucial to acceptance of the new federation. Few were aware that a great deal of energy and money would be spent, in the next century and longer, trying to resolve the inherent contradiction implicit in separate sovereignties. The number of members in the House of Representatives from each state was to be proportional to population, but the Senate was to have equal representation from each state in the hope that those elected to it would serve the interests of their states rather than those of a party. It was an ideal to which the reality of political life soon put paid.

Federation did not come about quickly or easily, especially in New South Wales where a combination of uncertainty on the part of politicians, unease within the Labor Party and a reluctance to abandon free trade helped to confuse the electorate. In South Australia some manufacturers were unhappy about unrestrained competition from Victoria and their employees shared their fears. The negative vote in Queensland, where over forty per cent of the those who participated in the referendum was against federation, remained inexplicable except on the cane fields in a north distant from the centres of political power and where many workers did not feel themselves to be a part of Australia in any useful sense.

The majority of Australians were federationists although few became emotional or excited about the whole affair. The creation of the Commonwealth was a simple, public act ratifying what they internally accepted, the reality of white Australia. They had always been able to move from one part of it to the other. They met the same kind of people who spoke the same language with only minor variations for slang and accent and who ate, drank and dressed as they did. They were all proud of Melba as she won acclaim in the opera houses of Europe, and of their soldiers who, like lion cubs, had 'rallied to the dam' in South Africa. In vain the *Bulletin* called the new flag of Union Jack and Southern Cross a bastard symbol of Australia. To most Australians the symbol was insignificant and nothing was made of the fact that federation, the most significant long-ranging step in Australia's white history, had been achieved without any civil discord of an extreme kind. Only thirty years before a much smaller country, Italy, had won its unity after centuries of struggle and bloodshed.

There were three main groupings in the first Parliament. Edmund Barton, an urbane Sydney lawyer, was Prime Minister and leader of the Liberal Protectionists, who were convinced that progressive but judicious reform was the right path to progress. The Labor Party held the balance of power in both Houses. Led by John Watson, it differed from the Liberals in that it wanted more radical and rapid reform, but Barton could rely on its support to govern. George Reid led the third group made up of Conservative Free-Traders. In effect they became the opposition and had little to say except that they were against protective tariffs, which meant that they were opposed to the Liberals, and that they would have no truck with socialism, by which they meant the Labor Party. There were some very able men in the first Cabinet – Deakin, Lyne, Turner, Kingston and Forrest – who added considerably to the prestige of the new Federal Parliament.

The days of early, penal Australia were also represented in the person of William Groom, member for the Darling Downs. Groom had come to Australia, aged sixteen, as a convict on the *Hashemy* in 1849. Six years later he was sentenced again on a charge of stealing gold and served time on the roads. Notwithstanding his past, he was six times mayor of Toowoomba and sat for over thirty years in the Queensland Parliament. His time was short in the Federal sphere as he died on 8 August 1901. His passing symbolized the end of an era – convict Australia was dead and buried and most Australians preferred to forget that it had ever been. William Groom, member of the House of Representatives, had reminded them briefly of its importance, although the last imperial convict, an original Fenian from the days of the *Catalpa* incident in Western Australia, was not pardoned until 1906.

Lacking its own place to sit, the Federal Parliament met in Melbourne although the Constitution had decreed that its eventual site was to be in New South Wales and at least 100 miles from Sydney. All those elected to

Parliament showed a determination to keep Australia British, and all but two were bent on maintaining the continent as the possession of an exclusively white population. Barton knew that if they could run financial matters smoothly, deal firmly with the question of non-white immigration and leave the old colonies, now transformed into states with their own political and vice-regal apparatus to run their own affairs, all would be well. In his resolve to keep the country white, Barton was ably assisted by his Collingwood-born Attorney-General, Alfred Deakin, who was member for Ballarat.

Deakin's temperate racism was oddly quirked in that he wanted to deny entry to the Japanese because of their good qualities, which he feared would result in their outstripping the more leisurely Australians in endeavour. Labor, backing Barton to the hilt, had members who talked about the danger of making 'a mongrel nation' if 'the coloured sheep' were not culled to preserve its 'racial purity', and there was general agreement in the Parliament on these propositions. The decision to introduce a White Australia policy was a conscious one with which the vast majority of Australians agreed. It had its economic overtones, but no one reading or hearing the debates in the Commonwealth Parliament could have mistaken the general thrust of the arguments for the exclusion of non-whites – they were essentially racist.

Asiatics and the hapless Kanakas, who it was decided would be refused entry after 1904 and who were to be returned to their home islands by 1906, were the main butt of the exclusionist argument, but colour itself was proposed as the forbidden factor by the Labor members. Those Kanakas who were born in Australia or who had been residents since 1879 could remain. Some of the rest had come voluntarily, a few happily, and there were those who feared to go back to the islands, but the law took its course. They were black and hence unwanted, and in the end 4,269 were returned 'home' while 1,654 were permitted to stay. For other coloured races the Parliament devised a dictation test of fifty words in a European language to which undesirable immigrants would be subject. To appease the Japanese, European was later changed to any prescribed language, but the effect, in its power to exclude non-white or other undesirable entrants, was the same. In this way the Commonwealth, now ruling over a continent that 113 years previously had been the exclusive domain of a black race, ensured that, temporarily, its citizens would only be whites.

The Aborigines, depleted by disease and murder and disheartened at the loss of practically everything that had made them a people, had all but vanished from large parts of the continent. The remainder, nevertheless, continued to resist being submerged in the culture and social structures of the whites. The pernicious idea of the Great Chain of Being which placed the blacks one degree above brutes, the pseudo-scientific pronouncements of phrenologists who measured skulls and attempted to prove that the intellect of the black was inferior, and Darwin's survival of the fittest theory combined to soothe the conscience of those who, for their own material gain, had contributed to the decline of a whole race. The tragedy of the part-Aborigines who could not merge into either society was apparent in the history of the Breelong blacks with the violent outbreak led by Jimmy Governor in north-central New South Wales in 1900. In 1972 Thomas Keneally's novel, *The Chant of Jimmy Blacksmith,* told the Governor story powerfully and brutally and it was made into a film in 1978.

In places where they still lived on in significant numbers, it was decided that protection was the best means of allowing the Aborigines to die out in peace and with some dignity. Reserves were set up in which they had to live unless they were permitted to take approved employment elsewhere. They were legally in the charge of their protectors, they could not receive old-age pensions and they had no status as citizens, which meant that they could not be counted in a census. Above all, they were subject to the constraints of institutionalism and were often under the control of inept and unsympathetic bureaucrats. It was almost as if, now that the whites had taken all from them, the Aborigines were judged as unable to cope for themselves in a land whose fullness they had once possessed.

There is no evidence that the Aborigines, reduced now to a remnant of less than 40,000, were either aware of, or responsive to, federation. Their problem was survival which no flag or symbol could make secure. The new century, however, saw them granted a form of equality in one area of importance to the whites. When their skills could be used cheaply, they were welcome in the workforce and the Aboriginal reserves became nurseries providing a cheap source of labour for the pastoral industry in particular. The union movement, so resolutely opposed to coloured labour, encouraged them to join its ranks and, because of their particular aptitude, they were welcome as shearers and some participated in the shearers' strikes of the early 1890s.

At Broome, Beagle Bay and La Grange in the Kimberley, Christian missionaries had worked among the Aborigines since the 1880s. Working as stockmen in the outback and as pearl divers, the blacks had been treated badly in the polyglot community that grew up around Broome. The efforts of the missionaries, whether Protestant or Catholic, were often without apparent success. Bishop Gibney of Perth thought the Aborigines were a 'splendid race' and another missionary said they were industrious, co-operative and friendly. Daisy Bates, her first marriage to 'Breaker' Morant now long in the past, worked with Gibney for the betterment of the Aborigines and lived herself among the Kimberley blacks for some months. Her vast, personal knowledge of Aboriginal languages, customs and beliefs, and her dignity as a white woman who went to live among them caused the blacks to name her Kabbarli or grandmother.

Many later critics took pains to decry the work of the Christian missionaries, condemning it as harmful and destructive at the worst and mere paternalism at the best. The missionaries did, however, perform one priceless task in that they awakened some form of conscientious response to the Aborigines among the whites. Without their civilizing influence there would have been scarcely any full-blood Aborigines left because the missionaries worked at a time of unenlightened governments and a white community imbued with barbaric ideas which could have, as in Tasmania, resulted in the virtual extermination of the blacks in the north of the continent.

In the same way as the population retained the major aspects of the parent societies in the British Isles, so also the religious denominations repeated in Australia the composition and flavour of their origins, and their beliefs were preached with the same emphasis and accents of their homelands. Religion was observed in a quiet and orderly manner without outbursts of fervent enthusiasm because the ostentatious, the unusual or the foolish were not the way of Australians. Methodism went through periods of restrained revivalism in New South Wales and South Australia, and its daughter, the Salvation Army, first established in South Australia in 1881, grew rapidly and had representatives in all the colonies by 1891, when its founder, General William Booth, visited Australia to see for himself the progress it had made. No sects of any consequence were born, no martyrs made, and no saints proclaimed but every so often a bigot declaimed against the Catholic Church and its largely Irish adherents. Yet when the Archbishop of Sydney, Cardinal Moran, stood, unsuccessfully as it happened, as a candidate to represent New South Wales at the Constitution Convention in 1897 he was supported by many Protestants.

Men of principle, who remained firmly committed to the Judaeo–Christian tradition with its accompanying moral standards, carried out the secularisation of education and of the state. They were also committed to the idea that church and state needed to be separate, although they did not recognize that the virtual elimination of the Bible from the schools would result in future generations losing one of the most precious well-springs of their culture. In this society there was a determination to bury forever the patronage, power, hatreds and divisions that had so marked the history of the old world, but the spirit of Christianity remained alive and only one person in 500 stated that he or she had no religion. Nonetheless, the diverse denominations claiming to be Christian resembled a spiritual Tower of Babel as they ranged from Bush Baptists to Callithumpians with every other shade in between.

Hospitals, for which the governments met the capital costs, were mainly run by charitable organizations and staffed by women – lay and religious – and countless acts of unsung private charity sustained the needy, especially in times of hardship like the 1890s. The positive change in religious attitudes and the adherence to Christian values in England after the middle of the nineteenth century had an effect on social legislation when many convinced Christians immigrated to the colonies. Votes for women, factory acts, pensions and other similar enactments, often hailed as indicative of a new spirit at work, had their basis in Christian morality. Among those who thought, worked and made sacrifices of time and money for the 'good' society, there were many who found inspiration in Christian socialism. Edward Bellamy, whose influence on the early Australian workers' movement through his novel *Looking Backward* was greater than that of Karl Marx, taught that Christian socialism was the fulfilment of Christ's teaching on love for thy neighbour, and many Australians worked with that as their ideal.

As a result, in the trade unions, throughout the Labor Party and among the Liberals, there were many men and women prepared to stand up, not only for the poor and disadvantaged, but also for the right of the ordinary citizen, by virtue of work and frugality, to enjoy an ensured and decent standard of living. The voices of Marx and other justifiable exponents of international solidarity among workers were heard, and in their wake followed claims to universal economic equality. Such claims aroused unfilled hopes among some and moved others, who saw their own wealth threatened, to attempt to negate the gains made by the workers and their representatives.

By beating up the hare of international socialism, conservatives were able to create unity among themselves and arouse groundless fears among timid Australians. The Labor Party, while embracing wide divergences of opinion within its ranks, settled down as a valid representative body of the generality of Australians and its, not infrequent, bouts of flirting with doctrinaire creeds were always of short duration. Those ardent spirits whose purpose was the destruction rather than the containment of capitalism found the Labor Party a weak vessel and deserted it while others, no less ardent, remained in the Party to defend the defenceless and help to bring some measure of relief to the weak.

The signs of a new age were everywhere apparent. They gradually appeared in the extension of street lighting to the large country towns, together with water, street curbing and guttering, although drainage and sewerage, even in the cities, were often lacking. The cinema and silent pictures, x-rays, the motor car, fast dances and fancy drinks all vied with the theatre, the quack, the horse and buggy, stately waltzes and rum. With the introduction of the hydraulic lift, higher buildings became feasible and, in 1889, the construction of the twelve-storey Australian Provincial Life Assurance Building on the corner of Elizabeth Street and Flinders Lane gave Melbourne one of the tallest buildings in the world. The bicycle had become the most popular means of transport with the introduction of low wheels and pneumatic tyres, and by 1900 there were two cycle paths in Sydney. In the bush the bicycle meant that workers no longer had to walk from place to place in search of a job. Progress, sacred to some and acceptable almost to all, was ascendant and to stand against it was useless.

On 9 May 1901 Melbourne staged the opening of the first Federal Parliament in its Exhibition Building. The Duke of York did the honours, 'Australia' was sung and Tom Roberts painted the scene. In the House of Representatives a formidable group of members took responsibility for the new Commonwealth. Very few of them were new to politics, because ten had been premiers of their colonies, twenty-two had been ministers and fifty-eight were experienced as former members of colonial parliaments. Proud that they were the foundation members of the new democracy, they undertook their task with much seriousness and, because Christianity was still the firmly accepted religion of the majority of the people, they began their deliberations with a plea for God's help and the recitation of the Lord's Prayer.

Despite the pageantry and the optimism, all was not well in the Commonwealth for the longest of all droughts had not broken and sheep numbers had dropped by half, but gold, sugar and wheat helped hold up the economy. Nevertheless, there was much optimism, for unity had been achieved without much rancour or division and the social cohesion that existed was the product of material success. Spiritually, the new Australia was an infant because no great cause, no overwhelming catastrophe, no response to a sign transcending the mundane had contributed to its birth. Australia had been federated because a few men of commonsense, motivated by high motives of patriotism and lesser ones of profit, had said, 'Let there be an Australia'. It was left to others to consummate the vision.

12

A Fledgling Commonwealth

The first and, for a short time, only Commonwealth public servant was Robert Garran, who was appointed on 1 January 1901 as secretary to the Attorney-General's Department as well as parliamentary draftsman. He acted as his own clerk and messenger, wrote the first *Government Gazette,* personally delivered it to the printer and then, without the benefit of an electoral law to guide him, he organized the first federal elections almost single-handed. Garran said that he felt reasonably sure justice had been done to the contending parties. As seven out of nine of the founding Cabinet were lawyers, he probably felt that he was being closely scrutinized. In his spare time, Garran saw to the setting up of the new Commonwealth departments.

A totally new structure had to be developed at the federal level although it could draw upon the previously existing colonial departments in the case of the new Commonwealth Departments of Customs and Postmaster General's. The defence forces, of the former colonies, naval and military, also passed to the Commonwealth with the establishment of a Department of Defence. The others – Prime Minister's, Home Affairs, Treasury, and Attorney General's itself – were entirely new. Garran worked indefatigably, and he was chiefly responsible for the smooth beginning of the Commonwealth structure. His insistence on clear, straightforward language, free from technical jargon became, for a time, a model which others imitated. In collaboration with John Quick, Garran wrote the classic *An Annotated Constitution of the Australian Commonwealth* (1901). By his retirement in 1932 he had served as permanent head of a Commonwealth Department for thirty-two years and had been the trusted counsellor of sixteen governments.

A Public Service Commissioner was appointed to ensure that entry into the service was competitive and that promotion was based on merit rather than patronage. Were the federal structure to work effectively it was readily accepted that judges who possessed the skills necessary to determine the meaning of the Constitution had to be appointed to the new High Court. The matter was particularly important in the sphere of state rights given that each state was to retain a large measure of self-government. By 1903 the High Court was set up. Its prestige was enhanced by the fact that Barton resigned as Prime Minister to sit on it as Senior Judge, Samuel Griffith, who was the principal framer of the Constitution, was Chief Justice and the third member was Richard O'Connor, who had also worked on the Constitution. Therefore the first High Court was in a position to interpret a document which its members had helped formulate.

Meanwhile, the custodians of the parent society in Britain watched the fledgling Commonwealth closely. Some saw evidence of 'racial decline' proved, in their eyes, by the relentless pursuit of wealth, a mania for sport, lack of an intellectual life and an appalling pronunciation. In their judgement the eight-hour day and trade union activity had led to laziness, which allegedly gave birth to the depression of the 1890s. Despite their acquisition of voting rights in the federal sphere, some observers accused Australian women in general of lacking education and refined manners. In short, Australia's first, tentative steps towards a form of nationhood particular to the place and people of its origins did not enhance the estimation of Australians held by their British 'betters'.

Nellie Melba had been acclaimed an opera singer without compare since her debut at Brussels in 1897, her subsequent successes at Covent Garden and throughout Europe. She came home to a tumultuous welcome in 1902 and made £21,000 from concerts in Sydney and Melbourne alone. She noted that the country was still gripped by drought and that much in it was crude and antiquated. Nellie was pained to find that people everywhere had little appreciation of their proper role in society. This point on female servants was well made in her eyes when her cook refused to work on a Sunday. Nellie failed to observe that most female domestics still worked in harsh conditions with keep and wages as low as 10s per week for up to a hundred hours work. In her turn the English writer and commentator on social conditions, Beatrice Webb, said that bad manners, pretentious dress and a marked lack of refined taste were predominant among the women she deigned to meet in Australia.

Amidst the rhetoric and petulance there were serious voices, including that of the former Victorian Minister for Education, Charles Pearson, who said that Australia, with its reliance on state interference in the economy and social life, the increasing public debt and the swollen growth of the cities was a deplorable example for other white peoples. In general, the common denominator of English opinion was that somehow Australia had been wayward. It had not been content to remain another England in the south, it showed every sign of being turbulent and, above all, it had mismanaged British capital. John Fortescue, previously noted as a military historian, summed it up by saying that worshipping state socialism was an inevitable road to disaster, although the effective survival of Australia through the depression silenced him.

Despite these criticisms, it was clear that there would be no social revolution in an Australia where the reformers were apace with, if not ahead of, organized unrest. After all the talk of a social laboratory, there was a degree of irony in the fact that Tom Mann, the British trade union leader, was disappointed when he visited Australia in 1904. He was surprised that leaders of the Australian workers, whether of trade unions or the Labor Party, seemed bent on 'civilizing' rather than destroying capitalism. As an antidote, Mann, who was both an idealist and theoretician, formed the Victorian Socialist Party in Melbourne in 1905.

The leaders of the Labor Party, however, remained conscious that their strength lay in practicalities. They were prepared to use power sensibly when given the chance, but as yet the party, formed on the federal level on 8 May 1901 and named the Australian Labor Party in 1908, could not govern alone. John Watson's first Labor government in 1904 lasted four months, which proved that power was so transient as to be futile without a majority in Parliament. Clearly the road to a majority was to persuade enough voters that Labor would govern in the best interests of all. As the *Brisbane Worker* said, it was possible to do greater harm to capitalism with a vote than with a strike.

One remarkable feature of the early years of the Commonwealth was the resilience of rural Australia during the long drought. Nothing had prepared squatters and farmers for such a catastrophe. With sheep numbers fallen dramatically, the wheat crop yielding less than a tenth of the pre-drought harvest, rabbits eating what feed remained, and dust clouding the skies, many small settlers left their few acres with all hope lost. Their wives battled the hardships alongside their menfolk, working long hours inside and outside the homestead and trying to make ends meet when there was a shortage of food or clothing. Often the survivors on large properties were unable to tap a source of capital to tide them over. As a consequence, they were forced to run up debts with local stores and mortgage their land to stock and station companies. The eight-year drought was generally eased by 1903–4 and good times came again, but its effects were not forgotten, especially in the inland parts of New South Wales and in Queensland, although in coastal areas the effects were not as bad.

Amid such matters as drought and depression and the return of the troops from the Boer War, only a few of the more serious-minded noticed the warning of the eminent statistician Timothy Coghlan that the birth rate had declined to 27 per 1,000 in 1900 after reaching 38 per 1000 in 1870. A Royal Commission blamed the decline to selfishness and stated that white Australia could not be maintained unless the rate of national procreation went up. The depression and unemployment, the previously unrestrained development of grim suburbs and the increasing cost of maintaining a family under a policy of compulsory education were not seen as other factors contributing to the decline. Nevertheless, with its own statistical analysis, the Commission, unaware of the rise in immigration before World War I and after World War II, was not wide of the mark in predicting that, with such a trend, there would only be seven million Australians in 1948 and twenty million would not be achieved until the year 2017. In the first five years of the Commonwealth, the economic climate persuaded trade unionists to oppose any widespread immigration, including that from Britain, so no one hoped for relief from that quarter.

The young Commonwealth attempted to continue the work on social legislation begun earlier in the colonies, particularly in the field of disputes between employers and employees. Labor politicians saw industrial legislation as the means to ensure good conditions and adequate wages, while the more conservative view was that such legislation served only to restrain employers or employees from harming the community by lockouts or strikes. The problem for the Commonwealth was whether it possessed powers in a dispute that was restricted to one state. In 1903 a week-long strike among railway workers brought the role of the Commonwealth to the fore. The strike was called off under threat of a Coercion Act.

Labor, holding that the states were powerless in disputes affecting industries with an inter-state element such as the seamen and the railway workers, wanted an arbitration system that would apply to the whole continent. Deakin held out for state rights, but when George Reid became Prime Minister in 1904 he managed to establish a Federal Court of Conciliation and Arbitration, which, as required by the Constitution, only had power over interstate disputes. The very creation of the Federal Court helped to clarify the relationship of the Commonwealth to the states. It also gave the trade unions a more public and responsible role and brought out the great talents of Henry Bournes Higgins, who became the second President of the Arbitration Court.

Higgins brought down the most far-reaching decision in Australia's industrial history on 8 November 1907. The facts in the case were simple, but the social ramifications immense. For each harvester made by H.V. McKay at Sunshine, Victoria, McKay had to pay the Commonwealth £6 in excise duty, unless he could prove that his workers received 'fair and reasonable' wages. This requirement was part of Deakin's 'New Protection', which had been introduced to ensure that manufacturers who benefited from tariffs on competing imports should charge reasonable prices and pay reasonable wages, as well as ensure decent conditions for their workers.

To order a Court to interpret 'fair and reasonable', was, to Higgins's, an act that lacked both qualities, but he brought in his judgement nonetheless and ruled against McKay. He decided that profits did not enter into the matter, likening the hiring of labour to buying raw materials. Taking as his norm the requirements of an unskilled labourer with four dependants who needed to live in 'frugal comfort' in a civilized community, he ruled that the adult male wage should be a minimum £2 2s for a six-day working week. Higgins ignored the fact that many men had no dependents, or more or less than four. Equally he ignored women with dependants, many of whom worked in factories for less than £1 per week. In effect, his judgement enshrined the principle of a male minimum wage based on the need of the worker to receive, rather than on the ability of industry to pay. It also established the family as the central unit of the industrial workforce and, as a corollary, the economic dependence of women on men. The history of wage fixing in Australia for nearly seventy years always looked back to the Harvester judgement. Over the years, it assumed legendary status, almost in the way Magna Carta had done in the disputes between the king and the barons and few recognized that Higgins had drawn his fundamental concept of a just wage from Pope Leo's XIII's encyclical, *Rerum Novarum*, published in 1891.

The second Prime Minister, Alfred Deakin, was first and foremost a philosopher, but he threw himself wholeheartedly into politics. He never reaped the rewards that sometimes befall those whose gifts are unsurpassed by their peers. Needing the support of Labor to govern, he found that he could only apply his principles provided Labor concurred. In some ways he led, in others he was pushed, but in the end, dispirited and broken in health, he had nowhere to turn for constant support except to that group of so-called liberals, protectionists and conservatives which he assuredly despised. They had already discovered that, by making noises against the 'socialist tiger', which, in the words of Reid, would turn 'the free citizens of the Commonwealth into members of one great Government gang', they could awaken a response in those who feared socialism. Deakin was sensible and just and he realized that Labor's posturing about collective ownership of the means of production were mostly high flown sentiment and, to the extent that they were not, would be rejected by a staunchly conservative electorate, which applauded moderate change when it served its own interests.

Labor itself was beginning to sense that the time to govern in its own right was coming because its vote kept increasing at succeeding elections, the trade union movement was growing and the Catholic vote was solidly behind it. In 1908 the Party withdrew its support from Deakin and Andrew Fisher formed the second Labor government. Under this pressure, Deakin fused his liberal followers with those who had previously espoused Free Trade and a new Liberal Party was born. The result was that Labor could not maintain its majority, and after only six months in office, Fisher, bemused at the turn of events, was out of office. Deakin's act inaugurated the beginning of two party politics and thereby gave the electors some chance of knowing where candidates stood on policy issues. Furthermore, the 'Fusion' among liberals clearly identified the Labor Party, for the first time, as a distinctive force in its own right. Under these circumstances the Labor Party had no choice but to try to win sufficient support from the electorate to govern securely without the need to seek support from other parties. To embark on such a course was to ensure that the voices of those socialists who still remained within the Party would henceforth cry in the wilderness of rational pragmatism.

For the third and last time, Alfred Deakin was sworn in as Prime Minister on 2 June 1909, and he continued to foster and implement moderate and progressive policies. By his life's work, he deserves to be remembered as the part creator and foremost defender of federation. In his resistance to state aggression, his bridling of centralist tendencies and his promotion of harmonious relations between the Commonwealth and the states, he remained firm to those qualities of the Constitution that were lasting in value. Charming, brilliant and totally committed to the welfare of his country, Deakin was also, according to Garran, utterly sincere and straightforward and he hated 'political tricks, manoeuvres, and opportunism'. In Deakin, genuine liberalism had meaning because he believed in destroying class privilege and in abolishing laws against trade unionism. His ideal was a just and progressive Australia in which the poor, the sick and the old would all be protected, and policies would be implemented to give equal political rights to all citizens without regard to wealth or standing. With his passing as Prime Minister in April 1910 and his retirement in 1913, Australia lost the services of one of her finest sons.

During the first decade of the Commonwealth, Australians began to perceive that their future was bound up, not merely with the mother country but also with other countries in the region. The realization was dawning that Australia was a large island continent with a small, white population situated in the south of the vast Pacific and Indian Oceans. In any case, Britain had its own worries with the emergence of a powerful Germany, which was increasing its presence in the North Sea. Although 451 volunteers from New South Wales and Victoria left to help put down the Boxer Rebellion which had broken out in China in 1900, surprisingly, no fears were raised of a Chinese invasion of Australia. Closer to home, there was, however, concern about the responsible administration of Papua. As early as 1883, Queensland had 'annexed' the south-eastern portion of New Guinea but Britain refused to ratify the act, and in 1884 it set up a British protectorate there based on Port Moresby. Four years later Britain formally annexed the territory itself and, under the moderately enlightened rule of William MacGregor as administrator, the urge of the settlers and traders to exploit the natives was at least curbed.

The Commonwealth reluctantly undertook responsibility for British New Guinea in 1902 and in 1906 it became the Australian Territory of Papua. However, effective Commonwealth control was spasmodic and chaotic until the appointment of John Hubert Plunkett Murray as lieutenant governor in 1908. Murray was a generally benevolent ruler who supported the settlers while remaining friendly with the natives, whom he defended and encouraged. Australian involvement in Papua, however, could not disguise the fact that other nations had firmly entrenched interests in the Pacific. The Germans were in charge of north-eastern New Guinea, New Britain and New Ireland, the Dutch had held the western half of New Guinea since 1828 and France's involvement in New Caledonia and its interest in the New Hebrides were well known. All of these were distant, European powers, but Japan was geographically located in the Pacific and it was undergoing rapid change.

Britain had signed a treaty with Japan in 1902 which, ironically, made Japan Australia's ally in the Pacific. In 1904 the Japanese inflicted ignominious defeats on the Russians. This aroused fears that Japan was no longer a slumbering volcano but one that had awakened and was likely to erupt the 'Yellow Peril' down upon Australia, thereby endangering its people and its peaceful prosperity. The Japanese protested that they were a peace loving race and lacked any imperialistic intentions, but Henry Lawson begged in vain 'Hold them, Ivan' but Russia, although a major European power, was no match for the Japanese.

With no foreign policy of its own, no defence forces of significance and no diplomatic representatives overseas, Australia left concern for its security to Britain. Nevertheless, a first, scarcely noticeable, crack in the bond of imperial relations took place in 1905 when Deakin said that 'next to our own nation we place our kindred in America' and tentatively looked to the Americans as possible defenders in the Pacific. Washington refused this role, but the visit of the sixteen ships of the 'Great White Fleet' from the United States in 1908 reassured all Australians that American dominance in the Pacific was sufficient to dispel any fears from Japan.

Despite the cries of nationalists at the time of federation, it was decided to continue hiring an Australian squadron from the British Navy, thereby avoiding the huge cost involved in having one built. Likewise, it was agreed that a small standing army would be sufficient for defence, although it had to be commanded by an Englishman, Major-General Edward Hutton, because the Defence Minister thought it proper to get 'one of the best men in the Empire to start this machine'. The title 'Royal Australian Navy' was made official in 1911, and in 1913 an Australian Navy of seven vessels sailed into Sydney Harbour, led by the battle-cruiser HMAS *Australia*. Under Vice-Admiral Creswell, who rightly became known as the 'Father of the Royal Australian Navy', the Australian navy was no longer under British command. The event stirred up much national pride, of avowals of loyalty to England and of a determination to maintain responsibility for Australia. This in turn would contribute to the 'fabric of Empire', which was held to be the guarantor of peace in the world.

If there was minimal strategic significance in such a minuscule navy, it was clearly possible to build a citizens' militia, as distinct from a standing army. The Labor Party, with William Morris Hughes beating the drum of national defence, had included compulsory military training in its platform, despite opposition from members of the trade union movement who asked what it was that the working class found worthy of defence. The trade unionists were threatened with prosecution and reminded that sufficient individuals, invariably sanctified with the title 'the people' on such occasions, were in favour of compulsory military training, which made all opposition absurd. No one needed reminding that a policy as odious to other races as that called White Australia might eventually require that it be defended in ways that were not merely verbal.

The British Field Marshal, Kitchener, arrived by invitation in 1909 and visited the military installations in each state. He set the seal of authority on the planned militia, and 1911 saw military training made compulsory for all males, starting with children aged twelve and going through to young adults aged twenty-five. Isolation from any form of organized and militant solidarity among workers, the prevailing ethos of pragmatism and loyalty to Empire, and the already formulated plans of German mobilization in Europe had turned the ears of the Labor leaders away from the voices that proclaimed the insanity of war.

Temporarily, minority opposition to compulsory military training was silenced by grossly unjust and repressive measures resulting in nearly 28,000 prosecutions and the imprisonment of 5,732 citizens in military gaols between 1911 and 1914. Rumours of war did not prevent the government proceeding with other developments in the new Commonwealth. In early 1913 the valley of the Molonglo River, nestling among gentle hills on the southern tableland of New South Wales, was still a place of much solitude, as well as being in the grip of a drought. By Wednesday 12 March, all had changed. The river was swollen and the land green and lush from rain. More significantly, the tranquillity had gone forever because on that day the new capital of Australia was launched and christened with its ancient Aboriginal name of Canberra. The choice of the site had taken until 1908 with much travel, restless nights, banter and band waggoning among federal politicians and their staffs. Dalgety, Tumut and the Yass–Canberra area were the final contenders and the latter won in the House of Representatives by six votes over Dalgety and by two over Tumut in the Senate.

The Minister for Home Affairs was King O'Malley. Of uncertain origins, possibly Canadian or American, he fluctuated from the sane and wise to the flamboyant and unbalanced. Two of his ideas for the new Capital Territory were of the latter variety, for he wanted to call it 'Shakespeare' and keep it dry of all alcoholic beverages. He succeeded with his wowserism – to the intense discomfort of a generation of residents of the capital who had to travel to nearby Queanbeyan to quench their thirst. The proceedings by the Molonglo on 12 March failed to impress many Australians, who thought that the whole undertaking of building a capital city was insane, extravagant and pointless. The die was cast, however, and the bush capital was started in a place of such natural beauty that others eventually concluded that only Providence could have guided politicians to choose it. As a symbol the capital was already one of white supremacy for almost all the Aboriginal people of that region, heedless in any case of such matters as chieftains and their need for a capital, had long since departed. They left their traces in the lilting softness of place names and in a few of their mixed-blood descendants.

The generality of Australian citizens went about their business paying little heed to the doings of their politicians except at election time. After the introduction of compulsory voting in Queensland in 1914, the practice spread to the Commonwealth in 1924, and then to the other states, although South Australia resisted the move until 1942. Such a procedure caused the citizens to go through the formality at least of casting a vote. It also reinforced the weak, the marginalized and the uneducated who may have been disinclined to exercise their right to vote without some minimal form of coercion. As time went on it became the case that most Australians voted out of habit, rather than through compulsion.

Sometimes voices were raised about the expense of maintaining seven separate Parliaments, six Governors and the Governor-General, all of whom were imported from Britain to keep up the vaunted ties of Empire. The voices went unheeded. The growth in rulers, elected and nominated, was matched and outstripped by a greater one in public servants. This growth was partly due to the determination to maintain the full apparatus of government in the colonies until 1900 and, latterly, in the states. It also came about because of the successive waves of new people who had come to Australia since the 1830s. In the ten years 1904–14, the reawakened desire to populate the continent saw another wave of 400,000 immigrants from Britain. Their reliance on government assistance, in most cases both for their passage and settling, helped the growth of the public sector as had been the case in previous generations of immigration. All in all, counting teachers, nurses, the police, railway workers and similar enterprises, few countries had a higher percentage of their workforce serving the public than Australia. That fact said a great deal about the strength of its economy and even more of its overall social wellbeing.

The renewed influx of immigrants depended upon the maintenance of a boisterous economy because half of the immigrants was assisted by state governments. The healthy economy resulted from a remarkable regrowth of flocks after the drought, which yielded a record clip of 1,400,000 bales of wool in 1906, mostly sold to Britain. The management of flocks on such a scale would have necessitated a much-increased workforce had it not been for the remarkable development in the breeding of border collie and kelpie sheep dogs in the 1870s and 1880s. Notable among the developers of the kelpie was John Quinn of Cootamundra who won a sheep-dog trial at Temora, New South Wales, with a black-and-tan kelpie, Clyde. This dog sired the legendary blue kelpie, Coil, which won trial after trial and became the progenitor of a noted strain of prize-winning working dogs. In time it became possible for comparatively large flocks to be managed by one man, mounted on a horse and accompanied by one or two dogs. The unity and understanding of man and dog in the control of sheep became a fundamental feature of the whole pastoral industry. It soon became a pastoral axiom that a good sheep-dog was worth two men and the skill and faithfulness of the drover's dog was commemorated in verse:

> And whether its Toby, or Toss or Nell,
> And whether its wool or meat,
> He will work all day, and at night as well,
> Till the pads wear off his feet.

There were similar and equally valuable developments in the breeding of dogs for the cattle industry. The Australian blue-heeler cattle dog, the only pure-bred cattle dog in the world, evolved in the 1890s from crossing the smooth-haired Scotch collie with the dingo, Dalmatian and kelpie. The blue heeler fulfilled all the requirements of a cattle dog. It proved capable of working with horses and bullock teams, as well as looking after stock in the wild bush, and guarding the owner's property in days when stealing horses, saddles and bridles was a lucrative profession. As with the flock owners, cattlemen said 'a good cattle dog is a man's living'. The cattle dogs proved especially valuable with the opening of the Canning Stock-Route in Western Australia in 1906. It was the longest stock-route in the world stretching for more than 900 miles and on it cattle could be overlanded from Halls Creek in the Kimberley to the railhead at Wiluna by passing through some of the most arid regions of the continent.

The increase in the production of wheat was due in no small measure to the work of one man. William Farrer arrived in Australia in 1870 and worked as a tutor at Campbell's property, Duntroon, at Canberra, which became the site of the Royal Military College in 1911. Farrer had become convinced that many of the wheat strains then in use were not suited to Australian conditions and settled near Queanbeyan in 1886 to devote his life to improving them. Without any specialist knowledge of genetics, he crossbred Indian, Canadian and older, established Australian strains to produce one he called 'Federation' in 1901. It became the basis of wheat growing for many years across the continent. Farrer was never entirely successful in developing a fully rust-resistant strain, but his devotion and skill put wheat growing in a position from which it did not look back, especially when it was combined with the introduction and then the widespread use of superphosphates, trace elements and chemical fertilizers.

Despite the introduction of migrant workers, the demand for labour remained high, especially in places, like Western Australia, where railway construction was still going ahead. Nonetheless, unemployment still failed to fall below a six per cent national average. Much labour was seasonal and many young people were still drifting to the cities where industrial unemployment rose despite the rapid development in the manufacturing and building industries. Unemployment caused resentment among a workforce which thought that state expenditure on immigration was foolish and strikes took place at Broken Hill and on the coalfields in New South Wales. The Labor Party expressed concern at these trends and seemed to sound the right note with the electorate, because it was the first party to achieve a majority in both Houses when, in the elections of 1910, it won over half the seats with 49.97 per cent of the votes.

Andrew Fisher, as Prime Minister, implemented the decision taken at the 1905 Labor Conference which decreed that the Cabinet be elected by all the Labor members in Parliament. This procedure became a source of irritation and frustration to successive Labor Prime Ministers. Faced with an array of ministers chosen on factional, state or mateship lines the Prime Minister could do no more than designate their portfolios and hope that time and luck would prove him right. Fisher retained the Treasury for himself and made Billy Hughes his Attorney-General. Although Scottish in origin and formerly a coalminer by trade, Fisher decided to order a motor car for his use, unlike Alfred Deakin who either rode a bicycle or took the tram to Parliament daily. Fisher was a man of wide, sound and moderate views, and he fondly hoped to see women representatives in the Federal Parliament, a hope that was not realized in his lifetime. In fact, in 1903, Vera Goldstein and three other women stood, unsuccessfully, for the Senate. Goldstein was the first woman in the British Empire to stand in an election.

The Labor government lasted until 1913 and oversaw a period of hitherto unmatched reform. In the minds of many of its members, there were memories of the bank crashes of the 1890s and they were determined to avoid any repetition of a catastrophe which had brought much suffering to the poorer classes. As a result, they were committed to the foundation of a Commonwealth Bank, which King O'Malley in particular had spoken of for years, and legislation for its foundation was passed in 1911. The new, government-guaranteed, savings bank was a competitor with the private banks for deposits. It introduced a national currency and thereby displaced the notes put in circulation by private banks. With the addition in 1913 of the role of a trading bank, it was financially profitable and was directed by a governor appointed by the Parliament, to which he was responsible. For a time, its very existence, like that of the Labor Party, helped to restrain capitalism in some of its excesses. Attitudes to the Commonwealth Bank remained a fundamental difference between conservative and progressive political parties for the next seventy-five years.

As the first Labor government of any consequence, Fisher's had a chance to implement in its own right a series of policies, some of which derived from the Deakin era while others were distinctively its own. Old age pensions were extended, those for invalids started and a maternity allowance of a £5 'baby bonus' was granted in 1912, though Aboriginal, Asian and Pacific Islander mothers were excluded from receiving it. Piecemeal arrangements were made to solve federal and state financial relations, with the states being compensated £1.5s per capita of population for their loss of revenue from customs and excise. Railway construction was undertaken to the extent that Australia ranked first in the world on miles per head of population and in 1912 construction began on the line from Port Augusta in South Australia to Kalgoorlie in Western Australia so as to link east and west. At the same time Reverend Joseph Flynn's Inland Mission also began.

In 1910 the first Australian coins were minted to replace English coins, and in 1913 the first Australian postage stamps were introduced when the Commonwealth took over the whole of the postal services from the states. The government courageously implemented a land tax on unimproved properties worth more than £5,000 in order to break up the large holdings into small farms. Much resentment was aroused at this measure despite the fact that it achieved little in land reform, but some urban holdings were affected and the revenue raised was considerable. Fisher was irritated that the Constitution restricted the powers of the Commonwealth in industrial disputes and, wanting to extend its control over trade and nationalize monopolies, he tried twice, unsuccessfully, to have it changed by referendum.

The men who wrote the Constitution had ensured that no one could idly tamper with their legacy to the nation. To this end they had written clauses into it that safeguarded its text and meaning by requiring that it could only be changed when a majority of the electors in a majority of states voted in favour of a change. In these instances, on trade and on monopolies, as in so many subsequent ones, the electorate voted against change, although narrowly in respect of monopolies. No one had ever asserted that the Constitution was graven on stone; equally no one henceforth imagined that it could be toyed with at will, or even that it could be changed at the wish of a majority of Australians, which eventually resulted in some of its clauses being anachronistic.

The early years of the Commonwealth widened the horizons of politicians and public servants, who hitherto had seen themselves as responsible only for one or other colony. Their new concerns were particularly evident in regard to the Northern Territory and the Antarctic. The settlement of the Northern Territory, an area of half a million square miles, had been one of fits and starts since 1849, when Port Essington was abandoned for the second time. In 1863 it was annexed to South Australia although it retained its name – Northern Territory. The government in Adelaide, with that zeal for good order and land development so evident there since the foundation of South Australia, proceeded, unsuccessfully, to introduce Wakefieldian theories into settling the sub-tropics. The town of Palmerston was renamed Darwin and became the main centre, but all interest in the coastal north was lost after the gold discoveries at Pine Creek and other places in the 1870s. In the appalling conditions of heat, distance, lack of water and general amenities on the fields, only some Chinese survived to help found the cosmopolitan population of Darwin. Meanwhile, the north remained unattractive to white settlers.

It was agreed that, without a railway linking north and south, no progress in developing the north would be made so, gradually, a line crept from Darwin to Pine Creek and from Adelaide to Oodnadatta leaving a not inconsiderable gap of 1,800 kilometres. In 1907 South Australia gave up the burden of trying to administer the north and passed the whole Territory to the Commonwealth. This step finally took effect on 1 January 1911. The Australian taxpayer thereby incurred a public debt of over £10,000,000 while the total annual revenue from the lease of 150,000 square miles of the Territory was a meagre £9,000. It was not an auspicious beginning to Commonwealth control although great pastoral properties running cattle herds had flourished since the 1880s, especially on the Barkly Tableland. An administrator with a staff of nine was appointed to run the Territory, but further development of any consequence had to await the beginning of World War II.

For well over a century, there had been interest in the vast land mass to the south of the Australian continent, but it was spasmodic and ineffective. Few even knew anything practical about Antarctica, although its connection with the origins of white Australia was close. On his second voyage of discovery, Cook had left Cape Town on 23 November 1772 and struck south. A few weeks later his small vessels were surrounded by islands of ice and, penetrating these, they crossed the Antarctic Circle on 17 January 1773. Twelve months later Cook ventured even deeper into the unknown and rightly claimed that no man before him had gone further south. His Antarctic voyages helped to seal his reputation as one of the greatest navigators of all the ages.

After Cook, intermittent voyages were made in the nineteenth century, but it was not until 1895 that a party of Norwegians landed at Cape Adare and Carsten Egeberg Borchgrevink was the first man to set foot on the Antarctic continent, an area twenty per cent larger than Australia and the coldest, highest and windiest of the continents. Among those who followed were Amundsen, Scott, Shackleton, Edgeworth David and Mawson. Professor Edgeworth David claimed the whole area for the British Empire when he and Mawson reached the south magnetic pole on 16 January 1908. By 1911 the Antarctic was the object of attention by parties from Britain, Japan, Germany and Norway, so Mawson was commissioned to sail south and hoist the flag on land deemed to be geographically Australia's own province.

Mawson was Professor of Geology at Adelaide University, but his interest in the Antarctic was such as to link his name with it for all time. He set up headquarters at Commonwealth Bay where his party suffered great hardship, but much useful exploratory work was done in the next two years including a survey of a thousand miles of the continent's coastline. As a result the Australian public, already aware of the Antarctic through the tragic loss of Scott, began to think of it as closely connected to their own continent, although what use it would ever serve was not readily discernible. In 1936 an area comprising forty-two per cent of the continent was declared to be the Australian Antarctic Territory, and eventually three permanent bases were established there for scientific purposes.

Throughout the Australian continent, the motorcar was already the chosen means of transport for the people of more ample means. Those with lesser means, or a taste for the flamboyant, often used a motorcycle. Cars had rapidly captured the general interest and their use resulted in changes in women's clothing, especially when it was realized that bustles and trains were uncomfortable on the seats of T-model Fords. Furthermore, cars so disturbed pedestrians and horses as to warrant them and their drivers being required to have licences and the Automobile Club of Australia was founded to protect motorists' interests. Melbourne's Harley Tarrant managed to start a local car industry, but competition from overseas importers, especially Ford, restricted his market so that he only built sixteen cars. His Tarrant was clearly suited to

Australian conditions, and its prototype came equal with imported cars in the 1905 Melbourne to Sydney reliability trial over roads that were still so primitive as to be little improved on the bullock tracks of half a century before.

Among the most creative of all Australian inventors was Henry Sutton, born in Ballarat in 1856. Although without formal scientific education, Sutton proved to be a prodigy in the scientific and technical field. He was the first Australian to experiment with heavier than air materials for flight, his electric motor contributed substantially to the growth of the electrical industry and his work on the electric storage battery was widely acclaimed. He improved on Bell's telephone so much that the inventor visited him in Ballarat to see the complete system Sutton had installed in his own home. Independently from Thomas Edison, Sutton had successfully experimented with a carbon lamp. He invented a mercury air pump and a vacuum pump, and, by the late 1880s, claimed to have designed an instrument which would televise the Melbourne Cup and allow it to be shown in Ballarat, but he did not proceed with his invention. Engraving, colour photography and car carburettors were other interests and he built a portable radio set with a range of a little under 500 yards. In the midst of all this creative work he remained engrossed in the family musical instrument business, Suttons Pty Ltd, and died in 1912 with no one sure of his greatness because, wanting 'to benefit fellow workers in science', he had taken out very few patents in his lifetime.

By 1914 Australians could take a ticket by post in Tattersall's lottery based in Hobart, go to a night out at a moving picture show or perhaps listen to the gramophone at home. They avidly read the adventures of the Linton family in Mary Grant Bruce's 'Billabong' series of stories although the author had decided that there should be no love interest in them. They could use the first postage stamp, featuring a kangaroo and an outline map, post a letter by airmail between Sydney and Melbourne which would be delivered in two to three days, visit C. J. Coles's stores in Melbourne where a shilling was the highest price for any article, read, in any of the more than 1,000 newspapers, that Norman Brookes had helped beat the Americans four times in the Davis Cup and that an Australian had no opposition when winning the first air race from Botany to Sydney in 1912. His American opponent had refused to trust the weather. The telephone had linked Sydney and Melbourne since 1907 and in that same year Australians were able to slake their thirst with the first beer produced by Carlton and United Breweries and eat Peter's ice cream. Australia had become a world leader in the use of electric power which was used in lighting and to propel trams. The first official wireless station was opened in Melbourne in 1912 and speed, in measures hitherto unsuspected and applied to communications and transport, became a reality accepted, if scarcely understood, by all.

Increased prosperity made leisure the prerogative of all except the very poor. Such festivals as the Melbourne Cup and the Royal Shows attracted huge crowds and an international exhibition of women's work was held in Melbourne in 1907. The dominant form of religion, Protestantism, discouraged sport on a Sunday, but the weekend started to emerge in 1909 when workplaces began to close on Saturday afternoons. This encouraged a multitude of sporting activities so that football, tennis, golf and less publicised activities such as fishing and shooting attracted thousands. In New South Wales, Queensland and Western Australia glorious beaches and fine weather drew crowds who, as yet, refrained from exposing most of their bodies to the sun, surfing became popular, the 'Australian crawl' (used for centuries in the Pacific Islands) was learnt and voluntary lifesaving clubs were spreading from Sydney where they started at Bondi in 1906. In January 1907 a nine-year-old schoolboy Charles Kingsford Smith, the future airman, was noticed struggling in the surf at Bondi. He was the first to be rescued with a reel and line which had been invented by the captain of the Bondi Life Saving Club, Lyster Ormbsy, a few weeks previously.

Amid all this beach going there was a degree of unease expressed by some clerics who warned of hedonism and were especially alarmed at mixed bathing. A Presbyterian minister spoke of 'promiscuous hoodlums' infesting some beaches; the Catholic archbishop of Melbourne breathed the word 'abomination' and the Prime Minister, Andrew Fisher, sprang to the rescue of the errant ones saying he had seen no signs of 'hideous immorality' at the beach. But there was much seriousness in life also. The main churches were spending enormous sums, both in money and human effort, on charitable works with the Catholics carrying the added burden of educating their own children in schools to which the state contributed nothing. Education was extending very slowly to the secondary and technical levels. Only one student in twenty went on to secondary schooling while a mere handful graduated at a university.

The first woman doctor had been registered in 1890 and the first woman lawyer graduated from Sydney University in 1902. She was excluded from practising until after the passing of the Women's Legal Status Act in 1921. A universally free, secular or even fully compulsory education system was still a sought after ideal. Teacher training was inadequate and, of the 867 teachers registered in the secondary system in Victoria, only nine were properly trained. The beginning of the Commonwealth Literary Fund and the offering of tutorials by the Workers' Educational Association, which stood for an alliance between 'Labor and Learning', all helped to contribute in the field of adult education. D. S. Mitchell gave 10,025 books, 50 art works and £70,000 to the State of New South Wales and, in 1910, the Mitchell Library in Macquarie Street, Sydney, was opened and rapidly became a treasure house of learning and enjoyment for the public and scholars alike.

Despite apparent prosperity, many of the poor still went hungry, wages were often insufficient and home ownership was, for most, only a dream. In many factories, conditions remained primitive and exploitation of women by sweated labour continued despite the legislative acts to prohibit it. An outbreak of bubonic plague had caused great consternation in Sydney in 1900, which had led to measures being taken to clear up slums, although the work went ahead slowly. Pure Food Acts did not operate with much effect until 1912, pneumonia killed the young and the strong, as well as the old, and diphtheria ravaged the lives of many children. Blood poisoning after operations, especially for appendicitis, was a common occurrence, and it was tragically illustrated when the nineteen-year-old swimmer, Barney Kiernan, who held eight world records from 200 yards to a mile, died in Brisbane during the Australian swimming championships in 1905. Life for many was still brutal and short, but throughout the continent the ideal of Australia as a paradise for the workers was maintained, especially by those with something to gain from its acceptance. The concept of a fair go for all, already firmly embedded in the Australian psyche, manifested itself also in a reluctance to see children brought before the apparatus of an adult court. The first Children's Court was opened as an experiment in Paddington, Sydney, in 1905. It was a success.

Most white Australians were scarcely aware of the continued existence of the Aborigines, the majority of whom dwelt in the far outback or on the fringes of inland towns. They had been excluded from civic and political rights in the Constitution and were not counted in the census despite the fact that the majority of them had lost their ability to live according to the traditions of their ancestors. A Royal Commission in Western Australia resulted in an *Aborigines Act* in 1905 that was a mixture of morality flavoured with patronage. The surveyor, Alfred Canning, after whom the famous Stock Route was named, had admitted before the Commission that he had chained Aborigines at night on his journey south from the Kimberley in 1906. He pleaded that it was necessary for him to 'make use' of them and that the only way to stop them leaving his expedition at night was to chain them by the neck. Canning was exonerated, but the *Act* prohibited the use of chains on Aboriginal prisoners, the police could not force Aborigines to remain with an employer, Aboriginal women were forbidden to board pearling vessels and measures were introduced to punish immoral acts committed against Aboriginal children. The subjection of a once proud people was almost complete.

Very few Australians were alarmed at an apparent constitutional crisis in 1914. By now political choice was clearly narrowed to the two parties – Labor and the conservatives, who were often known as Liberals. Joseph Cook led the latter. He too was a former coal miner and had alternated between Labor, Free Trade and Protection to settle down as a conservative Prime Minister when, in the federal elections of May 1913, Labor lost its majority in the House of Representatives. Cook had a majority of one in the House of Representatives, which he used to overturn Labor legislation giving preference to unionists in Commonwealth employment. The Senate, with a strong Labor majority, rejected Cook's bill twice and the Governor-General, faced with a lack of precedent, decided that Parliament could not function and dissolved both Houses. After an election in September 1914, the Labor Party, under Fisher, returned to govern with thirty-one of the thirty-six Senate seats and forty-two out of seventy-five in the House of Representatives. In the meantime events had taken place in Europe, which were to test the proclamation of the Australian Natives Association of 13 December 1913 that 'Our home is Australia'.

13

Innocence Lost

Compulsory military training, the acquisition of a navy, the setting up of a college to train army officers at Duntroon in 1911 and an aviation school at Point Cook in Victoria had all helped to prepare Australia for participation in a war. Involvement in the Sudan and Boer conflicts combined with an increasing interest in European and Pacific affairs to develop public opinion on Australia's readiness for war. The psychology of a pioneering society had also done its part. Australians, it seemed to many, had faced hardship and sacrifice with manifest endurance and wrested control of an old land. Pride in manhood, the ability to struggle and improvise against the odds, widespread use of, and familiarity with, the horse, rifles and shotguns, and the emphasis placed on sticking to one's mates were other factors shaping a mentality that was not adverse to war.

In literature and legend, in stories told around the fireplaces of homes, the 'glories of war' had been held up as an ideal to young Australians and many took it for granted that the true worth of a people was tested in battle. Over-riding all other considerations was the bond of Empire forged in blood, sentiment and commerce. Since 1905 Australians had solemnly celebrated Empire Day on 24 May and pledged themselves to stay loyal to their British origins. In 1910 the Catholics in Sydney claimed that 'Australia, not England, is our motherland' and they decided they would call 24 May, Australia Day. Yet, despite their differences, the majority of Australians were bound in some way to Britain and there was much enthusiasm for, and apparent unanimity in, the cause of the 'Mother Country' – England. That bond was the decisive factor determining Australia's participation in the First World War. A nation that had begun its origins tainted by convictism could perhaps prove that the stain was finally eradicable in blood.

Joseph Cook was still Prime Minister on 5 August 1914 and it fell to him to announce that war with Germany was now a reality because 'when the Empire is at war so is Australia at war' and that 'our duty is quite clear – to gird up our loins and remember that we are Britons'. The wider implications of that reality, and Australian involvement in it, seemed apparent to none at the time. A few days earlier, when Labor leader Fisher had promised to come to the defence of Britain with 'our last man and our last shilling', no one remarked that such a wildly profligate offering of blood and resources may not have lain in Fisher's, or anyone else's, keeping. The thing that seemed to cloud rationality, inflame passions and stir anger, even in the breasts of the peaceful, was the allegedly barbaric behaviour of the Germans as they 'raped' Belgium.

Other causes of war, ranging from unbridled nationalism to the desire for territorial conquest and more trade outlets, were scarcely considered. Britain was at war with a nation of so-called primitive 'Huns'; Australia would come to her aid with her little navy and, as an initial token of support, 20,000 men. Few voices questioned the wisdom or justice of it all except those on the far left like the Industrial Workers of the World, to whom war was the bloody exploitation of the workers by the capitalists. A few feminists and other 'small voices' such as the Quakers, who regarded war as the antithesis of Christ's teachings, joined them. When the Labor government came to power on 17 September and showed every sign of wanting to prosecute the war with enthusiasm, the consciences of most dissidents were eased and, temporarily, there was unity.

Australia threw herself into the conflict with such a will that it was claimed the very first shot of the war was fired from Point Nepean to stop the German steamer, *Pfalz* as she was about to pass through Port Phillip Heads. This occurred at about noon on 5 August and it was the only act of belligerence on Australian territory during the war if one excepts the episode in which an Indian and an Afghan, using their horse-drawn ice-cream cart for protection and flying the Turkish flag, attacked a train of picnickers at Broken Hill. They killed four and were soon killed themselves. Germany did, however, have naval forces of two large cruisers in the Pacific and a strong squadron and garrisons in New Guinea, while there were potential spies in Australia itself. The capture of Rabaul was the first significant act by Australian soldiers. The fleet put to sea to hunt German warships and Germans of military age in Australia were interned, shops and clubs raided and all German clubs closed. Melbourne University refused to re-appoint a German music teacher to its staff and among internees later in the war was the Sydney brewer Edmund Resch, who had neglected to take out Australian naturalisation, unlike his brother Emil, the first managing director of Carlton and United Breweries, who remained free.

No pleas were needed to attract volunteers and over 50,000 men enlisted as rapidly as they could be processed. On 1 November thirty-six transports and three cruisers, with 20,000 Australians and New Zealanders aboard, sailed from Albany in Western Australia. The fears of Asiatic hordes were set aside as Japan, Australia's ally, provided a powerful escort cruiser, the *Ibuki*. A few days later, a naval engagement took place near the Cocos Islands where the Australian cruiser, *Sydney,* destroyed the German raider, *Emden*. The news of the successful episode caused great rejoicing and pride throughout Australia.

Turkey's entry into the war in October had caused concern for the safety of the Suez and the Anzacs, so named after the Australia New Zealand Army Corps, were diverted to Egypt rather than going on to England for training on Salisbury Plain. On arrival at Suez they helped repel a Turkish force bent on cutting the Canal. To the consternation of the British command, and of some of the locals, the Australians, after training in the shadow of the Pyramids by day, gambled, drank and whored on their 6s a day in Cairo at night. With their loosely fitting khaki uniforms, hats swept up on the left and the badge of the 'Rising Sun' worn proudly, they were a formidable group of men eagerly awaiting action. They had little time to wait because Winston Churchill, and others in England, had decided to conquer the Turks on Gallipoli Peninsula about 200 miles south of Istanbul. The plan was to open up the Dardanelles to the Allies and relieve pressure on the Russians. On 25 April 1915, at a place they called Anzac Cove, the 3rd Australian Infantry Brigade of the Australian imperial Forces (AIF) came ashore at dawn.

The Australians scrambled up the slope from the beach under the ceaseless fire of the Turks positioned on the heights. Cries from the dying and wounded, anguished appeals to mates for help and the incessant whirring, shrieking and thudding of bullets and shells filled the air with ear-shattering noise. The Australians were at Gallipoli where they had been told to defend an Empire and, far from the peace of the old continent of their origins, the ancient feuding ritual of blood was enacted on them. They were in a place that had seen all this through the ages when men killed men for land, money, religion or other causes. By nightfall their steps were irretraceable, for 16,000 had been landed with over 2,000 casualties and they had nowhere to go except into the earth. Many of their forefathers had been diggers and now the sons dug in to hold an alien soil. At home, ministers of religion visited houses to tell of the dead and wounded; names went up outside newspaper offices where wives, mothers, parents and friends stood to grieve and only partly understand. At last, it seemed, white Australia had a history.

By early 1915 all Australians had learnt a good deal about involvement in a war. The federal government had imposed an income tax, prices had risen considerably and no price controls were introduced until 1916, there was a marked decrease in shipping and overseas trade combined with uncertainty in the manufacturing sector to cause unemployment. Imports, especially from Britain, were scarce and wages were frozen, which caused many workers to become resentful because some people were making huge profits. Meanwhile, there was another of those perennial hardships to be faced, drought, which had begun in 1911 and lasted until 1915. A Commonwealth War Crimes and War Precautions Act brought in previously unknown forms of control over the lives of ordinary citizens and allowed for censorship. Patriotism in many guises gripped scoundrels and the decent alike. Whether person, place or product, anyone or anything to do with Germany, suffered discrimination or internment, name change or rejection. In South Australia forty towns or districts with names of German origin were changed and Germanton in New South Wales became Holbrook in 1915.

Another face of patriotism was shown in the extraordinary level of recruitment, partly engendered by the news from Gallipoli. June (12,500), July (36,000) and August (25,700) 1915 were its peak months with the British calling for more and more troops and the Australian authorities drumming them up with recruiting campaigns. The numbers, however, began to drop away which prompted a group of men, determined to see the war prosecuted to a successful conclusion, to form the Universal Service League. The principal creed to which the League subscribed was that only conscription for military service would fill the ranks of the dead and wounded and thereby win the war against the 'Hun'.

After weeks of battle, August 1915 saw the Australians assault and take Lone Pine on the south of Gallipoli Peninsula, but fresh British troops had failed tragically at nearby Suvla Bay because of indecisive command, and the whole campaign, in which both sides engaged in brutalities, was in jeopardy. Hamilton, the British commander was replaced, and, in London, the War Office, was at last ready to cry 'enough' after eight months of futile bloodshed. In a manoeuvre remarkable for ingenuity, 20,000 Australians were withdrawn from the Peninsula under cover of darkness on 18 and 19 December 1915 with the loss of only two lives. They left behind over 8,000 Australian dead near Anzac Cove while nearly 20,000 had been wounded. Major-General Bridges, commander of the AIF, died as a result of wounds he received on Gallipoli and his body was brought home to rest at the Royal Military College, Duntroon, of which he had been the first commandant.

The British and Indians lost 27,000 men, the New Zealanders 2,701, the French almost as many as the Australians. The Turks, who defended their land with great courage under a valiant commander, Mustafa Kemal Ataturk, counted 86,000 dead, but to them, presumably, the whole campaign had not been a waste as they had successfully defended their homeland. Seventy years later the Turks, who had proved a worthy enemy and had conquered with dignity, named the place Anzac Cove. They erected a plaque there with the words of Ataturk inscribed upon it: the Anzacs were called heroes who now lie 'in the soil of a friendly country' and their mothers were reminded that their sons, who 'have become our sons as well, now rest in peace'.

The courage and endurance of the Anzacs had been staggering as, with their agonies and fears shrouded in sardonic good humour, they endured the impossible. The New Zealanders had fought alongside the Australians and suffered their own awesome meed of sorrow, which formed a bond of lasting trust across the Tasman. The words 'Anzac' and 'Gallipoli' were etched in the memory of the nation while the dead of the Peninsula became, in time, a symbol and measure to test its quality. From the agony of those months, no nation was created because such a thing happens only through the unity of a people with its land and with each other. Nevertheless a precious bond among Australians was formed on the bloodied slopes of Gallipoli and the Anzac legend speaks truly for its bearers walked upright, fine and noble of bearing as they went to death, to maiming and defeat. The nation born in convictism, on the goldfields, in the suburbs of the cities and in the bush had sent its sons to battle bearing its values already in their hearts. No people could have asked more, permitted more or expected more of their sons and received such a response. In the end it was fitting that a non-combatant, John Simpson Kirkpatrick, 'the man with the donkey', who brought in the wounded day-after-day amid fierce shrapnel fire and died as he did so, became the enduring legend and symbol of the pure, selfless and heroic at Gallipoli.

The debacle of Gallipoli was of minor consequence in London, where victory on the Western Front was seen as the key to a final triumph. By 1916 the opposing armies had dug in along long lines of trenches and the war had become one of attrition of human life. Territorial gains were minimal, but both sides hoped that the death toll and the bleeding of their respective economies would cause the other to capitulate. The Allies saw the summer of 1916 as the time for a decisive strike for which more men were needed. In Australia, a census showed that there were still 600,000 able men available, so William Morris Hughes, who became Labor Prime Minister in October when a dispirited Andrew Fisher resigned to go to London as High Commissioner, called upon them to help crush 'Prussian military despotism' for all time.

Hughes was a complex character who was born in London in 1862 although he always claimed to be of Welsh origins. After a sound secondary education, he taught in England for a while and arrived in Australia in 1884 to become in turn a fettler, seaman, shearer, and actor. Later he studied law, owned a book shop, organised strikes as a union leader in the 1890s, helped found the New South Wales Labor Party, entered Parliament, became a federal member in 1901 and later a King's Counsel. He managed to contain in his own diminutive person a spirit whose elements were explosive in passion and enthusiasm, including a love for Empire, a fierce loyalty to Australia and a penchant for militarism.

To Billy, as he was known by thousands, there were plenty of men to draw on in Australia and he wanted 50,000 without delay and a further 16,000 each month. He claimed that those who opposed recruitment were 'foul parasites' on the body of the Labor movement, knowing 'no nationality, religion or principle'. It was an unwise way to confront a movement in which many were already suspicious of his refusal to hold a referendum for price control by the Federal Parliament. They saw this as craven capitulation to the forces of capitalism, which were growing fat on war while the workers were called upon to fight it. By 1916 prices had risen by twenty per cent, real wages had dropped by ten per cent and unemployment, despite the number of males who had enlisted, stood at six per cent.

Many were largely unaffected by the war preferring football matches, horse racing and sundry other diversions, although inflation was constantly rising, war loans were being called for, and income tax now added to other increased taxes. Manufacturing grew due to the opening of munitions factories and the need to make other necessities no longer available by import. Broken Hill Proprietary Limited opened a steelworks at Newcastle and the production of pig-iron rose from about 130,000 tons to over a million tons during the war years. The drought was over by 1916 and farmers and woolgrowers were benefiting by British demand for their products.

Hughes had failed to find any remedy to rising prices, but wages did not go up commensurably, which caused the workers to think that they were being asked to bear the burden of the war at home and at the front. Trade union leaders, despite being reviled as disrupters of the war effort, called for strikes on the waterfront, and among metal workers, coal miners and shearers. As a response 1.7 million working days were lost in 1916. By then the war appeared to be dragging on interminably and the workers were less and less inclined to be swayed by the heady rhetoric of Hughes, who called for greater and greater sacrifice. Easter 1916 saw a rising of insurgents in

Ireland, which was followed by the execution of James Connolly and other Irish leaders by the British. It was not a happy event for the Irish in Australia to ponder on while their sons were being called to put their own lives at stake for the Empire.

Early in 1916, Hughes visited England, where he arranged for the purchase of fifteen ships by the Commonwealth to carry freight to and from England, helped formulate a tough line on how the Allies should deal with Germany once victory was secured, stomped the country preaching total war, and was feted and applauded by royalty, politicians, the wealthy and the powerful. He also met the Australian troops in France where, affectionately, they called him the 'Little Digger'. He had left the Western Front before their first disaster at Fromelles on 19 July, and was on his way home to receive a hero's welcome. Despite the enormous losses, the British commander, General Haig, had stubbornly persisted in trying to breach the German lines on the Somme. In and about Pozières, two months of late summer and early autumn saw 23,000 Australian casualties with the gain of about one mile in territory.

Gallipoli was another world away compared to the ferocity and horror of the Somme. The sheer enormity of the slaughter, the dreadful noise of the shells, the stench, poison gas, mud, filth and, finally, the uselessness of it all drove the men into shock and depression from which some failed to recover. In its own way, the Australian army was never the same again. Distrust in the British High Command, almost contempt for the British troops, bitterness at the loss of so many lives, hopelessness when no avenue of escape was possible from further horrors; all overwhelmed the men. So many of the finest of the nation soaked their blood into the fields of France that Australia, in that generation at least, suffered a grievous blow.

Despite some heartening news from Egypt that Henry Chauvel's Light Horse had forced the Turks back into Palestine, all was not well at home. Women sent white feathers to men who had not enlisted and the recruiting officers did their best, but the number of volunteers fell from 22,000 in January 1916 to 6,000 in July, which was said to be far short of the numbers demanded. On his return Hughes said that 32,500 volunteers were required immediately and 16,500 a month thereafter which was unrealistic and provocative. If realised, it would have caused industrial and agricultural chaos with the loss of a third of the able-bodied, male workforce in a year.

Undaunted Hughes pressed ahead with a proposal to hold a plebiscite on conscription for overseas military service. He did not have the numbers in Parliament to enforce conscription by legislation, and he paid no heed to the clear signs of resentment in large segments of the Labor Party, both federal and state. As a result of his determination to pursue conscription, he found himself, together with his fellow Labor conscriptionist, William Holman, Premier of New South Wales, expelled from the New South Wales state branch of the Party in September 1916, and the same happened in other states as well. With a further rash act of provocation, he called up young men for home service and announced a plebiscite for October. It was a step that dramatically divided the people – after all the claims that involvement in war had united them.

The basic reason for the division stemmed from two broadly divergent concepts of Australia. One held that Australia was white, civilised, British, mostly Protestant and part of a great Empire, which itself was God's gift to mankind. To people who held this concept the Germans threatened the very bastion of civilisation – the Empire. For them it was difficult, if not impossible, to comprehend how anyone but a traitor could disagree with conscription, which was the logical extension of their belief given the military situation. Practically every public figure in Australia, the press, except for publications of the broad Labor movement, the judiciary, all but a handful of the Protestant clergy, and the wealthy held this view, often fiercely. Many thousands joined them in the feelings of patriotism and loyalty to Empire, which inclined them to vote for conscription. The press inflamed passions with the *Age* castigating those who failed to enlist as 'muddy-mettled wastrels', while David Low and Norman Lindsay used their brilliance in the *Bulletin* to draw cartoons showing the miserableness of the anti-conscriptionists and the glory of the soldiers fighting to defend civilisation from the 'Hun'.

The other concept of the nation was held by a numerically significant sector, represented particularly in the Labor movement and in large sections of the Catholic Church. To them Australia was part of the Empire, but it was also an entity in itself. Their emotional ties with Britain were weaker than those of the conscriptionists and for many Catholics, led by Archbishop Daniel Mannix of Melbourne, the bloody reprisals taken by the British in Ireland after the Easter Rising had effectively severed the ties. To such people, whether of the Labor movement or not, it was not as easy to represent the Germans as the embodiment of all evil, nor the war as a holy crusade to preserve civilisation. Furthermore, with the losses in casualties since April 1915 and the daily news of increasing slaughter in France, the idea was increasingly held that Australia was doing enough in manpower and resources. Vida Goldstein led the Women's Peace Army, which was pacifist and struggled for women's rights. While speaking at a peace rally in 1916, she was disrupted by irate soldiers.

In the main the anti-conscriptionists were not against involvement in the war, although many held deep-seated convictions on the evils of militarism, which they saw embodied in conscription and some, such as the resolute and courageous Quakers, were implacably opposed. Among the workers there was also the fear that military conscription would be followed by industrial conscription, the importation of coloured labour and perhaps the repression of the trade union movement. Many women were strengthened in their resolve to resist the blandishments of those who exhorted them to make further sacrifices of their husbands and sons and they were determined to vote 'No'. The voting strength of many farmers, worried about their harvests and the manpower needed to reap them; small businessmen and factory owners who feared that a further depleted workforce would endanger their economic interests, became anti-conscriptionists. Such people, having voted 'No', could return to their traditional conservative political allegiance afterwards.

Much passion, ranting and pathos confused the issues in the two conscription campaigns of October 1916 and December 1917. Alfred Deakin was so ill he could not speak publicly, but the old patriot wrote the sorriest document of the whole affair. He begged Australians to vote 'Yes' to keep Australia 'white and free for ever' – to vote to save civilisation. He concluded with a plea and a promise, both of which remained sterile: 'Let our voices thunder "Yes", and future generations shall arise and call us blessed'. A very narrow majority of 72,476 out of nearly two and a quarter million voted against conscription in 1916, but the majority increased in 1917 and Victoria joined New South Wales, Queensland and South Australia in opposition. At the Front the soldiers on active service were almost evenly divided, as if to say that it was bad enough in France for those who went there willingly.

The first important consequence of the conscription era was a deep and lasting split in the Labor Party, which stemmed from past differences that were heightened by the war. In the broad labour movement there were some who saw the Labor Party as a vehicle of social change, but whose commitment to the cause of the working masses was either emotional or merely one of convenience in that it gave them a stage to work on. Conscription forced them to evaluate their position and act on it. After the first plebiscite, Hughes replied to a caucus motion of no confidence on 9 September 1916 by saying, 'Let all who support me, follow me'. He walked from the party room with twenty-four followers out of the sixty-five present. By January 1917 he had formed the Nationalist Party with the support of his former Labor colleagues and the parliamentary opposition. Holman did the same in New South Wales and the Labor Party was divided in all states except in Queensland. Frank Tudor was elected federal Labor leader and went onto the opposition benches with forty followers. Labor was changed in that it now relied almost completely on trade union and worker support.

Another consequence was that many Australians who remained loyal to Labor, whether as parliamentarians or voters, were Catholics. The Party was seen for several ensuing decades as Irish and Catholic, which was sufficiently true as to arouse sectarian fears that were given added strength because, after 1916, some Australians regarded Catholics as traitors. Radical elements of the workers' movement were inspired by the Russian Revolution and became convinced that the solution to the ills of society lay in the overthrow of its dominant capitalistic structure, which they judged the Labor Party incapable of achieving. Thus the seeds were sown which blossomed into the Communist Party of Australia in 1920. Meanwhile the Labor Party, reduced in numbers and with the press against it, with an untried leader and much of its base eroded by jingoism, lost the federal election called by Hughes in May 1917. The Nationalists, who campaigned effectively under the banner 'Win the War', dominated the seventh Parliament having more than twice Labor's numbers, and patriotism seemed the preserve of those who were anti-Labor.

Meanwhile the war went on relentlessly with little yielding of ground, although the Australian Flying Corps joined with other Allied airforces to bomb German positions effectively. Haig, who never seemed to weary of the butchery, had a victory when five miles were gained in October 1917 near Ypres. Both sides lost half a million men – the Australians suffered 38,000 casualties in four months. The Australian soldiers now called each other 'diggers', and the survivors became more embittered as they watched their comrades being maimed or killed. The only note of optimism was the entry of America on the Allied side. At Villers Bretonneux five Australian divisions went over the trench tops on 8 August 1918 assisted by two Australian squadrons in the air and 450 British tanks. French, Canadian and British troops fought along a twenty-mile front and it was Germany's blackest hour. The Australians took thousands of prisoners and saw their final engagement in France on 29 September, as the war drew to a close.

In France, the Australians won the respect of their allies and their enemies as they had on Gallipoli and in Palestine, where their mounted troops had helped to gain victory and took Damascus on the morning of 1 October

1918. On leave in Egypt, France and England, the troops had enjoyed themselves, to the not infrequent discomfort of their hosts. Among them there were some mutineers, deserters and malcontents, but the majority were the pride of their officers and a source of confusion to the British commanders, who often found them discourteous, insolent and undisciplined. The Australian dead numbered 60,000 out of the 330,000 who had served in theatre-of-war zones and their overall casualty rate at 68.5 percent was the highest of the Allied forces. The news of the Armistice of 11 November was heard with happiness and relief throughout Australia, but in many homes hearts were broken. Mute, material relics of Australia's passing on Gallipoli remained for generations, as its memory did in the homeland itself. Time perhaps healed much sorrow and the broken earth bloomed again in Flanders' fields where poppies grew on graves. In the words of Australia's official historian of the Great War, C.E.W. Bean:

> What these men did nothing can alter now. The good and the bad, the greatness and smallness of their story will stand. Whatever of glory it contains nothing now can lessen. It rises as it will always rise, above the mists of ages, a monument to great-hearted men; and for their nation, a possession for ever.

Many Aborigines enlisted as Maoris to disguise their racial origins, but 289 were officially counted as members of the AIF of whom 44 died and 59 were casualties. There was a significant number of Aborigines among Light Horse regiments in Palestine. Two Aboriginal privates from Victoria, William Rawlings and Harry Thorpe were both killed and awarded the Military Medal while Corporal A. Knight of New South Wales was twice wounded and won the Distinguished Conduct Medal. Grief struck at Aboriginal families just as it had done at those of the white soldiers. Three Coe brothers became casualties; two of the three Firebrace brothers were killed, as were both the Lister and Gage brothers. Private Douglas Grant spent several years in a Berlin war prison where he became the object of serious study by German ethnographers and was treated leniently as a result.

Tarnished permanently in the minds of some by his conscription stand and by his destruction of a Labor government, Hughes, nonetheless, revealed himself as the forthright exponent of Australia's traditional foreign policy. Because the nation was determined to remain white, coloured races had to be excluded and, as an island far removed from its cultural roots, Australia had to be defended. The former was to be achieved by ensuring that no exceptions were made to the policy on colour, and the latter by preventing any hostile, or potentially hostile, power from getting a foothold close to

Australia. Despite the fact that it had been an ally, Hughes remained uneasy about Japan as a Pacific power, and he was determined to keep her people and her forces at bay.

At the Paris Peace Conference in 1919, Hughes firstly established Australia's right to speak as an independent signatory in the name of 60,000 dead. When the Japanese tried to have a racial equality declaration proclaimed, Hughes saw it as a threat to the White Australia policy and would have none of it, so Wilson, President of the United States, refused to accept the Japanese proposal. The Japanese claimed, and were granted, a mandate to control the north Pacific islands formerly held by Germany. Hughes objected unsuccessfully, but he did, however, succeed in his main objective of obtaining a mandate for Australia to control the former German colonies in the southwest Pacific and especially in New Guinea. He thereby ensured that there was a barrier between Japan in the north and Australia in the south. Hughes was satisfied and came away from Versailles feeling victorious, to be acclaimed by large crowds at home, who wildly cheered him on arrival.

To a small nation of five million people, a war debt of £350,000,000 was huge. Admittedly, most of this money had been spent in Australia to the benefit of the public utilities in every state. The opening of the transcontinental railway through to Perth in 1917 was an example. Furthermore, the economy had prospered with assured markets for wool, metals, wheat, butter and other primary products, sold mostly to Britain. The inability to import many items resulted in a wide variety of articles being manufactured locally, ranging from ships to Aspro tablets. There were other effects of the war which, though not as tangible, left a lasting legacy and served to put the negative aspects of Hughes's prime-ministership in perspective.

At the very start of the war, Hughes had played down the implications of the wide powers granted to the Commonwealth by the War Precautions Act, but eventually its implications became clear. The Act covered aliens and, although they were rarely treated with the harshness shown on Torrens Island in South Australia where 300 harmless, Australian-born Germans were flogged and in other ways treated inhumanely, the paranoia caused by the war ensured that to be an alien of any kind was to suffer a sorry lot. By 1917, an incident occurred in Queensland which showed how Hughes's enthusiasm for the war had so unbalanced the Prime Minister as to cause him to behave like a despot by misuse of the Act.

Thomas Ryan was an extremely able politician and Premier of Queensland, which was the last state to retain Labor in power in wartime. Ryan's government brought in a range of reform measures of lasting benefit such as a mandatory eight-hour day and state controlled enterprises that competed with privately owned concerns. Moreover, Ryan was a forthright opponent of conscription, and he spoke strongly against it in the Queensland Parliament. Hughes decreed that the *Hansard* containing Ryan's remarks could not be processed by the Post Office. Ryan repeated his statement outside the Parliament and was charged under the Act with making statements prejudicial to the war effort, for which he was tried and acquitted with costs against the Commonwealth. At the time Hughes was in Queensland and, when making a speech at Warwick, an egg was thrown at him which met its target. A sergeant of police refused to arrest the egg thrower, Patrick Brosnan. This so enraged Hughes that he returned to Melbourne and set up the Commonwealth Police Force. That body proved to be the forerunner of future secret organisations culminating in 1949 with the establishment of the Australian Security Intelligence Organisation, commonly known as ASIO. The purpose of such bodies was always the security of the country, but they often proved to be a source of concern to some Australians who were innocent of any subversive acts.

Hughes's War Precautions Act had been invoked to launch a wide variety of successful prosecutions by the end of the war. They included exhibiting the red flag, showing disloyalty or hostility to the Empire, disturbing loyalist meetings, giving shelter to unnaturalised Germans and dyeing military overcoats. Such prosecutions by the Commonwealth were scarcely a good precedent for its behaviour in peacetime. Governments, once having secured wider powers in the name of an emergency, invariably show a remarkable reluctance to relinquish them once the crisis has passed, and the Australian government was no exception.

The nation at war was subject to much industrial disharmony despite the prevailing attitude that all strike action was disloyal. On the extreme left, the Industrial Workers of the World, determined to destroy capitalism, preached a highly idealistic doctrine with violent undertones. They kept hysteria high by allegedly plotting to burn down Sydney, by helping Tom Barker, editor of their paper, to escape from prison and, generally, by conspiring to incite sedition. Twelve of them were arrested and were sent to prison for long terms. A judge enquired into the matter in 1920 and found that their convictions rested on Crown witnesses who were 'liars and perjurers', which resulted in ten of them being released.

In 1917 Hughes blamed the Industrial Workers of the World, Sinn Fein and other allegedly disloyal elements for inciting a general strike in New South Wales. It began among railway and tramway employees who refused to accept a new system of recording work done. A total of 70,000 men were on strike by the time it was halted when volunteers and other assorted 'loyalists' helped to fill the vacant jobs. The Premier, Holman, enunciated the uneasy principle that there were times in which the state was supreme over the individual, without delineating the exact terms in which that principle operated. His statement indicated that the war had so increased the power of government that in some minds, including Holman's, it bordered on the absolute. The general strike itself was a psychological response to the bitterness caused by war with its losses and deprivations, to the conscription plebiscites and to the way in which Hughes had partially destroyed the Labor Party.

After the war, there were so many strikes that it seemed as if the battles of the Western Front were being fought again, this time in the factories and on the wharves. Members of trade unions and returned soldiers rioted over their respective loyalties to Russia or to the British Empire, to capitalism or socialism. In Brisbane nineteen people were wounded when returned men attacked the office of the Russia Association, while the Returned Soldiers League, founded in 1916, played its part in ensuring that nothing which resembled a Bolshevik Revolution would take place in Australia. Despite these upheavals, Lieutenant-General John Monash, the most outstanding Australian military commander of the war, directed a remarkably smooth operation by which some 160,000 servicemen returned home in eight months. By November 1919 all except 14,000 were in employment while another 20,000 were receiving technical training.

To the returned men, much had changed in Australia since they left. Some had gone to war in hope and determination. Many were swayed by a spirit of adventure because, to young men who had perhaps never been beyond Tasmania's north-west coast, the northern rivers area of New South Wales, Victoria's Wimmera, the wine-growing valleys of South Australia, the Darling Downs or the wheat belt towns of Western Australia, it was a chance to see the world. They came home with a new way of looking at things, for they had seen their friends killed and many had taken human life; they had been close to a world old and wearied in its ways with little hope of renewal. As many of them saw it, they had fought for the integrity of Australia and the Empire, but on return they discerned, here and there, the signs of an

Australia that had lost its conscience and direction with everyone seeking the best for themselves irrespective of others.

Australia was no longer an isolated island, even to disease. The diggers brought the Spanish influenza with them, which forced the wearing of masks, closed public buildings and killed 12,000 people in 1919. In politics, there was a new creation called the Country Party, which began informally when it won its first seat at the Corangamite by-election in the Western District of Victoria in 1918. The Party relied on the simple slogan of 'Production first' and the vote of those farmers who believed that the city and all those who represented it were against them.

Initially the closing at six p.m. of hotels in several states may have seemed trivial to the returned men but it was a symbol of the passing of the old ways. Since the 1830s the temperance movement had never lost its drive, but even its most ardent supporters could not have dreamt what a golden chance the war would give to their cause. In early 1916, at Liverpool near Sydney, 15,000 troops mutinied in protest at their prolonged training hours. They rioted, consumed vast quantities of beer and fought among themselves as well as against civilians. One soldier was shot dead and there was general disorder in Sydney's streets. In June the people voted to close the hotels at six o'clock, so New South Wales joined Victoria, Tasmania and South Australia in the practice.

In this way the degradation called 'the six o'clock swill' began. It saw men line up in hotel bars after leaving work to get down as much beer as possible before 'Time, gentlemen please' signalled the closure. Ninety per cent of beer consumption took place in the one hour between five and six and bottled beer, previously ill favoured as a beverage, became universally acceptable. Six o'clock closure was an undignified, narrow and fruitless response on the part of wowserism to what certainly had long been a social problem in Australia – the over-consumption of alcohol. The swill produced more drunkards in the ensuing generation than any other single factor and was not got rid of in Victoria, long the heartland of wowserism, until the 1960s.

Australia welcomed the returned men with fervour and genuine gratitude. In every city and right through the land, even in the small country towns, stone monuments to the memory of the fallen were quickly erected, or were being built, for it was agreed upon everywhere that permanent recognition had to be made of the sacrifice of the diggers. Often the monument was a single figure, upright, rifle and bayonet in hand, slouch hat shading fixed eyes. There was little attempt at religious symbolism, with classical models chosen by preference to avoid sectarian differences although Moruya on the south coast of New South Wales failed to erect a monument because of religious tensions. On the plinth a roll call proudly listed the names of those who had served and every list had its dead. Sometimes there were brothers and cousins, for many families were doubly stricken. Around the monument the townspeople and the returned men gathered on 11 November 1919 to observe two minutes silence for all the dead.

Anzac Day, 25 April, the day of the landing at Gallipoli, overshadowed memory and made all new and vital in significance for it was seen as the day on which the nation had shaken off the bonds of subservience and Australians had come to know themselves. Billy Hughes saw it a little differently. To him victory in the war meant national safety, liberty and the safeguarding of the White Australia policy. Despite some signs to the contrary, Hughes was still convinced that Australians were 'more British than the people of Great Britain'. The two views of the nation revealed so clearly on the conscription issue had survived the war. Time would reveal their respective validity. Something else, however, had endured in that the longing of the native-born for equality and acceptance had been partially requited on Gallipoli and the Somme. In many of them ran the blood of their convict ancestors. Blood had redeemed blood.

14

A Mirage of Progress

Australia came out of the war with a new sense of its identity and Australians felt that the ways of the past were changed irrevocably. The application of technology to the purposes of war, on land, at sea, in the air and in the factories at home, meant that a large proportion of the population had grown accustomed to developments in science, communications, medicine, engineering and transport. The involvement of the nation in war had radicalised those who rejected violent conflict as a means of solving international problems, while many, who previously had seen Australia with the eyes of patriots, now looked upon her as more firmly embedded than ever in the web of Empire.

That development was notable in the *Bulletin*, which joined the newly-founded *Smith's Weekly* as a voice of conservatism and firm devotion to the British and their Empire. In the case of the *Bulletin,* its founder, Archibald, who said in 1894 that it had started as a 'clever youth' but that it would become 'a dull old man', had foreshadowed this development. Conservatism was notable too in the new legend of the digger as the bearer of the national legend. The digger showed the old virtues of his forerunners in the bush and on the goldfields, but he added conformity and imperialism to them, which blunted the creative urge and made the 1920s for many a period of material but not spiritual development.

The role of women underwent some changes during the war and with differing roles came developing attitudes. Some served as nurses in the Armed Services, but at home they were employed in greater numbers in shops, banks, and light industry. They worked as typists and telegraphists and, generally, where the lack of manpower or, given the differential wage structure, the avarice of employers made their employment convenient. Nevertheless, two women became police officers in Sydney in 1915 and five female doctors worked for the Victorian Education Department. Participation in the workforce gave many women a personal understanding of how society operated outside the home, but their overall position remained one of subservience to males. For the minority who were married workers, the need to organise a timetable to fit in a day's work with child minding, leaving the home environment and dressing up to do so, the contact with others, and finally the acquisition of a wage helped towards a greater understanding of their own value. The conscription struggle had radicalised a few women who began to take more interest in union activity and to strive for women's rights.

The role of wife and mother still dominated and marriage was seen as the acceptable norm to which young women were educated, but there were some changes. Domestic service no longer attracted most of the female workforce because industrialisation continued after the war and by 1925 females made up half the workforce in light industry. A typical woman worker was young, unmarried and received half the male wage. If widowed with children, her burden was severe because there were no child-minding facilities, no national health scheme, and no child endowment until 1927, and then only in New South Wales.

For the young and independent woman, life offered avenues of fulfilment and enjoyment not open to her elder sisters of the pre-war period and still not available to most women in rural areas, where distance, the lack of amenities, the need to work on farms and the absence of female companionship made life hard. The divorce rate doubled in the decade from 1911. The imbalance in the sex ratios, plus the hospitalisation of so many returned men, 23,000 in 1926, and the deaths of many others, combined with wider knowledge of birth control techniques to reduce the birth rate. In 1931 there were over a third less births by percentage of population than in 1921.

Reaction to the war years, with their deprivations and sorrows, took place in many material ways. Dress styles changed with the introduction of short skirts known as 'frock shocks', silk stockings and lower bodices. Mixed bathing in increasingly revealing costumes became popular, while dancing the foxtrot, Charleston and waltz was a favoured pastime in public halls and cabarets. Women smoked, often using long cigarette holders, rode pillion on motor bikes, a few learnt to drive cars and all went to the pictures where romance dominated as the theme, culminating with the excitement of the 'talkies' in 1929, when enthralled thousands listened to and watched Al Jolson in *The Jazz Singer*. Picture palaces of vast and often sumptuous proportions and style were built and Australians, partly reflecting their continued sense of being aliens in a continent far from their lands of origin, became the world's most regular patrons of the film with attendances reaching 126 million in 1929. The popularity of the cinema helped to develop a local industry, although it began to wane in the late 1920s due to competition from imported American films.

Middle class and some conservative women joined organisations such as the Country Women's Association, the Australian Women's National League and a host of others that had their counterpart in the religious world, where the evergreen Temperance bodies still survived. In 1921 Edith Cowan became the first woman elected to an Australian parliament when she won the seat of West Perth for the Nationalist party in the state parliament. She uttered the sentiments appropriate to her Party's ideology of conservatism and nationalism, but she also proclaimed that she would stand by women and demanded their right to vote in union ballots to prevent strikes; she worried about class-consciousness and wanted the shilling impost on prams carried on public transport to be removed. The appropriate Minister promised to comply immediately with her last request. In 1922 a deputation of women from several organisations complained to the New South Wales Premier that single men were receiving a basic wage based on a family component. They claimed that such a wage was absurd in that it ignored the needs of large families and harmful because it encouraged birth control and sapped the health of the community. The Premier promised to deal with the matter 'later on'.

The middle class, urban dwelling woman of the 1920s was, in general, as distant in the fruits of progress from her mother of thirty years before as she in her turn was from the woman of the seventeenth century. Technology and work had wrought the change for both, and the war was a turning point for modern women, while steam power and industrialisation had been responsible for the earlier changes. Time payment meant that a range of appliances including washing machines, electric irons, stoves and kettles, hot water services and radiators were procurable while gramophones and wireless sets, of which over 300,000 were licensed by 1929, provided music and other entertainment in the home although subscribers could only receive from the station they paid for. The poor enjoyed few, if any, of these amenities, but the gradual spread of electricity, even into the bush, helped to bring about change.

For children, life was an orderly process governed by parents who insisted on set patterns of behaviour in the home as much as teachers did in the schools. A church service was followed by the Sunday roast and then an 'outing', possibly to visit relatives when children were often called upon to recite or sing. Clothes were handed down and fruit eaten sparingly. After school, jam was spread on bread, sometimes with cream to top it off, and at the main meal there was usually a pudding of some kind, even if only of rice or sago. American contributions in the form of sundaes, Life Savers and

Kellogg's Cornflakes came on the market and were occasional treats by the early twenties. 'The health food of a nation', Peters ice cream, was widely consumed with delight by 1929.

In many schools, the children still used slates, the readers contained the long-after remembered stories of awakening consciousness, while sums, parsing, spelling and tables were everyday fare for home work, which, depending on economic circumstances, was done in exercise books or on brown paper. Boys grouped in 'gangs' in which the shanghai, a Y-Shaped, hand-held catapult, was a favourite weapon, while, after school or on Saturdays, to go rabbiting or yabbying (called lobbying in Queensland) for small, freshwater crayfish was always a source of excitement for both boys and girls. In the bush, children rode horses to school, often two or more to the one horse. On cold mornings, a warm, bare back was preferable to a cold, stiff saddle.

Inevitably, elders asked children the question, 'What are you going to do when you grow up?' which implied that the precious days of childhood were only preparatory to the real stuff of life. The answers from the boys were mostly fanciful – fireman, policeman, sailor or whatever happened to be in vogue, such as aviator. The girls had only one choice marriage – perhaps preceded by a career as a nurse, shop assistant, schoolteacher, office worker or whatever was deemed a genteel task. Yet for children to grow up in the twenties was to sense security. War was over and had not yet come again, the economy seemed to work moderately well and the phenomenon of the broken home was rare. At the end of the year seemingly endless summer holidays arrived when it was always hot and Santa Claus was looked forward to eagerly, although in every schoolroom there was the child sceptic who declared Santa to be a fraud. Above all childhood was a time in which to go to bed dog-tired and wake up looking forward to another day, when 'to go out to play' at some time, was a normal expectation. They were still days in which the human capacity to stretch the imagination and invent ways to play flourished.

The predominant factor, which affected the lives of the thousands of men who came home from the war, was the need to settle back into society and find a role in its economy. Preference for jobs for returned men was accepted federally and in all the states except Queensland where trade unionists always came first, but unemployment rose to twelve per cent in 1921 and varied from five per cent to eleven per cent during the decade. The unmarried men rapidly spent their deferred pay and gratuities but behind all the returned diggers stood the Returned Soldiers League which had 30,000 members by

1925 and eventually built clubs in the suburbs and country towns, especially in New South Wales.

The League rapidly became a powerful body with access to government, and it ensured that the provisions of the Repatriation Act of 1917, designed to help the returned men, were followed. The League fiercely propagated the legend of the Anzacs, held to a hard line on White Australia and generally took an anti-radical stance on matters it failed to understand or accept, such as Bolshevism, although it would be legitimate to argue that they instinctively understood the essence of the latter only too well. The contribution of the League, and that of the non-political Legacy movement founded in 1923, to the welfare of the returned men and to the widows and children of the dead, was immense.

The old myth of an empty land, with vast numbers of nameless Asians poised with grasping hands to flood into it, still held strong among the people and the planners in Australia. The land, it was thought, could produce abundantly, which would help people Australia and keep out any would-be invaders. By exporting the produce of the land the economy would thrive. To get all this up and running a few things were needed. Suitable land, people, credit, roads, water, railways, determination and hard work had to be at hand and the rest would surely follow. It was a neat and circular argument given shape in the phrase 'Men, Money and Markets' and had its remote origins with Hughes who had postponed the dream of Australia as a social laboratory in order to get on with the war. Pragmatism had replaced ideals, and, by the time Billy had come back to his senses there were other men with different ideas, based essentially on the marketplace, ready to take over affairs.

Among the new men was Earle Page, a medical practitioner from Grafton, New South Wales. He was elected to the Federal Parliament in 1919, where he joined and led ten others who represented the Country Party. The Country Party was essentially conservative and had its origins in the conviction that city-based politicians would invariably neglect the needs of 'the man on the land', but the Party managed for a while to work in moderate harmony with Hughes. Under Hughes, Parliament stumbled along, with its most useful acts being the acquisition of control of the Commonwealth Oil Refineries and of Amalgamated Wireless. The Prime Minister irritated the Melbourne and Sydney financial establishments by his attacks on their power; but he placated all conservative elements in society in late 1919 by forcing the expulsion from Parliament of Hugh Mahon, Irish-born Labor member for Kalgoorlie, on the grounds that Mahon had uttered seditious and disloyal sentiments in referring to 'this bloody and accursed Empire'.

Hughes could only maintain the uneasy alliance between Nationalist and Country Party members by offering sops to both rural and industrial interests. He introduced a tariff bill, which effectively wanted to make protection the basis of domestic policy. Few seemed aware that such a step was also a fundamental act of foreign policy because to protect one's own industries was to disadvantage others. Page and his members feared protection because they knew that farmers would buy agricultural machinery and items, such as fencing wire, at the lowest price, irrespective of their origin. The Country Party was pacified by subsidies to local production, which was another form of protection. As a result, Australian citizens paid to keep both primary and secondary industry economically viable and to retain the levels of employment in both. Another consequence was that secondary industry had little incentive to improve its efficiency, or to compete for sales on overseas markets.

Given the fickle support of the Country Party, Hughes decided to bolster his position in late 1921 by appointing the National Party member, Stanley Bruce, as his Treasurer. Bruce, though born in Australia, was in all respects English. Melbourne Grammar, Cambridge and the British Army, in which he fought at Gallipoli with distinction, formed his spirit; an Oxford accent and the best of English fashions cloaked his exterior. His inscrutable calm and air of detachment hid a mental agility of which Hughes seemed unaware. Bruce and Page combined to force Billy's downfall and the former Laborite was made to step down from being Prime Minister by the quintessence of Australian conservatism.

To the Country Party, Hughes had become much too radical for comfort so they refused to maintain the coalition, which left him without the numbers to govern. Although Bruce had openly pledged his support to Billy as his leader, he accepted the post of Prime Minister, made Page his deputy, and five of the eleven cabinet posts went to the Country Party. Billy neither forgot nor forgave, and he went to the backbench probably uncomforted by the thought that his undoing had been his inability to rid himself of some of his Labor principles. Reviled and called a 'rat' by many in the Labor movement, Billy's tragedy was the exaggerated patriotism that had led him into conflict with those to whom, at heart, he always belonged.

The new government, formed in February 1923, set about implementing Bruce's policy of 'Men, Money and Markets'. In essence, it meant populating the rural areas with settlers, whether native-born or immigrants, providing the money for settlement, and finding the markets for the wool, wheat, dried fruits and other produce. The states, again all under Labor governments except Victoria, where the Country Party held too great an electoral advantage, were wary of immigration given the unacceptable levels of unemployment. Nevertheless, Bruce went to London and negotiated an agreement whereby £34,000,000 was made available to assist British migration. In the following decade 261,000 Britons arrived of whom eighty per cent were given assistance and a quota system saw a few thousand Italians arrive, many of whom went to sugar cane farms in Queensland.

The greater part of the British immigrants remained in the cities and towns helping to produce and, in large measure, consume the increase in manufactured goods, which rose by one third in value from 1919 to 1929. Light industry, chemical, metal, engineering and electrical firms, all prospered, helped by cheap coal and steel, high tariffs and electrification of the suburban railways. Tariff-protected secondary industries made goods for the Australian market, thereby swelling profits for some and raising living standards for many, but the increasing trend to place almost total reliance on primary exports to service national accounts was apparent. Any marked decrease in overseas demand with a consequent fall in primary exports could spell ruin. In the decade before 1930, borrowing, mostly from Britain, amounted to £250,000,000, and after 1925 no year had a favourable balance of trade. Very few saw this imbalance as an ominous sign for the future.

If the new immigrants, like their predecessors in the nineteenth century, were unwilling to risk life on the land, the returned soldiers showed no such reluctance, and 37,000 of them, with their wives and families, decided to try to become farmers. A market seemed assured in Britain for tinned and dried fruit, wheat, wool and hides, and the fatal myth was peddled that the land could be worked cheaply. A former politician stomped about proclaiming 'A million farmers on a million acres'. The Commonwealth was prepared to put up £1000 per settler, but the actual settlement process was left to the states, which also incurred huge costs thereby. Often the selected land was infertile, acreage too small, improvements too costly, labour too expensive and livestock, or trees for fruitgrowers, unsuitable. Nevertheless, the settlement scheme went forward with reckless disregard for either planning or consequences.

In the Mallee, in Gippsland, in the Western District and in the Goulburn Valley in Victoria, on Queensland's Darling Downs, in the west and around Griffith in New South Wales, in the northwest and in the Tamar Valley of Tasmania, new settlers tried to wrest a living from the land. The experiment proved a costly failure in public and private money, in torn emotions and misery, with appalling conditions in which families frequently lived on rabbits and parrot stew. In Western Australia, the group settlements for British immigrants equally turned out to be a failure, although a dairy industry was established. The whole episode of post-war rural settlement should have learnt from the experiences of small selectors in the 1870s and 1880s. The miracle was that about half the settlers somehow survived, although for many it was a short-lived reprieve because the Depression of the following decade saw many more leave their blocks.

A judge was asked to examine the settlement scheme and explain why it failed, especially as the states lost well over £200,000,000 as a result and rural debt was high. He saw some evidence that hard work and persistence had been rewarded and cited the Murrumbidgee irrigation areas and parts of the Victorian Mallee as instances. Without malice, he stated bluntly that many of the men were unsuited to farming, but suited or not, they could never have succeeded on inadequate land, little or no capital, mortgages and falling prices for their produce. Notwithstanding this, the rural myth persisted with its unshakeable promise to keep out the 'hordes' and bring home the bacon. To balance the ledger somewhat, more land had been opened to the plough and for the fruit tree. More importantly for the future, some insight had been gained into how rural settlement could be successfully undertaken.

Bruce, impeccable in word and manner, was essentially a prudent man, whose concern was to make the federal system work. He was especially troubled in the area of industrial relations, with the workers wanting higher wages as prices rose and the employers remaining intent on increasing profits. Arbitration, intended to temper both drives, could work effectively only when a careful equilibrium was maintained. When employers or trade union leaders pushed the scales too far in one direction, lockouts or strikes followed. If industry was unable to expand because wages were too high, the economy suffered, while workers in a period of rising prices were always disadvantaged. It was an intricate maze to Bruce, especially at a time when Labor premiers appeared to favour the workers.

In Queensland, where Labor was in power from 1915 to 1929, Premier 'Red Ted' E.G. Theodore brought in a living wage, unemployment insurance and abolished the Legislative Council. His plan to expand the economy with state steel works and coal mines was defeated when London bankers refused him £9,000,000 in loan money because he proposed to increase rents on pastoral properties. As a result, unemployment rose in the state to nearly twenty-two per cent and there was a recession until Theodore capitulated on pastoral rents. Jack Lang became Premier of New South Wales in 1925 and was accused, wrongly, of flirting with socialists and 'Reds'. In fact he abhorred both. His government introduced widows' pensions, compulsory insurance paid by employers, child endowment, abolition of fees in secondary schools, a Government Insurance Office and better conditions for rural workers. All of this seemed to threaten social equilibrium when viewed from the conservative standpoint.

Another source of concern to conservatives was that the Labor Party itself appeared to be tainted by socialism given that its 1921 Federal Conference had set as an objective 'the socialisation of industry, production, distribution and exchange', although the Conference carefully refrained from stating in which millennium this goal was to be achieved. Conservative anxiety was heightened when a series of strikes occurred, including some by public servants and schoolteachers in Western Australia in 1920 and by Melbourne policemen in 1923. Rioting and looting took place during the police strike, and a right-wing group of militants, called the White Guard, was formed under the direction of Sir Brudenell White, retired chief of the general staff of the A.I.F., to resist the feared and often imaginary advances of Bolshevism which he considered a threat to Australian society.

Under these circumstances, Bruce was assured of widespread support. The fact that future economic stability was jeopardised by continued and large overseas borrowing in London and New York was not yet apparent. Nonetheless, Bruce formed a Loan Council to control public borrowing and the electorate showed good sense by agreeing at a referendum in 1928 to give centralised powers to the Federal Government which made the Premiers accept a curb on their spending.

In 1926 Bruce had decided to tackle the arbitration question head on by increasing Commonwealth powers, but he lost a referendum on the matter, basically because the electorate was unsure of what was proposed. Undaunted, he went ahead with legislation designed to curb union power and sharpen the teeth of the Commonwealth Arbitration Court. By this time union strength had risen to sixty per cent of eligible workers and the Australian Council of Trade Unions had been formed to present a united front to employers and the government itself. Union reaction was predictable and a worker's life was lost during riots on the Melbourne waterfront in 1928. It was a period of direct conflict between capital and labour with a mounting number of days lost in strikes everywhere. In the upshot, Bruce decided on a remarkable turn about. He would pass all power in industrial matters to the states, retaining for the Commonwealth control over its own territory, its own employees and those engaged in overseas and interstate shipping.

Hughes seized his chance and moved to amend Bruce's bill, winning by a single vote. This led to an election being called for October 1929. The electorate had not understood either Bruce or his motives, but had trusted him when the feeling was widespread that he knew what he was doing. At this stage he seemed to have lost his equilibrium and lost the election, miserably, with Labor winning forty-six of the seventy-five seats, including the Prime Minister's own blue ribbon seat of Flinders. It was good for Bruce and his country that he lost because he had become a centre of extreme discord. Bruce, despite the spats and the voice, was a patriot and a man before his time with an urge towards moderate interventionism, a feeling for technocracy and a realisation that governments had to be structured on an objective rather than an emotional basis. He served Australia well as High Commissioner in London, where he spoke the language of power to perfection, and elsewhere as a roving diplomat. In his latter years, Bruce accepted the first Chancellorship of the Australian National University, and, when he died in London in 1967, he asked that his ashes be scattered over the bush capital, Canberra, which he had helped found.

In May 1927 the Federal Capital moved to Canberra, the dream child city of an architect of rare genius, Walter Burley Griffin. From America, Burley Griffin had admired the radical developments in politics and social legislation of the young Australian democracy. In response to an international competition, he and his wife, Marion Lucy Mahony, planned a capital to express those ideals. Griffin, a difficult and unyielding character, came to Australia to oversee construction of the city in 1914 but, in 1921, he had become disillusioned at bureaucratic interference and departed to leave others to fulfil his plan. He was absent when the Duke of York opened the new Parliament in a temporary but pleasing structure among the gum trees and with sheep grazing peacefully in a nearby paddock. Nellie Melba led the singing of the national anthem by 9,000 whites and a solitary Aborigine, who left no record of his reaction to the ritual, watched the whole proceedings.

Bruce took seriously the need for research into problems besetting the rural sector, and in 1926 the Council for Scientific and Industrial Research was firmly set up and properly funded. It helped in the elimination of the prickly pear, a pest that had ravaged millions of acres of good land, especially in Queensland. To eradicate it, the cactoblastis insect was brought from South America and did its work of destruction so efficiently that grateful farmers at Dalby in Queensland, which had been particularly affected, erected a monument, said to be unique in the world, to an insect. Despite the high sounding name of the research body, the rural myth was strong in its ranks also and very little attention was initially paid to the needs of research for secondary industry. Manufacturing lagged behind developments elsewhere, which affected profitability, made exporting products difficult and shored up the accepted tenet that the country rode on the back of the sheep.

As early as 1894 Lawrence Hargrave had become airborne at Stanwell Park, New South Wales, with the help of four box kites. He was never able to adapt his great invention of a compressed-air engine, powered by three rotating cylinders, for use in flight. Australians remained fascinated by the progress made in aviation and by the 1920s it was an area of great technological advancement. Again the rural sector benefited greatly given its need for fast, safe transport and reliable communications. In 1928 John Flynn, a pastor of the Presbyterian Church, established an aerial medical service in the north-west of Queensland with headquarters at Cloncurry. Communication with outback stations was possible by means of a pedal wireless, and the Flying Doctor Service treated patients on the spot or flew them to the closest hospital. It was a service unique in the world and its contribution to the people of the outback was immense in the social, medical and educational spheres.

In 1928 Bert Hinkler flew the longest solo flight in the short history of aviation. In a small, single-engine plane, he flew from London to Darwin, and his epic and courageous journey earned him £10,000, as well as a dahlia and a soup named in his honour. Shortly afterwards, Kingsford Smith, Charles Ulm and two Americans flew from San Francisco to Brisbane and then across the Tasman. By the time of Hinkler's great feat, the Australian continent was already crisscrossed with airmail services. Qantas, (Queensland and Northern Territory Aerial Services), had linked the outback towns of Queensland since its formation at Winton in Queensland in 1920 and the conquest of the air was a reality.

Holden's Motor Body Works at Woodville, South Australia, was producing over 20,000 car bodies to fit an American chassis by 1924, while at Geelong, Victoria, Ford, in conjunction with General Motors, began assembling, and was soon producing, 36,000 bodies annually. The T-model Ford had come into widespread use. By the end of the twenties, half a million cars carried six million passengers to work, leisure and romance, whether in the Ford or in a more stylish model – Renault, Essex, Chandler or Chrysler. The horse, both as a means of travel and of traction, still held its own in country areas, although tractors in small numbers had begun to shatter the silence of the bush. Car transport meant that roads had to be upgraded, but sealing them was costly, accounting for a quarter of public expenditure by the end of the decade, which added to overseas debt.

Henry Lawson died on 2 September 1922. Lost for years in the mists of alcohol and eking out a miserable existence on charity, his literary talents were spent. For countless Australians, his passion for hopelessness entwined with endurance was epitomised in the dying words of his famous character, the woman of the bush, Mrs Wilson, who told her children to feed the pigs and calves and 'to be sure and water them geraniums'. Lawson became the symbol of the embattled visionary whose sad but all-embracing eyes had looked on a world in which the sounds were gradually muted by increasing deafness and in which, to him, neither the flora nor fauna had mattered. Lawson had seen through to the land and its people both in city and bush and there was a frailty in all he wrote which resembled the land he loved. Like it, he left a gentle but indelible mark on those who peopled it.

All Australians knew Gladys Moncrieff affectionately as 'Our Glad' after she sang the lead role in *Maid of the Mountains* at the Theatre Royal in Melbourne in 1921. It was the first of her 3,000 appearances. In the following year Jack O'Hagan's song, 'The road to Gundagai' became popular after Allen and Company published it in sheet music. Arthur Hoey Davis, creator of *On Our Selection* lived on but wrote little as his Dad and Dave became celebrities of stage and screen, while Paterson, whose penname 'Banjo' taken in memory of a favourite horse, passed from memory for a time. Only Christopher Brennan – his head filled with languages, literature, scholarship, laughter, love and the fumes of alcohol – strode on, for he was a poet who belonged neither to time nor place. In the end he was struck down in the place of his birth, Sydney, to which he had given all his great qualities of mind and heart. In 1925 Sydney University dismissed him as associate professor and head of the Department of German and Comparative Literature for adultery and drunkenness. Its gesture was symbolic of an age in which many of those who loved life seemed to be outsiders threatening the stability of entrenched morality and order.

The great literary work of the period was the trilogy, *The Fortunes Of Richard Mahony*. It was written by Ethel Robertson, who called herself Henry Handel Richardson, and the work had the golden days of the 1850s as its setting. The main character, based on her father, struggled between an old world and a new one and found rest in neither, much as W.C. Wentworth had done. The book remains a poignant testimony to those whose lives were broken because Australia to them never became home, whether in heart or in mind. Because he was wholly Australian, John Shaw Neilson achieved what eluded Robertson and he wrote of the mystery and lure of his native land with mastery. Half blind, often appearing to be stupid, Neilson grew up at Minimay in the Victorian Wimmera and worked around Sea Lake in the Mallee until the late 1920s. Unmarried and lonely, his verse was tender and delicate and 'in that poor country' he was no stranger, for he neither knew nor longed for another. Neilson's pen was matched by Elioth Gruner's brush for Gruner painted the landscape with the same delicacy. Margaret Preston was the Brennan of the brush, turning into still life the eternal truths the poet had put into verse.

Millions of Australians had never heard of Neilson or Gruner, but they all knew something about Ginger Meggs, of Ginger's girl friend Minnie, his enemy, Tiger Kelly, his rival for Minnie's affection, Eddie, his mates, Benny and Ocker, and Mrs Meggs, the archetypal mother of strength and stability. James Bancks was the Sydney-born cartoonist and creator, in 1922, of the lovable figure of Ginger with his mop of red hair and his black waistcoat, who at one moment was wheedling ice-cream from an Italian vendor and the next was softening-up two 'sooks' named Cuthbert and Wentworth. Through thousands of escapades in the Sydney *Sunday Sun* and other papers, Ginger was an essentially urban larrikin, philosopher, battler and humorist. Children and adults laughed with him, worried about him, hoped and dreamt with him. On the twenty-fifth birthday of his appearance, the occasion was celebrated in children's wards of state hospitals. Ginger bore the stamp of his creator Bancks, who was generous and warm, and Ginger carried also the old legend of the bush in his reactions to figures of authority – parents, policemen and schoolteachers. At his death in 1952, Bancks left Ginger as a legacy to a generation of battling Australians who had gone through war and depression with him and came through in the end to the good times.

To an increasing proportion of Australians, especially adherents of the Reformed Churches, religion was steadily more closely identified with such matters as opposition to drinking, gambling, and Sunday violation, and the rejection of anything that threatened stability in the social order. Publications such as John and Ezra Norton's weekly *Truth*, with its emphasis on sexual, domestic and political scandals, alarmed them, but it was widely read nonetheless. Sectarianism had been given a new dimension through the involvement of Catholics with the Labor movement. In New South Wales the unhappy story of the flight of a young, deranged nun from a Wagga convent in 1921 caused waves of resentment and thinly veiled hate to flow over the embarrassed Catholic community. Catholics seemed a race apart with their preoccupation about birth control, divorce, feminine immodesty and their refusal to eat meat on Fridays. They were protected in their own schools and adult organisations such as the Holy Name and Saint Vincent de Paul Societies, while Freemasons often denied in covert ways their entry into business institutions. The teaching orders directed their Catholic pupils into professions and the public service, but in the main they lived alongside Protestants in peace, played the same sports, suffered the same anxieties and worshipped the same God because the Australian Commonwealth was still, professedly, in large measure, Christian.

Probably less than one in ten white Australians had seen an Aborigine, and perhaps one in ten thousand knew anything about them that was not derisory. An academic Association for the Preservation of the Native Races was founded, and Professors Baldwin Spencer and A.P. Elkin had become useful advisers to state and federal governments. In 1927 an Australian Aboriginal Protection Society secured the abolition of Aboriginal child labour, but the Aboriginal population throughout the continent had shrunk to about 60,000 'full bloods' and there were grim warnings about the spread of diseases among them. Around the towns the blacks were an irritant to the righteous, but on some government reserves and mission stations there was a measure of good will, if at times ill-directed, and they could live there peacefully, unmolested by those who now inhabited their land. In the north the cattle industry relied heavily on their labour, and in the south many more were itinerant workers. Many children grew up without parents or race for the government decided to separate part-Aboriginal children from their Aboriginal mothers in an attempt to integrate them into white society. It was an exercise in inhumanity that bore its fruits in sorrow for decades.

In some places in the desert, in the Kimberley, at Cape York and on Arnhem Land the Aborigines still lived in the ways of their ancestors, and like them they were subject to the same barbarisms from the whites, although now only spasmodically. In 1926 a police party killed up to twenty Aborigines and burned their bodies in the Kimberley and probably killed another thirty in the same year. Two police were charged, ineffectively, with the murders of four of them. An Anglican minister, the Reverend A. Gribble, said before a Royal Commission that the Aborigines in Western Australia were the worst treated in the world. In his judgement up to 10,000 Aborigines had been 'exterminated by devious means' there in the previous 50 years. Another atrocity, again implicating the police, took place in the Northern Territory in 1928 involving the killing of thirty-one Aborigines.

The day had passed when such behaviour was acceptable and there was a sense of outrage among whites in southern and eastern Australia although in the West it was rumoured that station owners poisoned meat with cyanide and laced flour with arsenic when Aborigines became a 'nuisance' which was a repetition of the behaviour of whites after the Myall Creek massacres in 1838. Nevertheless, after 140 years of intermittent slaughter, the last public atrocities closed a chapter in the history of the Aboriginal race.

Until the late twenties, it was possible to look back on the decade as one of development after the years of the Great War. The value of production rose, the workforce grew, home ownership was slowly becoming a reality and 260,000 immigrants had arrived from Britain of whom eighty per cent were assisted. The population, over six million by 1928, saw signs of progress everywhere. The Melbourne tramway system was under electrification, as was the railway line from Sydney Central to Oatley, and the first traffic lights were installed in Melbourne. Vegemite was produced and gradually accepted, Anna Pavlova came on a ballet tour, Melbourne University Press was founded, the Surfers Paradise hotel was opened in 1923 and the hoodlum-killer, 'Squizzy' Taylor, died after a duel with another gangster, who also died, in Carlton, Victoria.

Other signs were not so promising. The birth rate fell, prices rose, unemployment hovered from six to eleven per cent, the cities grew but the rural population fell, while a submerged urban poor suffered without much comment. Over two million koala skins were exported from the eastern states, resulting in the virtual extinction of the animal in Victoria and New South Wales. There had been unprecedented conflict in industry, militancy grew, right-wing elements took shape and there was much bitterness between capital and labour. Despite the efforts of the Loan Council, the states had continued to over-borrow, and, generally, Australians over-spent as if there would be no day of reckoning. The twenties, outwardly so full of gaiety and promise and underneath marked by harshness, tinsel and a lack of seriousness, had brought progress but they also gave a hostage to fortune, which the next decade would be asked to redeem.

15

The Unforgotten Thirties

The thrust of Australian nationalism had been realized in the person of James Henry Scullin. Son of a railway worker, Scullin was born in 1876 at Trawalla, near Beaufort in Victoria, and educated to primary level. He was the product of the Western District of Victoria and of Ballarat, where he won prizes as a public speaker. The bush, trade unionism, the Labor Party, the conscription conflict and the Catholic Church shaped his ideals. The influence of the latter was not obtrusive and throughout his political career he never directly favoured his Church. The essential platforms of the Labor movement – humanity and justice – were the forces that motivated him, but they were frail weapons in the battle for survival Australia was about to enter.

Elected federal leader of the Labor Party in April 1928, Scullin made many speeches in Parliament warning of impending economic disaster as shown by rising unemployment, unfavourable trade figures, a large national deficit, mostly owed on loans raised in London, and the parallels with the economic downturn that led to the depression of the 1890s. Just as his cry of doom seemed vindicated, he succeeded Bruce as Prime Minister. Stock prices were falling and London investors were becoming shy of lending; wheat and wool prices fell by a half and a quarter respectively; industrial conflict on the coalfields and waterfront abounded; a drought had begun; and no solutions seemed in sight. Scullin's government took office in late October 1929 during the very week which saw the collapse of Wall Street in New York with a catastrophic drop in share prices and a loss of confidence among investors followed by a spate of suicides. The London Stock Exchange also witnessed catastrophic falls and the Great Depression had begun. Its paralysing impact on the economy and workforce was readily apparent, but few understood its causes and fewer still had any clear idea as to how it could be combated.

An economic depression on a large scale embraces almost everyone in its human devastation. It debases even further those to whom life is a quest for riches and power. In a failing economy they either increase their wealth and power at the price of others' degradation, or they lose both. They rarely, if ever, forgive, and they never forget. The poor, the homeless, the widows and the orphans, the innocent of all ages and kinds, especially those who previously lived in moderate comfort and then found that they had been reduced to penury; all these are broken in body and spirit. Many never recover.

In Australia the effects of the Depression were clearly discernible in both the private and public sectors. The Federal Labor government was reduced to a shambles of conflicting factional interests with those on the right and left having diametrically opposed solutions, roughly summed up as spend less or spend more. In the centre of the Party stood Scullin and his Treasurer, Ted Theodore, who opted for a little of both. Meanwhile, the conservatives sat back, effectively opposed any legislation they deemed unsatisfactory by using their huge Senate majority to block bills, nibbled away at the waverers in the government, and waited for the whole sorry edifice to collapse.

The private sector, like its public counterpart, was divided. The poor, the unemployed, the small businessman whose economic base was shattered, the shopkeeper who no longer had customers or who had to extend credit beyond his resources, the professional whose services could not be afforded, the entrepreneur who had gambled and faced unpayable debts, the farmer who had overcapitalized in hope and had walked off his property in despair; all these suffered deprivation to a greater or lesser degree. On the other hand, the rich whose capital was safe, those of the employed whose jobs were not at risk and especially those in government services, the clever who had enough capital to take advantage of those who were forced to sell a home or a business; all of these survived and some prospered. Those on salaries could absorb cuts because the drop in commodity prices compensated. To such people, the Depression was mostly a stage on which they played a part, but as mere observers, although some were not even that as they remained sheltered in their affluent suburbs with their rounds of social events, where misery did not penetrate. The rich, the employed and the secure did not join the ranks of those who bore the marks of the Great Depression for a generation, and passed its memory on as a caution to their children. For the first time Australia had been divided into two nations, the rich and the poor.

In the psychology of the nation, the gap that opened between promise and reality was the deepest source of concern. Since the days of the goldrushes, with the one exception of the 1890s, there had always been the assurance of steady progress. Only the heartless or the obtuse ever denied the existence of both rural and urban poverty in that triumphal march towards the workers' paradise. Yet the unemployed had never previously averaged at least twenty-four percent of the workforce, which it did for five long, hard years from 1930 to 1934, with over twenty-eight per cent out of work in 1932. Only Germany topped that figure, and it says much for Australian resilience and common sense that there was no shift to the totalitarianism that took place in Germany with the subsequent rise of Hitler.

Nevertheless, unrest caused some to turn to utopian solutions. The Communist Party increased rapidly in numbers and fought valiantly for people who had been evicted from their homes because they could not keep up rental or mortgage payments. As a result of their manifest concern, Communists were elected to key positions in several important trade unions. Meanwhile, the followers of Social Credit propounded a doctrine of supply and demand probably only understood by its originator, Major Douglas, and his devotees. Some Sydney Rotarians formed the 'All for Australia League' with business and professional men at its core and a rapidly growing membership in New South Wales, Victoria and South Australia. The League was especially concerned at the ineptitude of politicians, and it determined to rid the political arena of those elements it disliked, which, after the League's merger with the opposition parties, were seen to be chiefly in the Labor Party.

Another sign of unrest was apparent in rural areas where the Country Party was dominant. In Western Australia the Wheatgrowers Union adopted some of the organization and tactics of industrial unionism to fight foreclosures for debt. In New South Wales, both in the Riverina and in New England, movements that looked to the formation of new states flourished, because Sydney was judged to be the source of mismanagement and neglectful of people's interests, especially those of country dwellers. In time, such moves for separation came to nothing. The White Army continued in Victoria. In New South Wales some returned soldiers, alarmed at what they saw as a thrust to demoralize the institutions of democracy, associated themselves and others in a body called the New Guard. Armed, enthusiastic and secretive, they were a pale imitation of Mussolini's Blackshirts but their numbers grew to about 60,000 in Sydney. The Guard busied itself mainly in the violent disruption of meetings it suspected to be communist inspired. Its one original act took place on 19 March 1932. The newly-constructed Sydney Harbour Bridge was the pride of the city and its future symbol. Premier Jack Lang had decided that he was the most worthy person to cut the ribbon at its opening. The New Guard leadership had decided equally as determinedly that neither Lang nor his followers were the appropriate representatives of the law-abiding, Empire-loving citizens they claimed to defend. As Lang was about to cut the ribbon, a Guard member rode forward on horseback and slashed it with his sword. He was promptly removed to a centre for the mentally deranged.

The ordinary citizenry of New South Wales, and throughout Australia, stood bemused at this event, which implied that the state was unable to preserve its own integrity. However, the New Guard and similar movements proved to be short-lived surges of fanaticism because most Australians had little taste for radical or absurd solutions to social ills. In a departure from the norm of peaceful coexistence and prompted probably by unease about foreigners taking jobs from Australians, an outburst of racial violence took place on the Kalgoorlie goldfields. An Australian miner had died in a hotel fracas with an Italian barman and about 1,000 miners, inflamed by alcohol, rioted against Italian, Greek and Yugoslav communities, killing two and burning and looting buildings.

The Aborigines and their own particular miseries of deprivation, whether cultural, economic or social, seem to have been enveloped in the general malaise that swept Australia in the 1930s. Their treatment in the Northern Territory in particular was condemned as a 'blot on the national escutcheon' and their general situation was increasingly regarded as impossible of solution unless the young among them were integrated into the wider community. Without education and skills, that solution was impractical except for a very few, among whom Albert Namatjira of the Arunta people was one. His artistic skills, by which he depicted the often harsh beauty of his native-land, were increasingly recognized, possibly because he painted in a way that was derived from European material and functional models.

Australia Day, 26 January, had been accepted as worthy of celebration by all the states since 1934 and, on the 150th anniversary of Governor Phillip's landing, the occasion was marked by a grand celebration in Sydney in 1938. Hitherto the Aborigines had remained impassive in the face of white celebrations of their occupation of the continent. On this occasion, a group of Aborigines led by William Ferguson's Aborigines Association refused to celebrate a day which they regarded as more rightly one of mourning.

During the Depression, there were bankruptcies and suicides, heart-breaks and anxieties, which bit deep into psyches, especially when the loss of work meant the loss of a home. Men, married and single, tramped the roads, rode the rattler between the towns, begged and hawked trinkets. Later, some cynics, who had not suffered the depressed times suggested that they gave some men an opportunity to flee their marital and paternal responsibilities. Dole queues of men lined up for 7s per week if single, 14s if married and an additional 7s for each child. It was no longer a crime to dye an army overcoat and the government itself issued thousands of surplus coats left over from the war, but now dyed black. Wearing one became an outward sign of misery and defeat. In the ranks of those who wore the old army cast-offs was John Ryan who had marched with the 'Kangaroos' from Wagga to Sydney in 1915 to enlist. He won the Victoria Cross during the attack on the Hindenburg defences in the last weeks of the war. After his return home, he had adjusted badly to civilian life and, by 1935, he was destitute and on the road again seeking work. By his death in 1941, John Ryan, VC, was a victim of both war and Depression.

Partly by a wages tax, State governments financed the dole and some public works, but their support for the unemployed was inadequate and partly grudging. In Victoria the Shrine of Remembrance, opened in 1934, the Yarra River Boulevard and the Great Ocean Road became monuments to the Depression because men working on sustenance, called 'susso', built them. Some of those who lost their homes often went with their families to shanty towns, like 'Happy Valley' in the sand hills near Sydney's La Perouse, where they erected ramshackle dwellings from bags and beaten out kerosene tins and where they at least enjoyed fresh air and were given unsaleable produce by the local fishermen and the Chinese market gardeners. There were such places in the other big cities and none worse than Jolimont at Melbourne, where homeless men lived in conditions that many of them had seen paralleled on the Western Front fifteen years previously.

The rabbit filled many a pot and empty stomach and gold prospecting became much more than a pastime. A sustenance worker, Jim Larcombe, found the last of the big nuggets, the Golden Eagle weighing 78 pounds, in Western Australia at Coolgardie. At times there was violence when the unemployed marched in protest in the cities, but mostly acceptance of their lot was the norm. For those who could get government assistance, survival was reduced to the purchase of basic necessities. Bread was spread with dripping in many a home, onions became a staple, hotels induced drinkers with a free sandwich, blankets were replaced with wheat bags in the bush, and in the cities cardboard covered holes in footwear. The horse sometimes came back into its own as a means of transport and traction, replacing cars and tractors.

Many children born in the twenties grew to the age of reason and then lived as teenagers in the thirties without knowing either affluence or much comfort for there was still ten per cent unemployment in 1939. In the cities their parents moved from one boarding house to another, while the father tried to earn a 'quid' by selling something, possibly one of the new gadgets such as a sewing machine or a vacuum cleaner – mostly bought on hire purchase. Moving from school to school, the children picked up the rudiments of an education, but above all they learnt to survive without revealing their poverty to their better-off schoolmates. In the bush some children grew up rarely wearing shoes, eating the plainest of food and working on the family farm for hours before and after school. The children of the Great Depression were a generation that endured to go into another war, only to see the semblance of good times come with the 1950s. For many it was too late for enjoyment. Despite the fact that the majority could not avail themselves of luxuries there was an increasingly evident influx of American innovations, including milk bars. In the Sydney schools, however, a degree of unease was expressed at the tendency of the children to use such expressions as 'Attaboy', 'sure' and 'I guess', but it was less easy to suggest Australian alternatives. The advent of an epidemic of infantile paralysis in 1937, especially in Victoria, warranted much greater concern. Forty schools were closed in Melbourne and border police tried to prevent Victorian children crossing into New South Wales.

One prominent Melbourne citizen was among those who did their utmost to combat the Depression. Sidney Myer was born Simcha Baevski of Jewish parents in Russia in 1878. He joined his brother Elcon in Victoria in 1894 and prospered as a merchant, initially at Bendigo, and then in Melbourne. By 1930 the Myer store in Bourke Street was renowned throughout the state with its only rival in Australia being Hordern's vast Italianate emporium on Brickfield Hill, Sydney. Myer issued shares to his staff, but cut their and his own wages in 1931 so that no staff need suffer retrenchment. He gave an example to other capitalists of how to stimulate the economy by selling Australian made goods, enlarging his own premises, donating over £20,000 to the Yarra Boulevard scheme and holding a vast Christmas dinner for the unemployed on Christmas Day 1930. Myer's life was one marked by philanthropy, love for and encouragement of the arts and education. His quiet revolution in the retail trade changed Melbourne in a way that made him one of the outstanding figures of his period.

Labor's short period of office, 1929–31, was eventful. Scullin's overwhelming numbers in the House of Representatives, forty-six to twenty-four, ought to have ensured a moral ascendancy despite his lack of a majority in the Senate. The capabilities of Theodore, Brennan, Lyons, Fenton and Anstey in his Cabinet also ought to have given him the human agents through which to govern well. A few steps were taken to relieve the general economic situation – personal income tax on the better-off was raised in order to boost government finances, defence expenditure cut, tariffs raised and the gold market controlled. Scullin was faced with a hostile Senate and an uncooperative chairman of the Commonwealth Bank in the person of Robert Gibson, who was determined to make governments balance their budgets. More importantly, he and his Cabinet lacked clarity as to what course to follow. The Prime Minister turned firstly to the farmers whom he exhorted to grow more wheat in the hope that increased production would compensate for falling prices. Wheat in abundance was grown, but prices remained low and it proved impossible to ensure the promised 4s per bushel of wheat, which consequently alienated a whole generation of farmers from the Labor Party. Despite the huge wheat crop, export income in 1930 was half the 1928 level. The basic wage had to be dropped by ten per cent.

Scullin's other course of action was to invite, reluctantly, an expert from the Bank of England to advise on the Australian economic situation. The expert, Otto Niemeyer, duly arrived in the winter of 1930 and, after investigation, advised the government, with some degree of ingenuity, that Australians had been living beyond their means, that they now had to cut back in public and private spending, that governments had to run their affairs without borrowing and that wages had to be reduced. In short, he had concluded that Australians were over optimistic and far too carefree in their attitudes and behaviour, especially in the way they spent money. Federal and state governments made vague promises about balancing their budgets, which they, and Niemeyer, knew were unrealistic because to do so at the time would have resulted in even greater social disorder. Niemeyer's financial advice was simple, but his political impact was considerable because he personified the very thing that many Australians abhorred – subjection to England and her bankers. On the other hand, to many wealthy and comfortable Australians, Niemeyer was the embodiment of respectability, decency and financial integrity.

Many contemporaries considered Scullin's Treasurer, Ted Theodore, as highly competent and capable of creative innovation in financial matters, but he was lost to Scullin when charges of fraud allegedly committed while Premier of Queensland forced his resignation from the Cabinet in 1930. In any case, the climate was such that Theodore could not have survived because he favoured an inflationist approach to the economy by stimulating it through bank credit, public works, a reduction in incomes and a devaluation of the currency. Lyons replaced him as Treasurer and Scullin made the grave mistake of leaving the country to its own destiny between August and January 1930–31.

Scullin attended an Imperial Conference which helped define the status of the dominions, travelled around Britain and Europe, and persuaded an unenthusiastic monarch that it was appropriate to appoint an Australian-born Governor-General to represent him in the person of Isaac Isaacs, a move branded by the federal opposition as 'practically republican'. The Prime Minister arrived home in mid-January 1931 to find his government and Cabinet in such disorder that recovery seemed impossible. However, increasing tariffs and devaluing the Australian pound by almost a third against sterling were useful steps. These measures rapidly helped to reduce imports by two-thirds. Within weeks the two men who had run the country during his absence, Fenton as acting Prime Minister and Joe Lyons as Treasurer, resigned from the Cabinet when Scullin reinstated Theodore who had been exonerated over the fraud charges.

Economic policies were the principal cause of the divisions within the Labor Party and the labour movement generally. The more cautious elements were determined to cut spending and acknowledge the financial obligations to overseas creditors, especially Britain. Responsible members of the government agreed with such measures, but saw the need for some inflation and extension of credit while the left had a range of solutions from socialization to the repudiation of debts. In New South Wales matters were further complicated after Jack Lang led Labor back to power in the state elections of October 1930. By March 1931 he was trumpeting debt repudiation to London on the grounds that the Depression was a gigantic swindle by capital to force the workers to their knees. Lang's rhetoric was mostly heady nonsense, but it met a positive response among the left elements of the labour movement. Scullin found that he was isolated from both left and right when he met the interest payments owed by New South Wales in London.

Gibson, still reigning supreme as director of the Commonwealth Bank, had threatened to completely cut off loans to the governments unless they reduced spending. A meeting was held in Melbourne in June at which the federal and state governments agreed to reduce pensions and public service salaries by twenty per cent. This lead was readily followed by private enterprise. In the meantime, business interests centred on Melbourne had decided to form a new party under the leadership of Lyons and call it the United Australia Party. When Scullin lost a confidence motion in the House in November and went to the polls, the result was a foregone conclusion. Lyons, less than a year before Labor Treasurer, now became a conservative Prime Minister. Nonetheless, the Depression continued and by the middle of 1932 unemployment was close to thirty per cent.

Scullin had tried to grapple with the financial and social problems thrown up by the Depression but he failed. Without justification the Australian electorate was unable to associate Labor with financial expertise – a quality more readily seen in their opponents. Furthermore, the Labor Party had not been in power since 1917, and it came to the Treasury benches precisely when the profligate spending in the 1920s had begun to reap its fruits to the extent, as Niemeyer pointed out, that Australia's credit rating was lower than India's. Nonetheless, the inability of the Federal Government under Scullin to present to the electorate a carefully thought-out plan for economic recovery, even were it defective, was a major cause of its downfall. In New South Wales two parties calling themselves Labor were in existence by the time of the federal elections, and the official federal party won only three seats in that state. Scullin's government was destroyed not merely by a coalition between conservatives but one which, for the temporary purpose of destruction, included those segments of the Labor movement who saw Jack Lang as the saviour.

In New South Wales, Lang commanded a huge and enthusiastic following which failed to recognize that his determination to default on interest owed to Britain on loans, while fine and flamboyant rhetoric, was an untenable position to take in the circumstances. Australia was so closely tied to British finance that to default would have brought worse and more long-lasting economic ruin. In 1932 Lang's followers remained convinced of his courage and wisdom in sufficient numbers as to persuade him to repeat his act of repudiation of interest due on loans in London. The Commonwealth again picked up the bill, but this time it decided to recover its money by a new Financial Agreements Enforcement Act, and, in April 1932, it used those powers to take over the revenues of New South Wales despite Lang's having the state Treasury barricaded.

When Lang instructed public servants not to pay money into the Federal Treasury, as the law required, the state Governor, Sir Philip Game, sacked him as Premier on 13 May 1932. In June the electorate returned a United Australia and Country Party coalition to power with a resounding victory and the reign of Lang, the 'Big Fella', was over. He went from office convinced he was right, and placards all over the country and the largest crowd in Australia's history of 300,000 people in the Sydney Domain testified to their belief that he was indeed right. Perhaps he may have been right in that his action of repudiating debts, if followed at the federal level, would have so alienated Britain and Australia from each other that some form of an Australian Republic could have eventuated. Despite his record of legislation in social matters, many Labor supporters justifiably remembered Lang as a decisive element in the destruction of the Scullin government. He lived on until 1975 after his re-admission to the Labor Party in 1971.

Despite the rigours of the Depression, there were still ways in which the generality of the people could find some outlet and enjoyment, although the banning of James Joyce's *Ulysses* deprived a few of them of participating in that initially bizarre pleasure. Attendance at football and cricket and listening to them on the wireless continued, as did having an illegal bet on the races with the local starting-price bookmakers. The automatic totalizator (tote) had also come into widespread use since its introduction at Cloncurry Park racecourse in Perth in 1916. The picture theatres never failed to attract crowds to films which allowed those present to escape into the unreality of Hollywoodian opulence, while on the stage Roy Rene, known simply as 'Mo', with his inimitable blend of earthy humour and humanity, gave a universal touch to an essentially Australian performance and delighted audiences in Sydney and Melbourne. Outdoor recreation, especially on the beaches, was inexpensive, although seven fatal shark attacks in 1934 made many bathers unenthusiastic. Bondi proved how dangerous it could be when a huge wave of 35 feet crashed onto the beach sweeping over 200 bathers out in its wake and drowning four despite the valiant efforts of lifesavers.

To go to the race course was an event in itself, and it was a rare pleasure to watch the skill and knowledge with which jockeys rode their mounts and the course bookmakers set a field. Racing's event of the year was the Melbourne Cup, held annually on the first Tuesday in November. Declared a public holiday in Melbourne, the Cup attracted huge crowds, and, by the mid-thirties, a few minutes silence descended on Australia as people everywhere listened to it on the wireless. The Cup always attracted the best trainers, jockeys and horses in Australia and New Zealand, including Carbine – who carried ten stone five pounds to victory in 1890, beating the largest ever field of thirty-nine horses – and Peter Pan who won in 1932 and 1934.

In 1929 a New Zealand bred horse, Phar Lap, ran third in the Melbourne Cup, won it in 1930 with Jim Pike as jockey, but was weighted out of a chance with ten stone ten pounds in 1931. The horse won thirty-five times in thirty-nine starts in two years and died suddenly in California in 1932, where he was taken to prove he was the best. His death, said by some to have occurred when the wind swept residual poison from nearby fruit trees onto the paddock he was grazing, reminded Australians of the death of the young boxing champion Les Darcy by blood poisoning in the United States in 1917. During Phar Lap's short career, he had given a little hope and pride to countless Australians in those depressed times, when a small wager on him could return the price of a Sunday roast. His name became a lasting legend.

During the same period, a human wizard was carving his own legend. Many old-timers still spoke in awe of the 'immortal' Victor Trumper, whose artistry with a cricket bat had held crowds spellbound both in England and Australia in the early years of the century. In 1930 Don Bradman, aged twenty-one, returned to a hero's welcome after an outstanding season in England. Unlike Trumper, to whom every stroke was a creative act, Bradman had a single purpose – to score runs and thus win matches. He had done this so effectively on the tour of England in 1930 that he had scored 974 runs, including four centuries, in seven Test innings with an average of 139, and a highest score of 334.

Bradman's equal had never been seen, and the English cricketing hierarchy knew that he had to be tamed were England to win the test series in Australia in the summer of 1932–33. The method used, bodyline bowling, was against the spirit of the game, but it proved effective. It consisted in fast bowlers concentrating their deliveries on the body of the batsman who had to choose between ducking under the ball, weaving away from it, being injured or being caught out to a packed leg field. England won the series amidst widespread recrimination and the truthful accusation by the Australian captain, Bill Woodfull, that, 'one team is playing cricket, the other is not'. Nonetheless, Australians were diverted from their own worries while the bodyline series was played even though Bradman was temporarily subdued, averaging fifty-six runs per innings. He went on to become the greatest batsman of all time scoring 6,996 runs in fifty-two test innings at an average of 99.94.

Other heroes helped to lighten the gloom of the Depression. Walter Lindrum, whose skill at billiards was never equalled and for whom the rule book was constantly rewritten, held fifty-seven world records when he died in 1960, but his greatest feats with the cue took place during the early thirties, including a world record break of 4,137 in 1932. Jack Crawford won both Wimbledon and the French tennis singles in 1933. 'Bobby' Pearce won the Diamond Sculls at Henley in 1930, a gold medal at the Commonwealth Games in Canada in the same year and Olympic gold medals in 1928 and 1932. Every Saturday saw thousands go to football grounds to watch Rugby League, Rugby Union and Australian Rules.

In the very height of the Depression, 6 June 1932, a record crowd of over 70,000 watched Australia lose a Rugby League test to Great Britain at the Sydney Cricket Ground. However, in the 1930s club and suburban loyalties shared by players, officials and spectators were the basis of all football codes, adding cohesion both to sport and society itself. South Melbourne won the Victorian Football League's premiership in 1933 despite the absence in America of their champion forward flanker, Austin Robertson, who was also world professional sprint champion. The players were happy to receive an average of £3 per match throughout the season, and total payments weekly to the team and coach rarely exceeded £75. South Melbourne's win was an historic event in itself because, over the following seventy years, it failed to win another premiership. In 1982, forced by economic pressures, it went to Sydney where the team became the Sydney Swans.

No great literature was published during the Depression, although a few writers later drew inspiration from their experiences of it. Kylie Tennant and Christina Stead tried to give literary expression to poverty and to the slum dwellers. Xavier Herbert began to grapple with the plight of the Aborigines in his great work *Capricornia,* but few Australians at the time were able to share either his love for the land or his respect for her original people. It was not until 1964 that one of the finest novels of the Depression came out, *My Brother Jack*, by George Johnston. Unlike the novelists, who needed time to distil their experiences, the artists could express their sense of reality directly, but they had nothing to say in the face of a society in trauma and produced little of value, except for Noel Counihan's work in a later period with his harsh but truthful rendering of the despair of the helpless.

In 1925 an American visitor informed his Department of State that Australians, lacking any significant historical event, had no soul. He thought that an attempt by any of the states to secede from the Commonwealth might sharpen perspectives and enliven the general scene of acceptance of the status quo. Since 1906 the 'yell of the secessionist' was loud in Western Australia, and in 1933 the farmers in the West outvoted the gold fields two to one in a referendum to secede and become an independent part of the British Empire. The farmers' vote was based on the fact that they had to sell their wool and wheat on a competitive international market and buy Australian secondary products from the eastern states which were protected by high tariffs. The Premier, James Mitchell, said that the West was the victim of 'Protection that does not protect and Free Trade that is neither free nor fair'. A visit to the West by Lyons and Hughes had done nothing to pacify feelings, and a plan to throw Hughes into the Swan River misfired.

In the election held at the same time as the referendum, the same people who voted to secede also voted out of office the conservative government that had put the referendum to them. Premier Mitchell and his Attorney General both lost their seats and the Labor Party came back into office. In this way the majority of electors in the West protested against the neglect of Canberra by voting for secession and against their own government for its failure to take decisive action to lessen the effects of the Depression. There was little interest or concern in the affair, whether in Canberra or at Westminster. A Committee set up by the British government decided that it was not proper to receive the petition to secede, which proved that once a colony had become part of the Commonwealth there was no escape from it by constitutional means. Although there was a Fremantle Sugar Party, which planned to throw sugar into the harbour in the manner of the Boston colonists at their Tea Party, unlike the Americans no one in the West was prepared to take up arms to make secession a reality.

A similarly apathetic attitude was taken to the Statute of Westminster, which was formulated in 1926 and gave independence in domestic affairs to the dominions while at the same time requiring common allegiance to the Crown. It was ratified at the Imperial Conference in 1930, passed by the Imperial Parliament in 1931, and rapidly put into legislation in the other dominions, but remained a dead letter in Australia until 1942. Some Australians thought that implementation of the Statute would weaken the ties with the Mother Country, but, in the main, most Australians saw no need to assert their national independence in the face of a Crown, which for 150 years had been looked to as the cornerstone of unity and the guarantor of safety.

There were occasions when the Australian government was prepared to question British foreign policy in the Pacific. The appointment of R. G. Casey to the new post of Australian Liaison Officer in London in 1924, and an improvement in the status of the External Affairs Department in the early thirties, helped to make information available to the government. The awareness of Australia's lack of defences and the possibility of an eventual war involving the Pacific region led to a slight reassessment of the traditional relationship with Britain and a realisation of the need to speak up, even if in hesitant and respectful tones, on Australia's behalf. In 1933 a complaint was lodged with the British Foreign Secretary when Britain unilaterally embargoed the sale of arms and munitions to China and Japan. In 1934 John Latham, Minister for External Affairs, told his Japanese counterpart that any attempt to land an army on Australian soil would result in Japan finding that she had 'a very lively nest of hornets' on her hands. The argument was clearly put to Britain that unless the Japanese were allowed to expand in their own region, specifically in Manchuria, they would probably soon turn their attention to the South Pacific, and the Americans were told that, if they continued to neglect Australia's interests, its government would have no alternative but to continue to appease the Japanese.

Latham was aware of the need to develop good relations with Australia's near neighbours. The lack of diplomatic links and the existence of only minor trade relations made close contact difficult, except with New Zealand, although relations with the Dutch government in the East Indies were maintained. Despite the broadening of Australian attitudes, no realistic assessment was made of the preferential treatment given to Britain in trade, which was further extended reciprocally in 1932. This completely ignored the growth of Japan as an industrialized nation and Australia's favourable balance of trade with Japan in primary products.

Lyons had come to office determined to balance the federal budget and thereby give a lead to the states. He embarked on a rigorous program of salary cuts including, creditably, those of politicians; he reduced the number of persons entitled to allowances and pensions; and, in an almost revolutionary move, he slashed tariffs. By mid-1932 the figures revealed that the objective of a balanced budget had made considerable headway, both federally and in the states except New South Wales, and that the trade balance had begun to register a surplus. Such developments did little to relieve the misery of the unemployed, and the 1933 budget was noteworthy for the way it favoured the affluent and the rural community. Census figures showed that one in four of the nation's breadwinners was unemployed or on a pension. More starkly still, two thirds of the male bread-winners had no income or received less than £3 per week, while three-fourths of the female breadwinners received nothing or less than £2 per week.

Nearly thirty years previously Henry Bournes Higgins had set the basic wage at £2 2s per week, which proved possible in a time when the economy was booming and there was almost full employment. The Depression revealed the frailty of the Australian social laboratory and its inability to withstand a world-wide recession. Yet, even during it, there were those who denounced 'subsidized idleness' and predicted that, come prosperity, the evil would continue because there would be a generation reared on doing nothing. Such a generation of idlers would, they feared, prefer to remain in that state of alleged bliss. To the Melbourne *Argus* the hope of the unemployed was in the restoration of 'profitable private enterprise' which was partially true, but did not recognize the fact that the principal enterprise which helped people survive the Depression was the government and the public service. They were funded by taxes, but staffed by citizens of the

Commonwealth who, for the larger part, remained in work and maintained traditions of genuine service and integrity on behalf of the nation.

One lusty child of the Depression which endured was the Australian Broadcasting Commission (A.B.C.). From the beginning, wireless stations had been supported financially by listeners' licence fees or by advertising. The government decided to take over those stations financed by fees, and, in 1932, the A.B.C., modelled on the British system, was set up with eight metropolitan and four regional stations. By the end of 1932, there were fifty-five stations and 370,000 wirelesses, and Australians had become avid listeners to soap operas, plays, sport and classical music. The establishment of studio orchestras in all states in 1936 opened the way for the development of symphony orchestras in the following decades. The people in far-flung or inaccessible rural areas were thus given the benefit of entertainment and of the informative and educational aspects of the wireless, increasingly known as radio. An elderly lady in Western Australia, who had come to Australia on a sailing vessel in 1857, listened in awe to the coronation of King George VI in London in 1937. The government permitted those stations funded by advertisements to enjoy wide autonomy, but, whether through an act of providential genius or merely to protect private interests, the A.B.C. was debarred from advertising or sponsorship. Generations of Australians looked back on that decision with relief.

The Depression did not prevent Reginald Ansett from founding an empire in the field of transport. He was born in Victoria in 1909 and, using a second-hand Studebaker car, started his own business, Ansett Roadways, running a passenger service between Maryborough and Ballarat in 1931. He had obtained a pilot's licence in 1929, and, when legislation restricted road services, he turned to the air by opening a line between Hamilton and Melbourne in 1936, which became Ansett Airways Ltd. Despite the unfavourable economic climate, his enterprise flourished and developed further into Ansett Transport Industries. It later became Ansett Airlines of Australia and the private sector of the government's two airline policies. In private enterprise, the other Australian who made a very considerable contribution was Edward Hallstrom with his Silent Knight kerosene-powered refrigerator. Even during the Depression, it sold in thousands, bringing comfort to homes in the city and rural areas, although most people still used ice chests and some the primitive but effective Coolgardie safe, which cooled the contents of the chest by water evaporation. History will surely acknowledge that the greatest contribution to the well being of homes and the comfort of housewives was refrigeration.

Another, more fanciful, child of the Depression was Lasseter's Lost Reef. Lewis Hubert Lasseter was an Australian-born dreamer who claimed to have located 'a vast, gold-bearing reef', 14 miles long, in Central Australia at some indeterminate date between 1897 and 1911. Gold had the added attraction of being a quick means of achieving wealth in bad times, so an expedition set out in July 1930 to find the reef. After a three months unsuccessful search, the party returned, but Lasseter remained behind and died in the Centre a few months later. He was clearly unbalanced, and it is extremely doubtful whether he had ever been in that part of Central Australia previously, but he had probably read some of the earlier novels based on gold finds in the central desert. In September 1931, Ion Idriess published his *Lasseter's Last Ride* that stirred the popular imagination and went through seventeen editions by 1935. The book helped to transform Lasseter into a myth, perpetuated by the name of the Lasseter Highway between Alice Springs and Ayers Rock.

The signs that the Depression was lifting because of economic restraint showed faintly in 1933, and the following years saw a gradual but discernible improvement. Five years of economic recovery followed with revenue exceeding expenditure, balanced budgets on both federal and state levels, tariffs slightly reduced. Credit was restored in London where Bruce had been able to persuade British bondholders to accept a cut of twenty-five per cent in interest. The mining industry, especially gold, but not including coal, prospered and the upturn in manufacturing after 1934 was remarkable, resulting in a slow increase in industry's share of national productivity, the creation of an industrial base for later years and the reduction of unemployment to eight per cent by 1938. After the Depression, the overall standard of living rose. Many Australians at the price of much suffering had learnt the old virtues of thrift, hard work and prudence.

Many other Australians, however, never recovered financially and wheat farmers, struck by lower crop prices and accumulated debt, were the worst hit of primary producers. Later debt-adjustment schemes were able to help only a few, although most farmers managed to hang on through a long period of deprivation. Wool growers fared better with firmer prices and greater demand, but dairy-farmers, with an increasingly restricted British market, suffered badly. By the mid-thirties jobs, especially in the manufacturing industries, became more readily available, and some children in the cities who had known only bleakness began to find that life could hold the promise of better times.

Through all the days of Australia's misfortunes, little Billy Hughes had battled on with an ever-alert eye cast on the world outside her shores. Reinstated as a member of Joe Lyons's Cabinet as Minister for Health and Repatriation, he published a book in 1935 entitled *Australia and War Today: the Price of Peace*. Billy looked out from Canberra and saw that 'The East, roused from its age long slumbers, has awakened'. For years he had been crusading for the need to prepare for war, and he saw Australia endangered by Japan which appeared to have an uncontrollable military and naval oligarchy. Lyons was embarrassed and sacked him, but Billy had the better insight, because he realised that Australia's long dependence on the British Navy, as an assurance against aggression, was drawing to a close.

16

War and the American Bonding

In 1938 an attempt was made to celebrate the 150th anniversary of white settlement in Australia, but no one showed much interest in the proceedings except in New South Wales where the anniversary had some meaning. A re-enactment of the landing of the First Fleet took place, accompanied by a protest by a group of Aborigines who refused to rejoice in the '150 years of misery and degradation imposed by the white invaders'. Despite these differing views of the meaning of the festivities for whites and for blacks, one thing was certain – Australians of whatever origin were irrevocably bound to live together and to find a common destiny. As always that destiny was inseparable from the decisions made by more powerful nations, and the 1930s had made Australia's dependence even plainer than in previous generations. Dependence heightened insecurity and combined with the aftermath of the Depression to make Australians feel insecure about their role in the world.

It was increasingly clear that little had been learnt from the experience of the Great War and some nations, notably Germany and Japan, were gearing up their military machines with aggression in mind. In those countries the same kind of reaction that had led to Australian conservatism after the Depression was in the process of consolidating regimes that led to fatal extremes. The fascist movements of Mussolini and Hitler were born, in part at least, of the wrecked hopes of millions, to whom the suffering and humiliation of their countries after the Great War were intolerable. They looked to dictators to restore national and personal dignity.

Inevitably, Australians began to take an interest in the development of the fascist regimes and, equally inevitably, differing views were held on them. Generally, those whose view of the world revolved around the desirability of moderate, structured progress governed by law and order judged such regimes benignly. Some commented on them favourably, especially on Mussolini and the alleged progress of fascist Italy. Those who regarded social change as demanding the recognition of human rights and the involvement of all sections of the community in the democratic process were cautious and critical. That small minority who looked to Soviet Russia as the model for all countries to follow, rejected fascism outright.

Despite these differing attitudes, there had been widespread displeasure in Australia when Italy used its vastly superior military power to invade Abyssinia in 1935. The government followed Britain's lead in the largely useless step of applying sanctions on Italian trade, which, nevertheless, met general approval in the electorate. Prime Minister Joseph Lyons, a man to whom peace was paramount, held strong pacifist and anti-conscription convictions, which he managed to enforce on his Cabinet. Perhaps his pacifism led him to trust Mussolini, and, at the Imperial Conference in London in 1937, he said that Mussolini had expressly requested him to say that Italy wanted peace and most especially friendly relations with her old ally, Britain. There can be little doubt that the Italian Duce would have preferred to stand beside Britain as he had done in combat in World War One, but few steps were made to ensure his adherence. In any case, opting to play both sides, he had already proposed an alliance between Italy and Germany in 1936 and signed the Anti-Comintern Pact, together with Japan and Germany, in 1937.

Germany was proving much more aggressive and recalcitrant than Italy, but Lyons was determined to add his government's voice to those who wanted to appease Hitler. Although he was horrified in 1938 at the barbarities perpetrated on the German Jews, Lyons was as anxious to deter Britain from entering into a war against Germany on behalf of Czechoslovakia as he had been in 1936 when Germany asserted its sovereignty over the Rhineland. Australia retained the cornerstone of its hastily erected foreign policy, which determined that any threat to Britain was conceived as a threat to Australia. In consequence, involvement in the defence of the 'Mother Country' would be the automatic response of Australia although a few wise commentators felt a degree of unease. Were Britain to be engaged in a war in the European theatre at the same time as Australia was involved in the Pacific, it would prove difficult for either country to help the other. The steady deterioration of Australia's relations with Japan, Japan's military and naval buildup, together with its alliance with Germany and Italy, all gave point to Australian concern about the future.

In Canberra it was felt that a Pact of Non-Aggression signed initially by Japan, the United States, Canada and Australia would ensure peace in the Pacific. President Roosevelt readily gave warm support to the idea of a Pact in 1937, but Japan was lukewarm, especially so its naval warlords, who regarded the navy as the spearhead of any future thrust into the South Pacific. Furthermore, Japan had withdrawn from the League of Nations, consolidated itself on the Chinese mainland with the seizure of Peking and

Tientsin, and showed signs of moving into the same fascist ideological orbit as Germany and Italy. Unsurprisingly, the Pact of Non-Aggression came to nothing, and the British government made it plain that in the event of a war with Germany, accompanied by Japanese involvement in the Pacific, priority would have to be given to the European zone and the war won there first. An assurance was, however, given of maintaining a 'defensive policy in the Far East' of which the essential feature would be 'economic pressure'.

No one was entirely clear what this 'defensive policy' meant, although there was general agreement among British and Australian military authorities that Australia would be incapable of repelling a full-scale Japan invasion, unless the British fleet based on Singapore were to intervene. John Curtin, Labor leader after Scullin resigned because of ill health in 1935, thought that the sensible course to follow was to engage in an immediate build up of the Air Force, which he considered the only effective form of defence for Australia. Curtin was doubtful whether Britain's naval base at Singapore would prove to be invulnerable, and he saw air power as a partial answer to Australian exposure to occupation. On one issue the Labor Party remained unmoved – it rejected all forms of conscription, while maintaining its determination to defend Australia against aggression from any source.

Curtin was a quiet, determined leader who was bent on healing the divisions in his Party caused by Lang and his followers. To him party unity was paramount although the widespread diversity of opinion within it needed to be recognized. The first inklings of a repercussion within Australian society to international events had taken place in 1937, when there was conflict between Catholics in the Labor Party who regarded Franco as the saviour of Spain, and those on the left of the Party who judged him to be a mere tool of 'the military captains of capitalism' bent on destroying a genuine workers' republic. There were very few Australians committed enough to either Franco or to the Republic to volunteer to go to Spain and fight in the civil war there, but the division within the Australian labour movement was sufficiently deep to indicate that, were a choice to arise involving conflicting ideologies, the democratic process upon which the Party was based would be in jeopardy. Curtin was fully aware of the danger of a split in the Party were the Spanish issue pressed too far, so he carefully avoided permitting it to come to prominence.

A negative reaction to Communism had been building up for some years, bolstered by the conservatism of a society bent upon economic recovery. There was a zeal to exclude Communists altogether, which led to a ludicrous situation in 1934. Egon Kisch, a Czechoslovakian agent of the Comintern, arrived to attend a Congress against War and Fascism. Kisch was refused entry, but he leapt from his ship onto the Melbourne wharf, broke his leg and was later subjected to a test in Scottish Gaelic as a condition of obtaining entry. Unsurprisingly, he failed the test, but when taken to the High Court his case was upheld on the grounds that Scottish Gaelic was not a European language. Kisch was given a further test and failed again. He was deported after attempting to convert others to his view of the world, but the case seemed to illustrate the ineffectiveness of the democratic process in attempting to curb those bent on its subversion.

At the same time, the censorship of books, conducted by clerks in the Customs department, resulted in 5,000 titles being banned on the grounds that they would tend to offend morality or good order. Their authors ranged from Defoe to Hemingway, and it was axiomatic that works by Marxist theorists were regarded as unfit for public consumption. This repressive atmosphere resulted in a reaction among intellectuals, some of whom started to move to the left. Another variation of the old 1890s nationalism was revived. P.R. ('Inky') Stephensen, a controversial writer and publicist, appealed to other Australian writers to turn from Britain to their own country as the true source of their creative spirit, while his follower Rex Ingamells founded the Jindyworobak movement to foster the same aim, as well as to encourage Australians to draw inspiration from the culture of the Aborigines. Stephensen himself went on to found the extreme nationalist movement, 'Australia First', which, through its journal the *Publicist*, expressed pro-German and pro-Japanese sympathies in 1942. This resulted in the suppression of the movement and Stephensen's internment for the duration of the war.

Living a simple life with his wife and large family at the Lodge in Canberra, Lyons was perhaps faintly aware that one of his colleagues sensed his frailty and was determined to succeed him as prime minister. Robert Gordon Menzies was his attorney general and they appeared to get along well, but events in Europe were gradually convincing Menzies that strong leadership was needed in Australia. He took it upon himself to mention his conviction publicly in a climate fraught with rumours of war. Yet, the news of a settlement of the Czechoslovakian crisis reached at Munich in September 1938 between Hitler, Chamberlain, Daladier and Mussolini seemed to promise 'peace in our time'. The passengers on the Sydney–Melbourne express, forced to change trains at Albury because of the differing rail gauges, congratulated each other when they heard the news.

Other news from Germany caused alarm because the pogrom against the Jews, involving confiscation of property, deportation and death was now widely known about. The Catholic news commentator, Denys Jackson, called it 'a new form of barbarous fetishism'. Its human evidence was soon apparent in the Jewish refugees who arrived in Australia on the *Dunera* in 1939 and whose later contribution to Australian society was considerable. Australian concern had been shown when attempts were made to found a Jewish homeland in the Kimberley, but they proved abortive, although 7,500 of the 15,000 Jews Australia had promised to receive arrived before the outbreak of war. Despite their exposure to overseas events, there was general ignorance among Australians on foreign affairs with few commentators of any quality able to proffer informed opinions. The country was isolationist and overseas news was filtered through Britain. The government timidly followed British policies closely and any suggested departure from them was quickly dubbed as disloyal.

Lyons died of a heart attack on Good Friday, 7 April 1939. His life as Prime Minister had been full of distress and he wrote to his wife some time before, 'I wish they (the Labor Party) would defeat us and we'd be out of our misery and get a little happiness.' Except by those zealots in the labour movement to whom he would always be a 'rat' because he left the Party, Lyons was a widely loved figure. There was some slight truth in his words to his wife, Enid: 'Neither you nor I can put everything right and we saved Australia from ruin. Think of the homes that are happy because of what we did and realise that no one is unhappy because of what we did'. He was buried in his native Tasmania and three weeks later Menzies became Prime Minister.

Clearly Europe was moving towards war and, were Australia to be involved, the support of the workers would be needed. The opposition to Menzies by a now revitalized trade union movement did not help him. To trade unionists he was known as 'Pig-Iron Bob' because, when attorney-general, he had tried to use the law to force striking wharf workers at Port Kembla on the New South Wales coast to load pig-iron for Japan. The government's position was strengthened, however, when it became known that Germany and the Soviet Union had signed a Non-Aggression Pact in August 1939. Many conservatives were delighted at the news of the Pact as it seemed that both the Nazis and the Communists were now in the one camp, thereby simplifying matters. Some Australian communists were confused at this turn of events, and they were not much enlightened when one of their leaders explained that the preservation of the Soviet Union had to be the main concern of the workers everywhere.

The Depression and the consequent downturn in imports had sown another seed, which bore fruit in preparing for war because Australian industry had expanded very considerably. Under the direction of Essington Lewis, Broken Hill Proprietary Limited had been modernized and diversified, and its steelworks were developed so as to rival its European counterparts. General Motors and Ford had expanded to the extent that, by 1939, most cars bought in Australia were made in Australia, although the engines were still imported. A mill at Burnie was turning out excellent paper entirely made of Tasmanian hardwood, while the first Australian war plane, the Wirraway, was built by the Commonwealth Aircraft Corporation set up by Lewis. Munitions were in production at several government-owned factories. There had been an increase in skilled factory workers who now worked a forty-four hour week, although the unions had already tentatively begun to agitate for a reduction to forty hours. Finally, a national register of all males aged eighteen to sixty-four had been introduced, which the Labor Party opposed because it seemed a first step towards industrial and military conscription.

Britain and France declared war on Germany on 3 September 1939 after her invasion of Poland, and no one was surprised when Prime Minister Menzies went on radio that same Sunday to inform Australians of the melancholy fact that their country was also at war. He elaborated this position with the words 'where Great Britain stands, there stands the people of the entire British world'. In the clearest possible terms Menzies thereby declared his nationality. It was British and, in his eyes, Australians shared it. There was no jubilation among the people, because, after the Great War, Australians knew what was entailed in a bloody international conflict. Most calmly accepted the fact although, unlike 1914, the question of national security was involved. Tears were again shed in some homes where the sorrows of Gallipoli and Flanders were remembered, but, generally, people accepted Menzies's advice of 'business as usual' and life went on.

Recruitment of a Second Australian Imperial Force began quickly, but the main problem was where to deploy the available troops. Initially the war was fought only at sea with no British troops committed to the European theatre. The conflict was quickly dubbed a 'phoney war', especially by segments of the trade union movement and communists who wondered whether the Allies were serious in their fight against fascism. Behind the problem of whether to send the troops overseas lay the preoccupation about Japan's intentions. The British Secretary of State, Anthony Eden, assured the Australian government that Japan would remain neutral 'for a time', and the British government promised to defend Singapore and Australia from any attack by Japan, although an invasion of Australia was regarded as unlikely given the lengthy supply lines which would be involved. With these comforting assurances, two Australian divisions left for Palestine in early 1940. Meanwhile, an Empire Air Training Scheme got under way in Australia, England and principally Canada, which prepared Australians to fight as air crews in the European zone.

By the end of June 1940, all talk of a 'phoney war' was over. Northern Europe was in German hands, Paris had fallen, Mussolini had entered the war as Hitler's partner and the British Expeditionary Force was withdrawn from Dunkirk. These developments heightened Australian fears, because, with her ideological allies winning in Europe, it could only be a matter of time before Japan struck in the Pacific. R. G. Casey, recently appointed as the Australian representative in Washington and thereby Australia's first accredited diplomat to a foreign power, strongly advised that the Japanese claims to Chinese territory had to be appeased because 'beggars cannot be choosers'. Concern was further strengthened by a message from London stating that no additions could be made to the fleet based on Singapore, because all available British naval strength was needed in the Mediterranean, as well as on the home seas.

Australia, it seemed, had herself become a 'beggar' with no one to defend her. The navy was committed in the Mediterranean where the sinking of the Italian cruiser, *Bartolomeo Colleoni,* by HMAS *Sydney* made Australians proud. The successes of the Australian army in Egypt against the Italians, of whom 40,000 were captured, added further to local pride, and the troops were convinced that their cause and their qualities were as good as those of their fathers. A sense of reality was brought home when 6,000 Australians of the Sixth Division were killed, wounded or captured in Greece and on Crete in April and May 1941; but the defence of Tobruk through 194 weary and dangerous days by the 2/13th Battalion of the Ninth Division, in unison with British and Polish units, added another legend to that of Anzac. The port's defenders became known affectionately as 'the rats of Tobruk' and took their place with the heroes of 1915.

When Germany invaded Russia in June 1941, the still illegal Communist Party decided that the war effort, in which it could now join, was in the best interests of the Soviet Union. With a new and different attitude taken by the previously condemnatory press to the Party, it grew in numbers to reach a peak of 23,000 in 1944 and Fred Patterson, the only self-declared Communist ever elected to an Australian parliament, won the state seat of Bowen in Queensland. Throughout Australia there was much enthusiasm for the Russians, and a campaign to procure 'Sheepskins for Russia' was launched. As time passed, the Soviet Union and its courageous people, shunned both physically and mentally since 1917, were regarded as valuable allies.

The great majority of Australians were now united in the war effort. It was easy for the government to introduce press and radio censorship as well as price control over consumer goods. The National Security Act's already wide powers were broadened so that individuals could be directed to contribute their services and property to advance the war effort. Essington Lewis was appointed Director-General of Munitions Supply, and Keith Murdoch was given a similar role in directing wartime propaganda and information. For their part, the farmers were urged to grow more wheat and wool. Daylight saving started, petrol rationing was introduced and the A.B.C. employed its first female announcer in order to free male announcers for active service.

As wartime leader, Menzies did not enjoy the confidence of the electorate, partly because of his previous ambivalence to the Fascist regimes. His own party was divided, the coalition was shaken and, when he appealed for a National Government in mid-1941 as the Japanese moved into Indo-China, Curtin's refusal on behalf of the Labor Party brought the Prime Minister's resignation. Fadden, leader of the Country Party, became prime minister for six weeks, but resigned in October so that, after ten years in opposition, the Labor Party was back with John Curtin as prime minister. H.V. Evatt, brilliant, impetuous, but erratic, resigned from the High Court to enter Parliament and became attorney general.

Curtin's main burden was becoming leader at a time without precedent in Australia's short history. The Japanese were moving quickly, without a declaration of war, and their successful attack on the main American naval base at Pearl Harbour in Hawaii on 7 December 1941 brought the immediate entry of the United States into the war. Within days, Thailand, Malaya and the Philippines were invaded, Hong Kong bombed and the pride of the British Navy, the battleship *Prince of Wales* and the battle cruiser *Repulse* sunk, thereby opening Singapore and, consequently, the Australian north to invasion. A few weeks beforehand Australia's defence capabilities were lessened when HMAS *Sydney* sank off Geraldton after a battle with a German raider, with the appalling loss of all the 654 men aboard.

Australians heard of these matters with foreboding and of the loss of the Sydney with great sadness. The government, not waiting for British approval, declared war on Japan on 9 December. Japanese forces took only weeks to occupy most of South-East Asia, driving the Australian, British and Indian troops back into Singapore. By mid-February, the so-called impregnable fortress of Singapore was in Japanese hands, together with 15,384 members of Australia's Eighth Division. Subsequently, a third of them died on the Burma Railway and in Changi Prison Camp, thereby earning for the Japanese a reputation for cruelty that would take decades to erase. This reaction was exacerbated during the early part of the war by the hate campaign conducted by propagandists in Australia itself. More than 2,700 Australian troops were captured in Java by March after the Allies surrender there and, by April, the Philippines and the Dutch East Indies had fallen. Rabaul was captured in the same month. The ancient cry of the enemy at the gates had become real for Australians. At last they were beginning to grasp that the true meaning of nationality entailed a unity of the people with the land and with each other.

Even before Singapore fell, the Japanese advance meant that, unchecked, it would lead to Australia at a time when three of her trained divisions were in the Middle East. As early as 1936, Curtin had said, 'The dependence of Australia on the competence, let alone the readiness, of British statesmen to send forces to our aid is too dangerous a hazard on which to found Australia's defence policy'. On 27 December 1941, the Prime Minister said that necessity had irrevocably shifted the balance of Australian dependence from Britain to America. His end-of-year message, published in the Melbourne *Herald*, bluntly stated, 'Australia looks to America, free of any pangs as to our traditional links or kinship with the United Kingdom'. British reaction was not recorded, but President Roosevelt was ill pleased to find his country so unequivocally adopted as Australia's sheet anchor.

The Japanese stepped deftly and quickly from island to island and they were soon in a position to threaten the Australian mainland. The first of sixty-three bombing raids on Darwin took place on 19 February 1942 with the loss of 243 lives; eight vessels were sunk in the harbour; the town, airport and port were extensively damaged, but the severity of the first raid was concealed from the general public. This decisive event convinced Curtin that his main responsibility was the defence of the nation, and he refused Churchill's request that the Australian Seventh Division, which was on its way home, go to Rangoon and help prevent the Japanese take Burma. The Australian government did not share Churchill's opinion that Australia was temporarily expendable, and it would not have been accepted by the people had they been aware of it.

The bombing raids on Darwin, Broome, Wyndham and Townsville early in 1942, the laying of mines by submarines and raiders off the coast, the sinking of seventeen vessels on the east coast with the loss of 80,874 tons of shipping and 503 lives between 1942–43, the attack by three midget submarines against shipping in Sydney Harbour, and the shelling by submarines of Sydney and Newcastle in May and June, although played down by the government, had nonetheless an enormous impact. Even before these events, at schools and in many backyards, trenches were dug. Public air raid shelters were built, blackouts enforced, beaches and headlands fortified and anti-aircraft guns and searchlights erected in the cities. In Queensland there was a virtual state of panic and in some northern towns, such as Ingham, many homes were deserted as people fled to the south. Plans were made for an evacuation had the Japanese attempted to invade the north. Resistance to the invader was also prepared and the Japanese would have met a type of guerrilla warfare in Queensland before which, even with their superior forces, success would have been dearly bought. Rupert Lockwood published *Guerrilla Paths To Freedom* in 1942 and used Mao Tse-tung, Garibaldi, Ned Kelly, the Soviet Army and others as models for Australians to 'terrorize and demoralize' the Japanese invader.

In the event, there was no invasion, and the arrival of American forces commanded by General Douglas MacArthur, who had made good his escape from the Philippines, was partly the reason. As he travelled from Alice Springs to Melbourne by train on 20 March 1942, MacArthur was shocked to learn of the small numbers of American troops, in all only 30,000, and the general weakness of the Australian forces. He said, 'God have mercy on us', when he was given an outline of the situation, but his tumultuous welcome in Melbourne cheered him and he spoke at Spencer Street Station of his great admiration for the Australian soldier and promised to 'keep the soldier faith'. Many Australians said, 'Thank God for Mac'. MacArthur, despite his long-held conservatism, formed close ties with Curtin, who had been imprisoned for his opposition to conscription in the Great War. To MacArthur, Curtin was 'the heart and soul of Australia'.

The first units of the Australian divisions arrived home in March, and, when added to the number of enlisted men who had not been sent overseas, there were over 100,000 fully-trained Australian soldiers available to MacArthur by the middle of the year, half of whom had seen action in the Middle East. To these were added the Americans who began to arrive in

April 1942 and soon numbered 120,000 men. The Americans represented a great military power and their affluence as well as their access to luxuries – cigarettes, liquor, and chocolates – made them welcome in homes, and, to the chagrin of some Australian men, also in the hearts of many local girls. One wit lamented that the Americans were 'overpaid, oversexed and over here'. Riots and brawls erupted at times between Australian and American servicemen, especially in Brisbane where MacArthur's headquarters as Commander-in-Chief in the Pacific were located. Generally, however, the presence of the Yanks, as they were known, did much to create a relationship of understanding on both sides and particularly in America, where previously Australia had been practically unknown.

The general population endured severe restrictions from 1942 until after the war. The Commonwealth took complete control of taxation, identity cards were introduced and food, including meat, tea and sugar, clothes, tobacco, liquor, but most severely petrol, were all rationed. Few grumbled seriously except at the black marketeers, who seemed to be able to provide anything at a price from Scotch whisky to silk stockings and, with the coming of the Americans, nylon stockings. The population was now a little over seven million, and women aged 18–30 were required to undertake work for the war effort. Many motorists compensated for the lack of petrol by attaching huge and awkward charcoal burners, called gas producers, to their cars. Even in cooking, the ability of Australians to make do with basic ingredients became apparent when women concocted dishes such as the Austerity Loaf and Austerity Beef. Morale, nonetheless, remained high, bolstered by such things as community singing in halls, theatres and on the radio, by newsreel segments in picture theatres, which gave war news with much emphasis to victories, and the gradual realization that the danger of invasion had receded.

In the Pacific, the war turned against the Japanese when they were contained in the Coral Sea and Midway Island naval battles in May and June 1942, although they remained on the offensive in 1943. Although they were repulsed in the Bismarck Sea, in May 1943 they sank the hospital ship *Centaur* off the Queensland coast with the loss of 268 lives and bombed installations at Exmouth Gulf, Western Australia, which was their most southerly attack on the Australian mainland. On the islands of the Pacific, the struggle was long drawn-out and costly in men and material on both sides. A key event had occurred on 2 November 1942 when, after grim fighting, the Japanese were driven back from near Port Moresby along the Kokoda Track, which added its name to Tobruk in the recent history of

Australian war legends. With some opposition in the labour movement – notably from Arthur Calwell, Minister for Information, who, like Curtin, had memories of the anti-conscription campaigns of the Great War – the Labor government introduced conscription for the South-Western Pacific zone in early 1943 and the now respectable Communist Party supported the measure.

Although the Australian commander, General Thomas Blamey, found it an irksome experience to serve under MacArthur, the two armies fought together amicably enough, especially in Papua and New Guinea, which MacArthur regarded as the true battleground for the safety of Australia. To back up the campaign in the islands, the Americans engaged in huge construction works in Australia in roads, bridges, airfields and buildings, and Australians saw bulldozers, brought by the Americans, for the first time. With this kind of support, the armies in the islands gradually gained the upper hand, although the Japanese fought grimly, gave no quarter and knew nothing of surrender. Their desperation was apparent on 5 August 1944, when, in the largest outbreak in the course of the war, 234 prisoners and three Australian guards died in a mass, suicidal attempt at escape from the prisoner of war camp at Cowra in New South Wales.

In the islands, Australian servicemen came into contact with peoples whom they had not encountered before. Many remembered with gratitude the assistance given in New Guinea by some courageous and generous sections of the local population who became known as 'fuzzy-wuzzy angels', although others collaborated with the Japanese. In Timor the indigenous people made great sacrifices to help the Australians, which was remembered by many in the 1970s when East Timor was again in trouble, despite the reluctance by the government to support the cause of independence of East Timor from Indonesia. Generally the Pacific War was marred by the continuation of 'mopping up' operations throughout the islands long after there was any need for them. They caused unnecessary deaths and injuries to both combatants and non-combatants and served only to glorify the commanders in charge of them.

Early 1943 in Africa saw the Germans defeated at El Alamein, where the Australian Ninth Division helped conquer Rommel's Afrika Korps. In Europe the war slowly turned in favour of the Allies in the west and of the Russians in the east. By May 1945 Berlin had fallen and Hitler's Third Reich had collapsed in ruins with death and destruction as its legacy. The Japanese continued to fight on in the Pacific, until the destruction of Hiroshima and Nagasaki by atomic bombing in August 1945 caused formal surrender. Into the future there were arguments as to whether the act of annihilation of civil populations by such total means was ever justifiable.

The RAAF had contributed gallantly to the defence of Britain where many Australians fought with the RAF while several squadrons under Australian command operated from Britain, the Middle East, North Africa, Italy and Corsica. As the war developed in the Pacific zone, the RAAF was called upon to contribute in the air, which it did with great effect until the very end. A total of 190,000 men and 27,000 women enlisted in the Air Force and there were nearly 14,000 casualties of whom over 10,000 died.

In all the zones in which it operated, but notably in the Pacific, the small Australian Navy of nearly 40,000 men and women made a great contribution. The Australian army suffered the loss of over 20,000 dead. The total of 33,826 dead of the armed forces was about half the dead of 1914–18, although this did nothing to appease the grief of those who lost their loved ones. The wounded and injured came to 180,864, and 23,059 had been prisoners of war while the monetary cost of the war was over £200,000,000. Six years of sacrifice, austerity, determination and grim resolution had seen the Australian people united as never before.

The social and economic effects within Australia of the war were far reaching. The demands of a wartime economy, at its peak in 1942–43, meant that 40 per cent of the national income was spent on the war effort, and the federal government took over all personal income tax collecting using the pay-as-you-earn (P.A.Y.E.) method after 1943. As a result, there were no longer anomalous discrepancies in tax ratios between the states as had previously been the case when Queensland had a maximum level of 1s in the pound and Victoria only half that amount. Another important consequence was that, henceforth, the states had to look to Canberra for their main source of revenue. This step gave the federal government centralized control over state development. To help further in raising revenue, a tax on company profits, a pay-roll tax and an entertainment tax were imposed but, despite the cessation of hostilities and the removal of the need for their imposition, they remained in place. A National Welfare Fund was established to provide a pool from which social security benefits would be funded as well as a child endowment payment for families with more than one child under 16 and a widow's pension.

Although the Military Board early in the war regarded the recruitment of non-whites as undesirable, public opinion was aroused against the measure and 3,000 Aborigines enlisted while many served as patrollers and coast watchers in northern Australia. Reg Saunders, whose father had served in the first AIF, became a commissioned officer and his brother Harry was killed on the Kokoda Track. Leonard Waters, a Queensland shearer, flew 95 operation sorties with the RAAF and several Aborigines were decorated. Many worked on construction projects in Northern Australia at award wages and all received social service payments. Aboriginal women also contributed significantly to the war effort. Oodgeroo Noonuccal, among others, enlisted in the army while others worked in factories and at military camps. As a consequence, some Aborigines began to enjoy a degree of equality with white Australians and the government, in 1949, extended the franchise to Aboriginal ex-service personnel. Nonetheless, many resented the fact that the equal standing they had been granted in wartime did not extend fully into post-war life and in particular that they had to apply for a 'dog tag' so as to enter a pub and enjoy a beer with their former army mates on Anzac Day.

The demands on manufacturing industry during the war were such that a genuine quantum leap was taken, especially in the making of all kinds of arms and munitions, vehicle and aircraft engines, as well as optical glass, without which many weapons would have been useless. Under the direction of Essington Lewis, to whom both Menzies and Curtin gave enormous power, industry contributed to the war effort in a way that helped make Australia an effective partner with America in the Pacific. The chemical industry advanced rapidly in petrochemicals and synthetic rubber, and also in drugs, vitamins and other products, often produced from native shrubs. In steel making, power production, in heavy and light engineering and in electrical goods there were also advances. To assist in all of this development and to maintain productivity, especially in the rural sector, over 200,000 women entered the workforce. Together with the 52,000 women who joined the services and the other half a million already in the workforce they were able, at least for the duration of the war, to feel that their contribution was necessary and valuable, and all Australians recognized it as a highly significant social development.

Despite the acquiescence of most people in the imposition of wartime restrictions, they were prepared to tolerate curtailment of their freedom for the period of the war only. Although Curtin won a resounding victory in the 1943 general elections, including a win in the Senate, a referendum held in 1944 to continue Commonwealth government control over the labour force and the economy was lost. Undaunted, Curtin worked on and, looking to the future, he set up a Ministry of Post-War Reconstruction under John Dedman in 1945. Unnoticed except by those who were closest to him, the prime minister's health was breaking under the strain, but his wholehearted leadership of Australia had won the respect of all, including that of Churchill with whom he had so strongly differed. John Curtin died in Canberra on 5 July 1945 without experiencing the joy of seeing the end of the war in the Pacific. In the meantime, the forces of Australian conservatism had regrouped when Robert Gordon Menzies founded the Liberal Party of Australia at Albury in October 1944.

17

A New Wave

A few days before the end of the Pacific War, Arthur Calwell, with the new title of Minister for Immigration, spoke in the House of Representatives. He was the embodiment of the now venerable traditions of the Labor Party in that place, where it alone had been represented continuously since federation. Nevertheless, he had a policy to propose that ran contrary to the firmly held traditions of his Party. Long before the days of the organized labour movement, the workers had always been uneasy about governments assisting migrants to come to the Australian colonies. It seemed too easy for employers to use such people as a weapon to break down working conditions and to lower wages. Such, in fact, had never happened, but the mythology was strong, and the trade unions and, later, the Labor Party itself had generally opposed assisted migration.

Despite the past, Calwell, with the full approval of the Party and the acquiescence of the unions, proposed a scheme of assisted migration on a large scale that would also embrace refugees from Europe. Calwell's scheme was introduced in 1946 with the aim of achieving 70,000 immigrants annually by 1948. Those from the United Kingdom were expected to pay £10 for their passage, with the British and Australian governments making up the remainder. The whole scheme was so successful that the government was forced to cut back the intake from 170,000 in 1952 to less than 80,000 in 1953. In 160 years the population of Australia had grown to less than eight million. As a result of the realization of the vulnerability of the country with its small population, the most remarkable and far-reaching effect of the Second World War was to increase that number as quickly, efficiently and smoothly as possible.

Calwell was as committed to the White Australia policy as any purist of the past had been, and it was initially intended that only immigrants of European extraction would be welcome. Few Australians had any real objection to the British or, as they were mostly affectionately called, Poms, but many took a different attitude to southern Europeans. A survey, conducted in 1948, indicated, with signs of deeply ingrained ethnic bigotry, that Germans were more acceptable than either Italians or Jews. When it became clear that not enough migrants were available from northern Europe, especially the British Isles, Calwell turned to the south for more. Moreover, the European war had cast up vast numbers of displaced persons who were not Anglo-Saxon in origin, but who possessed the qualities to settle in new lands and over a million of them were prepared to do so. The Australian government was willing to take some of them despite a degree of local disapproval. Calwell went to work and obtained the shipping necessary for transport; toured the camps of displaced persons; set up offices in European capitals to facilitate the selection process and prepared a climate among Australians to receive the new settlers. The first to arrive from Europe were from Latvia, Lithuania and Estonia.

With one exception, the success of the scheme was astonishing. Some thousands of immigrants, including many Italians, had spent months in 1952 in the Bonegilla migrant camp in Victoria. They had been promised work within a month of their arrival in Australia, but it was not forthcoming. Eventually becoming desperate, they demanded 'Give us work or send us home to Italy.' They took to lying on the train tracks and finally, led by Giovanni Sgrò and a small group of delegates, they marched in thousands on the administration building, smashing windows and firing some of the huts as they went. Four tanks and over 200 soldiers with arms in their hands met them. A repeat of the bloody affair at Eureka in 1854 was narrowly avoided and, in time, the men obtained work, often by their own efforts.

With their skills and determination to make good in Australia, the immigrants helped lay the foundations of a labour force with which to build manufacturing and construction industries and to secure economic prosperity for the next twenty years. By 1949, when the Labor Party lost office, 500,000 immigrants had been welcomed. Only a third were from the British Isles, and many of the rest were 'Balts', 'Dagoes' or 'Reffos' – nicknames which did not necessarily imply either suspicion or rejection, but merely an acceptance that the 'new Australians' were different to those of the old variety. Many immigrants initially had to go into camps where they often experienced hardship. Most were obliged to work in specified jobs for two years, frequently in work unsuited to their qualifications so that doctors became ward attendants and scientists were put to work as laboratory cleaners. Indeed, the medical profession proved to be a 'closed shop' for the great majority of medically qualified immigrants who found that their only pathway into the profession was by repeating their training at an Australian university. One profession that proved to be open handed and just in its dealings was engineering. Careful scrutiny was made of qualifications, and those who satisfied the criteria were accepted as engineers. In the main, the immigrants eventually settled in the new society, with varying degrees of acceptance on their own part and on that of the 'old' Australians but, in the main, acceptance by both was entirely positive.

As with other waves of immigrants in previous decades, the great majority began in a lowly way, living in the less desirable suburbs, taking the jobs least sought out by others and enduring the hardship of relegation to second-rate and third-rate citizenship. European women in particular found the new society strange and integration, especially for those who remained at home, was slow and, at times, heartbreaking if indeed it ever occurred at all. With time, the rest settled even if painfully, and their differences, whether of language and accent, food, drink, outlook or cultural attainment, blended with and gradually transformed the society they entered. Often in a broken way at the start, the great majority learnt to speak English with the accent forged since the first settlement at Sydney Cove.

The experiment in nation building in the post-war period had no parallel in Australian history. The gold rushes saw more people, as a proportion of the population, arrive in Australia, but that wave was unplanned and mainly Anglo-Saxon in origin. This time the initiative rested with the government, and non-Anglo-Saxons were in sufficient numbers to make them noticeable. The fact that the Labor Party, which had pledged itself to full employment, accepted the risk that a vastly increased workforce posed to its policy, made the whole scheme more significant. With this development, Australia entered the third phase of its history. Up to 1850, the theme had been one of survival and settlement. After 1850, consolidation of the Anglo-Saxon dominance was the aim. From the mid-1940s, perhaps unwittingly, diversification in the origins of the immigrants and hence a diverse population became the keynote. Arthur Calwell little knew that the policy of 'populate or perish' he so passionately and effectively made work, would lead inexorably to the eventual dismantling of the White Australia policy, which had been fundamental to the idea of federation.

In 1946 Ernest Burgmann, Anglican Bishop of Goulburn, (later Canberra and Goulburn), asked in prophetic tones whether the time had come for Australians interested in planning their country's future to be more concerned with culture rather than colour. He courageously suggested that a finer race would emerge if, overcoming prejudice, there was 'a gradual infiltration of other colours into the blood stream'. In this, as in so many of the social policies he supported, Burgmann was ahead of his time, but when he died in Canberra in 1967 his dream of 'infiltration' was about to take place.

At the same time as the new immigrants were arriving, the 700,000 Australians who had served in the war had to settle themselves into a way of life markedly different to the one they had grown accustomed to in the services. Their experience of travel inside and outside of Australia, the exposure of many to learning and culture, the work of the Army Education Service, the rank they had held and the authority they wielded, had opened up expectations that made them a new generation. When they entered civilian life, some were dependent for the first time upon their own ability to earn a living in a workforce. Many had to readjust to the demands, as well as to the warmth and comfort, of family life. Little things, such as the six o'clock closing of hotels, which remained the law in New South Wales until 1955 and Victoria until 1966, proved irksome to men and women who considered that they had made enough sacrifices and whose exposure to more mature cultures led them to judge such restrictions as absurd.

Cigarettes, clothes and luxury items were scarce and rationing of clothes and meat continued until 1948. Housing was very difficult to obtain and some new homes were built using fibro sheeting for the exterior walls, which made them hot in summer and cold in winter. The deference shown to the uniform disappeared and few people outside immediate family circles wanted to hear tales of the exploits, the heroism, the horror, or the mere monotony of life in action. Fortunately, the prediction made by some economists that the post-war period would see up to eight per cent unemployment did not materialize, and grants given to returned men to further their education at any level, including university, were readily available and eagerly accepted. With the influx of returned servicemen into the universities, especially Sydney and Melbourne, an intellectual and political ferment began to emerge which in retrospect seemed a golden age to many later students. In 1946 the Australian National University had opened in Canberra, initially as a research and postgraduate institution. Among its first Ph.D. scholarship holders there were several ex-servicemen.

While the rural economy had suffered from a severe drought in 1944 and 1945, the demand for wool and wheat in countries ravaged by the war brought a speedy recovery, and the outbreak of the Korean War in 1950 increased the demand for primary products. The price of wool increased from 2s per pound in 1947 to 12s in 1950, and graziers breeding superfine merinos sometimes received the hitherto unheard of price of 20s per pound. The acreage under wheat increased, as did the price of wheat, and 20,000 tractors were bought by farmers in 1952. Under the direction of a newly established Wheat Board, which guaranteed a minimum purchase price, farmers who had been through hardship and drought began to prosper so that they were able to replace run-down equipment and engage in improvements to their properties. The scientific use of superphosphates and trace elements in deficient soils also helped to raise productivity.

The main factor creating employment and boosting the economy was a demand for goods produced by industry. During the war, Australian industry had of necessity rapidly developed skills and efficiency and proved that it could produce quality goods. After the war, industry responded to demand, most markedly in the automobile sector. Inspired by the drive and foresight of Lawrence Hartnett and with the full backing of Prime Minister Chifley, the Holden car, to the accompaniment of a ten-piece orchestra, was launched at Fisherman's Bend, Victoria, in November 1948. The Holden was a sign of Australian progress and independence, because no American money was used to finance the venture. The on-the-road cost of the six-passenger vehicle was £760; it did thirty miles to the gallon (10.6 kilometres to the litre) and had a maximum speed of eighty miles (129 kilometres) per hour. Long waiting lists quickly exhausted the flow of 20,000 units a year and to own a Holden became a badge of prosperity and a source of pride in Australian ingenuity. By 1962, when Australians had become the fourth largest car-owning people in the world, a million Holdens had been manufactured, but in the first years of production its cost was prohibitive to most Australians being double the annual average wage.

The initial period of recovery was under the Labor government led by Ben Chifley who was determined not to allow the economy to run on unbridled. Personal income taxes rose with the need to pay for social services but, because the medical profession still blocked a national health scheme, the poor, who could not contribute to private health funds, continued to suffer. The use of x-rays to make an early diagnosis combined with a government campaign to bring about the virtual elimination of tuberculosis, which had been the greatest cause of death for the twenty to forty year olds. Poliomyelitis continued to ravage the young until the Salk vaccine effectively wiped it out after the mid 1950s.

The Labor government also initiated the most comprehensive construction scheme in Australia's history, which began in 1949 under the direction of the Snowy Mountains Hydro-Electric Authority. Using a network of tunnels and dams, the scheme was designed to irrigate dry land for food production and generate electricity at half the cost of power stations that burnt coal or oil. The Authority attracted 5,000 to its workforce, most of whom were immigrants, and its low record of labour unrest was probably due to high wages and the community spirit engendered by the almost pioneering conditions under which the men worked. When the scheme was completed twenty-three years later, its objectives had been completely achieved. In its planning it seems to have escaped general notice that a by-product would be the reduction of the once strong-flowing and gracious Snowy River, itself a kind of icon of the bush, to a virtual trickle. Fifty years passed before the Victorian and New South Wales governments decided to rectify the damage, in part at least.

Part of the Labor government's commitment to an overall objective of post-war reconstruction was expansion of the tertiary sector in education. The Australian National University attracted a group of eminent, expatriate scholars to found its research schools and, in the following years, the older universities were transformed by an injection of funds, thereby augmenting staff numbers as well as teaching and research facilities. Trans-Australia Airlines was set up under government ownership to compete against private carriers on internal routes, and, in 1947, the government bought Qantas from Qantas Empire Airways to be the national carrier on international routes. The necessity to buy vessels to transport migrants after the war led to the establishment of a national shipping line, which helped to maintain a shipbuilding industry and provided a mercantile marine service.

These steps were acceptable even to those who regarded every move into the private sector as another expression of Labor's design to socialize the economy. As the people at large were enjoying a new prosperity, it was, however, difficult for Labor's opponents to make much headway by cries of socialization. With the general introduction of the forty-hour week by 1948, there was time for a variety of pursuits and the money to enjoy them – to go regularly to the pictures on a Saturday evening while the kids had been to the matinee shows in the afternoon, to take the family to the beach or to the mountains, to have a picnic on a Sunday, to visit relatives and generally resume the activities that war had interrupted. Even so, there was still the reminder of the austerity of war because petrol rationing was retained until 1950. More children stayed on at school, and the universities began to see entrants who were neither wealthy nor on scholarships. Furthermore, there was the chance to take some pride in Australia as a minor power in peacetime, rather than to look back at war as the testing ground of the nation.

With H.V. Evatt as Foreign Minister, a policy emerged which, unlike in the past, was not solely connected with Australia's defence. New Zealand had always been regarded as part of the family as well as a friendly neighbour, so it was logical to cement the bonds in 1944 with an Anzac Agreement designed to ensure the two nations co-operated in furthering their common interests. Having helped in the creation of Israel, Evatt was elected President of the United Nations in 1948; he surprised those Australians who thought that he was under communist influence and incurred the displeasure of the Russians by his protests against the treatment of Cardinal Mindszenty in Hungary. He fully supported the independence of India and his initially reluctant, but finally firm, stand for Indonesia in its bid for freedom from Dutch rule, enthusiastically backed by the Waterside Workers Union which banned Dutch supplies, gained him and his country the warm gratitude of the Indonesians, which long afterwards, in less amicable situations, was sometimes remembered.

When China became communist controlled in 1949, Evatt insisted that such a situation should not preclude commercial and eventual diplomatic relations with her, although his own government did not recognize the new Chinese one. Nonetheless, he was genuinely concerned at the development of the communist movement in Asia and also in Europe where Russia had begun to extend its control over most of the Eastern states. Evatt was probably swayed by these considerations when he agreed to the formation of a secret body, later called the Australian Security Intelligence Organization, which eventually and ironically helped bring about his own downfall.

Australians did not want any form of national independence for themselves and in 1947 a Gallup poll indicated that sixty-five per cent, as against twenty-eight per cent, preferred having British nationality to a separate Australian one. Eighteen months later, another poll showed that Australians ranked first of six nations (the British ran third and the French last), in response to a question as to whether they were happy. This may have meant that they saw happiness stemmed from a lack of concern about larger questions than personal fulfilment. In any case, the fact that the retention of British nationality, and consequently British passports, was increasingly meaningless was not as important to Australians as the symbolic tie with Britain, but in 1949 the Nationality and Citizenship Act became law and Australians ceased to be British subjects.

The Labor government attempted to retain its sense of responsibility for the direction of the economy despite the good times and some Labor members were determined to control the banking system. Some of them had youthful memories of the bank crashes during the depression of the 1890s, and all retained a taste of bitterness from the days of Niemeyer and Gibson in the 1930s with their reminder that the Australian government was helpless in the face of the banks. Chifley tried to reform the system in 1945 by abolishing the Commonwealth Bank Board and making the Bank responsible, through a governor, to the Federal Treasurer. All banks were required to deposit a proportion of their reserves with the Commonwealth Bank, which set interest rates. Finally, only those banks controlled by government could be repositories for the accounts of all Commonwealth, state and local governments and their instrumentalities. There was a degree of outrage at this measure, which the Melbourne City Council challenged in the High Court in August 1947. The Court judged the measure to be unconstitutional and therefore invalid.

Given that the electorate was still prepared to trust Labor provided it restricted its control to areas not generally accepted as fundamental to private enterprise, Chifley's reaction to the High Court decision was impetuous, but understandable. He persuaded his colleagues that the only course of action was to bring the whole banking system within the ambit of the Commonwealth Bank, in effect to nationalize the banks. The outcry was immense, despite the fact there was no evidence that public or private money was in danger. An avalanche of propaganda, orchestrated by the press, fell on the government, which was portrayed as only one step removed from ushering in a socialist state. A year later the High Court again found against the government, and the Privy Council in England upheld the decision. This meant that the Commonwealth Bank, while retaining its centralized powers, was no more than one other competing agency in the banking market place. By the 1990s, when the banks, including the privatised Commonwealth Bank, had become vast, profit-making ventures only minimally related to the community on which they fattened, some looked back with nostalgia to what might have been.

The domestic argument about the banking system highlighted the concern about socialism that the tensions of the Cold War was making evident on the international scene. The success of several leading communists in winning important trade union elections had fostered a considerable attitude of reserve in the Australian electorate towards any organization showing left-wing tendencies. This was heightened in June 1949 when the communist-controlled Miners' Federation called a strike in New South Wales. The union wanted a 30s weekly rise in wages plus three months paid leave every seven years, and claimed that the request for a thirty-five hour working week was not being processed rapidly enough. As the strike spread to other states and stocks of coal ran low, electricity usage was rationed, firms laid off their workforce for weeks, and the country was thrown into industrial and domestic chaos.

The government froze the union's funds, some communist leaders were imprisoned and troops were sent to work open-cut mines. To the left wing of the labour movement this proved that their leaders were mere tools of capitalism. To many other Australians the attempt to nationalize the banks combined with the strikes to prove how unsafe the country was under Labor. The anti-communists exploited this feeling and sought to alarm voters. It was also unfortunate that, at a time when many voters were enjoying their new Holdens or imported cars, Chifley insisted that petrol rationing was still needed to maintain the exchange rate and help Britain with her trade balance. The electorate was fed up with wartime controls after a decade of restrictions and welcomed promises by Labor's opponents to remove them. For all these reasons, the end of 1949 was not a good time for Labor to go into an election.

Menzies went to the polls proclaiming that to vote for Labor was to bow under the yoke of socialism – to him an 'alien and deadly growth'. He had a basket of choice offerings for the electorate labelled 'putting back value into the pound'. They ranged from the abolition of petrol rationing to the banning of the Communist Party. The result of the elections was a handsome reward for the coalition parties, who were able to take office knowing that they were governing in a period of prosperity not enjoyed since the 1880s. The fact that Australian troops, a mere five years after the end of World War II, began to arrive in South Korea in September 1950 and went into action almost immediately, did nothing to dispel the air of contentment. When the war began to take its human toll, it went almost unnoticed except in the families of the 1,396 casualties and 277 dead, including some Aborigines. Hostilities ceased on 27 July 1953 and, a few weeks previously, Private Toby Hazel had written home to his Aboriginal parents from Korea. He told them that his Battalion was to go 'up to the front on Sunday night' and added that, though he 'a bit windy' about going into action, he supposed 'it will be okay after I get used to it'. He had little time to become accustomed to combat. Toby's brief war ended when he was killed in action a week later on 25 June 1953.

There were some promises that Menzies stuck by, although he was only able to deliver less than half of his electioneering basket. Child endowment was extended to the previously excluded first child in a family, milk was distributed to school children, and medical care given freely to pensioners. In 1953 Earle Page was able to introduce a modified version of Labor's envisaged Medical Benefits Scheme, when he persuaded the medical profession that neither their wealth nor their social position would thereby be endangered. Compulsory national service training for selected eighteen-year-old males was introduced caused by concern that the Cold War in Europe would lead inexorably to real war. Harold Holt, a young protege of Menzies, who had become Minister for Labour and National Service, explained that the six months' period of training would improve the physical fitness of the trainees, and many of the youths in question subsequently agreed.

To his, and the coalition's, credit, Menzies continued the Labor government's immigration program, and he warmly praised Calwell for his initiative in setting it up. Holt was also Minister for Immigration and, in January 1951, he enthused publicly about the benefits of taking in close to 100,000 immigrants annually. Holt thanked the trade unions for their co-operation and noted that even militant unions had accepted immigrants with ten per cent of the workers at the Newcastle and Port Kembla steelworks being displaced persons. The remarkable thing about the whole program, however, was the way in which the Australian people, led by government, churches and neighbourhood groups had accepted, or at least tolerated, the new wave of immigration. For Labor the irony was that many of the displaced persons had fled from Europe with a horror of communism, which made them disinclined to vote for a party that cynics and opportunists, and a few honest persons, labelled as pro communist.

In April 1950 Menzies brought in a bill to ban the Communist Party, seize its assets and declare persons who belonged to it 'unlawful'. At the time there were about 10,000 communists in the country and only a small fraction of the electorate ever voted for communist candidates, but it was unquestionably true that communist strength in key trade unions was marked. It was also true that most communist trade union leaders showed a sense of responsibility to their fellow workers, which was the main reason for their election to such positions. As a secular creed, communism or Marxist-Leninism had begun to fill a void in the minds of many intellectuals to whom Christianity, often untried but found still wanting, was pernicious or merely irrelevant.

Within the Labor movement there were some who, impatient with mere reformism and the long struggle to tame rather than overthrow capitalism, looked to the kind of more decisive action that they saw exemplified in the Soviet world. Yet neither they nor the communists, many of whom were loyal Australians, wanted to destroy the existing structures of government and society by force, although the chairman of the Communist Party,

Lawrence Louis Sharkey, was sentenced to three years' imprisonment in 1949 for having stated that Australian troops would welcome Soviet forces were they to enter Australia 'in pursuit of aggressors'. Probably a majority of Australians genuinely thought that the Communist Party should be banned nonetheless, although it never became clear why, except to a group of militant Catholics who had been tireless in denouncing communism as far back as the days of the Spanish Civil War.

In 1931 Archbishop Mannix had encouraged a few Victorian Catholics to form a society that they named after an English Jesuit martyr, Edmund Campion. By examining the history and intellectual heritage of their faith, they realized its universality, which over-rode its Irish Australian content. To them it seemed clear that the main, contemporary threat to the Church was international communism closely followed by rampant capitalism. They published a vigorous weekly, the *Catholic Worker*, and eventually Industrial Groups were formed to contest union leadership against communists which, with Labor Party blessing or mere tolerance, were often, and increasingly, successful. The Labor Party had a long history of opposition to communists involving themselves in union affairs – based as much on political expediency as on the desire for ideological purity – and the Industrial Groups thereby fitted into a well-known category to be tolerated as long as they proved convenient.

Understandably the success of the Industrial Groups bred opposition to them by some powerful members of the Labor movement. Seeing their base in the industrial sector eroded, they were quick to deny to Catholics who opposed them in the Labor Party the right to the same kind of political activity they had temporarily granted to communists. B.A. (Bob) Santamaria, a young Catholic lawyer, led a secretly organized Movement that stood behind the Industrial Groups. To the extent that it was an official body of the Church, criticism of it and the Church itself was valid. Otherwise some criticism of Santamaria's Movement was an expression of mere bigotry, or was based on the desire to retain factional and personal power within political Labor and the union movement.

Within the Labor caucus, there was a solid Catholic minority that shared Santamaria's attitude to communism. Chifley as leader and Evatt as deputy realized that the unity of the Party was threatened and decided to compromise on Menzies's Communist Party Dissolution Bill and the Senate eventually passed it. Evatt appeared for the Waterside Workers before the High Court in a case against the Act, which caused accusations that he was soft on communism. The Court ruled that the Act was unconstitutional and the upshot was a double dissolution, with Menzies promising a referendum, which, if successful, would give Parliament power to ban the Communist Party and all its followers.

In April 1951 the Liberal-Country Party coalition won the election and took control of the Senate. A state ball was held in June to celebrate the Golden Jubilee of the Commonwealth Parliament, but Chifley, re-elected leader of the Party, remained in his Canberra hotel to work. Weakened by strain, worry and work he died that night leaving behind a legend as the Labor leader par excellence – loyal, intelligent, determined and always a worker. But above all he was an Australian who, in his own words, had seen and struggled towards 'the light on the hill' which lit up the path to a just and humane society. His other legacy was H.V. Evatt whom caucus elected as leader. With Menzies's referendum set for September, the caucus choice was one which, in the long run, would admirably suit Menzies.

Those who remembered 1917 saw in essence a re-run of how a community can be divided on a moral issue. Again the powerful organs of the media were lined up to persuade people to vote 'Yes' and thus ban the Communist Party and its followers. Unlike 1917 the Catholics mainly joined with the conservative forces, but Archbishop Mannix, true to conscience again, publicly declared that he would vote 'No'. Menzies campaigned with brilliant vigour, but Evatt did even better. In September 1951 a very narrow majority, (50.48 per cent) of the whole electorate, voted 'No', and only Queensland, Western Australia and Tasmania voted 'Yes'. The referendum was probably lost because a majority of Australians did not think it just to place the onus of proof on the person accused of illegal communist practices rather than on the prosecution. One curious side effect was that the Communist Party lost ground, but it did not mean that the problem of communism would be allowed to disappear.

In the same month that the Australian people rejected what virtually would have been the persecution of communists at home, their government took a step designed to contain communism in the Pacific. Australia, New Zealand and the United States signed a treaty alliance called ANZUS at San Francisco, binding them to meet and consider the common danger, were a signatory attacked. For Australia the basis of the treaty was the firm conviction that only the United States would be able to come to her aid in the South Pacific in the face of any potential aggressor, although the treaty contained no assurance that it would do so. Nevertheless, the treaty was signed in the awareness that, like 1941, Churchill was alarmed at Australia's slide towards America.

A turning point for Australia was the victory of communism in China in late 1949, just as Japan's entry into the war had been in 1941. Percy Spender, Minister for Foreign Affairs, spelt out a theory in March 1950, which was based on China being a communist power. Spender foresaw first Vietnam and then Laos and Cambodia falling to communism. Thailand, Burma, Malaya and finally Indonesia would then be under threat. All he needed to say to sum up Australia's position, and its consequent foreign policy for the ensuing decades, was 'No nation can escape its geography'. This was a conclusion white Australia had been groping towards since 1788, but it had never previously been understood in the way Spender intended.

The official public life of a nation is never as indicative of its vitality as is the growth in communal awareness seen in its culture, both high and popular. During and after the war, high culture developed in art, music and literature in a manner not seen since the 1890s. The development had its roots in the 1930s when the lack of abundance forced a rethinking of provincial values, and the artists, in particular, began to realize that new forms of expression had arisen in the northern hemisphere. European art had begun to reflect the agony of a society, which, since the sixteenth century, had gradually moved from its Greco-Roman and Christian wellsprings towards atheistic humanism and secularism. Traditional values were no longer seen as bulwarks for societies faced by new forms of totalitarianism of the right and the left, and art, being more universal than language, began to respond. The Melbourne *Herald* staged an exhibition of modern painting in 1939 including works by Cézanne, Matisse, Van Gogh, Chagall, Picasso and Dali. The exhibition produced some negative reaction, but it was also part of the excitement and creativity that led to the founding of the Contemporary Art Society in Melbourne and Sydney. In Sydney, William Dobell painted a range of portraits, which combined technique with acute insight into human nature and culminated with his Archibald Prize winning portrait of Joshua Smith in 1943. A court was asked to judge whether it was a portrait or a caricature and decided that it was both, which was one way of saying that an artist had some right in what he saw. With stark realism and understanding, Russell Drysdale painted the outback, and his women of the bush stood upright in adversity, as Lawson's women had done. Drysdale then did a series of paintings on Aborigines, which was a new field for Australian artists if one excepts those done in earlier colonial times.

In Melbourne, the days of McCubbin, Streeton and Roberts were invoked and a genuine expression of the national spirit evolved, which was no mere mimicry of the masters of the Heidelberg school. Sidney Nolan went to the flat, long plains, dotted with trees, dams and wildlife, of the Victorian Wimmera for inspiration. Later he turned to the legends of Kelly, Gallipoli, Eureka and the early explorers, while himself exploring the inland in an attempt to come to the heart of the continent. Arthur Boyd turned from landscape to surrealism, to religious themes and then back to the bush, calling upon a long family tradition of identification with Australia, while Albert Tucker went from social realism to surrealism with his *The City in Wartime*. His strength of intellect and character marked him as a leader among his contemporaries, until he left Australia in 1947 as a refugee from the culture he was helping to create.

In music Peter Sculthorpe developed an aggressive but eloquent Australianism, which was first apparent in *Irkanda 1* (1955), based on Tasmanian Aboriginal lore, and most notably, in his *Sun Music* series and subsequent compositions. Sculthorpe, Richard Meale and others reflected Australia's new awareness of Asia in their use of the forms and textures of East Asian music, which would have greatly pleased Percy Grainger, perhaps Australia's best-known composer, who died in 1961.

R.D. Fitzgerald, Judith Wright, Douglas Stewart and James McAuley were poets of the national spirit, but among them a cause célèbre occurred that overshadowed the Archibald Prize affair and became itself a memorable cultural event. *Angry Penguins* began in 1940 as the journal of the Adelaide University Arts Association with John Reed and Max Harris as coeditors. Reed, president of the Contemporary Art Society and founder and director of the Museum of Modern Art in Melbourne, was a courageous man of large heart and spirit. With his wife, Sunday, Reed had sheltered, fed, encouraged and loved a generation of young artists and poets from whom he demanded all and received much in helping to give Australian high culture flesh and form. Both Reed and Harris used *Angry Penguins*, in Harris's words, to attack, 'the tired and mediocre nationalism which passed for poetry and the pedestrian bush whackery which gave Australia a novel of unequalled verbal dullness'. Their enthusiasm in the cause of modernism was the undoing of their journal.

In autumn 1944, *Angry Penguins* published sixteen poems written by Ern Malley, whom Harris praised as a poet of extraordinary talent. In fact Ern only existed in the fervent imaginations of James McAuley and Harold Stewart, who had compiled the poems to protest against 'the gradual decay of meaning and craftsmanship in poetry' and to debunk *Angry Penguins* as a purveyor of the absurd. They were so successful that some critics claimed that they had written excellent poetry, despite themselves. The literary world, local and international, laughed but modernism in Australian writing received a severe setback and the scoffers seemed to have won in a way never intended by McAuley and Stewart, who had taken a stand for rational modernity.

The universities began to teach Australian history and the first, full course was introduced at Melbourne University in 1946. Historians already had a small body of valuable material from which to draw including Ernest Scott's pioneering *Short History of Australia,* 1916; the four volumes by Timothy Coghlan, *Labour and Industry in Australia,* 1918; and the first and unsurpassed edition of *The Australian Encyclopaedia* in two volumes in 1925. Keith Hancock's seminal *Australia* came out in 1930, and in 1935 Stephen Roberts's *The Squatting Age in Australia* was published. It was a remarkably evocative study of the pastoral days, although it was completely insensitive to the history of the Aborigines in the period. Charles Bean's great work in twelve volumes, *The Official History of Australia in the War of 1914–1918,* was finally completed in 1942. Modern historiography in Australia began with the publication in 1937 of E.M. O'Brien's *The Foundation of Australia,* which argued from the original sources that Australia's origins as a white settlement stemmed from the need of the British to dispose of their unwanted criminals. Manning Clark was appointed to a lectureship at Melbourne in 1944, and began his life's work on Australian history with the publication of *Select Documents in Australian History* in two volumes (1950, 1955). His talent, diligence and flair saw their flowering with the publication in 1962 of the first of his six monumental volumes on Australia, which take the story of his country from pre-European times to the mid 1930s.

The founding of literary journals such as *Southerly* (Sydney, 1939), which after 1944 turned its attention to Australian writing, and *Meanjin* (Brisbane, 1940) gave the new intelligentsia, who were mostly of a radical bent, an outlet as contributors and readers. The *Bulletin* still retained an audience although it had become a shadow of its former self. These developments, together with the fostering of full orchestras by the A.B.C. in Sydney and Melbourne and the production of ballet and opera by the Tait brothers, helped throw up a cultural wave unnoticed by most Australians. They preferred to draw their relaxation from Gwen Meredith's immensely popular radio serial 'Blue Hills' which ran from 1949 to 1976, from listening to Bob and Dolly Dyer's quiz show 'Pick-a-box', reading the *Women's Weekly,* or the 'girlie' magazine *Man,* and going to the football or races. In 1952, they were delighted, and their national pride bolstered when Frank Sedgman started a twenty-year epoch in tennis by becoming the first among fourteen Australian victories in the Wimbledon Men's Singles Championships, while 1950 had seen the first of the fifteen Australian wins in the Davis Cup achieved in the next seventeen years.

War and its aftermath, with the frequently proclaimed threat of Chinese Communist expansion in the Pacific, had helped to foster a national awareness at all levels because the question of Australia's survival as a white, European outpost seemed in jeopardy. It had become essential to face the question whether there was anything distinctive enough in Australian society to make its preservation worthwhile. Most Australians, of whom there were almost nine million by 1954, but probably not including the 39,319 'full-blood' Aborigines who were counted separately in the census, thought that there was something distinctive and, in differing ways, they attempted both to create and enjoy it. Perhaps as an expression of the differences between the two post-war generations and the increased importance given to material values, there were few monuments erected to the dead of World War II. Instead towns and municipalities throughout the land laid out parks and built swimming pools as memorials. The fact that donations to them were tax deductible was an incentive, but the outcome was fruitful.

18

Modern Australia

Australians gradually began to discover their own continent in the 1950s. Prior to that period, family holidays, honeymoons or trips away by sporting and other bodies were generally taken in the state of residence. In Victoria some people took a change of air at Mount Macedon or Daylesford, while in New South Wales the Blue Mountains and Bundanoon were popular and the other states had similar resorts. A few venturous souls in the eastern states visited the snowfields for sport and recreation, but the majority went to the beaches surrounding the continent. On the Queensland coast south of Brisbane, an enterprising publican had named his hotel the 'Gold Coast', which name rapidly embraced the whole adjacent area. The Gold Coast and the Great Barrier Reef were attracting many local and some interstate visitors by the mid-1950s.

Some Melburnians took a journey by train across the Murray on the *Spirit of Progress* to make their own judgement whether Sydney was truly Australia's most beautiful city and to compare, fruitlessly, their bay beaches with Bondi and Manly. Some Sydneysiders came timidly south to test the rumours that it was possible to have four seasons in one day in Melbourne and that the city closed down on a weekend. Proportionally, there was more movement from the other states to New South Wales and Victoria. A journey east from Perth and Adelaide, south from Brisbane and north across Bass Strait from Tasmania was necessary in order to visit the financial, political, cultural and, in population, numerical strongholds of the country. The wealthy and adventurous still went 'overseas' which, rather than Asia, meant the British Isles with perhaps a week on the continent for good measure. Some brave souls made the trip by air to arrive stupefied and exhausted at their destination. In the main, however, Australians were still state-bound.

The car was crucial to the movement of young people in the 1950s, and its use, mostly in second-hand models, spelt the end of some small country towns as centres for community life. Petrol became more readily available and some improvement was seen in the road system although the Hume Highway between Sydney and Melbourne and the Princes Highway along the coast remained in a disgraceful condition for years, as did the Eyre Highway to Perth. Very few were adventurous enough to take a 'run down the Darling' from Bourke to Wentworth, and the outback remained a mystery to most city dwellers. Tourism was helped by the availability of money, the widespread use of bus tours and the gradual introduction of better accommodation for travelers. Ever-the-same motels, with their breakfast peepholes, rapidly added to Australia's first motel, opened in Canberra in 1956. The war was also partially responsible for an increasing awareness of Australia when the names of places most people were scarcely aware of previously – Wyndham, Townsville, Broome and Derby – had become part of the national consciousness. People outside Australia also had become aware of the southern continent during the war when servicemen of other nations had trained and were based in Australia, or passed through it on their way to the Pacific War.

Australia, consequently, became interesting, relevant, worth taking time to see and, to the surprise of many, a place of awesome splendour, vast and lonely distances, great rolling beaches, rain forests, tropical luxuriance – in fact a microcosm of everything it was said the rest of the world could offer. It didn't seem to matter that, in the main, the meals were much the same from Cooktown to Geraldton – steak and eggs with or without tomatoes or a mixed grill – and that the regulations governing drinking hours remained uncivilized. The Indian Pacific train service from Sydney to Perth was commenced in 1970 and contained the world's longest stretch of straight track of 480 kilometres. From then on there was a gradual improvement in train services, which, with few exceptions, had been a recipe for boredom at the best and extreme discomfort at the worst. In any event, by the late 1950s it was apparent that Australia was there to be visited and Australians began to do so.

Conservation of the land was a preoccupation of very few, although some farmers took steps, by tree planting and contour ploughing, to repair the ravages of soil erosion that had degraded five per cent of the country. Soil salinity was already showing ominous signs of becoming a problem because of tree removal and over-irrigation in the Murray–Darling Basin. Three-quarters of the native forests were gone or endangered, seventy-six species of native flora were presumed extinct, while many others had become rare. In some places, the countryside seemed to be dying through over clearing, which had upset the ecological balance and produced serious effects on mammals and birds, some of which were extinct or close to becoming so. Little had been learnt from the Aboriginal habit of regular burning-off, so that noxious shrubs and inedible grasses were endangering vast areas. Thirty years later a clearer realization of these factors was apparent, but by that time there was little hope of turning back the clock.

Science, however, had its role and, partly through the work of a remarkable scientist, a significant change came about on farming and pastoral lands, thereby contributing to a rise in sheep numbers by sixty per cent in a few years. Annie Macnamara was born in Beechworth, Victoria in 1899 and graduated in medicine with much distinction at the University of Melbourne in 1922. She devoted herself to the prevention of poliomyelitis, and her orthopaedic work for victims of the disease brought her great renown. The first centre for spastic children was opened, in the Royal Children's Hospital, Melbourne, at her recommendation in 1940. With her rural background, she had taken an interest in attempts to eradicate the rabbit, including those made by Dr Danysz of the Pasteur Institute in France, who had conducted unsuccessful experiments with a virus, but nevertheless aroused interest in such a method of rabbit control. Until 1950 little was done until Dr Macnamara persuaded the government to resume field-testing along the Murray River on the effects on rabbits of the South American virus myxomatosis. The work on the virus was carried on further by Professor Frank Fenner and others at the Australian National University.

The virus, carried by mosquitoes and later also by fleas, spread rapidly from Victoria into South Australia, through the New South Wales river system and on into Queensland. Within two years, the rabbit population was ravaged, pastures improved, the flora and some native fauna began to prosper again and sheep in ever-increasing numbers began to graze on land that had previously been the domain of the rabbit. The return from wool was augmented by £30,000,000 in three years. The woolgrowers rewarded Dr Macnamara with a present of £800 and a clock. At her death in 1968 thousands whom she had treated as victims of paralysis mourned her.

Myxomatosis was spread through the work of the CSIRO and a mortality rate among rabbits of over ninety per cent was achieved in the early years, but the vermin increasingly developed resistance to the virus. By the mid-eighties, the pre-myxomatosis levels were returning, and some farmers were turning back to the old methods of rabbit eradication such as burrow fumigation.

Previous experiments in soldier settlement had finally taught the lesson that, instead of opening new lands, it was better to subdivide proven land for settlement. This ensured that most returned men who became soldier-settlers after World War II were successful. Nevertheless, despite the attraction of farming, many young men, who had tasted other and more attractive forms of life in wartime, chose not to return to country areas. Within a few years, many small country towns began to decline as the local population fell and better means of transport enabled country people to shop at major centres. Farmers began moving into larger towns where there were better educational facilities, and social life and amenities, especially for women, were available. In some areas, farmhouses were often left derelict or turned to other uses such as shearing sheds. Small rural schools, especially of the one-teacher kind, began to disappear as the rural population declined and buses came into widespread use to convey children to central schools.

The most positive aspect of farming among more aware members of the rural community was the realization that the days of haphazard agriculture and husbandry were over. Land management was designed scientifically to maintain fertility and increase crop yields, while flock and herd development on specialized breeding and nutritional grounds was practised more widely and successfully, thereby raising the whole standard of farming. The increasing complexity and expense of modern farm machinery led to over-capitalization in many instances, resulting in debts to banks and agricultural companies. Among some city dwellers, especially of the more affluent kind who could write off losses as tax benefits, the old rural dream revived and gradually the land near the cities was subdivided and sold to hobby farmers. Some of them took a genuine interest in their farmlets, but it was often the case that the land was neglected, weeds and rabbits abounded, and the productivity that resulted was negligible in comparison to that achieved by genuine farmers.

In manufacturing, further great strides were taken and, from 1949 to 1959, the value of factory production rose four-fold to nearly £2,000,000,000. A trade agreement was made in 1957 with Japan, which had become Australia's second largest customer next to Britain. Even the Labor Party, the trade unions and the Returned Soldiers League showed little opposition to the agreement because it was plain that, without it, wool sales, heavily dependent on Japanese buying, were at risk. The former enemy countries agreed to give each other 'most favoured nation' treatment for imports, which meant that continued wool sales were assured and there were good prospects of exporting Australian wheat to Japan. Despite Australian shops quickly beginning to display a wide range of quality Japanese goods, Australian industry seemed to withstand the shock easily, at least while tariffs were maintained.

A workforce for industry was readily available through the continuing immigration programme. Few immigrants were either interested in, or able to go onto, the land except for Italians in the cane growing areas of Queensland, on fruit blocks in the Murrumbidgee area around Griffith and along irrigated sections near the Murray River in Victoria. Migrants helped produce steel at Port Kembla from iron ore mined at Cockatoo Island in Western Australia, oil was refined on Cockburn Sound near Fremantle for the Anglo–Iranian Oil Company and Caltex, an American concern, began refining at Kurnell near Sydney. In 1952 Lang Hancock had discovered fabulous iron-ore deposits in the Hamersley Ranges of Western Australia. In 1949 uranium was discovered near Rum Jungle in the Northern Territory and the mine was developed by Conzinc Riotinto with a ten-year agreement to export the material to the United States. Within a few years of the destruction of Hiroshima and Nagasaki, Australia had become both an atomic test site and a resource for an industry that few people understood and many feared.

On the Monte Bello islands off Australia's western coast, Britain had begun a series of atom bomb tests, which neither the government nor the trade unions perceived as having serious implications for the future. The tests were continued at Woomera in South Australia and finally completed at Maralinga in the same state in 1957. The areas in question were said to be devoid of significant populations, although there were Aborigines living near the South Australian test sites. While Britain's actions were understandable – in that it wanted to compete with other large powers in the nuclear energy and arms race, and it could not carry out tests at home – the complaisance of the Australian government was not. It took thirty years and an official enquiry, called for in 1980, to reveal the careless planning and the long-term deleterious effects of the tests.

Industrial development on a large scale often required community facilities and services, as well as housing for the employees, which resulted in a similar growth in service industries of all kinds. High demand for labour, materials, machinery and buildings, coupled with the import of manufactured goods, often in the form of luxury items, caused the economy to boom. But, by 1951, a rising national trade deficit, marked increases in incomes, and inflation alarmed the government. Severe restrictions on imports were imposed in 1952 followed by a decision to cut that year's immigrant intake from 150,000 to 80,000. The unions demanded this decrease as unemployment, especially among unskilled workers, had risen, and in Victoria they wanted a complete cessation of immigration. The myth had prevailed of immigration causing unemployment, although, in fact, it boosted the economy and helped to provide further employment. As always, it was easy to seek causes for economic dislocation in factors external to the real ones affecting Australia.

The atmosphere of anxiety engendered by fears of Communist expansion had not abated. There were accusations that communists had infiltrated both the organizers of the Commonwealth Literary Fund, which subsidized books and periodicals of literary merit, and the staff of the Australian National University. On 13 April 1954, Menzies told Parliament that a Soviet diplomat, Vladimir Petrov, had asked for and been granted political asylum. Petrov stated that he had lost faith in communism and, having lived in Australia, he now wished to remain. He also said that he had been a Soviet spy and that a Russian espionage system was operating in Australia. Mrs Petrov had allegedly decided to return home to Russia, but she changed her mind and Australians were treated in the newspapers and on newsreels to the unsavoury spectacle of her release at Darwin from the clutches of her armed, Soviet escorts by Commonwealth police. That incident did more to cement the idea in the minds of Australians that Soviet communism was an ugly, repressive system than Petrov's own admissions had done, and very few were upset when the Soviet Union cut diplomatic relations with Australia. With the support of the Federal Caucus of the Labor Party, Menzies set up a Royal Commission to investigate Soviet espionage.

There was an election scheduled for 29 May 1954, but Menzies's prospects did not look good as all states except South Australia were under Labor governments. Largely because of a system of electoral distribution, his Liberal-Country Party coalition, with 47.07 per cent of the total vote, won sixty-four out of 120 seats in the House of Representatives. The Labor Party, led by Evatt, managed to win only forty-seven seats with 50.03 per cent of the vote. It was a bitter blow to Evatt from which he never recovered and, in the aftermath, his Party fell into disarray.

In September 1954, the Royal Commission called members of Evatt's staff to appear before it concerning their possible connection with Soviet espionage. Evatt, the former High Court judge, rushed to defend them and the three judges of the Royal Commission listened with increasing bewilderment as he alternated between sense and hysteria. They withdrew his right to appear on the grounds that he was unable to separate his legal from his political role. In August 1955, the Commission, not surprisingly, reported that the Soviets did engage in espionage in Australia, but refrained from asking for the prosecution of any of the alleged communist sympathizers they had called before it. However, the real damage was done for which Evatt, as much as either Menzies or the Commission, was responsible. Among a large portion of the public, the whole affair seemed to show that the Labor Party led by Evatt was favourable to communism, and Evatt's act of asking the Soviet Foreign Minister whether documents produced by Petrov were genuine – Molotov replied that they were forgeries – was merely a symbol of his move into unreality and the ineffectiveness of the Party executive which had been unable to control him.

Within the Labor Party, the argument over communism served to hide the real struggle being enacted between right wing and left-wing factions for control of the Party machine. The whole conflict was capable of resolution by compromise between the warring factions, as indeed happened in New South Wales. There the left wing was weak and the first Australian-born cardinal, Norman Thomas Gilroy, Archbishop of Sydney, worked for a peaceful settlement to the dispute. His auxiliary bishop was close to the Catholic faction, which controlled the ALP in the state, and both Church and Party needed each other for their own interests. Evatt, however, was aware that his leadership was threatened in Victoria where the Party was controlled by the right wing. He stated publicly that his Party was suffering from the behaviour of disloyal and subversive members directed by an outside body. All concerned in the matter knew he meant Santamaria's Movement.

In the upshot, the Victorian branch was virtually destroyed as a political force; the official Party abandoned the Industrial Groups and John Cain's Labor government lost office in May 1955. The Party did not return to power in Victoria until Cain's son led Labor back to government in April 1982. More importantly, the nature of the Labor Party changed radically. In the past, its most fruitful elements had been composed of idealists of both left and right, many of whom were Catholics. In 1917 during the debacle over conscription, the Catholics remained in the Party. But in 1955 so many Catholics were expelled and so many Catholic voters repelled that the old, uneasy but fruitful alliance between the idealists was destroyed. In the long run, some of the former idealism also disappeared, and the gulf between Labor and Liberalism narrowed.

In the immediate aftermath of the 'split' in Labor ranks, a new party was formed, which eventually called itself the Democratic Labor Party. Many of its members were expelled Labor members and former Industrial Groupers. Although its stronghold was Victoria, it stood candidates in all states. Its birth helped Menzies considerably. He called a federal election in late 1955, which he won handsomely with the help of preferences from the new Party, and he relied upon it for support and electoral success for the rest of his years in office.

Whether in a conscious attempt to gain a Liberal foothold in Catholic households, or because the urgency of the case had become so apparent by 1956, Menzies decided to use Commonwealth funds to pay interest on loans raised by church bodies to build new schools in the Australian Capital Territory. After eighty years, state aid to religion re-emerged and its spread and increase throughout Australia was inevitable. The main beneficiaries were Catholics, who supported ninety per cent of the private schools and whose need was pressing in parochial schools. It was anomalous though that some of the wealthiest schools, charging the highest fees in the land, also benefited. State aid inexorably meant a marked change in the texture of Catholic parochial life that had revolved around the demand to raise funds for education and the presence of religious orders whose members staffed the schools. Both responses required great sacrifice. Time also revealed that, given the choice, many non-Catholic parents would opt for a private education system in which, they fondly hoped, and sometimes found, higher standards of teaching and discipline would prevail in comparison with the state system. The debates, acrimony and expenditure of energies of the 1860s and 1870s were repeated a century later.

In 1954 Menzies welcomed with effusive warmth the first reigning British monarch to visit Australia, Elizabeth II, and took great pride in the reception given to her throughout the country. At the same time, he presided over a period in which emotional, economic and political ties with Britain were lessening perceptibly. Asia had always been a place of little interest to him, but he encouraged Australian participation in the Colombo Plan. With nearly all Southeast Asian countries participating, the Plan succeeded in serving human and social needs in Asia. Australia contributed generously with technical assistance, equipment, training of personnel, agricultural development, capital aid and in many other ways. Australia also benefited considerably in that the thousands of Colombo Plan students who came to study in its universities and schools helped to soften racist attitudes to Asians. They also became ambassadors for Australia on their return to their home countries. Furthermore, the thousands of Australians who worked for the Plan as experts and advisers in Asian countries served to educate and awaken the general community to the needs and potentialities of Asia on their return home.

Australia continued to refuse recognition to China on the grounds that her communist government was hostile to America. There was also concern about Vietnam after the fall of the French held Dien Bien Phu in 1954 and the consequent partitioning of the country into north and south. Some Australians held the view that the Vietnamese liberation movement, led from the north by Ho Chi Minh, was mainly an expression of nationalism rather than a concerted drive to make the whole country communist. John Foster Dulles, U.S. Secretary of State, and his Australian counterpart, R. G. Casey, thought otherwise. A body called the South-East Asia Treaty Organisation was consequently born with the specific purpose of combating communist aggression in the area.

With exemplary pragmatism, Menzies announced in April 1955 that Australia and New Zealand would join with Britain to help Malaya combat subversive elements operating there. In his opinion, if a battle had to be fought against communism, it was better for it to take place as far away from Australia as possible. The agreement committed Australia to the deployment of naval, air and land forces in Malaya and met strong opposition from the Labor Party, where the opinion was strongly held that nationalist, anti-colonial movements in Asia had to be understood rather than be pushed into becoming communist.

If there was confusion in some Asian capitals about Australia's role in the region, Menzies's ineffective intervention in attempting to negotiate with President Nasser of Egypt over the nationalization of the Suez Canal served only to heighten the uncertainty. By his act, Menzies adopted the old stance of European colonialism, which indicated that he thought the national interests of former colonies should always remain secondary to the interests of their former masters. The old idea of Empire, power and economic advantage died slowly.

While the politicians argued and made treaties, the Australian people went about the business of living in a more affluent and relaxed manner than had been possible since the 1920s. In 1954 the voters of New South Wales, by a narrow margin, took the venturous step of extending drinking hours. After nearly forty years, it came as a surprise to see people being allowed to enjoy themselves by drinking publicly at night. South Australia followed suit. The Victorians waited until 1966 before deciding to extend hotel hours until ten o'clock at night and restrictions on Sunday trading remained in force.

Drunkenness, nevertheless, with or without six o'clock closing, remained a destructive vice. Under its influence, drinkers' health was ruined, families were broken up and road accidents caused. The problem of drink was clearly illustrated in the case of the famous Aboriginal landscape artist, Albert Namatjira. Unlike the rest of his race, he had been granted full citizenship, which permitted him to buy liquor for his own use. In the time-honoured custom of his people he shared his possessions with them, including liquor, thus breaking the law. He was given a prison sentence of three months served 'in the open' and died soon afterwards on 8 August 1959. His reputation as an artist of high skill and as an indigenous painter who was at one with the land suffered later at the hands of postmodernist critics who scoffed at his work. Fifty years later Namatjira had started to come back into vogue.

At the core of the Aboriginal problem lay the alleged inability of many Aborigines to cope with alcohol, in part or wholly because of their social situation. Despite some attempt to welcome them into white society, they remained second-class citizens. They had not become accustomed to using drink in moderation, no attempt had been made to educate them to its use and the very fact of its prohibition had tended to enhance its attraction, so that the figure of a drunken Aborigine had become one of scorn in the eyes of many whites. By concentrating on alcohol the fundamental problems of the Aborigines remained hidden. Deprived of their land they had become homeless in their own homeland.

By the end of the 1950s, the car had become both the symbol of prosperity and the assurance of mobility, especially among many young people to whom a journey by bus or train was a novelty. The cult of the teenager began, Bill Haley and the 'Comets' swept the country by storm and their record 'Rock around the Clock' was the biggest seller of all time. Boys who had previously dreamt of owning their own bat or football now wanted to buy a guitar. The 'generation gap' began to be spoken about when parents were unable to understand the new ways of musical communication and young people found their elders incapable of comprehending the aspirations of a generation that knew only plenty. 'Bodgies and Widgies' wore their distinctive clothing and hair styles, and parents despaired of the 'rising generation' in much the same way as others before them had done.

The preparation and choice of food gradually became more varied and people tentatively ordered European dishes. Some began to drink wine with meals, although it was often of the white, sweet kind. The housing shortage was overcome by 1960. Many new homes resembled boxes with sloping lids, while the old terrace houses of some charm and dignity in the inner cities often gave way to graceless blocks of flats that quickly became slums. By the mid-sixties, one in five new dwellings was a flat. Skyscrapers were replacing the older buildings in the cities but, because very few people now lived in the commercial areas, they became desolate, windswept places on weekends.

The suburbs expanded and drew people in hundreds of thousands who were now able to buy a block of their own on which to build. In these new areas they could enjoy the semi-privacy of a backyard, with its Hills Hoist rotary clothesline, and a sense of achievement in getting a stake in the land, however minimal. Inevitably, the distance between work and home took up precious hours of travel, and there was either the boredom of train and tram journeys or the frustration of negotiating city traffic, which frayed nerves, consumed petrol, increased exhaust fumes and often caused chaos. Frequently the outer suburbs were still unsewered years after the construction of homes had taken place, trees were slow to grow and new lawns struggled to survive heat or rain, which either shrivelled the new growth or washed the seeds away. At first, facilities such as schools, shops, doctors, chemists and hospitals were non-existent, municipal libraries a dream and places of recreation a rarity. Housewives endured day after day of loneliness, despite the wide range of labour saving devices that had come into the home and the now almost universal availability of the family car. Exhausted husbands returned mute from the workplace to look forward to the weekend, when they could have a bet, go to the football, drink at a local pub or club, wash the car and mow the lawn.

Few, especially among the town planners, remembered E.G. Wakefield's 'The essence of civilization is concentration' so the suburban sprawl went on and on. In European cities, people lived near their workplace, with shops, markets, theatres, churches, libraries and cafes in close proximity to their homes. As a result, a distinctive urban culture, high and low, could develop and flourish. Only a few Australians stayed in the city or came back there to find the heart of urban life although, gradually some of the older inner city suburbs came to life again. The urbanization of the continent seemed complete by 1959 as four out of every five of the estimated white population of ten million lived in the cities or in country towns. Immigration was the key to growth. Well over a million new people had arrived since the end of the war, and it was confidently forecast that by the Bicentenary in 1988 the twenty million mark would be reached. However, with increased prosperity in Europe, there were signs that the traditional sources of immigration were drying up.

Television was introduced to Australia in 1956 to coincide with the opening of the Olympic Games in Melbourne. As with radio, the ABC and commercial channels operated separately and the ABC offered programmes devoid of advertising. There were warnings that the new medium would be a setback to culture, make books obsolete and ruin children, whose lives would be dominated by the square box. In fact reading remained a major pastime for adults and was stimulated by television programmes as some people wanted to know more about subjects the television could touch on only briefly. The sick, the old and the lonely benefited incalculably. Knowledge of Australia and the world was also enhanced, although there were grounds for believing that students spent less time doing their traditional homework and that they rarely listened to radio except for popular music. Within a few years, schools and colleges were faced with a generation of television watchers to whom reading had become almost an abnormal pastime. At all events, the television set became as much a part of the furniture of the Australian home as the radio and refrigerator. The initial sufferers at its hands were the owners of picture theatres and drive-ins, who faced declining audiences.

The excitement generated by the Olympic Games reflected a fundamental characteristic of the Australian ethos – the love of sport in a myriad of forms. Good weather, open spaces, harbours, rivers and beaches abounded throughout the continent while the snowfields of the Australian Alps had begun to attract thousands of skiers. These natural features combined with a desire among many, young and old, to participate in forms of outdoor life, a propensity to match oneself physically against others, an admiration for the battler and the underdog, a tendency to gamble on practically anything that moved and an increasing degree of leisure. Participation in sport, whether as players or spectators was important in the lives of the majority of Australians.

A nation singularly unencumbered by individual heroes in the military and political arenas looked to its sporting greats as the embodiment of those qualities of skill, courage and endurance most people admired. The big thing was to 'have a go', and, if a loser, to accept gracefully that to do one's best, even in defeat, was honourable. The worst disgrace was not to try, to 'turn it up' and to whinge about the result. All sports had their heroes and some had become household names: Bradman, Lindwall and Miller in cricket; Dally Messenger in Rugby League; Les Darcy in boxing; Roy Cazaly and Haydn Bunton in Australian Rules; Hubert Opperman in cycling; Peter Thompson in golf; Bill Beach and Bobby Pearce in sculling; Lindrum in billiards; Barney Kieran, Fanny Durack, 'Boy' Charlton and Frank Beaurepaire in swimming; Majorie Jackson in sprinting and Frank Sedgman, Lew Hoad and Ken Rosewall in tennis. The most popular of all sporting pastimes had no heroes, for fishing made everyone who caught a fish, large or small, his or her own hero. In the second largest sport, horse racing, big and small punters made temporary heroes of the horse and jockey who won. Throughout the land, hundreds of thousands of men and women went lawn bowling, every small town had a cricket pitch and golf course, and tennis was played day and night everywhere.

The Games were staged principally at the Melbourne Cricket Ground and Australians revelled in their success, as well as the fact that their country became the focus of international attention for a few days. Australian competitors won thirteen gold medals, broke four world records in swimming and Dawn Fraser began her long career as the world's greatest woman swimmer with her first of three successive gold medals in the 100 metres freestyle. She went on to hold twenty-seven individual world records. Betty Cuthbert was victorious in the 100 and 200 metre sprints and Shirley Strickland in the eighty metre hurdles. These successes against the world's best seemed to bring to fruition all that sport had meant in Australian lives, and no one felt cheated when their great middle-distance runner, John Landy, went down to an Irishman in the 1500 metres.

The festival of athleticism was played out on a larger stage as the world watched the Games on television. The struggle for medal supremacy was won by Russia, and its victory was symbolized in the diminutive person of their supreme runner, Vladimir Kuts. A shadow hanging over the Games became reality when blood stained the Olympic Pool while Russia played Hungary in water polo. Across the other side of the world more serious matters were in progress as the Hungarian Revolution was put down by Russian tanks, and Australia gave some validity to her creed of a fair go for the underdog by promising to accept 10,000 refugees from that unhappy land.

The commencement of the Sydney Opera House in both its structure and purpose was a cultural highlight because it was destined to stand proudly in any century as one of the world's great buildings. With its vast, but graceful, sail-like wings wedding land and water, the Opera House seemed a natural extension of the city and its setting on the Harbour. Its eventual cost of over $100,000,000 was financed largely by a lottery but the project still had difficulties, due to financial stringencies, combined with the seeming reluctance of its inspired Danish designer, Joern Utzon, to be more specific in his detailed planning. In despair he left the project before it was completed. Despite the fact that some critics regarded it as inadequate for full-scale opera productions, the opening of the Opera House in 1973 was a seal on Australian cultural maturity and a promise that the arts would always remain precious to a people often accused of lacking refinement.

Australian literature was crowned with the work of the novelist Patrick White and the poet Alec Hope. White drew specifically on the Australian experience to write *Voss* (1957), but his more universal treatment of the larger theme of the human spirit in *The Tree of Man* and *The Eye of the Storm* helped him to win the Nobel Prize for literature in 1973. Hope's first collection of poetry, *The Wandering Islands,* appeared in 1955, and thereafter he published regularly. With a high concept of the sacred role of the poet in society, Hope at times irritated, more often uplifted, and always led his readers to question the values of their generation. The playwrights Ray Lawler and Alan Seymour used a more explicit Australian terminology and theme. Lawler's *Summer of the Seventeenth Doll* became a classic of the Australian theatre in its exploration of the inadequate, even fragile, nature of 'mateship' while Seymour's *The One Day of the Year* further probed the weakness of the male stereotype by using Anzac Day as its theme. In the person of Barry Humphries's suburban housewife, Edna Everage, a consummate satirical humorist first appeared on the Melbourne stage in 1955. For Humphries, it began a career that has lasted almost fifty years, during which he has made suburban Australians confront the realities of modern life.

Cultural immaturity was shown when the Commonwealth Government decided that there were 178 works to which the reading public was forbidden access. They included Frank Hardy's *Power without Glory*. This was a sordid, mischievous and blatantly ideological tale of corruption in Victoria which would have had a restricted readership had not the family of John Wren, a Melbourne entrepreneur, believing that Wren's wife was libelled by the book, taken legal action, unsuccessfully, against Hardy. More public attention could usefully have been directed to the fact that Russel Ward was denied a position as lecturer in history at the University of New South Wales in 1956 after a selection committee had unanimously recommended his appointment. Ward had been a member of the Communist Party from 1941 until 1949 and, in the opinion of the Vice Chancellor, he could not be employed in the university because of his 'character and reputation'. With the publication of his *The Australian Legend* in 1958, Ward made a memorable and significant contribution that ranked him with the foremost of historians specializing in Australian history.

There was continued concern at the state of the universities, where over forty per cent of entrants failed to graduate while the results in honours and post-graduate work were equally dismal. An Englishman, Keith Murray, conducted an enquiry into the matter and discovered over-crowded classrooms and laboratories, poor facilities, low staff salaries, too few scholarships and a general dearth of funds. The government promised to act. Although only one new university was opened in direct response to the findings of the enquiry (Monash in Melbourne in 1961), the setting up of the Universities Commission in 1959 meant that great expansion took place later in the 1960s. Menzies had always retained a reverence for learning and scholarship and his finest and most lasting legacy to his country was his genuine support of education, especially in the tertiary sector.

Apart from its sporting heroes and a few of its soldiers, especially the World War I hero General John Monash who was of Jewish origin, Australians of note in other fields, particularly scientific ones, were not generally internationally recognized. Exceptions were the author Patrick White, a handful of painters and the incomparable opera singers Nellie

Melba and Joan Sutherland. Some English scientists were familiar with the work of Louis Brennan (1852–1932) who, although Irish-born, was educated in Melbourne as a civil engineer. Brennan invented a torpedo, and researched a monorail locomotive. He also invented a helicopter which was successfully tested in 1922, but further work on it was abandoned in 1926.

Only in the field of medical and related research were Australians able to make a mark, but they received little local encouragement prior to the Great War, so that some promising researchers went overseas to work. The English-born and trained medical practitioner Joseph Bancroft remained in Queensland and, in 1876, he discovered the filaria parasite that bears his name, thus revealing the cause of a serious tropical disease. Bancroft also worked on the transmission of insect carried infections and his son, Thomas, developed his father's work. He was the first to suggest the mosquito as the carrier of dengue fever. In New South Wales, J. Ashburton Thompson and Frank Tidswell demonstrated that fleas carried bubonic plague from infected rats to humans. Other important discoveries were made in Queensland on lead poisoning and, in South Australia, on hydatids. Charles Martin was English, but he became the 'distinguished Master' of Australian medical research. He taught at the universities of Melbourne and Sydney in the 1890s, and, after his return to England, he often came back to Australia to encourage further work. At the Lister Institute and London University, he directed the research of many young Australians who always acknowledged his inspiration.

Eventually, research institutions and units were developed in Australia, mainly through government support, and further progress became possible. The Walter and Eliza Hall Institute was founded in Melbourne in 1916, and its major work was undertaken when Frank Macfarlane Burnet became its director in 1944. Working with Edward Derrick, he influenced Australian research and, in 1960, Burnet won the Nobel Prize for his research in immunology. Two other Australian-born Nobel Prize winners were Howard Florey and John Eccles. Florey shared the Prize in 1945 as co-developer of the first anti-biotic, penicillin, and in 1966 he became Chancellor of the Australian National University. Eccles shared the Prize in 1963 for his work on the nervous system. In 1966 he left the John Curtin Medical School at the National University, where he was a distinguished professor, to work in Chicago. The youngest ever Nobel Prize winner was Adelaide-born William Lawrence Bragg, who, together with his father, William Henry, received the prize for physics in 1915 at the age of twenty five. Bragg, however, had done all of his work outside Australia.

The economic boom of the 1950s was marked with social conflict arising from the unrest within the Labor Party. That unrest and the subsequent split in the Party partially reflected the unease of a society that refused to allow a shadow cast by radical ideology to darken the path to individual and communal well being. Elections were held in 1958, and Labor, everywhere suffering from disunity and ravaged by the loss of votes to the Democratic Labor Party, again lost ground. Evatt was by now ill and exhausted by his battles, and he resigned in 1960 to go to the Supreme Court of New South Wales as Chief justice. He died in 1965 after a life marked by a great passion for justice. As judge, historian and international statesman, he had served his country nobly. He was driven to the edge of despair as Menzies, whom he regarded as his inferior, ruled with such ease and aplomb as prime minister, and he allowed himself to use the two-edged sword of sectarianism to cleanse the Labor Party of those elements, which he feared would destroy it. Evatt was destroyed himself, and the labour movement shattered and rendered almost futile as a wave of bitterness over the split in the Party spread into workplaces, homes and churches. It was Evatt's great misfortune to have reacted in a way that forced so many to take up positions opposed to his own which they, also, held honourably.

19

At the Edge of Asia

Since the war in the Pacific, any doubt as to the significance of Australia's geographical location at the base of Asia had been dispelled. It would never again be possible for Australians to ignore the proximity of their neighbours. In Asia, also, there was an increasing awareness of the large, thinly populated continent to the south. This discovery of place helped to change radically the underlying assumption upon which the Australian nation had been built – that it would remain white and British in perpetuity. In the 1960s the outcome of that change was scarcely apparent. The path was open which led inexorably to a future when Australia, in the last quarter of the twentieth century, would be scarcely recognizable to its founders at the time of Federation.

Menzies summed up what he still felt was the essential link between Australia and Britain in a speech he gave in London in June 1960. To him, allegiance to the Crown was the binding element that made all the members of the Commonwealth 'brothers in a special international family'. He thought that the family would survive even such blows as 'the tragic incident of Sharpeville', when blacks died for their race and colour in South Africa in 1960. This had caused a shocked reaction against apartheid in Australia, as well as elsewhere in the world. It is probable that the majority of Australians shared the loyalty Menzies felt towards the Crown, although not to the same degree. Certainly talk of a republic had been muted for nearly a century, and the abdication of King Edward VIII in 1936 only temporarily shook the moral basis of the throne. In the origins of its people, the Australia that lay so close to Asia was still in large measure Anglo-Saxon, and its bonds were with a world centered on London. Indeed, as Menzies quaintly put it, London was at the centre of world affairs because it is 'where the Queen is'.

There was some unease felt at the time about the prospective entry of Britain into the Common Market by those Australians who looked to Britain as a major market. Among them were woolgrowers and producers of dried fruits and dairy products as well as Tasmanian apple growers. John McEwen, leader of the Country Party and Minister for Trade in the Menzies Cabinet, visited England, Europe and America to ensure that Australia's special trading relationship with Britain was retained and, in 1963, there was some relief when French President Charles de Gaulle temporarily blocked British entry into the Common Market. During the same period, Australia was rapidly moving into the orbit of Japanese and, to some extent, Chinese trade forces so that the question of the special relationship with Britain was slowly becoming of lesser moment.

In Asia, loyalties and allegiances were in the process of being destroyed, reshaped or created. The closest place to Australia affected by this was Dutch New Guinea, and the proposed new alignment had little to do with the attitudes or wishes of the people in question. When, with Australian support, the Indonesians took control of the former Dutch East Indies in 1949, the Dutch retained part of Papua New Guinea. The Indonesians always claimed that the territory, which they called West Irian, was rightfully theirs, although its inhabitants had few bonds with them. In 1960, President Sukarno demanded its cession to Indonesia, with war against the Dutch, backed by Soviet arms, offered as the alternative. The United States, fearful lest opposition to Sukarno would further increase communist strength in Indonesia, was anxious to see the question resolved, even if it meant that the people of Dutch New Guinea would have no say in their future.

Australia was concerned by the defiance of the principle of self-determination that annexation would entail and at the prospect of having Indonesia as a neighbour in New Guinea, where the Australian right to retain its control was at best shaky. Sukarno continued to talk of confrontation and war with the Dutch seemed probable, so the Americans, acting as brokers from afar, decided to let the Indonesians have their way. In January 1962, Australia had little option but to acquiesce in the annexation of almost half of New Guinea by the Indonesians. It was a bitter price to pay for peace and the future was unlikely to discount it.

Arthur Calwell warned that acceding to threats over West Irian was to invite a day when East Timor, then Papua New Guinea and finally northern Australia would eventually be looked upon greedily by Indonesia. His voice was heard as little then as it was a few months later when he said that to permit the Americans to establish a communications base at North West Cape was to jeopardize Australian sovereignty and to bring the country 'a step closer to the firing line' in any future atomic conflict. On that particular matter, Calwell and the Labor Party were out of step with the Australian people for a Gallup poll indicated that a large majority were in favour of the base on the grounds that only America was capable of defending Australia in the event of it being attacked by a hostile power.

Another source of concern to Australia was the verbal and military opposition of Sukarno to the proposed formation of the new state of Malaysia, which was intended to embrace former British colonies in South-East Asia. Sabah, or British North Borneo, had a border with the Indonesian-held part of the large island of Borneo. When the new state of Malaysia was proclaimed in 1963, the British Embassy in Djakarta was sacked. Once again Australia had to decide whether mere words were sufficient to dissuade Sukarno, whom Calwell called 'a little Hitler', from active hostility. Adroitly, if supinely, the government kept Australian troops out of direct involvement with Indonesian guerrillas in Borneo, although three Australian soldiers were killed there in 1965.

The whole sorry affair of confrontation dragged on until Suharto replaced Sukarno in 1965. Thousands then died in Indonesia itself as the army slaughtered anyone with the remotest connection with the Communist Party. Confrontation seemed to lose favour in Indonesia but it expressed itself in another form in Portuguese Timor in 1975. In that year, the Indonesian government took advantage of the civil war there to annex the territory. The United States sided with Indonesia over annexation for strategic reasons and the Australian Labor government accepted the Indonesian act without protest. Indeed Gough Whitlam, who was prime minister until December 1975, regarded East Timor as part of the Indonesian world, and made it plain that Australia favoured eventual annexation, although American pressure probably lay at the heart of the Australian decision. Australians at the highest level had done nothing to repay the debt to the valiant people of East Timor who had sheltered their soldiers from the Japanese in World War II and had paid a heavy price for having done so.

In the sixties, Menzies continued to govern with ease although he went through a rough passage when falling wool prices, inflation and a drought in 1960 caused him to impose a credit squeeze which convulsed the economy, alarmed private enterprise and brought widespread unemployment, especially in the vehicle and building industries. He delayed the elections as long as possible into 1961 and had a narrow victory when one seat, hanging in the balance for a week, was finally won by the Liberals with Communist Party preferences. The Democratic Labor Party continued to support the Liberal-Country Party coalition with preferences and in 1963 Menzies called another election, for which he scarcely offered any pretext although it was a year early.

Once again, state aid loomed large in an election and even the Labor Party softened its attitude on the issue in an attempt to woo lost Catholic votes. In reality, Catholics had not stopped voting for Labor because of its anti-state aid policy in the past, nor had they voted for Menzies when he handed out a crumb of assistance to private schools. The issue that had turned many of them from Labor, rightly or wrongly, was communism, and many Labor-voting Catholics returned to their traditional allegiance once it was clear that the communist threat had diminished. Other Catholics had found security in the professions and in business. They never returned to the Labor Party because the forces of conservatism now best represented their economic interests. The Reverend Samuel Marsden's dream in the early nineteenth century of an Irish-Catholic minority living in conformity with the ruling segment of Australian society had partly been fulfilled. By the 1960s the taming of the Irish in Australia was almost complete.

Menzies won the election with a twenty-one-seat majority in the House of Representatives and the two Democratic Labor Party senators allowed him a majority on essential issues in the Senate. Foreign policy was the area that was most significant; especially in regard to Vietnam where the government had sent thirty military instructors in 1962 to help train South Vietnamese troops in combating the communist North. The main reason for the deployment of the instructors was to show solidarity with the Americans who needed to be able to prove that other powers, even insignificant ones, were allies in the struggle to keep Vietnam out of the communist orbit. When the number of instructors was doubled in 1963, it showed that the domino theory – which envisaged Vietnam as the next Asian country to topple, bringing down others in its train, including eventually Australia – was beginning to dominate Australian foreign policy.

At the time, there was understandable confusion about what exactly was happening in Vietnam. Clearly the communists in the North, whom some commentators thought of as nationalists, wanted to dominate the whole country. Equally, it appeared clear that the majority of the South Vietnamese people did not want to be forced to live under communist rule. The main problem seemed to be the role of China. It was alleged, indeed trumpeted, in

America and Australia, by those who believed in the domino theory, that China was behind the struggle by the North to overrun the South. China assuredly wanted the Vietnamese communists to succeed, but there was never any proof that Chinese personnel went south to fight. The supporters of the domino theory in Australia kindled old phobic fires which saw China as the great Yellow Peril, threatening to pour its millions southwards to engulf Australia. That fear made a majority of Australians initially accept happily, or merely complacently, some form of military involvement by their own troops in Vietnam.

By 1965, there were 23,000 American troops in Vietnam, where they were the main obstacles to the swift overthrow of the South Vietnamese regime. Their presence assumed that, as foreigners, they had a right to be involved in a conflict in another country, but some Australians and more Americans did not accept that such a right existed. It was a question that did not bother Menzies who told a half-empty House of Representatives – after dinner on a Thursday night before a long weekend in April – that his government had decided to send a battalion of Australians to fight against the Viet Cong. He did not say that the troops had been readying themselves for action two months beforehand. It was a step of unusual significance, because the Australians were to engage in a military conflict without any formal declaration of war. Indeed, it was doubtful whether the troops themselves had any clearer understanding of why they were to go to Vietnam except in the most general of terms of fighting communist aggression.

Soon there were conscripted Australian soldiers engaged in battle despite the fact that, unlike the war in the Pacific, the conflict in Vietnam involved no direct threat to Australia. The government had recognized that it was not possible to strengthen the armed forces sufficiently by voluntary means, so a system was introduced of calling up selected twenty-year olds, using a ballot involving their birthdays. It was the most ironic birthday present the nation ever gave to her young men and it was not long before Private Errol Noack became the first conscript to die in Vietnam.

Prime Minister Menzies's last significant act was the involvement of Australia in the Vietnam War. After sixteen years in office as the longest-serving prime minister, he resigned in January 1966 and many were generous in their praise of his work. His most notable contribution to Australian political life was the foundation of the Liberal Party, which satisfactorily represented the aspirations of a significant and powerful minority. His other significant achievement was to work in moderate harmony with the Country Party despite the single-mindedness of its leader, John McEwen, who, however, had the ability to see beyond rural interests. Menzies's turn of phrase, powerful personality, self-assurance and dominant physique made him a formidable electoral opponent, but, like all successful politicians, he was granted good fortune. The years of his prime-ministership were notable for their overall prosperity and the split in the Labor Party gave him an unparalleled climate for success. He sometimes came close to the people in his affection for cricket, which to him was the supreme English game. A small minority took pride in seeing him arrayed in knightly regalia standing near the Queen, but thousands were happy to join plain Bob Menzies at a cricket match.

Harold Holt, an amiable and dedicated Victorian liberal, was elected leader of his Party and therefore became prime minister. He had been the loyal and trusted lieutenant of Menzies and was delighted that he had risen to the position without stepping over the bodies of others in his climb to power. Holt was often unperceptive when he came to deal with the powerful of the wider world, but his association with Menzies had bred a streak of inferiority in him. Within weeks, he had agreed to triple the number of Australian servicemen in Vietnam, and, in mid-1966, he went to visit President Johnson in America, where his fulsome promise to go 'All the way with L. B. J.' dismayed even some of those closest to him.

By this time, the contrast between the government and the Labor opposition had become crystal clear on the Vietnam issue and the latter was committed to bringing home the troops. Some intellectuals joined with some churchmen, mostly Protestant, to express grave doubts and even outright opposition to the war. In October 1966, a month before the next federal election, at Holt's invitation, Johnson came to Australia. His visit was a huge success for the government despite anti-war demonstrations, and the election resulted in a landslide victory for the Liberal-Country Party coalition that spelt the end of Arthur Calwell as leader of the Labor Party. The election had been fought on the war issue, or to be more precise on what would happen to Australia were the communists to win in Vietnam, so it was now clear that the majority of electors accepted that the basis of Australian foreign policy was the domino theory. A simple application of the theory was the need to defend the nation's interests on foreign soil, which became known as 'forward defence'.

Nonetheless, Australians were now deeply divided over the question of involvement in Vietnam. Opposition to conscription had always been a matter of conscience for many but the war in Vietnam exposed problems that had not previously been raised, either with the same complexity or intensity. There had been opposition to the Crimean, Sudan and Boer wars but British involvement had been decisive for most Australians. This was also true of the Great War. The Pacific War had seen Australia threatened, which led even the Labor movement to accept conscription. The difference now was that the Vietnam War forced Australians to ask questions about the morality of conscription and even of war itself as a means to resolve a conflict, which did not directly threaten Australia or involve a country to which Australia had strong traditional ties. For many the issue became that of Australian involvement in an undeclared war against the people of a poor, third world country, which had been exploited by Western colonialism for over a century.

To the thousands of Australians who attended 'Teach-ins', walked in street demonstrations or prayed at silent vigils, it was idle for the politicians to claim that to bomb, kill and maim Vietnamese, including defenceless civilians, was morally right. Those Australians were not convinced that such acts would make Australia a safer place to live in, or that they would help preserve democracy in South Vietnam. For the first time in history, the war almost literally came into homes because people were able to watch on their television screens the horrors that were being enacted in Vietnam. The big question was whether the end, defeating the communists, justified the means used of a total war. To this was added the question whether Australians had any right to be fighting in a conflict that essentially involved another people.

For those more directly concerned, and especially the troops in Vietnam, the problem of conscience was overridden by the fact that they had become victims of the war. They were to remain its victims for long years after the end of the conflict, because, often broken in body and spirit, they returned to a country which wanted to forget that it had ever sent them to Vietnam and where, at times, they were unjustly made to feel that they were the guilty ones. Arthur Calwell, leader of the Labor Party, also became a victim. Calwell was a Party man of the old school to whom Labor and the Catholic Church were the keystones of existence. He had pronounced the Vietnam War as both 'filthy' and 'unwinnable' and he stood by that conviction in the elections of 1966 and lost his chance to become prime minister. He resigned his leadership of the Party to be succeeded by Gough Whitlam, but Calwell went from politics and, in 1973, from life, secure in conscience.

Harold Holt also had a conscience, which moved him to the prosecution of war. When he augmented the Australian troops to 8,000, it was clear that he had not wavered in his conviction that it was right to do so although considerable American pressure was exerted on him to ensure that Australia continued to 'show the flag' by standing alongside American troops. On 17 December 1967, Holt imprudently went swimming in huge surf at Cheviot Beach, Portsea, Victoria and was never seen again. Some of the world's most important people, including Johnson, came to his memorial service in Melbourne. To a large number of Australians, Holt's forceful prosecution of the Vietnam War had become hateful. No one spoke harshly of him as a person, and many of his political foes, as well as his friends, mourned his passing.

The years that saw the convulsions of a remote war affect Australia also saw unprecedented prosperity. Minerals were part of that prosperity, although to what extent Australians, as distinct from British, Japanese and American investors, shared in the profits never became very clear. At the same time the development of mineral deposits meant movements in population, absorption of immigrants, industrial expansion and the provision of transport and housing to remote places. There was an air of optimism as Australians became more aware of the enormous potential in areas of the land that had previously been regarded as barren and useless, and which, consequently, it had been considered appropriate to leave to the Aborigines.

In the Pilbara region of Western Australia, the discovery of vast deposits of high-grade iron ore in the early 1960s meant that the export of iron ore, hitherto prohibited so as not to deplete local reserves, was now possible and by 1968 fourteen million tonnes were sold, mostly to Japan. In the early and middle sixties, oil began to flow from the Moonie field west of Brisbane, from Bass Strait and from Barrow Island, off Western Australia. Within a few years sufficient Australian oil was produced and refined to provide a considerable portion of local needs, and natural gas from Moonie was pipelined into some cities, beginning with Brisbane in 1969. Coal production developed dramatically with Japan again taking the major share of exports in the wake of the steep rises in oil prices which, when low, had seriously affected coal exports.

The newspapers and television began to use the names of minerals with which most people had been unfamiliar. Bauxite, rutile, zircon, tungsten, manganese – some the product of mineral sands mined on the beaches – were added to the old familiar names of gold, silver, copper, lead and zinc all of which continued or increased in production. Gradually, members of the public with something to spare or a life's savings to invest began to look at such mysteries as share indices and to read company names as unfamiliar as the minerals they sought.

The names of the new mineral barons became prominent. Among them were Lang Hancock who sold the richest iron ore deposit in the world in the Hamersley Ranges in Western Australia to Rio Tinto, and Lindsay Clark who relied on Australian capital to develop his Western Mining Corporation. Two companies, Tasminex and Poseidon, rashly claimed in 1969 that they had struck nickel in Western Australia and their share prices rose dramatically in weeks, causing a rising wave effect on other mineral shares. Both companies rapidly slumped and fortunes as well as small life savings were lost, but other names such as Mt Tom Price and Mt Newman reminded Australians that their minerals were real.

Despite the mineral boom, primary products still remained the basis of the economy with wheat and wool its staple. The area sown to wheat doubled to more than ten million hectares and farmers prospered under the sensible direction of the Australian Wheat Board that sold the wheat, mostly to China in spite of that fact that Menzies blamed it for instigating the so-called 'aggression from the north' in Vietnam. Wool prices fell sharply towards the end of the decade, so the prospect of accepting a minimum reserve price was attractive to graziers. As wool contributed twenty per cent of national exports, it was essential to stabilize its price and the graziers now demanded from the government the minimum price plan they had rejected in 1951 and 1965. In 1962 the first shipment of 60,000 live sheep was made to Kuwait opening a Middle East market of increasing importance.

The government was not successful with a plan to grow cotton and other crops in Western Australia under the Ord River Scheme, which was located over 1,600 kilometres from Perth in the remote Kimberley region. The concept blended with the oft-expressed desire to develop the north and keep out the Asians. The Scheme was very costly and initially produced little that could not be grown more efficiently and cheaply elsewhere, and Commonwealth funding was eventually withdrawn although the venture eventually proved more successful. Initial confidence in such developments was also a reflection of Western Australians' faith in themselves that had been fostered by the vast mineral wealth discovered in their state. They had long suffered as citizens of the forgotten outpost of Australian development but this was now at an end.

The politicians in Western Australia with such slogans as 'West is Best' were proud that their state, one third of the entire area of the continent, was 'riding the crest of a boom'. They looked increasingly to overseas investors despite concern in Canberra that it was not wise to sell too much of the national asset to foreign companies. The history of one hundred and seventy years had shown that prosperity based on production financed by foreign capital would hold up only as long as the resulting exports were a source of competitive profits to the investors.

A sign of prosperity, and a contributing factor to the relaxation of standards in sexual behaviour, was the contraceptive pill. After its introduction in 1961, the pill came into widespread use by married and unmarried women, including many Catholics despite its prohibition by Pope Paul VI who paid a successful visit to Australia in 1970. Work was plentiful, young brides went back to work after marriage and by the end of the sixties thirty-three per cent of married women were in the workforce. Much was made of the fact in 1965 that the birthrate was at its lowest since the middle of World War II, although ex-nuptial births, probably because of a sense of sexual freedom, were rising. Women comprised a quarter of the total workforce which fact reflected expanding industrialization rather than a feminist revolution. The expansion in the application of 'equal pay to work of equal value', which the Commonwealth Arbitration Court finally accepted in 1969, resulted in a twenty-five per cent rise in women's wages and made work more attractive to them. Hire purchase on little or no deposit made many necessities, and some luxuries, possible, but many young couples often found themselves in difficulties with their too ambitious repayments. Several finance companies disappeared, together with their funds of over one hundred million pounds.

On 14 February 1966, pounds, shillings and pence were translated into dollars and cents when the long awaited, and sometimes dreaded, change to decimal currency took place. With the full implementation of decimalization, footballers who had stood at six feet measured 183 centimetres; the furlong disappeared from racing; the world's oldest professional footrace, run each Easter at Stawell, Victoria, became 120 metres instead of 130 yards; gallons of petrol became litres; there was some argument as to the pronunciation of kilometre and housewives grappled with the mysteries of the gram. In Western Australia, it was found that conversion to a decimal currency cut the public debt of nearly $700,000,000 by one cent and that there were two cents missing from the expenditure side of $125,000,000. In most respects, the conversion worked smoothly and, within fifteen years, a generation of children had grown up to whom the penny and the yard were as unfamiliar as the cent and the metre had been to their parents.

Australians continued to read of, or watch on television, events which made them realize that others were suffering while they enjoyed prosperity and that disasters, man-made or natural, could strike a discordant note in the hymn to progress. The worst Australian long-term disaster was the road toll with over 50,000 killed in car accidents from 1950 to 1970. The total was almost twice as many killed in World War II and countless others were maimed. Seat belts were made compulsory in Victoria in 1970 and progressively elsewhere, while newspapers drew regular attention to the death toll. Police attempted to impose speed limits but on country roads, where many accidents occurred, complete control was impossible. From the 1970s the states gradually introduced random breath testing, which had the effect of reducing drunken driving. That measure, together with compulsory seat belts and greater public awareness of the folly of speed, helped keep the death rate steady, despite the increasing number of motor vehicle registrations.

In 1964, eighty-five men died when the aircraft carrier HMAS *Melbourne* sliced through the destroyer *Voyager* and the reputation of a fine officer, Captain Robertson of the *Melbourne,* was torn to shreds in a welter of recriminations and inconclusive investigatory commissions. An earthquake shook parts of Western Australia from Albany to Geraldton on 14 October 1968, and a wheat belt town 135 kilometres east of Perth, Meckering, was reduced to rubble but no lives were lost. Bushfires raged throughout Tasmania and Victoria in early 1967, and eighty people perished in two fires – one on the main Melbourne to Geelong road, and the other in and about Hobart when 650 homes were destroyed on 'Black Tuesday' 1967. On another level, a significant step to redress the balance of disaster was taken by the introduction of Lifeline and a Sydney doctor, William McBride, established a link between the drug thalidomide and deformities in babies.

His discovery had much greater long-term effects as it forced governments and drug companies everywhere to be more scrupulous in the testing of new products.

Instances of political violence occurred: a deranged youth, who had served in Vietnam, attempted to kill Arthur Calwell as he left an anti-conscription rally in Sydney; a girl had spat at Harold Holt, and various harmless missiles were thrown at visiting American politicians. Yet the inner core of decency in most Australians was shown when universal horror was expressed at the kidnapping and murder of an eight-year-old boy whose parents had won the Opera House lottery in Sydney in 1960. It was the first such case to be recorded. When the long-serving premier of Victoria, Henry Bolte, decided to require the hanging of Ronald Ryan in February 1967 for the killing of a warder in an escape bid, only one of the sixteen major daily papers supported the decision. There was some support for the hanging by those citizens whose attitude to human life was selective, but Ryan's execution was the last in Australia although, sporadically, there were calls for restitution of the death penalty.

Meanwhile, scientists in Britain were taking the first steps towards in vitro fertilization and at the same time more and more people in Australia, and elsewhere, were insisting that abortion was the right of a pregnant woman, although no one had proved that a foetus was not a human being. The Liberal Party in South Australia loosened the law on abortion and other states followed suit eventually, which did much to clean up the iniquity of 'backyard' operations. Under the second reforming government of Labor's Don Dunstan, significant steps were taken in South Australia with the abolition of capital punishment, the outlawing of racial discrimination, the recognition that homosexuals had a right to human dignity and, in general, a relaxing of the rigid codes of Adelaide society.

The majority of Australians were unaware of the dreadful toll taken of livestock and the decline in agriculture during the drought in 1964–65, which struck the eastern states particularly badly, especially New South Wales and Queensland. The wheat crop fell by seventy-five per cent, sheep numbers declined by fourteen million and cattle by one and a half million. Many farmers never recovered from their losses, while others struggled for years to do so. The realization that many farms were too small to produce a consistent, worthwhile living was strengthened and, as a consequence, after the drought a process began of consolidation into larger holdings and land prices again soared.

Drought had never much affected life in the cities, where, by the mid-1960s most of Australia's 11,500,000 citizens lived. Three hundred policeman were present to control a thousand fans, mostly girls, when the Beatles arrived in Sydney to a rain-drenched welcome in June 1964, but the sun shone for the highest paid model in the world, Jean Shrimpton, when, dressed in a mini-skirt which ended five inches above her knees, she caused a sensation at Flemington racecourse, Melbourne, on Derby Day in November 1965. After the initial shock many women followed suit, wearing mini-skirts as fashion dictated and continuing to do so until designers decreed otherwise. As with other things, there was always a discreet time lag between the European mode and the Australian acceptance of it.

In other ways, rapid change was occurring. Sydney had lived to the sound of horse-drawn, steam and electric trams for a century but, in 1961, trams ceased to run endangering the time honoured expression 'To shoot through like a Bondi tram'. In 1962 a standard gauge rail was opened between Sydney and Melbourne which ended eighty years of confusion, expense and unnecessary labour and by the end of the decade steam powered trains ceased to run. Roma Mitchell became the first woman judge in Australia in 1965 and women attempted to change archaic drinking customs which prevented their participation by organizing 'sitins' in bars in Canberra and Brisbane. The Seekers became the most popular recording group and were Australia's first group to cut a million copy record with 'I'll Never Find Another You' and Joan Sutherland returned home to be compared with Nellie Melba after her operatic successes overseas. In the literary world, the bans that had been imposed on D.H. Lawrence's *Lady Chatterley's Lover* and on Vladimir Nabokov's *Lolita* were withdrawn. At Siding Springs near Coonabarabran in New South Wales an observatory with a huge telescope known affectionately as 'The Dish' was opened; the first hydrofoil appeared on Sydney Harbour; the Ford Falcon XM car was launched and Australia applied economic sanctions on Rhodesia for its unilateral bid towards independence.

Far-reaching change followed the awakening of consciousness brought about by involvement in the Vietnam War, or, at least, was concomitant with it. There were repeated calls for the public renunciation of the White Australia policy. Turks and Lebanese had begun to immigrate in small numbers and some Asians had been allowed to remain in Australia on temporary permits while a selected few, judged to have useful qualifications, were permitted to enter with their families and to choose to stay on after five years. It was the first real sign of a change in racial attitudes although the New South Wales president of the Returned Services League still spoke of non-white people as 'wogs and bogs'.

The change in attitude towards foreign-born non-whites was accompanied by one embracing the Aboriginal population. In 1963 an Aboriginal leader, Charles Perkins, led a series of 'Freedom Rides' on buses to the north and west of New South Wales, which, with the aid of television, made more Australians aware of the offensive nature of discrimination against blacks in swimming pools, cinemas and hotels. With the support of all political parties, Holt put a referendum to the people in May 1967 that asked for constitutional changes that would give the Commonwealth 'concurrent' rights with the states in the area of Aboriginal affairs. In effect it meant that the fullness of civil rights enjoyed by other Australians were to be granted to all Aborigines. Less than ten per cent of the electorate voted 'No' in the referendum and all the states fell in line with Commonwealth policies except for Queensland where the old practise of 'protection' was continued for a time. In states and towns, where contact between whites and Aborigines was closest, a higher percentage voted against. The goldfield town of Kalgoorlie reinforced its history of racism that had been notably evident in wild riots there against foreign-born miners in 1934. Thirty-four per cent of the town's electors voted in the negative.

Although Aborigines in Queensland, the Northern Territory and Western Australia were given the right to vote in 1962, which had been granted to them in other states in 1949, they still suffered serious disadvantages. In 1963 police evicted the Mapoon Aboriginal community on Cape York Peninsula and their homes were destroyed to facilitate bauxite mining. This vexed question of Aboriginal land rights had lain hidden, but it had been the nub of black-white relationships since the First Fleet sailed into Port Jackson in 1788. Australians expressed hidden guilt when they said of poor land that it might as well 'be given back to the blacks'. The matter came to the fore on a British-leased pastoral run in the Northern Territory of 15,500 square kilometers called Wave Hill. The Gurindjis had worked on the cattle station for many years, but, in 1966, they walked off rather than accept the low wages they were offered. They proceeded to set themselves up on land at Wattie Creek, which they claimed was their own. William Charles

Wentworth, federal Minister for Aboriginal Affairs was a direct descendant of his illustrious predecessor who had borne the same name and had regarded Aborigines as little better than brutes. The Minister saw the justice of the Gurindji claim and persuaded the Cabinet to grant them occupancy of about twenty-six square kilometers in good country. It was not a policy decision on land rights, but it contained the seeds of dynamic change, especially as the majority of white Australians regarded it as a just measure.

In the 1960s the national capital started to show signs of becoming a city worthy of its title. Canberra, since the days when it was no more than a dream and then a drab reality, had always been the butt of sardonic humour or trenchant criticism. Money spent on it was considered ill spent by many and politicians, with an eye to their electorates, had been reluctant to lose votes to the ignorant, which meant that progress in the development of the capital was painfully slow. Public servants were still unwilling to move to Canberra from interstate, and especially from Melbourne, despite the generous incentives the government offered them to do so. The business sector could not develop in an air of uncertainty about land tenure and population growth, and many Canberrans felt that they were exiles from a genuine urban civilization.

With considerable courage, determination and foresight, Menzies had decided to build a capital befitting a young and prosperous nation. Canberra citizens watched with fascination in 1963–64 as, between the southern and northern portions of the city, a splendid lake slowly took shape after the damming of the Molonglo River. The lake took the name, fittingly, of Burley Griffin although its dam, equally deservedly, was called Scrivener in honour of the surveyor who had selected the site for the new city. Thought was then given to the so-called parliamentary triangle and the National Library arose by the shore of the lake, looking at night like a huge Greek temple in southern Sicily. A National Gallery and a High Court were planned and new 'towns', with their shopping centres, began in the Woden and Belconnen areas. In the space of a decade Canberra came to life. Most visitors called at the War Memorial, which, as a place of quiet and impressive dignity with not a trace of triumphalism over former enemies, was a fitting tribute to the men and women who had fought and died in wars, as well as to Charles Bean who had seen the vision of its future grandeur.

The most remarkable characteristic of Canberra was that, despite its design by an American, there was scarcely anything American about it with the exception of the American Embassy built on gracious colonial lines. A strikingly Australian aspect of Canberra was the weekend, when, in summer, the citizens sailed on the lake, fled in thousands to the south coast, played golf, and went to the nearby bush for a swim in the Murrumbidgee or Cotter Rivers and then had a barbecue on their banks. They washed down their steaks, chops and sausages with beer or flagon wines and soon were able to draw their wine from the Australian innovation of the cardboard cask with its plastic container. In winter, many Canberrans hibernated at home to watch either Australian Rules on television from Melbourne or one or both Rugby codes from Sydney, while others went to ski on the nearby Snowy Mountains. Hardy parents and their offspring ventured forth to the innumerable ovals to participate in, and to cheer on the contestants engaged in winter sports such as hockey, netball, soccer, and football. In the variety of its sporting codes Canberra was emphatically cosmopolitan.

At a place called Tidbinbilla there was a nature reserve to which all the levels of Canberra society – diplomats, public servants, members of the armed forces, academics and others who made civilized existence possible such as milkmen, surgeons, chefs and garbage collectors – sometimes went to picnic and look, mostly in vain, for koalas, although emus were painfully prolific and an odd kangaroo skipped cautiously by. In 1963 the Americans decided to erect a space relay station there, but John F. Kennedy, who dreamt that the day would come when humanity would conquer the stars, did not live to see its usefulness as he was killed in November of that year. On their black and white television sets Australians watched in July 1969 as the American astronaut, Neil Armstrong, took a small step on the moon and said it was' a giant leap for mankind'. The world was no longer merely one because now there were other worlds to walk upon.

An entirely different world was close by although few Australians had ever walked on it. In 1959 the Antarctic Treaty was signed and Australia, as one of the original parties to it, hosted the first meeting of the member nations in Canberra in 1961 under the chairmanship of Senator John Grey Gorton. The Treaty was a significant step with far-ranging implications. For years there had been concern lest open conflict arise between nations with interests in the Antarctic and that it may become a pawn in the Cold War between Russia and the United States. The original twelve nations who signed the Treaty managed to submerge their individual interests and agree to provide independent advice to Treaty members and coordinate international scientific programmes in the Antarctic.

For Australians the end of the sixties – a decade so full of change, protest, acceptance and an awakening of consciousness, a decade perhaps without parallel in the previous history of humanity – spelt the end of the old securities and much of the life style that had reinforced the values of a white outpost at the edge of Asia. Never again would Australians look only to Britain as their economic, cultural and strategic prop, although most of them continued to enjoy British television shows, which reflected their own humour, tastes and values, while the introduction of the great bus of the airways, the jumbo, brought London within a long day's flight from Sydney or Melbourne. America was everywhere present, but especially in popular music; in the dollar, both as symbol and reality of dependence on Wall Street; in the young United States servicemen who came on recreation leave from Vietnam to Sydney and in the mediocre, or worse, serials on commercial television. Finally, there was the acceptance, even among the most reluctant, that American involvement in Vietnam meant Australian involvement. It was precisely that involvement which turned the Americanization of its newest province sour.

20

Years of Hope

By the end of the 1960s, the bush was little more than a heritage to be treasured in art, literature and legend as the birthplace of the nation. In fact, the cities were always the human and physical anvils on which the characteristics of the people were hammered out. The myth of the bush retained its vitality, but it lacked reality to the urban dwellers in the capitals, or even to the residents of the inland cities. Reality to them was home, school, family, neighbours, job, car, health, superannuation, insurance, taxes, rent, mortgages, supermarket, holidays, club and pub. They differed only in accidental ways from the citizens of London, Dublin, Chicago, New York, Berlin, Rome, and Tokyo. Over one hundred and eighty years of living on this continent had produced little that was distinctive or new. Talk about a national identity was increasingly hollow because Australians had become part of the industrialized world with all its values of dependence, consumerism, uncertainty, creativity, vitality and ever-surging hope in progress. The bush remained, and would always remain, a symbol of nature's hold on Australians, but the cities would continue to shape them. Some Australians were beginning to realize that they ought to play a greater role in that shaping.

Compulsory voting in federal and state elections always tended to inflate returns and hence obscure the reality of a lack of political interest on the part of most Australian citizens. Few people listened to the broadcasts of proceedings of Parliament, but the advent of television had brought the faces, attitudes and personalities of politicians into living rooms. Concomitant with their economic and hence social power, considerable political power also began to move into the hands of faceless men sitting on boards in New York London and Zurich. Powerful corporations, oil cartels, international banking houses and large newspapers exercised a role and politicians felt bound to assert their own importance in ways that were in inverse proportion to the actual truth.

An opposition party can make an impact on an electorate only if it engages in constructive criticism of the government, spells out an alternative platform and offers attractive rewards. From the early 1970s such an impact began to make a mark on Australia. The Labor Party became a vital force in opposition with Gough Whitlam as its leader. The contrary happened to the Liberal-Country Party coalition. Years of unchanged leadership under Menzies, the untimely death of Holt, continued affluence and sociological change, especially among the young, partly caused the coalition to falter as it tried to grapple with new values, problems and expectations.

The biggest problem for the coalition was to uphold the meaning of liberalism in a new world with rapidly changing values. Changes in the content of education, the impact of the media with standards of ethical behaviour imported from America and the centrality of economics made the role of the Liberals difficult. They had to formulate and offer policies that revolved around beliefs inherited from a neat and compact imperial order where everyone knew their place, and which were redolent of an unmourned for past. For the Country Party the problem was acute in that the people of the bush, on whom it relied for electoral support, had dwindled in numbers and had become increasingly urbanised as they moved into rural centres. In so doing many of them took on the outlook of the city dwellers to whom such things as subsidies for farmers, adequate transport for agricultural products, the retention of tariffs and similar preoccupations meant less and less.

The same held true for Labor. Young, tertiary educated idealists had entered its ranks to join the old guard of trade unionists and their impetus was not to be gainsaid. The strength of a unionised workforce was diminishing, white collar workers were outnumbering those who had previously toiled on wharves, down mines and in heavy industry. The tradition of Labor loyalty, through which adhesion to the Party had been handed down within families and acted upon on voting day without questioning either candidates or policies, had weakened. New ideas, new ways of confronting problems that were increasingly international in their scope, a fresh outlook and presentation requiring an up-to-date public image on the radio, in the media and especially on television; all were required if Labor were to have any chance of winning power from a long entrenched government. In these circumstances the 1970s became a decade of politics.

Changes in attitudes were also reflected in a widespread collapse of traditional standards on the individual level. Two children became the norm for a family; teenage promiscuity was prevalent with the highest teen pregnancy rate in fifty years, despite the contraceptive pill; the divorce rate doubled and the irretrievable breakdown of a marriage became the sole ground for divorce; 'living together' was regarded as an acceptable prelude or alternative to marriage; Sydney rivalled San Francisco as a 'gay' capital and the role of religion diminished as an effective element in society, as well as in the lives of individuals.

The authority and wisdom of the Liberal and Country Parties in thrusting Australia into the Vietnam War were queried and deplored by many, as evidenced by continued street marches in the capital cities protesting Australian participation in the conflict. The marches clearly demonstrated that civil authority could be questioned, defied and, in part, ignored. One Melbourne moratorium march took place on 8 May 1970 when 200,000 people went to the streets to protest against Australia's continued involvement in the war. The crowd covered the Fitzroy Gardens and filled Bourke Street when they marched down it. An old veteran of both World Wars, Bill Connolly, of Plenty, Victoria, said, 'I'm proud to be here today'.

In the education field, militant teachers' unions combined with student activism to challenge traditional methods of teaching and the universities became places in which some teachers began to taste the fruits of free enquiry at first hand. In some states the voting age was reduced to eighteen, a few 'alternative' schools were set up, and there were moves to abolish external examinations in Queensland. Neville Bonner, a Queensland Aborigine, became the first of his race to enter federal Parliament when he won a seat in the Senate in 1971 and, in the Sydney suburb of Redfern, an Aboriginal Legal Service was started as the first community controlled Aboriginal service in Australia. Generally, the early 1970s was a period in which old political slogans, outmoded ways of approaching social problems, fear of facing the unknown or the risky on an international level and unwillingness to change had lost relevance and everywhere there was a feeling that the time for moderate but purposeful change had come.

When Holt died in 1967, the Country Party leader, John McEwen, briefly prime minister, blackballed the prospective new leader of the Liberal Party, William McMahon, by refusing to serve under him. John Grey Gorton was elected leader and consequently took on the leadership of the country. He possessed considerable ability, drive and vision and had in him some of the characteristics of the old Australian legend that revealed itself in a degree of recklessness and a distaste for formality which made him open to criticism of his style and, eventually, of his personal behaviour. As prime minister, he believed in keeping a firm hand over his Cabinet and using Commonwealth powers to their fullest, which made some state Premiers nervous. He continued to support the war in Vietnam, although he declared he would commit no more troops there. This did not satisfy the ever-increasing number of Australians, mobilised by Jim Cairns, a Labor member of Parliament, who had the courage to act on his conscience and protest against the war. Most of the electorate, however, ignored the war, while they enjoyed continuing affluence, high rates of employment and a general optimism about the future.

In May 1968 the Prime Minister caused much dissension, even among conservatives, when he told President Richard Nixon at a dinner in America that Australians would 'go a-waltzing Matilda with you'. Presumably this promise was made to resist the spread of communism in Asia, although within weeks Nixon made it plain that, henceforth, Asian nations would have to attend to their own internal security. In this context, it was never clear whose security was involved when another American communications base was set up at Pine Gap, near Alice Springs. Many concerned observers thought that the very presence of such bases on its territory infringed Australian sovereignty and made it a target in any eventual war.

The crux of Gorton's problem was that he had nowhere to lead his party and many of those who supported it. He tried to replace both British and American links with his own brand of attractive, Australian, larrikin nationalism that had no genuine base among conservative Australians at that time, especially as a substitute for the British ties some of them still held to firmly. The coalition retained office at an election in October 1969 because of Democratic Labor Party preferences, but it had gained only 43.35 percent of the vote to Labor's 46.95 percent. Gorton survived one challenge to his leadership, but in March 1971 a party motion of no confidence in him was tied thirty-three to thirty-three. From the chair, he voted himself out of office to be replaced by William McMahon.

McMahon had to face a formidable Labor opponent in Gough Whitlam, as well as an economy showing signs of faltering. The command Whitlam had in the Labor Party was clearly illustrated by 1970 when he broke the hold of left-wing extremists over the Victorian branch, who had been in control there since Evatt's coup in 1955 and who had come to the quaint conclusion that it was better to remain in opposition than to compromise itself by taking office. Moreover, Whitlam's image in the electorate at large was that of a vibrant, forceful, intelligent and articulate leader who had a clear set of policies. McMahon, though a moderately successful Treasurer, seemed frequently incapable of enunciating a coherent sentence, and suffered by comparison with Whitlam despite his genuine concern for his country. On the economic level, Australia was beginning to suffer a backlash from the falling prosperity of the wealthier industrialized nations – America, Germany and Japan – but China was rapidly becoming a principal market for wool and wheat. Although, two per cent unemployment and six per cent inflation were far from alarming they were signals that could not be ignored, or in the event rectified.

McMahon's period in office was marked by unusually strident reactions to conservative foreign policies and by strong concern about the increasing lack of clear direction on the economic level. The Labor Party had shed its White Australia plank in 1965, and thereby moved closer to a policy of accepting immigrants, irrespective of their colour. There was a general air of anti-racism in the community. When a South African Rugby Union team toured the country, widespread anti-apartheid demonstrations were mounted, especially in Sydney, Melbourne and Canberra. In Queensland the conservative, populist Premier, Johannes Bjelke-Petersen, declared a state of emergency.

Aborigines sensed for the first time that many white Australians had sympathy for their cause, and they set up an Aboriginal Embassy in a tent on the lawns in front of Parliament House, Canberra, to draw attention to their general living conditions and to agitate for land rights. Anti-Vietnam demonstrators were everywhere vociferous, and there was even concern in the rural sector as farmers wondered whether it was time to recognize China, which had failed to renegotiate its agreement to buy a third of the Australian wheat crop. McMahon decided to do nothing about China except express outrage when Whitlam visited Peking, where he promised to recognize the communist regime that had now ruled for twenty years, were Labor elected to government.

On 2 December 1972, McMahon went to the polls with little in the way of policy, but relying on the coalition's twenty-three years in office and the claim that the Labor Party was an untried and untrustworthy force. On this occasion, the Democratic Labor Party proved unable to deliver the preferences necessary for a coalition victory, and the newly formed Australia

Party gave its preferences to Labor. Despite these advantages, Labor did not have a resounding victory. Whitlam became prime minister with his party holding sixty-seven seats to fifty-eight in the House of Representatives, but the Democratic Labor Party, with five seats, held the balance of power in the Senate.

Whitlam had run under the slogan 'It's Time', and he proved that time was a commodity he did not propose to squander. There were still seats in the Parliament in balance and the newly-elected members had not been sworn in. Whitlam and his deputy, Lance Barnard, formed a ministry of two, and, in the next couple of weeks, Whitlam began, by regulation, to fulfil the promises he had made on the hustings. It was decided to stop all military involvement in Vietnam and to abolish conscription. All those legally in jeopardy or in prison for their non-compliance with the draft for military service, or for urging others to refuse compliance, had their charges dismissed or they were restored to freedom. Plans were made to spend large amounts on education and on Aborigines whose traditional lands were to be preserved from mining leases. Formal steps were taken to recognize China. The White Australia policy was dismantled so that in law, and partly in fact, Australians could reject the label of being racists.

For a time, Australians, eighty-five per cent of whom now lived in urban areas, had every reason to believe that genuine change was taking place. No government since Federation had so carefully worked out its policies and then began so readily to implement them, so in the beginning only a very few said that change was going too far or too fast. An air of urgency and excitement prevailed, while Whitlam, often accompanied in public by his charming and intelligent wife, Margaret, took the helm and turned the nation around. He wanted to form a more just, humane and civilized society in which the distribution of wealth was to be more evenly balanced.

Whitlam also knew that he could not change a bureaucracy, which the conservatives had shaped at its highest level for over two decades. He had little control over the choice of his Cabinet colleagues, none of whom had had previous ministerial experience. Whitlam and the Cabinet were forced to rely on the advice of public servants, who, in the main, were loyal and generous to the new government. However, some ministers surrounded themselves by young and inexperienced 'experts' who proved an irritant to the long-serving public servants and, not infrequently, a source of anger and bewilderment to the wider public with which they were not in touch and to which they were not responsible.

Matters of genuine substance frequently brought no adverse public reaction, while those of little moment caused unease. The American alliance remained firmly at the base of foreign policy and the government did nothing about the bases on Australian soil, but alarm was raised in conservative circles when there was outspoken criticism of the bombing of Hanoi in December 1972. 'Advance Australia Fair' was chosen as the national anthem to replace 'God save the Queen', except on special occasions, despite the partial absurdity of the replacement and the inability of most Australians to sing its words. The 'British subject' on Australian passports was removed when Britain joined the European Economic Community; Lionel Murphy, as Attorney General, organized an ill conceived and badly executed raid on the Australian Security Intelligence Organization headquarters in Melbourne in an attempt to discover documents on alleged terrorists; and Whitlam went on regular visits overseas. All these minor matters caused unease among conservatives, puzzled the uninformed and provided a field day for journalists.

The Prime Minister had the ill fortune to be absent from the country in late 1974 when a disaster of unprecedented proportions occurred on Christmas Eve. Darwin, capital of the Northern Territory, was virtually destroyed by Cyclone Tracy, and, after four hours of violence, the citizens were reduced to terror and stupefaction. The government acted promptly, and an evacuation programme was organized involving the airlifting of 26,000 citizens from the area and the Navy was sent in to help. The city was subsequently rebuilt with materials and structural designs more capable of resisting hurricanes, but the fact that a thousand were injured and sixty-five died was indicative of the major nature of the occurrence. Whitlam bore no responsibility whatever for the disaster, but criticism of him was strong.

There were other matters of considerable consequence for which the Labor government was given little credit. From the very beginning of its term of office, Labor pledged itself to independence for Papua New Guinea. It acted decisively and courageously, despite the cries of those who thought that many years should pass before the local inhabitants could be judged responsible enough to direct their own affairs. The territory was given self-government by Canberra in 1973 and then independence in 1975, although it continued to rely on considerable aid from Australia to maintain its economic and social equilibrium. A decade later there had been a big decrease in aid, Papua New Guinea was forming its own independent foreign policy and there was concern in Australia that the days of mutual trust were passing.

Other important steps taken by Whitlam's government were the reduction of tariffs by twenty-five per cent, the abolition of tertiary education fees, a substantial increase in spending on both public and private education, the granting to public servants of wage increases and improved conditions, including twelve weeks on full pay to pregnant employees, and the reopening of the case for equal pay before the Arbitration Commission. Colleges of Advanced Education were built in every state and in the Australian Capital Territory, new universities were opened and the arts and cultural activities given support, although there was much criticism of the buying, for the future National Gallery, of Jackson Pollock's painting *Blue Poles* for $1,300,000. In rural areas none of this mattered compared to the decision that farmers would no longer receive a $50,000,000 subsidy on superphosphates.

By mid-1974, it became apparent that a concerted attempt was being made in conservative circles to get rid of Whitlam's government even though it was only halfway through its term of three years. The self-appointed saviour of the country from the evils of what he called socialism was Queensland's Bjelke-Petersen who stomped about declaring that he would cleanse Canberra of Whitlam and all his followers. The farmers were by now bitterly resentful and were prepared to take any steps to remove Labor. Segments of the business community were wringing their hands over inflation but, at the same time, helping by their propaganda to destroy the prospects of a referendum, subsequently lost, to control prices as well as wages. By April 1974, the Senate had rejected ten bills twice and nine others once, even though they bore on matters that Labor had included in its electoral platform.

To the opposition, the electoral circumstances seemed favourable and it proceeded to refuse passage through the Senate to three appropriation bills unless the government promised to hold an election for both Houses. Whitlam was forced to secure a double dissolution and his prospects did not seem good. Inflation was running at fourteen per cent, his government was under fire from intense conservative criticism and the strength of the opposition was lined up against him. Although Labor was returned with the loss of only one seat in the House of Representatives, the result indicated that there was a mounting degree of unease within the electorate. Billy Snedden, leader of the coalition since McMahon's resignation after the 1972 election, was no match, in or out of Parliament, for Whitlam. In the Senate, Labor still lacked a majority and the balance of power was now held by two independents who could not be relied upon to vote for the government, but the Democratic Labor Party was a spent force.

The most significant aspects of the election were the means used to procure it in the first place and that the coalition was defeated despite its confidence in winning. In the aftermath, Whitlam implemented further measures that served to enhance the animosity of powerful elements in society. Wage indexation was introduced; a Racial Discrimination Act came into force, and a general health scheme called Medibank was implemented which gave free health care to Australians. Medibank worked moderately well and brought great advantages to the less fortunate members of the community. Despite general approval of Medibank by the public, many medical practitioners were opposed to it, although it served to enhance rather than diminish their economic prospects and some few were quick to use it for their own enrichment.

Influenced by a worldwide recession, unemployment began to climb steadily in early 1975 and rose to over five per cent by August. Women in thousands were out of work, especially in the textile industry, where the lowering of tariffs had caused havoc, and the building trades were in chaos. Queues lined up at Commonwealth Employment Service offices, and some who stood in them had never been unemployed, while, among the young, there were some also who were never to be employed. They had left school with the dole as their only expectation, and they put their names down for it much in the same way as they had done when enrolling in school subjects in the past. There was less and less chance of gaining an apprenticeship and one employer received 800 applications for the single apprenticeship he offered. Meanwhile, inflation roared along at over seventeen per cent, fuelled by rising oil prices and the expenditure of the government on welfare, as well as on public servants' salaries, which had been used as a pacesetter for the community.

By his tendency to 'Australianize' aspects of public life, Whitlam had caused considerable concern among a minority that still looked to Britain and its culture as the unique source of all things worthwhile. In July 1975, appeals to the Privy Council from the Australian High Court were abolished except in a few special cases. In February of that year, Whitlam introduced an Order of Australia to replace dames and knights. The highest award was a Companion of the Order, which outstripped imperial honours. Though the Order of Australia was retained, the succeeding Liberal government reinstated imperial honours and those Australians to whom such matters were important were mollified. The great majority of Australians remained, however, either cynical of such honours or at best indifferent, believing that

> When they pin the Stars and Garters,
> when they write the titles rare,
> The men who earned the honours
> are the men who won't be there.

The absence of women from the ditty and their fewness among the decorated seemed to escape general notice.

The opposition had begun to show some bite when the Liberals replaced Snedden with Malcolm Fraser as leader in March 1975. Fraser was quick to promise that he would never force an election by threatening to withhold supply unless he found that the behaviour of the government was 'reprehensible'. In the circumstances it was empty rhetoric, because to Fraser, and to those who supported him, a Labor government was a political and social aberration, which, by its very nature, lacked legitimacy. Its behaviour was accordingly 'reprehensible' by definition. In such circumstances the coalition partners still regarded themselves as the only force capable of running the country satisfactorily. They were determined to return to the Treasury benches, which they considered to be their right. The difficulty was that Whitlam showed no signs of wanting to go back to the polls after fighting two elections in less than two years. To force him to the polls again required 'reprehensible' circumstances, and, in some measure, they seemed to be at hand.

A miserable episode called the 'loans affair', in which the government was guilty of considerable ineptitude, was used to force an election. Rex Connor, Minister for Minerals and Energy, was determined to buy back a share of the stake that foreign investors had taken out in Australian minerals and oil. The Middle East oil owners, who had thrown the international economy into chaos by their price rises for crude oil, seemed logical lenders of the vast sum of $4,000 million needed. A few simple inquiries would have revealed that loans would be forthcoming from such sources only through the normal channels of high finance, rather than through intermediaries of doubtful reputation. With a flagrant disregard for propriety, the government bypassed the Loans Council when authorizing the search for a loan. When the opposition began to raise objections, the Treasury lowered the sum to $2,000 million in the vain hope that the affair would bear some semblance of proper dealing.

Whitlam's deputy Jim Cairns was dismissed from the ministry when he was found to have misled Parliament over his attempt to raise other overseas loans, and finally Connor resigned when it became public that he had continued to involve himself in loan raising activities after Whitlam had assured the Parliament that all such behaviour had ceased. No money ever actually changed hands, but the media astounded the public with the names and faces of shady characters who were involved in the 'money deals'. The circumstances of the whole affair revealed clear imprudence and obstinancy on the part of at least Connor and Cairns, but there was nothing to suggest that anything so 'reprehensible' had occurred as to warrant the denial of supply. Fraser and his advisors did not see the matter in that light. They decided on 15 October 1975 that the Senate would use the simple device of refusing to pass the government money bills for 1975–76 when they came before it. In that way opposition senators would not actually go as far as to block supply, they would simply make its fulfilment impossible until Whitlam met Fraser's terms with an election for the House of Representatives.

For three weeks, the whole country watched as the political game was played out. Whitlam remained consistent in his stand throughout the affair – unless supply were passed or rejected outright, he would not budge. In the last few days before 11 November, he came within an ace of success, as some of Fraser's senators, seized with the seriousness of the whole matter, began to waver. Whitlam knew what he was doing throughout the crisis and his one unwise step was to turn, fruitlessly, to the private banks for temporary funds to finance the government. This act alarmed even some of those who were favourably disposed towards him. It was clear to him in the last week or so that if he could not obtain supply, but refused to resign or ask for a full election, he could be dismissed.

Whitlam's gamble failed because he did not have in his keeping the man who could make or break him – the Governor-General. A sympathetic Governor-General, and Whitlam was entitled to expect some sympathy from his own appointee, could have taken the view that the situation did not warrant the dismissal of a prime minister who held a majority in the House of Representatives, and who, for the second time in eighteen months, was being prevented from conducting the business of running the country by an opposition that used a method hitherto unheard of since the Constitution came into force – the effective negation of Supply.

One course for the Governor-General would have been to await the outcome of the blocking of supply which could well have resulted in some senators refusing to comply with Fraser's demand that they stay firm in resolve. He could then have granted Whitlam's advice to him that entailed the holding of a half Senate election. Under those circumstances, Whitlam would have faced the electorate as Prime Minister and there may have been some slim chance of success. In any case, whatever the outcome of the election, the accepted procedures of the Australian democratic process as they had been understood and applied since Federation would have been followed.

On 11 November the Governor-General, Sir John Kerr, called the Prime Minister to Government House. At Kerr's invitation, Fraser had already taken up a position in hiding at the House. During his brief interview with Kerr, Whitlam refused to accept the ultimatum of a general election, because he wanted only a half Senate election, which, were Labor successful, would have given him control of the Senate. Kerr, already prepared with the document in hand, dismissed the Prime Minister of Australia from office.

When Whitlam departed for his home at the Lodge, Kerr called in the waiting Fraser and appointed him as caretaker Prime Minister pending an election. Within hours, supply was passed, as was a motion of no confidence in Fraser by the House of Representatives. By the late afternoon of 11 November 1975, the Parliament was dissolved amidst scenes of disbelief and dismay among Labor followers and to the strong resentment of many who believed that the course of Australian democracy had been perverted. Among the great majority of conservatives, there was satisfaction, relief and rejoicing. During the previous three years, many of them had held to the view that Labor had no right to govern and that the course it had set itself of the equitable distribution of wealth was inimical to their best interests.

November 11 was a day decreed by fate to be remembered among Australians. On this day in 1854, the Ballarat Reform League had been founded on Bakery Hill and the Eureka flag was hoisted there later as a signal to the oppressed that Australia under the Southern Cross was a land of freedom. On 11 November 1880 Ned Kelly was hanged in Melbourne Gaol, and for many his life had become a symbol of the struggle of the helpless against oppression. And 11 November 1918 saw the Armistice to end World War I in which Australians had come to realize that the sacrifice of her young manhood marked the end of innocence. To the degree that there had been political innocence in Australia prior to 11 November 1975, it too was at an end.

From the steps of Parliament House after the dissolution, Whitlam had called on his followers to maintain their 'rage' at his dismissal and bolster their 'enthusiasm' for the return of his government. In the circumstances, 'rage' was an understandable if fruitless emotion while 'enthusiasm', so evident in the early period of Labor government, was essential for re-election and future success. In the long run, it too proved fruitless. The electorate had been led to believe by powerful sections of the media, on the radio, in newspapers and on television, that the Labor government had become bungling and inept, that it was totally responsible for the economic difficulties that Australia was encountering (which discounted the world economic situation), and that it was socialist and therefore dangerous – a useful lie Labor opponents always fabricated when desperate.

The fact was that the Whitlam government had lost its way, especially in economic matters, which was an area where Whitlam himself claimed no competence, and the appointment of the prudent and competent Bill Hayden as federal Treasurer came too late to redress the balance. Unemployment was running at a higher rate than at any time since the Great Depression; the Henderson Report on Poverty in August revealed that ten per cent of the Australian adult income units were below the poverty line with another eight per cent just above it; and among most farmers and many urban dwellers there was a fear of Whitlam and Labor that no reassuring words could allay. The media combined with the opposition to fuel those apprehensions, so Whitlam's chance of re-election was slim.

In the elections of 13 December 1975, Fraser and his followers were rewarded with the largest majority since Federation. The coalition held ninety-one to thirty-six seats in the House of Representatives and had a majority of eight in the Senate. On the following day, Whitlam tried to stand down as leader of the Labor Party, but his deputy, Bill Hayden, was too dispirited to accept the position, and furthermore, he was still waiting to find out whether he would retain his own seat. The other person to whom Whitlam spoke about the leadership was Bob Hawke, president of the Australian Council of Trade Unions who had been for some years a prominent figure as a successful negotiator between the unions and employers. Hawke was not in Parliament and Whitlam's discussion of the leadership with him served only to create tensions among some powerful Labor parliamentarians despite their own frequently dismal performances when in office.

Meanwhile, Fraser became Prime Minister without any further question as to his legitimacy and Doug Anthony, who had succeeded McEwen as leader of the Country Party in 1971, became the deputy. Anthony was a tough, skilful politician, whose personally expressed principle of action was to 'kick a head' when he saw one, and the pair of them made up a formidable team. The debt owed to some rural voters for their constancy throughout the crisis and at the polls was paid almost immediately with the restoration of the superphosphate bounty.

The seven years that followed under Fraser were ones in which it was largely believed that moderation in government spending was the cure for economic ills, notably unemployment and inflation. In fact, spending was not substantially curtailed, the whole business of government grew and there was little attempt to transfer public agencies into private hands. In 1976 there were four rises in wages amounting to over fifteen per cent and under wage indexation the trend continued in the following years until 1981 when the system was abandoned. As a result, ironically, a later generation of conservatives lumped Fraser with Whitlam, when they sought a long-term reason for the economic instability of the mid-eighties. Inflation did, however, drop by about five per cent, but unemployment hovered at eight to nine per cent. Young people, to whom unemployment was becoming a way of life rather than a temporary misfortune, were lumped together and branded as 'dole bludgers' although responsible coalition politicians recognized that, in the main, the unemployed bore no fault for their condition.

In the universities, dissent largely died as a new generation of youth enrolled knowing that a degree was partly an insurance against unemployment, which was still rising through the late 1970s, and that work, rather than political activism, was the path to success. Some still protested, often successfully, about examinations which they regarded as an unjust method of assessment, about the content of their courses in which they claimed they ought to be involved, and about their right to sit on university boards and otherwise share with academics the running of the universities. Within the wider community of youth many, as a simple variant on alcohol or tobacco, gradually accepted the widespread use of marijuana. When the drug pushers felt the desire for greater profits they often stopped the flow of marijuana in order to entice young people onto other more injurious substances that they made readily available. By 1980 there were over 20,000 heroin addicts in the country. More positive developments were colour television, bankcard and, as a faint sign of a forthcoming groundswell, a rally in Sydney on 20 September 1976 which called for an Australian republic.

The common denominators of the youth culture were dress and music. Dress was largely functional with little distinction between that worn by either sex, jeans were universal and there was an infinitude of signs, symbols or slogans appearing on t-shirts. The protest for greater individualism was suffocated in exterior conformity. In music, jazz was almost dead and the Beatles were superseded, to be replaced by the preachers of a new age, who had a social message on everything ranging from love to nuclear war. Australian 'pop' culture was of the 'moonlight' kind in that it merely reflected or slavishly imitated that which prevailed among American youth. Nevertheless, the Vietnam War had penetrated the consciousness of young Australians to the degree that many of them began to reflect on wider issues such as racism, the role of women in society and respect for the environment.

The Vietnam War and unemployment combined to convince many young people that their elders foisted the ills of society on them deliberately, and even maliciously. In the homes bemused parents often found communication with their children well nigh impossible. In some schools the transmission of knowledge became less necessary and less formal as external examinations were replaced by internal assessment, and teacher unions expressed their militancy and drive towards higher wages and better conditions by calling strikes, which bothered mainly parents. At the same time, the young showed a readiness to be tolerant of each other, to share, to make sacrifices and to encourage the less fortunate in a way that no previous generation had done.

A change took place in the treatment of Aborigines and non-whites. Fraser, son of a grazier, came from the sort of background that had been mainly responsible for the worst atrocities committed on the Aboriginal population. Yet he was a genuine anti-racist, which he proved in his constant attempts to persuade the South African government to mitigate the grosser aspects of apartheid and in his influential support for the setting up of Zimbabwe. The tightened economic situation caused budget cuts in the area of Aboriginal welfare, but there was a general climate of greater good will towards them, although their position remained deplorable in health, housing, education and employment. They began to organize more effectively, to run their own councils and to support their own leaders, who represented their plight to governments. In the Northern Territory land rights were granted over twenty per cent of the whole area, the Wave Hill case was concluded when the Gurindji people obtained inalienable freehold title to almost all of the station while in Queensland leases were given on traditional lands. In South Australia, where 100,000 square kilometres of land were granted to the Aborigines, the Premier Don Dunstan appointed an Aborigine, Doug Nicholls, as state Governor. Evonne Goolagong, who was of Aboriginal descent and came from Barellan in New South Wales, became a world tennis champion and winner of two Wimbledon titles.

Although the end of 1972 concluded all Australian involvement in Vietnam, the war itself dragged on until 1975 when a communist government was established in Saigon. People began to flee from South Vietnam, and Australia was sought as a new home by some of them. An episode that stirred the imagination of many Australians and helped to make them more receptive to Asians was the epic 8,000 kilometre voyage by the Vietnamese trawler, *PK 504*, from Vietnam to Darwin with fifty-six refugees aboard in late 1976. They were not the first, but their courage, endurance and the skill of the captain, who had navigated with a compass and a school map, had special appeal. The government was sympathetic to the plight of the refugees, partially as a response to a national conscience ill at ease about the Vietnam War. As camps in Thailand began to fill with thousands who had fled from Vietnam, Laos and Cambodia, selection procedures took place, and, by January 1978, 22,000 refugees had arrived with the government agreeing to take 14,000 more and another 20,000 in 1980–81.

The Asian refugees were often welcomed by members of voluntary bodies such as the Indo-China Refugee Association and helped to settle, sometimes in rural communities. By the mid-1980s, some opposition to their continued arrival was expressed by individuals and racist organizations but, in the main, the refugees continued to be accepted, although the government cut back the intake severely except in cases of family reunion, and those with special skills or financial backing. To its great and enduring credit, Australia had accepted over 100,000 refugees from South East Asia by 1987.

From the mid-1970s, some industries had a fifty per cent immigrant workforce with the overall average in industry standing at forty per cent. Immigrant women, many of whom lacked English, tended to be found in low-skilled jobs where they were disadvantaged and, in part, exploited. Economic survival, as had been the case in the past with the Irish and other minorities, made work of any kind acceptable. In round figures, four million immigrants settled permanently in Australia in the years following World War II with over a million from the British Isles and 350,000 from Italy being the largest groups. A J. (Al) Grassby, former Minister for Immigration in the Whitlam government, had been appointed Commissioner for Community Relations, and with Professor Jerzy Zubrzycki, he began to raise the issue of a multicultural society in Australia. They meant one in which groups, differing in their ethnicity, would all receive just and equitable treatment, share the common bond of being Australians with those who had come here before them and retain the culture they brought from their homelands. Some took this to mean much more, such as the provision of public funds for the teaching of foreign languages, the setting up of ethnic language radio stations and other measures. Widespread criticism was subsequently heard of a policy which, when correctly understood and sensibly applied, was the only practical step towards the formation of a truly human society.

Most Australians, including some newer arrivals, were happy when Australia defeated England in the 1977 Centenary Test Match played in Melbourne. Players and spectators alike feted the great fast bowler, Dennis Lillee, for his magnificent performance. No one suspected that after the game an agent of the newspaper magnate Kerry Packer went about the dressing room handing cheques to Australian players who had consented to join Packer's World Series Cricket. The new series competed with the official version by introducing one-day and night cricket, coloured clothes, white balls and instant television replays. Crowds flocked to the new game attracted by the glamour and the certainty of a decision. The large revenue gained put the game on a firm commercial basis, but a decade later, Australian Test cricket was still struggling to recover from the decimation of its leading players.

Other sports followed suit into an era of entertainment, costly in tradition and financial backing. There was an epidemic of player buying led by Sydney Rugby League and, later, the Victorian Football League. Players were bought and sold like commodities and they transferred from club to club for previously unheard of sums. The whole basis of club and suburban loyalties was eroded. In a few years, some Victorian clubs were either so financially distressed, had so little success on the field, or both, that there were clear signs that the days of the Victorian Football League as the premier Australian Rules competition were finished. Supine officials, premiership hungry clubs and greedy players watched the dissolution of a great sporting competition. Within a few years, a National Football League, to rival basketball, Rugby League and soccer, was in the process of development in an effort to develop the Australian game and make it national in fact as well as name.

The decade of the 1970s suffered its share of usual natural and man made disasters adding to the shock of the Darwin cyclone. In 1970 the collapse of the Westgate Bridge in Melbourne was clearly a case of negligence with thirty-five dead. In 1972 seventeen miners were killed in a colliery in Queensland, and another fourteen died in similar circumstances at Appin in New South Wales. During this period coal was becoming Australia's biggest export earner. Brisbane was flooded in 1974 and the waters extended right into its commercial centre. On a summer night in January 1975, twelve people died when a ship collided with the Tasman Bridge in Hobart, thereby dividing the south and north of the city. The worst rail disaster in Australian history took place on 18 January 1977 at Granville, Sydney, when a bridge collapsed on a train, killing over eighty passengers and seriously injuring many more.

A whiff of exotic crime and of the underworld came to Australia in 1977 when Donald Mackay, a highly respected citizen of Griffith, New South Wales, disappeared without trace. Mackay was also an anti-drug campaigner in a locality where millions of dollars were being made from marijuana plantations and drug running. His murder cast a long shadow over the police and the political administration of New South Wales, which was still lengthening a decade later.

On 17 August 1980 Azaria, the nine-week-old baby daughter of Seventh Day Adventist Pastor Michael Chamberlain and his wife Lindy, disappeared from a tent in the camping ground at Ayers Rock in the Northern Territory. The body was never found and the mother claimed that a dingo had taken Azaria. The first inquest agreed with her but, after a further inquest and a trial, Lindy was sentenced to life imprisonment for murder. The High Court rejected Lindy's appeal in February 1984. She was released after spending over three years in jail. No body or murder weapon was ever discovered and no motive was proved, and, in June 1987, a Royal Commission found that 'the evidence affords considerable support for the view that a dingo may have taken' Azaria. Lindy and her husband, who had been convicted as an accessory after the fact, were both pardoned for a ghastly crime which no one had ever proved they had committed. They were neither exonerated nor compensated. The whole bizarre and mysterious affair revealed gross incompetence among experts, dark aspects of religious prejudice, ignorance, fear of the unknown and the outback, and official negligence.

Apart from its last few months, the three, short years of Whitlam had been ones of hope and excitement. The sheer volume of his government's achievements tended to be forgotten in the manner of its downfall. Despite opposition in the Senate, which had rejected ninety-three bills – fifteen more in three years than the same House had rejected in the previous seventy-one years – there were 507 pieces of legislation enacted, which was a record for any government. It was often thought later that the Fraser government undid the work of Whitlam, but in foreign affairs, especially in regard to China, which Fraser visited amicably and successfully, and in the defence area, the main thrusts were maintained. Government assistance to needy students in the tertiary sector and the abolition of fees remained, schools were funded on a needs basis, and tertiary education continued to expand, although severe cuts were made in budgets. Welfare was certainly diminished and, despite Fraser's promise to the contrary, Medibank was changed radically thereby causing the first national strike in Australia's history. Nevertheless, most of Whitlam's welfare initiatives remained in place including the indexation of pensions. Equal pay spread in the workforce, law reform was maintained with the establishment of the Federal Court, legal aid was developed, the office of Ombudsman established and family law set in place. Anti-discrimination laws on race and gender were introduced, a host of other reforms put into effect and the Fraser government passed, with modifications, the land rights bill for Aborigines in the Northern Territory formulated by the Whitlam government.

The public remained unconvinced of Whitlam's belief that it was economically more practical, and personally more just, to provide social services through the public purse than through private measures. Understandably, those whose lifeblood was the accumulation of capital held to the conviction that a wider and more just distribution of wealth threatened their own immediate interests, and the unions failed to perceive that an increase in social services was often more useful to the workers than a few more dollars in wage rises. Those who cried 'too much, too soon' were unable to point to important things that Whitlam did that should have been postponed, except his venture into decentralization with the failed schemes of developing Bathurst/Orange and Albury/Wodonga. Those who felt that Australia had been changed for the worse could not spell it out in any detail except in generalities that were meaningless to the millions of Australians who benefited during his government and afterwards. It was to Whitlam's credit that a new hope and a new vision were given to Australians and to Fraser's that, in considerable measure, he did not destroy either.

21

The End of White Australia

The changed and still changing face of Australia was everywhere obvious as the nation came close to two hundred years of white settlement. Much that was here when the first settlers came remained intact, while vital elements of the culture and tradition they brought with them from the British Isles had been preserved. On remote coastlines and in desolate parts of the outback little or nothing had changed since the passing of Cook on the *Endeavour* in 1770 and the landing of Phillip with his cargo of convicts eighteen years later. Yet these events had set the pattern of change in which the ancient continent was to be transformed both in its physical and cultural landscapes. The cultural landscape was shaped by the introduction of a new culture that partly displaced the older Aboriginal one that had grown out of the physical landscape for over 50,000 years ago. The new culture based on commerce, growth and competition itself altered the physical landscape. Pastoralism, agriculture, mining, deforestation and urbanization had changed the landscape, in some measure irrevocably.

By the 1980s the new nation was still predominantly white, spoke mainly English of the Australian variety, owed allegiance to the English Queen and observed laws derived from British sources. The structure of Parliament and the legal system was based on the foundations laid down at Westminster while the education system, from the primary to the tertiary sector, owed its origins to the British Isles and the latter especially to Scotland. Everywhere, from country courthouses to railway stations, from racecourses to cricket fields, the nation's new origins were apparent. With those things the majority of the people felt at ease, but they no longer spoke of England as home because Australia had become their homeland.

In the cities, there were other symbols. Chains, predominantly American owned, including Hungry Jack's, Pizza Hut, McDonald's, and Kentucky Fried Chicken led the fast food outlets and in some suburbs there were streets with shops displaying signs in Italian, Greek, Arabic and Vietnamese. The cuisines of many nations attracted satisfied patrons and the clothing styles of France and Italy were worn by the affluent, the cars of Germany and

Sweden carried them and Japanese models were parked on every street. With appalling regularity, commercial and private small aeroplanes continued to crash killing their occupants, but the main carriers Qantas, TAA (Australian Airlines) and Ansett held to the highest traditions of air safety.

Although here and there a mosque or an Orthodox church had been constructed, the religion of the British Isles, with its varied divisions of Christianity, still dominated and the Methodists, Presbyterians and Congregationalists successfully formed the Uniting Church. The Anglican and Roman Catholic Churches, despite ecumenism, retained their separate identities and neither had the impact on society they previously enjoyed. The largest denomination numerically was now that of Roman Catholicism with 26.5 per cent of the population. Its ranks had been invigorated increasingly since the 1950s by immigration from countries with large Catholic elements, including Vietnam from which thousands of Catholics fled communist oppression. In 1986 Pope John Paul II visited Australia and called for a return to old values, but he also asked for openness to change and especially that justice be done to the Aboriginal people. Most Australians still believed in God and in an afterlife and a growing minority worshipped Him in the name of Allah. The Jews continued to hope that the Covenant God had made with their forefathers would be honoured. Other anxious souls, seeking more immediate rewards and relief for their tangled emotions in an ever-changing world, followed new prophets whom they accepted as the teachers of divine truths.

One or both parents of many children at city schools were born outside Australia. In their homes, such children often spoke the language of their parents who were drawn from 140 ethnic groups and in the multi-lingual society of Australia as many a 100 languages were in daily use. With their school friends, the children communicated in the language and accent which went back in part to the convict era, and favoured pies, chips and hot dogs with tomato sauce, in preference to pizzas, salamis, noodles and spring rolls. A few Italian and Greek youths gradually realized that their cultural roots went back to the wellsprings of European civilization, which did little to balance the loss of the languages they had inherited.

In a population of sixteen million, one in four was an immigrant. They had come to Australia from 120 different countries. Together, since World War II, the immigrants formed one of the biggest migration waves in the world in the twentieth century. Seven out of ten of them lived in the continent's ten largest cities because Australia, the driest and flattest of all the great landmasses of the earth, held little appeal to them. The decline of the Aboriginal population had stopped, although, at about 200,000, they were still less than a third of the number who had lived throughout the continent in 1788. About half of the Aborigines lived in the towns and cities and only a remnant followed the way of life of their ancestors.

The struggle of the Aborigines for land rights, whether in actual territory or in some form of monetary compensation for what they had lost, persisted, but, after two hundred years, they held only about ten per cent of their original land. Most of it was in areas removed from white settlement, and little of it was of benefit to Aboriginal city and town dwellers. The opposition of pastoral and mining interests had combined with other groups, whose motives rarely extended beyond racial prejudice, caused federal governments to falter and halt on the path towards genuine land rights.

Since the days of John Batman, there had been no progress in making a treaty with the Aborigines and some of them, understandably, refused to participate in preparations for the celebration of the Bicentenary celebrations envisaged for 1988. They regarded themselves as victims of a lost war that had been waged against their people for 200 years and they judged any form of celebration of its beginning as derisory. Others of a less militant frame of mind had come to accept that there could be no complete return to the Dreamtime of their ancestors. They knew that they belonged now to a nation the members of which held no responsibility as individuals for the distant past and with whom they had to work towards a better future for themselves and all Australians. Among them even the most hopeful and fair minded realized that their expectations would be slow in fulfilment.

Their needs in health and education, housing and employment were so great that only a concerted national effort could even partially meet them. There were, however, some indications that a change was taking place. Infant mortality rates stood at about 80 per 1,000 in the early 1970s. It had fallen to a little above 20 in the mid-1980s and the death rate among adults was slowly beginning to change although it remained 19 years behind that of the white population. As happened elsewhere, rising life expectancy and declining infant mortality had an effect on fertility rates that fell from 6.0 in 1970 to around 3.0 in the mid 1980s. This drop of a half was the quickest transition ever recorded anywhere.

In the 1970s and 1980s the most enduring and far-reaching change in society was seen in the status of women. Their involvement as equals with men in the anti-Vietnam war movement made some of them realize they were powerless as individuals to change the nature of the oppression to which they long regarded themselves as subject. In 1972, the Women's Electoral Lobby was founded, thereby facilitating the development of bonds among women and making it possible to stake a claim to a voice in the political process. Its foundation coincided with the coming to power of the Whitlam government, which was sympathetic to their cause. The women's movement drew some inspiration from overseas sources, concentrated on such issues as equal pay, the right to abortion, sexism in the media and in advertising. In its extreme form, the movement attacked the nuclear family, which was seen as repressive and therefore pernicious.

Initially, the gains were striking as more women began to understand, accept and demand their rights as equal to those of men, while some men began to regard the attainment of such rights as fundamentally just. At the start only a few more women entered politics or attained positions of responsibility in their professions and workplaces. Three women were elected as Labor members of Parliament in 1974, the equal pay case was resolved in women's favour, statutory bodies saw women appointed to their boards, refuges and rape crisis centres were established and there were developments in child care and preschool facilities. The government appointed women to head bodies concerned with the status of women, equal opportunity clauses were accepted by some employers, the title 'Ms' became widespread, women in the Capital Territory founded their own licensed premises, and institutions such as universities began, tentatively, to redress the balance in staff appointments and to set up women's studies programmes.

Many Australians began to respond positively to the women's movement although most remained unchanged. More husbands assisted at their wife's confinement, others took an active role in the home, a few accepted half-time employment. It was increasingly unacceptable to tell sexist jokes and respect for women, rather than mere male patronage, gradually became an accepted standard of behaviour. When the newly-founded Family Court sometimes appeared to favour mothers to the disadvantage of fathers, when unemployment rose and there were grounds to fear that, in some areas, men were being discriminated against for jobs through a process called 'affirmative action', there was a reaction and feminism began to lose ground.

The more vocal and extreme forms of the movement, which fostered conflict as a means to overthrowing the ruling, patriarchal structure of a male-dominated society, alarmed and alienated increasing numbers of women, including Germaine Greer, whose writings had made her one of its forerunners. By the late-1980s, the movement had lost much of its dynamism. Marriage, the home, bearing and rearing children were showing signs of revival and the worsening economic climate cut away at the advantages gained. A few Anglican women argued that there were theological reasons why they should be ordained to the priesthood and the concomitance of their discovery with the changed sociological climate was underplayed. Nevertheless, because of its essential justice and universality, the movement for women's rights was a most profound development that, in Australia, brought radical changes. That, for a time, the struggle would irritate and even infuriate those who disregarded its essential justice was understandable, but regrettable.

Malcolm Fraser's government had been re-elected in 1980, but there was no turn about in the worsening economy arising from a severe and prolonged drought, an increasing national debt, a lessening demand for Australian primary products and falling overseas prices. Fraser tried to pump the economy by attracting overseas investors to the amount of six billion dollars in 1980, but most of the profits went straight back to the investors. Large firms continued to flourish such as Broken Hill Proprietary Limited and G.J. Coles and there were takeover bids by local investment entrepreneurs. The West Australian millionaire, Alan Bond, successfully moved into the brewing business and the Bank of New South Wales bid $699,000,000 for the Commercial Bank of Australia. After the merger the new bank was called Westpac, thereby ensuring that the Bank of New South Wales, whose origins stemmed from the early colonial period, lost its identity.

Starting in the late 1970s the term used for the economic downturn was 'recession'. By early 1983, the rate of unemployment had reached its highest level, 10.7 per cent, since the Great Depression, but no one yet dared to use the dreaded word 'depression'. At the time, an informed estimate put one in five Australians as living below the poverty line, despite the fact that for most others there was a continued rise in living standards. An indication of the economic climate was clear in Sydney where over half of the married women were in the workforce, but most of them worked for financial reasons because both prices and taxes were rising in a way that wage increases could not match. It seemed that Australia was running down as exemplified by the decline of the once booming Broken Hill where the enormous silver, lead and zinc mines, which had created the inland city of over 30,000 people, were nearing exhaustion. Broken Hill faced the prospect of becoming a vast ghost town or a curiosity of interest only to tourists because, in its isolation in the dry inland there seemed no prospect of creating alternative employment for the men laid off from the mines. Such dire prophecies took little account of the resilience of its citizens whose ancestors had toiled under adverse and extreme conditions to create their fine city in the first place.

The normally astute Fraser made the biggest mistake of his career on 3 February 1983 by calling an early election. On that very day, a majority of Labor members in the federal Parliament convinced themselves that their party could not win an election with Bill Hayden as leader. Hayden, an intelligent, honest, forthright and cogent politician, had the misfortune to be confronted by Bob Hawke, who possessed, in abundance, a quality dear to the media and to the electorate which had become popularly known as charisma. The result of the election seemed to justify Labor's decision to change the leadership for Hawke led the party to its best victory since World War II. Nonetheless, success in the Senate eluded it, where five senators representing the Australian Democrats, formed by the breakaway Liberal Don Chipp in 1977, held the balance of power. The Democrats promised not to block supply, which was a guarantee no one had deemed necessary to give to the coalition parties when in office.

Hawke and his government were determined not to repeat the mistake of bewildering the electorate with immediate and far-reaching changes. With prudent promises of reducing unemployment, cutting back the deficit and stopping inflation, a new ministry took office, some of whom had had ministerial experience under Whitlam. Possibly because of the divisions created in Australian society in the Whitlam era, Hawke was determined to govern by consensus between the major interest groups, business leaders, employers, trade unions and government. In other modern societies, consensus was only achievable in times of crisis or when a dictator ruled under the guise of consensus. At its best, consensus on economic problems could only result in the lowest common denominator being adopted, even if all concerned with it were sincere.

Australia was not then in crisis and Hawke was a committed democrat, as well as an honest Australian who would never use dictatorial methods. He could only be accused of optimism or naivety, for the chance of a lasting consensus being reached between labour and capital was slim. The 'Summit', which met in Canberra in April 1983, supported a prices and incomes accord. It lasted for nine months on wages, but there was little evidence that it ever started on prices.

Initially, there was much good will towards the government and under the direction of Paul Keating, later acclaimed by Hawke as the 'world's greatest treasurer', the economy gave promise of recovering. Even the weather and sport seemed to favour Hawke, as one of the worst droughts in the history of Australia broke in 1983 and then, in September, Alan Bond's *Australia II* won the America's Cup. The happy theme of sporting success was sustained when Robert de Castella, whose ancestors had come to Port Phillip and planted vines in the days of Charles La Trobe, won the Rotterdam marathon and became Australian of the Year. Despite the interest of the Prime Minister in sport, and the support given to it by the previous government, which founded the Australian Institute of Sport in Canberra in 1981, the long-vaunted prowess of Australians as sportsmen and women was in decline. Apart from de Castella and the golfer Greg Norman there was scarcely another Australian sporting identity of world class standard although, six years after the foundation of the Institute of Sport, there was some evidence that its efforts were proving successful. Another face of sport, but one never fully disguised, was shown when Fine Cotton, substituted, rather clumsily, for an inferior horse, won a race in Brisbane on 18 August 1994. Some punters won over a $1 million, but all bets were called off when the scam was discovered soon after the race. Intense interest in the affair was aroused among the general public, including those who never laid a bet on a horse.

Youth and vitality were apparent in Hawke's Cabinet, which was composed of mainly young, competent, hard-working and dedicated ministers. They received the consistent backing of the public servants working for them, although the head of the Treasury, John Stone, decided that he was unhappy with a government that did not follow his own conservative fiscal policies and publicly criticized it after his retirement in 1984. A few alarmed or otherwise disconcerted conservatives joined him to form a body named after H. R. Nicholls, who, as well as achieving some notoriety as a turn coat at Eureka, had been tried for contempt of the Arbitration Court in 1911. Presumably, it was this later act that endeared

Nicholls to Stone and to those who thought that the arbitration system had injured the Australian economy.

In 1982 the National Country Party had decided to break with its past and drop the word 'Country' from its title. The purpose was to attract a broader electorate and thereby have more general, appeal. The Nationals retained their conservative image and worked harmoniously with Andrew Peacock who led the Liberals with some conviction and much charm, but little direction. In 1985, a pragmatist, John Howard, replaced him. To Howard winning office at all costs was the primary consideration. The coalition seemed at last to have accepted that the Hawke government was the legitimate representation of the will of the electorate, and, with its usual forays into invective and name calling, its tiresome and time-wasting debates, the Parliament got down to business. The government was determined to follow a moderate course and the coalition was neutralized except on some non-essential issues A watered-down version of Medibank was introduced with the new name Medicare. Financed initially by a one per cent levy on all incomes, Medicare commenced to provide basic health and hospital care for all Australians in February 1984. As costs escalated, it ran a difficult course, and many medical practitioners became increasingly restless and some went on strike.

Together with the women's movement, the other popular groundswell was in the growth of conservation societies that grew to some 800 with half-a-million members by the mid-1980s. As early as 1863, Tasmania had passed laws to protect its scenic areas, and in 1879 the world's second National Park was established in an area of 18,000 acres south of Sydney. A century later, more leisure time, greater affluence, the increasing numbers who went bushwalking, urbanization, the lure of the outdoor life and the demands of the tourist industry all combined to make the conservation groups a powerful lobby.

As a political issue, conservation came to the fore with a debate over the Gordon-below-Franklin Dam in Tasmania's wild and beautiful south-west in 1982. The Fraser government had decided not to interfere with the Tasmanian government's intention to proceed with the Dam, although the whole area had been put on the World Heritage List. The Hawke government refused to allow work on the Dam to proceed when it took office, and, in July 1983, the High Court supported its right to do so. This decision threw into confusion the question of state rights, still in some measure sacrosanct since federation, and infuriated the Liberal government in Tasmania.

By 1982 five Australian locations had been put on the World Heritage List as places 'of outstanding universal value'. The Western Tasmanian Wilderness National Parks area included the Franklin and Gordon rivers. The Great Barrier Reef, as the largest coral reef system in the world, provided the most beautiful marine scenery on earth. The Lord Howe Island group was listed for its unique landform, intact ecosystems and evidence of independent evolutionary processes. Human beings lived, some say up to 70,000 years ago, in the Willandra Lakes region of New South Wales where large marsupials roamed before the end of the last Ice Age. Kakadu National Park in the Northern Territory and 6,000 square kilometres in extent contains more than 1,000 known Aboriginal art sites, dating back to the Ice Age. The Park is haunting in its evocation of primeval creation and, with an abundance of wild life including over 100 species of birds, it truly forms part of the world's heritage. When remarkable rock formations called the Bungle Bungles were added in 2003, fifteen sites in Australia were on the World Heritage List.

Despite the occasional and temporary setback, such as the Franklin Dam issue, the federal-state system was retained and proved to be moderately workable even when governments of differing political hue held office at either level. In social welfare, education, railways and matters that crossed state boundaries, the federal government accrued more and more power. One area it could not control effectively was crime, together with the associated legal structures, including the police, magistracy and judiciary, required to curb it. A Royal Commission into the Federated Ship Painters and Dockers' Union revealed in 1984 that large sections of Australian industrial life were permeated by crime. In New South Wales, and particularly in Sydney, criminal activity had grown alarmingly during the premiership of Liberal leader, Robert Askin, from 1965 to 1975.

Askin had come into some prominence during President Johnson's visit to Sydney in 1966, when, as their official car was confronted by male and female anti-war demonstrators lying on the roadway, Askin had urged the driver to 'run over the bastards'. A national weekly paper alleged after Askin's death in 1981 that the Premier was involved in crime and corruption by the taking of huge bribes annually, that there were two corrupt police commissioners and innumerable lesser officers involved with crime, and that organized crime had become the largest industry in the state. Crime still held a prominent position in the economy of New South Wales during the succeeding Labor government of Neville Wran, and was becoming prominent during the Bjelke-Petersen government in Queensland.

In the same period drug peddling became widespread and again Sydney was its centre, with the occasional prosecution of a policeman or the apprehension of a drug-ring satisfying the authorities that the situation was in hand. Marijuana was widely cultivated in isolated areas, Customs officials were baffled by the ingenious methods used to import drugs, young people died or were wrecked by addiction and big syndicates made fortunes out of misery. Some few, courageous people advocated the legalisation of drugs, in particular marijuana. No government was prepared to face the problem in such a radical manner, because the old forces of wowserism, which had never died, were still strong and the involvement of powerful financial interests made action difficult.

In May 1983, another face to human suffering was shown when AIDS first appeared in Sydney among homosexual males. It spread quickly to bisexuals, intravenous drug users, blood transfusion recipients and a few heterosexuals who had come into sexual contact with carriers. By 1987 it was clear that little could be done to stop the spread of infection except, perhaps, by the use of condoms and the distribution of free hypodermic needles to drug users at large in society and in the prisons where drugs were readily available. The Federal government used the media to frighten people into having 'safe sex' by an advertisement combining the Black Death of the Middle Ages and the modern bowling alley. Any talk about moral standards, much less sin, on the part of the churches or other concerned observers was unwelcome yet, not surprisingly, there seemed to be a partial return to the old values of sexual behaviour and the curtain slowly came down on uninhibited promiscuity.

Lionel Murphy, reformer, justice of the High Court and one-time Labor Attorney-General was a victim of the general corruption of some elements in New South Wales society and their long-held contempt for authority of any kind. Over his long career in politics and the law he had of necessity come into contact with shady characters and with some few of them, out of the depth of humanity which he possessed in abundance, he continued to associate when prudence indicated that to shun them was the better course for a High Court judge. In the end, he was brought down because some token gesture had to be made to assure the general populace that government would not tolerate criminality and because he, as Attorney General and judge, had earnt the deep-seated enmity of many to whom reform was a threat. Murphy had turned his back on the old conventions, and specifically on Christianity, as the reinforcer of the moral code of society. He died in 1986 when all around him it was clear that nothing had been put in its place.

In the deteriorating economic climate, the Hawke government was unable to continue the funding of education at the levels to which it had grown since the days of Menzies. Universities in particular suffered drastic budget cuts and, in some areas, staff numbers declined by a third with drastic effects on teaching and the standard of research. During 1986 the government decided to introduce a $250 annual fee for students in tertiary institutions under the pretext that it was not for education, but for administrative costs. The argument that education at all levels is the right of a tax-paying community was not addressed; university administrators generally accepted the decision and the student bodies, rent by their own divisions, were unable to mount an effective protest. Sixty per cent of the Australian population had no post-secondary-school qualifications and thirty per cent of those qualified to get into tertiary institutions were unable to gain entry despite the energy of the government in providing 30,000 more places. The imposition of the $250 fee was an unusual decision for a government that professed itself concerned both about human welfare and the future economic viability of the nation. There were calls for privately funded universities and the financier, Alan Bond, of America's Cup fame, proceeded with plans to set one up in Queensland which may have helped console him for the loss of the Cup at Fremantle in January 1987.

The old argument about state aid to education began to show signs of a revival, but in a different context. Enrolments in state schools were everywhere declining – in Victoria, by 56,000 in the five years to 1986 – while those in private schools increased – again, in Victoria, by 26,000. More than eighty per cent of the children in private schools completed the final year compared to thirty per cent in government schools. Social inequalities in education were even more glaringly evident in the tertiary sector because, while over half of the students in private schools went on to higher education, only fifteen per cent of those in the public sector did so. Much ink was spilt and many words bandied about in parliaments on these discrepancies, but the attempt to deny the existence of a malaise in public education, despite the efforts of thousands of hardworking and devoted teachers, proved hollow.

Generally, the arts and literature seemed to falter. Manning Clark and Patrick White continued to despair at the 'Great Australian Emptiness' in 'this country of dry bones' while calling for a new spirit to awaken its people. The playwright, David Williamson, continued to satirize Australian life in a powerful, witty and partly crude manner in plays that drew appreciative audiences who laughed and wondered at themselves, but went away unchanged. Australia lost one of its greatest creative performers with the death in October 1986 of Robert Helpmann, pillar of the Australian ballet as well as actor, choreographer, director and producer. The death of Fred Williams deprived painting of an artist of consummate ability who brought life to the bush in a distinctive style that bordered on the abstract, but remained true to the landscape. Williams was firmly in a tradition of Australian painting that always shaped its techniques on overseas trends, and, as the Heidelberg School of the 1890s and the Expressionists of the 1940s had done, Williams, Clifton Pugh, Sidney Nolan and others, when they sought to represent Australia on canvas, portrayed its landscape. They seemed to admit that the only distinctive thing to be said about Australia and its people was the land they moved in, but never conquered. In 1982 the National Gallery was finally opened in Canberra. With time it promised to become not merely a repository for art works, but also a creative centre inspiring and assisting institutions and individuals throughout the land.

In the 1980s, three autobiographies were published, each of which gave an insight into the Australian experience from differing perspectives and they stand as a testimony to its value and endurance. A.B. Facey's *A Fortunate Life* summed up in his own experience many of the tribulations that thousands of others had been through since the depression of the 1890s. He lived as a youth on the Western Australian goldfields, was wounded at Gallipoli, became a tram driver in Perth and had to walk off his selection in the Narragin district in 1934 when rabbits, drought, and falling prices for wheat and wool sent him broke. Despite all the hardship, Facey still entitled his book with a tribute to fortune and, in a long Australian tradition, he was always a battler who won out over adversity. The Vasari of Australian painting, Bernard Smith, and Kathleen Fitzpatrick, a teacher treasured by students and staff alike, of Australian history at Melbourne University, wrote of their upbringing and education in Sydney, Melbourne and Oxford in *The*

Boy Adeodatus and *Solid Bluestone Foundations*. Each presents a gentle, evocative, honest and penetrating analysis of a past that marks them as Australians who gave their all to the native land.

The film industry was one area in which Australians had shown a creative flair before and after World War 1, notably in the work of Raymond Longford, but American films replaced the local ones so that film making practically died out. The industry began its revival in the mid-1970s with the support of government and in the main the old, painfully brash themes of the past were avoided so that Australians could watch their own product without cringing. About 150 films were made in the decade and they dealt with mateship, women, the shearers, the landscape, the treatment of Aborigines, life in country towns and the bush. The bush was portrayed as hostile, even incomprehensible, to urban dwellers and throughout the films there was an underlying theme which tried to say that Australians had not come to grips with their environment.

Some of the films were of sufficient merit to be remembered. *Wake in Fright, Sunday Too Far Away, Picnic at Hanging Rock, Caddie, The Getting of Wisdom, My Brilliant Career, The Devil's Playground, Storm Boy, The Last Wave* and *Newsfront,* were followed with war topics in *Breaker Morant* and *Gallipoli*. All were successful attempts at tackling aspects of the national ethos, although the filmmakers kept clear of other national themes, notably Eureka, the goldfields and the Irish, which were left to television to take up. In 1986, Paul Hogan produced and acted in *Crocodile Dundee*. The film was an amusing caricature of the bush and the bush hero, who, in Hogan, became a crocodile hunter rather than a drover or cattleman. *Crocodile Dundee* became popular in the United States, for which audience it was made, because many Americans had begun to look at Australia as the last frontier.

By the beginning of 1986, Australians at all levels of society had become obsessed with the state of the economy. The dollar had been allowed to float, which quickly resulted in a loss of parity by thirty per cent against the American dollar and there was a similar drop against other currencies such as the yen, the Deutschmark and the formerly satirized Italian lira. During the course of the year, the American government subsidized wheat sales to the Soviet Union and China, which further threatened Australian wheat farmers. They had already suffered through falling prices and many of them were forced to sell up or walk off their properties as interests rates showed no sign of falling. When one of them dumped 35 tonnes of unprofitable wheat on Parliament House steps in Canberra, 9,000 others rallied to support their cause. Coal and minerals generally, with the exception of gold, were meeting overseas buyers' resistance. Oil reserves were dropping at a rapid rate and it was alleged that further exploration was hindered by high government charges on oil production.

Wool, long the staple of the economy, retained its place as a valuable export commodity, partly due to the fall in the dollar and the continued demand from Japan. However, wool could not uniquely sustain a diverse economy, especially as manufacturing industry had not kept pace with developments elsewhere, even in the Pacific region where South Korea, Taiwan, Japan and, latterly, China were dominant. By June 1986, the deficit was six billion dollars, $800 million more than anticipated, but few people realized that seventy per cent of Australian companies were owned by foreign interests and that sixty per cent of the huge overseas borrowings were by large corporations such as the newspaper groups which had started to vie with each other for control of the Australian media. When it became apparent that Rupert Murdoch, formerly an Australian citizen who had become an American, had a fifty-eight per cent controlling interest in the Australian media the government seemed pleased. In fact, over ninety per cent of Australian newspapers were in the hands of the Murdoch and Fairfax presses. In the area of television, the three major Australian networks constituted an oligopoly and that fact, together with the virtual duopoly pertaining in the press, had social and political implications that the government seemed unable, afraid or unwilling to address.

Throughout Australia, many small businesses were failing and the motor vehicle industry was in chaos with the lowest sales for new cars in thirty years. Interest rates were slow to fall, home construction was dwindling, thereby affecting an industry that directly and indirectly employed over half a million people. The country went to second last on a list of twenty-four in trade performances for technological products. Wage levels had not risen in proportion to the cost of living, as there had been little appreciable fall in inflation, but the trade union movement, led by Simon Crean, attempted to moderate wage rises and minimize industrial unrest. Nevertheless the Victorian nurses, in despair at their inability to receive awards commensurate with their work, struck for the first time in their history in 1986 and remained out for seven weeks. Despite repeated provocation by employers the unions generally behaved with restraint and the strike rate more than halved in the years 1983–85 compared with 1959–83. Australia's rate was lower than the international norm. There seemed every reason to suppose that the accord and the Australian Conciliation and Arbitration Commission, as well as the Labor government's industrial relations policy, had a good deal to do with this shift in the strike rate.

The government had taken several tough and courageous decisions that, in the case of the devaluation of the dollar, the subsequent rise and fall of which Australians followed as closely as their forebears had watched the weather, ought to have resulted in a rapid decrease in imports, but it was slow to occur. A capital gains tax and a fringe benefits tax did little for the economy in the immediate sense, but both were regarded as outrageous measures by a minority who benefited when such taxes were not imposed. In 1986, the government's desperation was shown when Treasurer Keating warned that Australia was in danger of becoming a 'banana republic', a statement that failed to amuse his Prime Minister. By October 1987 an ailing international economy resulted in an alarming stock market crash on a worldwide scale. Millions of investors, small and large and, in particular, those who had borrowed to invest in shares, suffered.

Contradictions at high levels were never more evident than when the government, against its own party policy and having taken a stand against French intransigence on nuclear testing in the Pacific, decided to resume sales of uranium to that country. The decision dismayed even some of the most ardent and loyal of Labor supporters and the Chernobyl disaster at a nuclear plant in the Ukraine did nothing to allay fears that the very use of nuclear energy, leaving aside nuclear war, threatened the future of the human race. There were falls in the level of popularity of the government and even of Prime Minister Hawke who had hitherto enjoyed unprecedented trust by the electorate. Many Labor Party branches were disturbed by charges that the Hawke government had departed from the high ideals of its Labor predecessors.

As never before in their history, Australians were bombarded with the warnings of prophets and the remedies of the wise on the state of the economy. The public was confused with the mysterious terminology of economics that engendered a feeling of helplessness. This resulted in a tendency to leave everything to the politicians and financial experts in the hope that they would come up with a remedy. The leadership of farmer organizations, convinced that Australian farmers were among the most technologically advanced, cost efficient and highest producers per head in the world, was not so prepared and there were demonstrations outside Parliament House, angry meetings in rural areas and big sums of money were raised to help get rid of the Hawke government.

Little attempt was made by the increasing number of critics of Hawke and Labor to understand that, with the best will in the world, no government could solve problems outside its control, such as the covert ability of international financial interests to quickly remove capital from a country where they failed to make large profits. Nonetheless, to his credit, the Federal Treasurer, Paul Keating, stuck to the course he had embarked upon and lived in hope that the turn-about would come. By mid-1987 the government claimed to have created 800,000 new jobs but, while a significant step, it could not help those who had been out of work for years and continued to remain unemployed. Little difference was made to the overall unemployment rate.

On the international scene, a report commissioned by the federal government assured Australians that there was no direct military threat to their security, that no one wanted to invade the country and subjugate its people, and that global war was a most unlikely event among the superpowers. 'Forward defence' was emphasized with the earmarking of four billion dollars for six new submarines. Meanwhile, a magnificent new Parliament House was nearing completion in Canberra and there were murmurs of criticism at its proposed final cost of one billion dollars. No politician was prepared to state publicly that a building which would stand as a testimony to Australian democracy for hundreds of years was worth as much in expenditure as a submarine, which would probably be obsolete well before the new Parliament building needed even a face lift. In the event only a few years passed before it became evident that the submarines in question were scarcely seaworthy.

The economic and consequent social problems that had arisen in the early 1970s and continued into the 1980s were not new in themselves. Since the 1830s Australia had always depended for its viability upon the caprice of overseas markets and the willingness of foreign investors to risk their capital locally. When, as in the 1840s, the 1890s and the 1930s, those outside factors had adversely coalesced to lessen market demand and to reduce investment, Australia and its people had suffered. In the 1980s industry had to strive hard to compete against imports and, more importantly, it had to begin to export profitably. The latter was a challenge that had never been faced and it came at a time when Asian competitors were much more advanced technologically and could rely on a cheaper workforce. Few Australians bothered to understand these problems and fewer still were prepared to take the repeated calls for belt-tightening seriously. Among the more affluent section of the community there were 30,000 millionaires, one tenth of the population owned sixty per cent of the country's assets but company tax receipts totalled only ten per cent of tax revenue, compared with twenty per cent in 1975. Small business people, wage earners, many farmers, the unemployed, those on old-age and widow's pensions wondered at a system which seemed to make the amassing of wealth possible while to them survival was a constant concern.

In February 1987 a new factor entered the national political scene in the person of the Queensland Premier Bjelke-Petersen who declared his intention of becoming the next prime minister. A phenomenon similar to Bjelke-Petersen had rarely been seen in Australian political life and his closest counterparts were John Dunmore Lang, Billy Hughes and King O'Malley. The difference was that in them a solid core of sanity tended to override the flamboyant or merely ridiculous. The standard bearer of old-style, Deakinite liberalism in Victoria was the Melbourne *Age* which became eloquent in its finely phrased vitriol on the subject of Bjelke-Petersen. To the leader writer he was 'an ageing bucolic demagogue' whose crusade for the prime-ministership was 'political humbug, economic quackery and social mischief' while his 'geriatric gibberish', which consisted mainly in cries for smaller government and a flat-tax rate of twenty-five per cent, provided no answer to the problems facing the country. When Hawke called an early election for 11 July, Bjelke-Petersen was in America, and, on his arrival home, he decided to forego his attempt at national leadership. The main effect of his incursion onto the federal scene was that the Liberal Party moved further to the right leaving Labor in a position to stand by its moderate policy of continued restraint.

The time was not ideal for the Labor Party to go into an election unless the disarray of its conservative opponents proved a decisive factor to the electors. To most Australians, the tax system seemed out of control and the government's attempt to reform it had failed, while the promise of the Liberals to drop the highest rate to thirty-eight per cent had to be tested against the cost. The growth rate of the public service had doubled that of the population rate and on all levels of life, from birth to death, the involvement of government was obtrusive. The national debt was still rising, overseas pundits remarked that Australians had a first-rank standard of living based on a fourth-level economy and prices were continuing to rise. A $10 increase in wages granted in March by the Conciliation and Arbitration Commission was a mere crumb to the poor, although it had caused employer groups to cry loudly in dejection at the profligacy of the decision. Other groups were dismayed as overseas aid fell to its lowest level in twenty-five years, making Australia one of the least generous of countries in the developed world, and overseas students were asked to pay fees, which effectively restricted the intake to the children of the Asian wealthy.

Apart from a call by one Aboriginal activist for a separate Aboriginal nation and a vote to secede from Australia taken by representatives from the fourteen islands in the Torres Strait, by mid-1987 Australians generally, and their government in particular, were faced with matters of great moment that tested Australian foreign policy. Papua New Guinea appeared to enjoy some degree of stability, but elsewhere in the Pacific there were causes for concern. The Russians were showing an interest in gaining a foothold on Vanuatu, the French continued their colonial administration of New Caledonia and Libya threatened to introduce its own brand of militant fanaticism wherever the opportunity showed itself, including offering support to Australian Aborigines. Finally, in May, a coup engineered by the army toppled the duly elected multi racial coalition led by the recently formed Labor Party in Fiji. The long history of Australian commercial interests in Fiji had finally come home to rest.

Colonial Sugar Refining Co. (CSR) began its century-long association with Fiji in the 1870s when, after building an industry closely dependent on black birding in Queensland, it gained a monopoly on sugar production in Fiji. To work its mills and estates, CSR brought in indentured labour from India, a practice that the Indian government stopped in 1916. By then over 60,000 Indians had arrived, of whom a third returned home. The rest became the basis of what quickly formed almost fifty per cent of Fiji's population while the Melanesians, who originally occupied the islands, dropped to only 45.19 per cent. CSR had sold its interests to the Fijian government in 1973, when they were no longer regarded as commercially profitable.

The coup was partly a legacy of CSR's indentured labour system because it was initiated by the Melanesians in response to the threat of political control by the Indians. Short of military intervention the Australian government could do little except make protestations and threaten trade embargoes. The Fiji economy, already weakened by falling world prices for sugar, stood reliant on aid rather than on embargoes but the continued presence of large Australian financial interests there, including the press, banking, insurance and television made the present reality combine with the historical past to demand a more constructive answer from Australia.

The first two weeks of July 1987 were days of winners. On Saturday night, 4 July, at a hotel in the marginal seat of Bendigo, Victoria, Prime Minister Hawke shared the pride of millions of Australians when, on television from London, they saw Pat Cash win Wimbledon. His victory was the first by an Australian in the men's singles since 1971. A week later the electors of Bendigo returned the Labor candidate. Throughout Australia Labor won the election and Bob Hawke became the first Labor prime minister to achieve office on three occasions. The election was not easily won and, in the Senate, the Democrats retained the balance of power. The victory was significant because Labor had not made a weak bargain with the electorate. The levels of taxation would continue, there would be cuts in social security benefits in some areas and the public service would be pruned. Interest rates were dropped significantly, inflation was slashed and unemployment levels fell. Many months, even years, would have to pass before the deficit could be reduced to acceptable proportions. Sacrifices in wage levels would still be required, industry would have to learn to compete and subsidies would be reduced. Labor's campaign was successful because, unlike 1931 in the days of Scullin, the electors knew that the country was in the hands of a competent team. The election proved that a majority of the Australian people were capable of setting aside immediate self-interest to opt for the good of the Commonwealth. The nation had matured.

22

Hope Deferred

The Bicentenary Celebration in 1988 went on for several days and attracted the highest number of revellers in the history of the nation. The Aborigines looked back with hindsight to 26 January 1788 and pondered on the fateful fruits of white occupation of their continent. Many Aborigines refused to attend the national birthday party, as they had done at the time of the sequicentenary in 1938, but others decided to make their presence felt in Sydney where, on the fringes of several events, they gathered in substantial numbers.

One such event was held close to the place where Arthur Philip had landed with his cargo of convicts in 1788. Prime Minister Bob Hawke was present in order to launch my *Penguin Bicentennial History of Australia*, which had been commissioned by the federal Government to commemorate the Bicentenary. I recognized that a group of Aborigines who were present had the right to protest and I had given them a copy of the book a few minutes before the launch commenced. The fact that it purported to celebrate the Bicentenary was enough to enrage some of the Aborigines; one of them, anticipating the prime minister, decided to make his own statement. Cursing as he ran towards the water, he launched the book into the Harbour where it floated near a small boat from which two boys were fishing. They rescued the book, came ashore, promptly obtained the prime minister's autograph on it, and returned to their fishing.

The Aboriginal launcher and the author had made a small contribution to the Bicentenary. Try as we might, the passing of two hundred 200 years had not proved to be enough for us to comprehend each other. It was one thing for me to write the big word 'reconciliation' and the little one 'sorry' in my story. It was another to mean those words and make it plain by actions what their meaning entailed. Only then could my words prove even partially acceptable to the Aborigine.

Notwithstanding the difficulties, some things struck a note of hope in the saga of white–black relations. After 25 years the Aboriginal Embassy still stood on the lawns sweeping down to Lake Burley Griffin in Canberra. It was both a reminder and a stark symbol of the degradation to which the people whom it represented had been reduced. Some Aborigines abused the Embassy by erecting dwellings in its vicinity and others, who refused to accept that it represented their interests, rejected it. Many whites decried it and some federal politicians spasmodically inveighed against it, but the existence and endurance of the Embassy testified to the strength of Australian democracy and to the wish of most citizens that the underdog be given a fair go. In most other countries it would have been removed forthwith.

Among the Aborigines, and in ever widening segments of white society, there grew an increasing determination to redress some of the wrongs. On 3 June 1992 the High Court of Australia handed down one of the most important legal judgements of the century. Called the Mabo judgement, after Eddie Mabo in whose name it was principally made, the judgement ruled that Eddie and the Meriam people of the Murray Islands in Torres Strait had a native title to their land. In effect, the High Court held that, where the Aborigines were able to prove that they had maintained a continuous connection with the land, their right to it remained intact. The judgement was clearly based on the acceptance of a form of genuine occupation of Australia by the Aborigines before 1788.

Those Australians who wished to see justice done to the rights of the Aborigines rejoiced at the judgement, but some pastoralists, a few miners and even people who feared that they would lose their right to occupy their own backyards, panicked. In 1995 the Wik case confirmed a coexisting native title to land held under pastoral leases, which meant that the pastoralists and the Aborigines could make appropriate use of the same land. This judgement caused further consternation among many pastoralists, of whom a few hundred in Western Australia held leases on land four times the extent of Victoria, for which some paid as lowly a sum as $20 annually. In the upshot, the full implications of Mabo and Wik, and their application on the practical level, remained uncertain. Nonetheless, because justice, respect for others' rights and common sense continued to prevail in large elements of society, there remained hope that a settlement of the land question would help substantially in bringing about a reconciliation between blacks and whites.

Another grim aspect of race relations in Australia was apparent in the continuing problem of the deaths of Aborigines in prison or in police custody. To make matters worse, governments in Western Australia and in the Northern Territory introduced mandatory sentencing for repeated criminal behaviour. Given that the application of the law largely affected young, male Aborigines, there were obvious racist overtones. Too frequently their crimes were derisory, involving such trifles as the stealing of biscuits. The gravity and justice of the legal system itself became questionable. Despite widespread national and international outrage, the Chief Minister of the Northern Territory remained unmoved until financial overtures by his federal colleagues induced him to modify the legislation.

An even more serious matter, with lasting effects on thousands of Aborigines and their descendants, was their removal from the care of their parents when in their childhood. This practice had operated for over forty years from the 1930s. One intention of government officials was to assimilate the Aborigines into the wider community so effectively that the race itself, as a separate entity, would gradually disappear. At the same time, just as within the white community, there were occasions on which the necessity to preserve the life, education or well being of children seemed to indicate the necessity of their removal from a parent or both parents. Furthermore, the majority of white couples welcomed the children into their homes with a generous intent. Numerous Aborigines acknowledged that they had lived happily in such homes.

The fact remained that thousands of young Aborigines were taken from their homes and no argument, other than the need to respect a basic human right, could gainsay that truth. Apology after apology in all manner of forums were heard, but John Howard, who became prime minister in 1996, remained obstinate in his refusal to apologize on behalf of the Australian people, although he did so in his own name. A humble word, spoken officially by the prime minister, could have helped to bridge the gap, bring the races closer and heal some of the wounds. John Howard would not mouth a sorry when the day was upon him, after which it became too late. At the same time, it was clear that reconciliation had stalled, but Howard's intransigence was not the sole reason. Too many Australians saw reconciliation as part of an agenda being pushed by the same elites they felt had betrayed and deserted them in the economic and social sphere.

In 2003 a few influential Aboriginal leaders publicly acknowledged some dark aspects of Aboriginal society, namely the violent abuse of women and of minors. Alcohol, unemployment, frustration and the loss of their human dignity had brought some Aboriginal men to this pass and mere words were helpless to overcome it. Concomitantly, the highest representative body of the Aboriginal people, the Aboriginal and Torres Strait Islander Commission [ATSIC], was made unacceptable to both indigenous and white Australians by two of two of its leaders who brought public shame on themselves and on their positions. With the concurrence of the ALP, the federal government disbanded ATSIC in 2004, although no one was clear what reformed structures would replace it.

Throughout the twentieth century, the native populations of North America, Canada and New Zealand witnessed a reversal of their demographic decline. The same thing happened in Australia where the Aboriginal population grew from less than 100,000 in 1901 to 410,988 by the Census of 2001. There had been improvements in census methods and more people, who had previously not declared themselves as indigenous, found greater ease in identifying themselves as such. Other changes also took place. The Aboriginal infant mortality rate was 14 per cent of live births in 1960 and life expectancy was about 50 years. By the 1990s, infant mortality had fallen to less than 2 per cent, and life expectancy had risen to over 56 for males and 63 for females. At the same time, life expectancy among Aborigines remained alarmingly low when compared with the rest of the population. More recently, there was a remarkably rapid fall in fertility rates to 2.2 per cent for each Aboriginal woman in 2001 from 6 per cent in 1960. Some Australians hoped that greater access to improved health services, education, housing and employment would enhance Aboriginal welfare in all respects. Many Aborigines knew, and stated publicly, that centralized government action and expenditure on welfare, which took little account of local conditions and failed to involve the Aborigines directly, would continue to fail.

During the Bicentennial year, Queen Elizabeth II opened the new Parliament House in Canberra. By deliberate intent its New York-based, Italian designer, Aldo Guirgola, snuggled the building into the side of a hill to prevent it becoming the dominant point of the city. Before the fear of terrorist attacks led to the erection of plastic barriers at Parliament House, citizens could walk on the long sweep of lawns under which their legislators were deliberating. Given the negative attitudes towards politicians held by a majority of Australians it was inevitable that the majestic structure that housed them would not attain the almost mystical proportions of the Sydney Opera House. However, it stands as a building of grace, of restrained majesty, and as a reminder that the seat of central government deserves respect.

The pedestrian formality of the nearby, pagoda like, offices of the Department of Foreign Affairs and Trade, as well as the faintly fascist contours of the High Court on the edge of Lake Burley Griffin, are mocked by the great dignity of the Parliament. In physical appearance the Court proclaims the power of its judges so strongly that few citizens could ever approach it with a feeling of being equal before the law. However, one building in the parliamentary triangle has already stood the test of time and bids fair to continue to do so. The graceful Old Parliament House, now sheltering the new National Portrait Gallery, recalls to the beholder the dignity of a past generation.

From the 1870s, the development of the minds and spirits of the younger generation had been seen as a paramount task shared by parents and by the public sector. Yet, since the 1990s that task was increasingly passed into the hands of private bodies, which were encouraged and financially supported by government. In the decade to 2003, public schools' enrolments increased nationally by 1.2 per cent while the increase was 22.3 per cent in private schools. Sydney had 41.7 per cent of its secondary students in private schools. From 1992 to 2001 cuts in government funding were so savage that, of the 28 developed countries in the OECD, Australia was ranked 23rd in the proportion of GDP it spent on education.

Some unworthy and short-sighted critics of government schools seemed almost to rejoice in the drop in literacy and in standards of behaviour among students, forgetting that the human resources of the nation were thereby negatively effected. The main factor influencing parents to opt for the private sector, provided they could pay for it, was concern over discipline in the public schools. However, most teachers in the public sector remained devoted to their vocation. They did so despite the downgrading of their status and their low rates of pay compared, for example, with those of public servants whose professional education was often much less demanding. They were sometimes treated as being of little moment by parents and by the ignorant, as well as being threatened and abused by students whose home background bred incivility. The number, especially of males who joined the profession diminished, sometimes because the latter felt threatened by possible accusations of sexual misconduct. Cries that girls were given more attention at school than boys seemed to be borne out by the higher percentage of them who remained at school and gained higher scores to enter the universities.

Meanwhile, there was an increasing reluctance to accept the adage that 'boys will be boys', in or out of a classroom. A society, which had built a system of free, secular and compulsory education, seemed, to be rendered helpless. Classroom discipline, except in some private schools, was hedged by cautions that often rendered it ineffective. Oblivious that their wellsprings were Christian, the schools were assuredly secular, but parents paid more and more for their children's education in a system still alleged to be free of cost, while compulsion became little more than a jest. The argument over how to confront the problems besetting the public sector continued unabated.

In an impetuous overhaul of tertiary education devised by faceless advisors and initiated by the Federal Labor minister, John Dawkins, in the late 1980s, the nature and essence of university education changed from its old-age purpose of the pursuit and the sharing of learning to the service of the state, business and industry. With remarkable rapidity, Dawkins and his successors, who seemed determined to reduce the universities to sterile mediocrity, doubled them in number at the stroke of a pen. Student enrolments tripled, staff-student ratios fell alarmingly, tutorials were increasingly abandoned, and standards in some disciplines slipped perceptibly. Even the older universities joined in the rush to become part of the market economy; some of them appeared to be wastelands of the human spirit run by servile administrators who treated the humanities with special contempt. They were led in the main by academics – transformed overnight into managers – who debased the formerly respected title vice-chancellor while their universities competed for customers as if they were stalls at a trade fair.

Staff morale dropped, salaries remained low in comparison to those paid in comparable universities abroad, as well as to those on offer in the broader market place. More adventurous or desperate staff left for overseas; students were attracted to courses, some of which were as specious in content as the new degrees which the new universities offered. The Federal government continued to maintain that funds had not fallen and that more radical changes had to be made to a system which increasingly bore little resemblance, except in name, to that which prevailed a generation earlier. The Australian National University, managed to stave off the threat to its future in 1989 by Dawkins who was determined to amalgamate it with a neighbour institution and thus change the nature of both. Despite the economic ravages it suffered with all universities, in 2003 it was ranked 49th among the 500 leading universities in the world based on its academic and research results. In 2003, Dr Brendan Nelson, the Liberal Federal minister of education, continued the work with a series of decisions on the fate of the universities that ignored their condition and concentrated more on financial than academic matters. Shortly afterwards Barry Jones, a Labor minister of the 1980s, said that the Dawkins' 'reform' was the greatest mistake of the Hawke government.

There were, however, brighter notes. Sydney, chosen as the venue for the 2000 Olympics, attracted over 70 per cent of the new jobs in a welter of frenzied building. Some international organizers and their local representatives remained impervious to the scorn and mockery heaped on their base antics. Notwithstanding, preparations went ahead with remarkable efficiency and the event gradually took on its own momentum. In the main, the new buildings would have graced any metropolis in the world and Sydney, already a city on which nature had poured down an abundance of beauty, was further enhanced by human ingenuity. Including East Timor, 200 nations participated and the Games proved to be a triumph that brought Australia onto the world stage. Millions of viewers laughed with a pair of peerless comedians, Roy and H.G., as they commented on the day's events on television, and few Australians failed to rejoice when Cathy Freeman, an Aboriginal athlete who lit the flame at the opening ceremony, later won the women's 400 metres.

Apart from the Olympic Games, another topic in the sporting world was the state of international cricket. To those who knew that cricket in its home country, England had, until the 1850s, involved betting and sometimes bribery and that the very reason Matches rather than Games were played was because sums of money were staked on the outcome, the scandals that overtook cricket in the 1990s were scarcely a surprise. The complete professionalism of first class cricket, the huge profits made from matches played almost incessantly around the world, the advent and the wide popularity of the limited-over game, the almost fanatical attachment to it in some countries, and the national pride involved with winning Test and One-Day series quickly eroded the gentlemanly concepts of fair play and decency that had once been cricket's hallmarks. The long hallowed term 'that's not cricket' soon became a mockery. Individuals in several countries were tainted, as well as the sport itself, and the ruling body of cricket proved unable to confront the problems that had arisen. Meanwhile, under the captaincy of

Mark Taylor, followed by Stephen Waugh and Ricky Ponting, the Australian XI showed such supremacy over its rivals that it began, justly, to be compared with the great team led by Bradman in 1948 who had himself survived into the new century.

Rugby League, a game much loved by its followers in New South Wales and Queensland, had continued to suffer from the intrusion into its affairs by capitalist tycoons bent on profit, especially through the control of television rights. Its recovery was marked by the annual State-of-Origin clashes that ignited the passions of thousands of sports lovers. By 2004 Rugby League groaned under accusations of sexual misconduct by players whose idleness, drunken orgies, fame and wealth had so blinded them that civilized standards of behaviour meant nothing. In Rugby Union, the Wallabies team captained by John Eales, who was succeeded by George Gregan, showed the same mastery as the Cricket XI although England deservedly won the World Cup in 2003. In Australian Rules Football a national league composed of 16 teams from five states successfully replaced the old Victorian competition, although some of the Melbourne based teams struggled to survive. Tony Lockett, the Sydney Swans and ex-St Kilda full forward, retired in 1999. He had joined the immortals by kicking 1357 goals, making him the highest goal scorer at the top level of Australian football. Old-time commentators judged the Essendon premiership team of 2000, led by James Hird, as possessing similar greatness. When the Brisbane Lions won the premiership in 2001, 2002 and 2003, that judgement seemed threatened.

Two tragedies in the decade had different faces. In the penal era intense suffering had been visited upon thousands of convicts in a place of much beauty in Tasmania called Port Arthur. On 29 April 1996, 32 innocent people bent on a day's enjoyment died at the hands of a deranged gunman while 18 were wounded. An uncomprehending nation was grief-stricken, but some good ensued with the introduction of new gun laws that achieved the destruction of thousands of weapons. In the Snowy Mountains a building collapsed in the early hours of 31 July 1997 killing 19 many people. One young man, Stuart Diver, lay trapped under the debris alongside the body of his dead wife. He survived and was saved after an ordeal of inconceivable mental and physical suffering. The nation rejoiced because, in Diver and his intrepid rescuers, the human spirit had conquered the threat of death.

For the first time in the history of Australian democracy a malaise spread, especially among young adults, involving a deep suspicion of the value of politics. Both major parties lost membership and pre-selection procedures seemed suspect in both of them. In the Australian Labor Party there was an increasing tendency for insiders, party officials, powerful families, and candidates with a tertiary education to win pre-selection. More importantly, it became increasingly difficult to distinguish key elements of the respective party platforms from each other. The difficulty became uncomfortably evident in the sphere of economic policies. In this atmosphere, Bob Hawke's long reign as prime minister was first assailed when Paul Keating stood against him in a leadership ballot in June 1991. Hawke won, but his days were numbered and, by December, Keating had replaced him as prime minister.

The new ideology of economic rationalism, sometimes called neoclassical economics, flowered under Keating after developing in Hawke's era. This happened despite the utter incapacity of neoclassical theory, indeed any economic theory, to foretell human behaviour. Nonetheless, driven by the ill defined concept of 'globalization' and by the government's determination to bring Australia into the world of modern capitalist practices, often known as 'best practice', business, money and profit became the dominant factors in the lives of a large proportion of Australians. Never before had they taken so much interest in the All Ordinaries Index, the exchange rate of the dollar and the interest rate regularly set by the Reserve Bank. The forecasts of economists were devoured with greater avidity than those of weather experts and the *Financial Review* became the fare of thousands who had previously gone little further for their intellectual sustenance than the sports pages of the daily newspapers.

Few Australians understood economic rationalism except in its effect of making the rich richer and the poor more dependent on government handouts in order to survive. At its broadest level it demanded that less was spent on producing more to ensure that profits would increase to the few. Australia, it was argued, had to become competitive in a global economy where no barriers would be erected to curb international financial dealings. Political and financial world leaders said that globalization and free markets – not fair markets – would raise the living standards of the poor. At the same time, workers in Indonesia were paid $2 a week to make shoes for an international company. In Victoria, 140,000 women, often helped by their children, worked at home making shirts and other garments for up to fifteen hours a day at $2–3 an hour.

Understandably, this bare face of capitalism attracted interest in organizations that produced nothing, but were capable of making huge profits. This occurred in the temples of the new order, the banks, which devoted themselves to paring back their services, for which they charged higher and higher fees. They also closed their branches in many places, causing disruption and, at times, helping to further the impoverishment of country towns. Foreign banks joined local ones in cosy oligopoly and they became exemplars of what could be achieved when profits were pursued single-mindedly. In August 2000 a leading representative of the banking sector was asked whether the banks had any social responsibility. He replied with a firm negative. By August 2004 the Commonwealth Bank, having made an annual profit of $2.7 billion, threatened to sack more staff, but asserted that its services would not suffer.

There were sound reasons why the banks, and other financial concerns, started to behave in such a way in the wake of their recent downfall. Increasingly they had been profligate with funds that did not belong to them. They had made loans to entrepreneurs and other self-proclaimed financial wizards who proceeded to lose them with unfettered nonchalance and remarkable celerity. In the course of a few years billions of dollars were squandered. In addition to those who suffered directly, other people began to learn a new litany of names led by Rothwell's Bank. In 1988 the State Bank of Victoria experienced what was then the largest loss in Australia's history – $1.345 billion. The Bank of South Australia foreshadowed a possible loss of $3 billion in 1991. The Adelaide Steamship group declared a loss of $3.7 billion soon afterwards. In 1990 the Fairfax Group went into receivership and, at the end of 1992, Westpac Banking Corporation lost the comparatively modest sum of $1.56 billion. In 2003 the chairman of the Australian Mutual Provident Society (AMP) apologized for the loss of $5.5 billion of its funds.

The list of corporate casualties had grown apace: Equitcorp, Hooker Corporation, Spedley Securities, Quintex and the Bell Group were among them. Some of those responsible found it difficult to remain composed; they were unable to comprehend why they were arrested or sent to prison. George Herscu, Brian Yuill and Laurie Connell were a few of the guilty whose names became known throughout Australia. The collapse of Victoria's largest building society, Pyramid, in June 1990, caused a huge reaction. The result was that 190,000 people stood by helplessly as they watched their meagre investments slide into sand. The Victorian Labor government, led by John Cain, had refused to guarantee Pyramid's funds and, after its closure, an elderly lady rang one of the managers, pleading, 'I've got $90 in my account, can I get out $30 to buy some food?' He replied that nothing could be done for her.

Alan Bond, English born, but Australian raised, was the most flamboyant of the new financial pirates who raided the unprotected barques of private savings. His list of financial holdings included brewing and building; several of his other ventures were renowned. In 1991 Bond was sentenced to three-years imprisonment for criminal dealings in the financial world, but was later acquitted. In the end his behaviour brought its own reward with a prison term in which each day of his incarceration compensated for a million dollars of the total he had fraudulently squandered. Quick to overlook the loss of individual savings suffered by many during Bond's career of fraud and theft, some gave him credit for 'facing the music' he had composed. Others despised Christopher Skase who fled into asylum in Spain where he died leaving the comparatively paltry debt of $170 million.

Meanwhile, most Australians went about their daily lives as best they could and, despite all, that best remained one of the most admirable and least intrusive of personal liberties in the world. The Northern Territory and the Australian Capital Territory both achieved forms of representative government that added further to the structures under which their citizens laboured. In the latter case, economics rather than democracy gave point to the measure in that the Federal government wished to rid itself partially of the burden entailed in directly financing the Capital Territory. Although Canberrans had made it plain that they rejected their specious independence, they took it in good spirits. At the ensuing election in 1989 the ballot paper was almost as large as a tablecloth, but so thin and firm that some voters cut their fingers on it. One group of wits, motivated by an inspired food writer, Michael Boddy, proclaimed their right to be rid of the artificially coloured, tasteless fakes sold commercially as tomatoes and stood on a platform called the Sun Ripened Tomato Party. They attracted few votes, much amusement and a large following of new tomato growers in the Capital Territory.

The betrayal of East Timor in the 1970s bore its fruit in 1999. Indonesia was rent asunder by its own instability and by inherent economic and political weakness, which stemmed in some measure from cronyism and graft. In 1999 it finally permitted a vote on independence by the East Timorese. The result was massively pro-independence, although it had been preceded by intimidation involving much violence perpetrated by police and indigenous thugs who were led by cadres of the Indonesian military. In the wake of the vote the onslaught on the people was renewed with unrelenting ferocity. The Indonesians destroyed East Timor's social structures and economy. They murdered, raped, burnt and looted homes, businesses, churches and deported over 100,000 civilians. No count of the dead or missing was possible, and perhaps never will be, but it may run to hundreds of thousands and five years later no one has been faced with responsibility for those actions.

The Australian government, true successor of those preceding governments that had betrayed East Timor for more than a generation, was initially timid as to whether it ought play a role in halting the genocide. In October 1999, Australian military forces, operating with United Nations' troops, redeemed some of the nation's lost honour by taking a leading role in bringing peace to that unhappy country. By 2004 the past was so much forgotten by the Australian government that it engaged in an unseemly, some would say unjust, struggle against East Timor for the right to oil wells in the sea off that country. Meanwhile, unrest in West Papua continued to grow so that, in the end, Australia may yet be forced to call in another hostage given to fortune by its government in the 1960s.

Noticed and remarked upon for generations in some areas, especially in Western Australia and in the Murray–Darling Basin, the degradation of millions of hectares of land by rising salinity reached alarming proportions by the end of the Twentieth Century and official concern was aroused. That concern, however, was not translated into practical policies and the States were reluctant to undertake obligations, which the Federal government viewed with distaste. No one was prepared to curb the seemingly insatiable thirst for water among cotton, rice and fruit growers along the rivers of the Murray–Darling system. More enthusiasm was shown for spending money on very fast trains intended to serve the eastern seaboard rather than on saving the wounded land. In the fiftieth year of the Snowy Mountains Scheme, no proposal was made to again make vital use of an immigrant workforce on a national project, this time to save the rivers, which would have vast implications for the future. Concurrently, many farmers in

Queensland hastened to clear trees fearful lest the government at last take steps to stop the degradation that white occupation had wreaked upon the land. It was more the case that, for every acre planted with trees, another hundred acres were bulldozed. When El Nino caused drought to ravage the land, especially Queensland and New South Wales in 2001–3, and in parts into 2004, the dust storms that swept over the eastern seaboard, carrying millions of tons of soil and seeds out to sea, were a portent of what was yet to come and the threat to the future began to penetrate the dullest of minds.

In the Northern Territory, long an almost forgotten segment of the continent and regarded as no more than a stop over to Asia and places further north, a story of almost untold potential began to unfold. With less than 200,000 people living in an area twice the size of Texas, its enormous resources in natural gas, oil and minerals were said to be worth over $200 billion. The growth rate in population was the highest in the country at over 12 per cent and its economic growth rate was over 6 per cent compared to 4.3 per cent nationally. The building of a rail line to Darwin costing $1.3 billion, completed in 2004, and the rebuilding of its port were seen as keys to greater economic expansion and growth in population. Darwin, closer to Singapore than to Sydney or Melbourne, teeming with diverse races and throbbing with vitality, impresses all who visit it. In its hinterland the vast and splendid abundance of natural wonders in places such as Kakadu and Uluru make the Northern Territory a mecca for thousands of tourists.

As the end of 1999 drew close the millenarian movements of the past, anticipating the return of the Saviour or the appearance of the horsemen of the Apocalypse, were mocked by fear of a bug that was said to threaten the technological wonders of the age, including traffic lights. The meaning of the millennium was forgotten except among a minority, but the bug proved to be of no consequence although billions were spent to prevent its ravages. Amidst much hilarity, accompanied by fireworks and champagne, the date some believed added up to a millenium passed without a technological mishap. A few months later, when a virus called the 'Love Bug' posed a genuine threat, little notice was taken of its potentiality among those who were flattered by its proffered embrace. The damage to computer systems was disastrous, especially in the United States where promise overshadowed reality.

For several years, some enthusiasts had prompted the Federal government to celebrate the centenary of Federation in 2001 with ceremonies befitting its importance. Most Australians remained nonchalant about the event, despite the millions spent on it and the fanfare organized to ensure participation. In a manner reminiscent of their forebears they took it for granted that Australia would remain an entity in itself in which the citizens would live under common laws in moderate peace and harmony. To a very marked degree their aspirations over a space of four generations had been realized. The pragmatism that gave birth to a federated Australia was so low key, so careful not to offend state sensibilities, so minimalist and gradual, even in its centralization in the hands of a government based in Canberra, that no one could seriously complain about it. Headlines in newspapers never wearied of trumpeting that Canberra had done or not done this or that but, apart from a mild moan or murmur, the vast majority of people went about their affairs with acceptance or bored resignation. There were always better things to do than get over excited about politics, and Federation, with all the trappings and irritants of a federal system of government, as well as its immense benefits, was here to stay.

Nonetheless there were stirrings of nationality in the last years of the old millennium that promised change of a radical nature. During and after World War I, republicanism had lacked scarcely a vestige of respectability. The threat of invasion, with the necessity of turning from Britain to America for protection in World War II, did surprisingly little to awaken the thirst for independence. In the 1970s some small voices had been raised in favour of a republic, but they remained unheard. By the 1990s, although many Australians wanted to know who they were and where they stood in the world, there was much of the high quality of nationality and little nationalism in the seeking of the great majority. All they wanted was to be themselves and proclaim their selfdom in a simple gesture.

Much had also changed in that, by 2001, there was a heightened awareness of Australia's geographical place and its social, economic and political role in the Pacific and on the edge of Asia. It was a part of the world where several other peoples had shed their dependence on foreign powers in the previous forty years. At the same time Britain became economically a part of Europe and the royal house of Windsor proved that its was as full of human weakness as any other dwelling in the kingdom. Within Australia, despite the loss of those who had fled its shores to use their talents in the cultural and intellectual capitals of the Northern Hemisphere, there had been a flowering. It took place in art, music and song, the stage and theatre, poetry and prose, in science and medicine, industry and agriculture and in countless other ways. Throughout the land, in city and bush, numerous Australians had stood up to proclaim that this land could produce its own precious fruits of the human spirit. It seemed at last that the day had dawned when a new development of conscious independence among the generality of the people could take place.

Prime Minister Paul Keating Keating knew that the economic restructuring initiated by him and Bob Hawke had produced a widening gap between the power elites and everyone else, as well as a new ideology that ended the essential difference between Labor and the parties of conservatism. Turning to the politics of identity expressed by the idea of a republic and to reconciliation with the Aborigines, Keating thought that he could offer a prospect that would serve to disguise the economic thrust and inspire positive feelings of hope in the people.

Keating expressed the arguments for a republic in simple terms. A strong anti-British strand dominated his emotions, and cutting the ties with the monarchy seemed to be his major objective. The retention of ultimate power by the prime minister and parliament was also dear to him. His whole adult life had revolved around his becoming a member of parliament and, finally, its head. To him, parliament and the role of the prime minister were sacrosanct and any talk of the people as the ultimate source of all political power was deemed to be arrant populism. He decided to replace the governor-general with a president and, by taking that simple step, Australia would be a republic. Minimal change to the Constitution would thereby be demanded and the Queen would become, in law, what she already was in fact – a foreigner. Keating, furthermore, was convinced that great danger lay in permitting the people any say in the creation of a president. The way to proceed in this matter was for the prime minister to decide who would be president after which parliament would rubber stamp the appointment.

Having consulted largely among themselves, the leaders of the Australian Republican Movement, formed in mid-1991, accepted Keating's ideas with enthusiasm. The movement claimed to represent Australian republicanism and continued to do so despite the fact that, when asked, up to 75 per cent of the people said they wanted to vote for the president. As if that were not sufficiently ominous for the ultimate outcome, the overwhelming victory of the coalition led by John Howard in the Federal election of 2 March 1996 put paid to any realistic hope of an Australian republic in the short term.

Howard was an avowed monarchist to whom Australian nationality was a cliché expressed principally in cricket. In February 1998 he engineered a so-called People's Convention to which he appointed half the delegates. Its purpose was to devise a formula on which the people would vote in a referendum.

Led by the Australian Republican Movement the Convention came up with a version of Keating's model that Howard gleefully accepted in the confident hope that the electorate would reject it. The real purpose behind the model was to achieve a republic, but also to eliminate the people from any meaningful role in the appointment of the president. In effect, the president was to be the creature of the prime minister whom he could both appoint and dismiss at will. In such a way an Australian, democratic republic was to come into being.

The referendum of 6 November 1999 did not ask the people whether they wanted a republic, but only whether they wanted the one devised by the Convention. As was expected, the referendum failed miserably in all States, as did the proposed new preamble to the Constitution, which had been manufactured jointly by Howard and a poet and was judged almost universally to be a silly, if not hilarious, document. In the event, the people proved that their sense of democracy was far keener than that of the leaders of society, including large segments of the media, the judiciary and other notables ranging from comedians to heroes of the playing fields. The new economic structures had already alienated the elites from the majority of electors who no longer trusted either them or the republican model created for their passive acceptance. In the end, the republican model was rejected because the ordinary people saw that those who had done more than anyone else to dismantle national sovereignty, Keating, Howard and the economic globalisers, were advocating a model that rejected their involvement. They had only one weapon left and they used it at the ballot box. Thus perished, temporarily, the promise of an Australian republic. It was done to death by those who conceived its form, rather than by the people who wanted its genuine substance.

During the first years of his prime ministership John Howard had often been reminded that integrity, compassion and a vision for the nation based on justice and truth would strike a high note in the conscience of the nation. To his increasing discomfort these values were embodied in the person of the governor-general, William Deane, who expressed them in deed and word and was widely admired and valued as a person. That Deane made no effort to hide his Catholicism possibly prompted Howard to act as he did when the opportunity came to replace Deane in 2001. He did so with the Anglican archbishop of Brisbane, Peter Hollingworth, who had become known to some sections of the public in his previous career as the hard working head of a worthy body, the Brotherhood of St Lawrence, which was devoted to the poor and the disadvantaged. Christian churches had ceased to play a foremost role in public life and no longer attracted the animosity of zealots and bigots as they had done in the past. Thus, the appointment of an archbishop to the highest civil office in the land aroused only mild opposition, even though it had the clear overtones of a violation of the distinction between church and state.

Hollingworth was unfortunate in two respects. He could not hope, or even dare [given Howard's attitude], to emulate Deane and he thereby became a mere puppet of the prime minister. The execrable and inhuman behaviour of the government in respect to refugees elicited no response from the former Christian clergyman. Hollingworth was also unfortunate in that he fell into the maelstrom created by the wave of accusations of pederasty by Christian clergy. When some Anglican clergy accused the governor-general of covering up cases of abuse during his period of office as archbishop of Brisbane, Hollingworth's reputation was severely wounded. Henceforward, what he said or did ceased to have genuine relevance in the eyes of the public. Howard thereby achieved his objective in that a silent, almost ghostlike, figurehead posed no obstacle to his determination to be the unique leader of the nation. By early 2003 the governor-general had no option but to resign. Howard replaced him with a former soldier, Michael Jeffrey, who had been lieutenant–governor of Western Australia.

From his first days of holding office Howard embraced the economic policies already in place and added to their rigor. Humane instincts were dampened among those Liberal politicians who had believed in the value of a social safety net, the duty of society to support the disadvantaged, and the need to moderate the gap between rich and poor. Few commentators seemed to realize that a new ideology was sweeping the world and that there were no barriers to its spread. Communism, Fascism and Nazism, with their worship of class, state and race, had all been replaced with the worship of the ultimate god of materialism. The concept of economic rationalism hid a grim reality because it was a form of totalitarian materialism. In this new world, no transcendent objective was judged to be desirable other than corporate and personal gain through the manipulation of market forces. The only yardstick was an economic one based on an absolute faith in the free market, which ignored the fact that the law of demand and supply cannot even be defined, thus rendering it meaningless. Furthermore, the existence of free trade as other than a catchcry was constrained by the fact that only 15 per cent of trade lies outside the control of governments or transnational corporations.

Governments had to conform or else the inflow of capital, upon which they relied for the good of their societies, would diminish. In the Nineteenth Century the Americans belatedly abolished local slavery. In the Twentieth Century they reinvented it at a distance in the countries of the Third World where millions toiled for a pittance producing goods that, as a by-product, threw many thousands of Australians, among others, out of work. This effect was most notable in firms making footwear and clothing. The wealth of the transnational corporations was impervious to accountability and they were easily able to avoid social responsibility by tax evasion. Meanwhile, it was calculated by a United Nations Development Program that $26 billion annually would suffice to provide basic education, water, sanitation, health services and nutrition for the world's millions who lacked such vital well springs of human life. The combined sums spent annually in the United States on cosmetics and pet food, added to that spent by Europeans on ice cream, was more than the required $26 billion.

The new fundamentalists, often more rigid than their religious counterparts, valued human beings on their capacity to produce and contribute to the growth of profits. Induced to retire by 'golden handshakes', or to be made redundant without mercy, many thousands, whose experience and dedication the nation could ill afford to lose, disappeared from the workforce. Making a mockery of the hard won 8 hour day and the 40 hour week that stemmed back to the 1850s, the new economy led to a rise in overtime seen previously only in wartime so that Australians worked more hours per week than any other people on earth. Enterprise bargaining began to destroy the basis of a just wage and a rash of amalgamations tended to remove the human element still possible in smaller bodies.

To the distress of many who had given their lives to an honourable service of the public, the government set about shaping a new order. Under it the public service, increasingly politicized at its higher levels, became a handmaiden of the government and was slashed viciously in numbers in the first years of Howard's prime ministership. Unsurprisingly, the health system bade fair to grind to a halt in some States. The union movement – annually decreasing in numbers and strength – represented only a quarter of the workforce and was reduced in numbers from 323 unions in 1985 to 157 in 1995. As an organized force it was often helpless when those wanting to work accepted whatever employers offered. In that situation the much vaunted and united strength of the workers became a whisper from the past. Uniformed thugs, accompanied by snarling dogs, crushed a revolt by the dockworkers in Melbourne in April 1998. On this occasion unrestrained capitalism bared its fangs too markedly. The High Court issued a ruling that saw the Maritime Union members return to the docks.

To the thousands, especially women, who were forced to accept part-time jobs, most notably in the service industries and especially in that of hospitality where 50 per cent of the jobs were casual, work bore no resemblance to a vocation and the bonds previously created within the workforce between employees and employers were destroyed or weakened. When unemployment fell to an official rate of around 6 per cent in 2000, it was idle to point out that 75 per cent of the new jobs were part-time, that there were about 700,000 unemployed and that only 100,000 jobs were on offer. To add further insult to common sense in reckoning the rate of unemployment, it was decreed that only two hours in a week had to be worked to cause one's name to be removed from the list of the unemployed. In 1987 Bob Hawke had promised that no child would be living in poverty by the year 2000. By 2003, poverty, everywhere increasingly apparent [as the Salvation Army, the St Vincent de Paul and other societies who worked among the poor testified], seemed to be accepted as a natural element in the new capitalist state. In the end some of the church organization received sums of money from the government to do work that hitherto they had tried, and often succeeded magnificently, in doing for nothing.

One fundamental plank of the new economics was that no government ought to own an asset or do work that could be more profitably owned, or done, by private enterprise. The new way was to contract out or sell to the private sector the assets and services of large elements of the public sector. In 1985 Prime Minister Hawke had described the privatisation of public assets as a recipe for disaster. In the event, and beginning under Labor, it became almost obligatory to sell off, in whole or in part, national assets, such as Qantas, Telstra and the Commonwealth Bank that had been initially paid for from the common purse. The sale of the Commonwealth Bank was opposed by 64 per cent of the electorate and at no time was there general acceptance of privatization. In the twenty years up to, and including, the sale of Sydney airport in 2002, $155 billion worth of public assets had been sold off. Most of them increased their charges immediately.

At the same time government departments vied with one another in outsourcing to private concerns, or to individuals, work previously done by public servants. The worthy task of settling refugees in the community, largely undertaken by voluntary bodies, was put out to tender, as was much of the work of government utilities designed to help the unemployed find work. Even the Australian Broadcasting Commission, hitherto a respected and treasured public utility, suffered drastic cuts including the sale to a Christian fundamentalist organization of its facilities for broadcasting into Asia. After disturbances in several parts of Asia and the Pacific in 2000, the government began to resurrect its Asian network at a cost far greater than would have been the case had it not been sold. Meanwhile a new head of the ABC set about dismantling its structures, replacing its managers and paving the way for its commercialization, thereby threatening its most valuable attribute, independence. General unrest within the organization led to the termination of his employment in 2002, as it did to that of the chairman, another Howard appointee, in 2004.

The 'Asian Meltdown', caused by the collapse of the 'Tiger' economies of the region in the late 1990s, occurred adjacent to an Australian economy that seemed relatively immune from the disasters overwhelming its neighbours. It was hailed as a sign of good management by both government and business. In response, the chief executives of leading business organizations began to receive annual salaries, with their associated perks, up to 200 times higher than that of the average wage of a factory worker. When scandals among financial managers in America were revealed, followed by similar ones in such failed enterprises as HIH and Onetel in Australia, the government finally began to notice the rapacity, fraud, incompetence and sheer thievery that had become widespread. One minister, oblivious of the gross injustice of such a system, lamented that the greed of the CEO's cast a slur on the dignity and integrity of market capitalism. In early 2003, one retiring executive was rewarded with $33 million but, despite a public outcry, the response of the government was merely a lament.

In the last decade of its 100 years of history, the leadership of the A.L.P. managed to turn the humane direction of the party around and, in so doing, abandoned the idealism and vision that had been its lodestars. Never before had the A.L.P. consciously chosen policies that would make the poor poorer, the rich richer, the nation meaner and the dole queues longer. All this happened, and was justified, excused and done in the name of economic rationalism. The nation was increasingly divided into two segments, the rich and the poor, with a struggling and puzzled middle class in between.

Concomitant with an apparently booming economy, thousands of children remained homeless, people queued up in public hospitals for operations and 'work for dole' schemes became normal. In 2001 the nation watched with incredulity as the once-flourishing and admired Ansett airline dissolved in debt with the loss of 15,000 jobs. House prices rose in all capital cities, generally to startling levels, and the Australian dream of universal home ownership became a nightmare for many. Those investors who bought an additional home, or more than one, remained unaffected until interest rates rose in late 2003 and the market responded in kind. Few young couples could afford a home unless both worked, sometimes causing the indefinite postponement of a family. Amidst all this the Liberal government persisted in proclaiming its fear that too many people were becoming 'welfare dependent'. Depending 'on welfare' replaced being 'on the dole' as a term of opprobrium. The old, and noble, ideals that society should bear some responsibility for its weaker members and that the purpose of an economic system is to provide for the whole of society were rapidly being lost.

In 1995, John Howard declared 'There is no way in which we can have it [a Goods' and Services Tax] as part of our policy for the next election'. He was soon to change his mind. In 2000 the government spent $360 million on advertising the introduction of this regressive tax that hit especially hard at low-income earners, pensioners and owners of small businesses. The latter were turned into tax collectors. Known as the GST, it was widely applied, although most foodstuffs, but not books, were grudgingly removed from its ambit. The ALP, led by Kim Beazley, promised to rollback some of the GST's more punitive measures and partly used the tax against the government in the 2001 election. Howard won the election despite every indication in the preceding weeks that he would lose it; Beazley resigned as leader of the A.L.P. and was replaced by Simon Crean.

The election in 2001, called by some 'The Tampa election', was won principally due to a series of events without parallel in Australian history. In partial response to changing international relations with Asia, from the mid-1990s a curious phenomenon arose on the political and social spectrum. The One Nation Party, led by Pauline Hanson, was a blend of nationalism, racism, jingoism, naiveté and fear. It exerted a wide appeal, particularly in country areas. Confused, and often worse off financially, suspicious of governments and slow to accept a changing world, some voters thought that they saw in Hanson and her message a reawakening of an old world and its values, in which they had been comfortable. One Nation would have had little impact and done little damage had it not also contained anti-Aboriginal and anti-immigrant elements destructive of social harmony and dangerous to national unity. Despite the fact that John Howard long remained silent on Hanson, and ensured that his government did likewise, the electorate – after an initial period of enthusiasm – rejected her and the One Nation Party, although it did win about 8 per cent of the national vote in the 1998 election. Those who imagined that the bitter roots of Hansonism – fear, envy and racism – would vanish with her political demise were mistaken.

Inexorably the new economics affected immigration. A large portion of the immigrants was restricted to those with money and/or, skills, while the number given shelter on humanitarian grounds was restricted. Continued disturbances and totalitarian regimes in parts of Asia, Africa, Europe and the Middle East bore heavily on millions who desperately sought a safe haven in a new country. The increasing phenomenon of 'boat people', arriving on Australian shores in frail and unsuitable vessels, after paying for their passage to unscrupulous human scavengers, occasioned alarm. On their arrival, the government used a series of 'detention centres' or prisons, which had been initially set up by the ALP in 1992, to contain and restrain them. They were, [and remain], compounds, mostly situated in remote localities, where they were surrounded by razor wire. Their minders or guards, more rightly called mercenaries, were equipped with means to restrain them, which were more suitable to concentration camps. Among the 'detainees' in these prisons there were many families so that, in contravention of every human impulse and the conventions on refugees of the United Nations, signed by Australia, children became, and were treated as, prisoners.

The regimes in Iraq, Iran and, eventually, Afghanistan under the Taliban in the late 1990s, caused thousands of homeless and persecuted people to flee, some of whom found their way to Pakistan and neighbouring places. Assisted, and often swindled, by 'people smugglers' their point of final departure became Indonesia, whence they set out in unseaworthy, overcrowded vessels for the shores of northwestern Australia. The Coalition government responded with alacrity to this new phenomenon although the numbers in question, even had they all been accepted into Australia, would not have upset the equilibrium of society in general. For example, in one of the crucial years, 1999–00, 4174 'boat people' arrived seeking asylum. They were entitled to do so under international law so that they were not 'illegals'. The accusation that they were 'queue jumpers; was groundless, given that no queues existed in the places from which they had fled.

In the same period there were 1695 unauthorized entries by air and 53,000 people overstayed their visas and remained in Australia illegally. Taking a strong stand against what was portrayed as a veritable deluge of 'boat people'; proclaiming repeatedly the right of a sovereign people to defend its borders; dwelling on the threat of imported diseases; hinting that there may be terrorists among them – all this came easily to the lips of a government which, in the wake of Hansonism, had perceived that votes were to be won among Australians by such propaganda.

In this atmosphere of suspicion and carefully nurtured fear, the event known since as '9/11' (11 September, 2001) took place in New York. Categorized immediately as terrorists, homicidal criminals, proclaiming their belief in Allah and their assurance of happiness in eternity, took their own lives when they murdered some 3,000 citizens going about their daily business in New York and Washington. Millions of words were spoken and written in an attempt to understand the reason for such barbarity. Since the death of the Prophet, the West was seen among some of his followers as the land of the infidel. From the days of the Crusaders onwards, the seeds of jealousy and hatred sown by the representatives of the West, and cultivated by some of the leaders of Islam, lay partially dormant. They eventually flourished in the bosoms of a ghostly murderer and his acolytes who gave September 11 to the world. If a new age dawned on that day, it was spawned as the vilest possible expression of criminality. In such a thin atmosphere justice and peace, to say nothing of love, remained frail flowers.

The stage was set for the government to reap a harvest from the understandable fear of terrorism and the unknown among the general population so, shortly before the Federal election of 10 November 2001, a public relations scheme was designed to convince the people that it was prepared to take even harsher measures against 'boat people'. The scheme began in late August when a Norwegian vessel, the *Tampa*, was refused permission to land on Christmas Island. The *Tampa* carried a cargo of 'boat people' whom its noble captain, Arne Rinnan, – mindful of his responsibilities towards those suffering a disaster at sea – had rescued from a sinking vessel. The implications of the use of the Australian armed forces in the affair, especially the army and navy, were grave. The complicity of high level public servants in covering up what was happening was worse. These high matters were lost in a welter of applause for the government's action by many and of disapproval by a minority.

To make its point on 'boat people' more starkly to a national and international audience, the government then set about the implementation of a 'Pacific solution' to the problem by processing the applications of asylum seekers on foreign soil which meant that, even were they declared to be genuine refugees, the government was not obliged to grant then asylum in Australia. The ravaged island of Nauru was especially chosen for this venture. The government also decided to implement a hair-brained scheme whereby 4900 small islands in Torres Strait would be officially declared not to be part of Australia and thus 'out of bounds', as it were, to refugees.

The darkest chapter in this ignominious assault on humanity was the fate of Suspected Illegal Entry Vessel Number Ten (known officially by its chilling acronym SIEV X). It was a small vessel overcrowded with more than 400 people which sank, drowning 353, in late October 2001. Some expert commentators went as far as accusing the government, and the armed forces, of complicity with the Indonesian police and army in the affair. If true, it only added to the infamy of an already tainted regime. One thing, however, was soon clear. The campaign was successful and 'boat people', understandably, ceased attempting to cross the waters between Indonesia and Australia. The actions of the government were thereby vindicated in the eyes of its supporters and some sick members of a nation duped by lies rejoiced when a vessel holding 14 people was stopped in 2004.

The government was presented with a further, and undreamt of, vote winner a few days before the election in 2001. At official levels it was stated that, when a final vessel, SIEV IV, had been apprehended by the Australian navy, some parents had attempted to throw their children overboard. The government persisted in piously proclaiming its horror at such inhuman behaviour on the part of parents, in this case doubly unfortunate parents because they were Iraqis and therefore naturally subject to suspicion in days when all Iraq suffered from ignominy of its dictator. Ministers and officials persisted in this treachery despite their being informed that there was no proof that throwing children overboard had taken place and that photographs used to prove that it had were false, the responsible minister, Phillip Reith, rather than being forced to recant, lied almost daily without compunction and was later rewarded handsomely for his perfidy.

Despite the fact that all such events had been strictly under the personal control of the prime minister, John Howard persisted in denying that he knew anything about what had truly happened. The historical data records for posterity that he had been unwearied in proclaiming a falsehood to the Australian people. No series of events in Australia's history ever approached the baseness of the means willingly chosen by a government to retain power. Those means were not to cease and when, despite the increased surveillance, a decrepit vessel loaded with 53 souls from Vietnam slipped past the net and reached Australian waters, Immigration Minister Ruddock, consistent in his determination to behave inhumanly to refugees, sent them off on a naval vessel to Christmas Island to be processed out of sight and mind.

In respect of immigration generally, the highest and finest tribute to the growth of Australian nationality was the way in which most Australians willingly embraced the dispossessed of other nations and races. Although the great riches that had been poured out on Australia by the new settlers were often praised, too frequently they were appreciated almost solely for the diversity they introduced in food and its preparation. Much timidity was shown in speaking of another precious factor. Homogeneous races, especially those confined to islands like Britain and Ireland, or peninsulas such as Italy and Greece, run the risk of growing old, inward looking, uninventive and smug. Australians, inhabiting an island continent, and made up predominantly of white races for 170 years, had begun to run that risk, but the influx of new peoples dispelled the danger for centuries to come. That new thing, that precious blending of races, lies at the heart of and courses through the blood of the new Australia.

In the wake of September 11, the Australian government had sent forces to participate in the pacification of Afghanistan where they carried on the high traditions of their forebears in combat. When the Taliban seemed subdued, at least temporarily, and an acceptable structure of government was set up in Afghanistan by mid-2002, the American government under President George Bush became preoccupied about the regime in Iraq. Bush saw it as a threat to world security given its possession of weapons of mass destruction. Prime Minister Tony Blair, stood alongside and even led Bush in threatening war against Iraq.

John Howard publicly proclaimed that he would not send Australian troops into Iraq to rid its people of their demonic ruler, Saddam Hussein. He eventually conceded that it would engage Australians in Iraq if George Bush decided that the threat of weapons demanded war. Despite the general acceptance of America as a firm ally and friend for decades among Australians, many saw the proposed war as fruitful of much greater evil, as well as unproven in respect of the grounds for its provocation. No weapons of mass destruction were subsequently found. John Howard then began to justify the war on the grounds he had previously rejected and asked everyone to rejoice in the overthrow of Hussein.

In early 2003 thousands of Australians assembled to protest at the sending of their armed forces to stand with the Americans in a war against Iraq. They were heard, partly mocked and not heeded by those responsible for the decision. The war, in which Australian troops were involved and much praised for their skills and valour, was duly prosecuted. Within a few weeks President Bush declared that victory had been achieved. In its wake Iraqi resistance continued and grew worse daily while the civilized world recoiled at photos of the obscene actions perpetrated on the bodies of Iraqi prisoners by American functionaries. Despite the setting up of a provisional government in Iraq in mid 2004, the conversion of the people of Iraq to Western forms of democracy seemed far distant.

An event, which both horrified and alarmed all Australians, took place in Bali on 11 October 2002. As unprovoked and indiscriminate in its effects as '9/11' in America, the murder of about 100 Australians, as well as many of other nationalities, including Balinese, brought the shameful antics of the same homicidal maniacs, still operating under the banner of terrorism onto Australia's doorstep. In this way the new age ushered in by 11 September 2001 continued into 2002 and beyond.

On 6 September 2000 a frail but vibrant man had visited the Australian National University in Canberra. It was ten years to the day since Nelson Mandela's release from 27 years imprisonment by a brutal, racist regime in his homeland, South Africa. He spoke of his past without a shred of bitterness, but in words that implored all people to live in reconciliation and peace and share those gifts with the whole of the human race. Humbly, he asked Australians to help his own people in the huge task of building a united, educated and prosperous nation. A Mandela passes rarely across the canvass of history, but his true meaning to others, especially to the timid, the weak and the downtrodden, is that the human spirit can rise up and conquer adversity. Belief in human rights, justice, and democracy, as well as in the innate dignity of every human being is not the prerogative of any individual, even of those few who become the Mandelas of the ages. These truths also belong to every Australian.

***

At the opening of the new millennium it is too late to return to the almost ageless days of Aboriginal occupation of Australia and try to recreate the ways and culture of those ages. Yet it is not too late to embrace and treasure the high values that were developed since the beginning of the Dreaming: a sense of oneness with the land and an ability to wonder at its mystery, to rejoice in its harshness and in its beauty. These things can flourish, grow strong and become vital again. A determination to protect the land in its frailty, and to preserve the unique gifts of nature that grow and move upon it, are sacred obligations that brook no other choice. To beg the Aborigines to proffer the gift of forgiveness and to join in being one people is an action that surpasses words. The dead, black and white, implore the living that the deed will be done so that all Australians may begin to live in honour and unity.

For many Australians there were reasons why their hope in a future Australia began to falter in the late 1990s and continued to do so into the new millenium. If they had only reflected on the past, their own past, the elderly should not have cast down their heads. Many of them had seen Australia go into a Great Depression and come through it scarred, but not beaten. They had helped at home and abroad to drive back the wave of invasion southwards from Japan. They had lived to trade with the Japanese and to welcome them in thousands as tourists. They had opened their doors and their hearts to almost six million new people from 100 different countries and watched with gratitude, as those new ones became Australians. With an enduring act of tolerance and acceptance they had wiped away much of the old phobia of race and colour and participated in the building of a nation transformed and immeasurably enriched. In their lifetime, some had seen the Australian population grow from five million to twenty million.

The old also had memories passed on to them in story and folktale from earlier times. Those memories spoke of drought, of falling prices, of land manias that burst, of bank failures, of poverty and epidemics, of strikebreakers and police oppression and all the other woes that beset the human condition. The same people who suffered these things built the homes, towns, cities and their suburbs, factories, bush churches and city cathedrals. They traced and mapped the land with roads, railways and bridges, telephone and telegraph lines to make communication through a continent possible. They formed the farmers' and workers' movements, and the political parties. They laughed and drank tea and beer together, even when they differed.

Because a sense of belonging to the land and to each other was growing in the fibre of their being, no one had to tell them that they were Australians. In that way they were able to take the step to Federation without anger, much less bloodshed. They knew that the work of nation building was never done because, daily, there had to be renewal, the surmounting of obstacles and a stretching out for a better future for themselves and for their children. At the base of much of their history was a common striving for democracy with its recognition of human values and equality. In many ways they succeeded in creating a simple form of democracy unburdened by theory and impossible visions because they knew its only blueprint was that of life. To live and grow and spread its values, democracy had to be born day-by-day in the hearts and minds of its upholders. When they said to each other, 'fair go, mate', they expressed the essence of both Australian democracy and of social justice.

The old should not despair of the future. The young, too, must resist ever thinking of the future without hope. They have no time to do so because there is so much to be done. They cannot sit idly by bewailing the lack of purposeful and clear-headed leadership, the loss of high and demanding goals, the demeaning of the parliamentary process, the clouding of democratic ideals and a widespread sense of futility that saps national confidence. Nothing is gained by their merely railing against privatisation and globalization, ringing their hands over the depopulation of country towns and the daily loss of services to them. The almost bewildering development of technology, with its impact on all aspects of society, should exhilarate rather than demoralize them because, with the right will and fruitful education, it can all be turned to great good. Above all, they must throttle the waves of cynicism that rise in them when they behold the pitiful chicanery impeding the thrust towards nationality and the shameful refusal to achieve reconciliation with the Aborigines. Reconciliation and the true meaning of nationality are waiting to become the genuine marks of the Australian people. All that will happen when the young proclaim in word and deed that they belong to the land and to each other. Nothing will part them from either.

Hope, deeper thought, planning and cooperation will give rise to new things. Political parties can be revitalized. If not they will die and give place to others. A new spirit can permeate parliaments and renew trust in the people. Globalization, like capitalism itself, will feed on its essence and collapse unless it is humanized. High ideals and noble deeds can only be upheld and done by men and women who believe in the inalienable rights and precious dignity of the human person. The inordinate growth of vast urban centres can be controlled once there is a firm dedication to plan and effect decentralization. There are no barriers to the human spirit, no problems created by other humans that cannot be surpassed by the brave. New powerhouses of education can arise where teachers and taught become a genuine community resisting every drive to make them into producers and products.

A new world of justice and peace cannot be created without the determination, the energy, the integrity and, above all, the hope of the young. In the past they were looked to and sacrificed as the bastions of national defence. The future makes another, and even greater, call. This time the young are called to create anew on those foundations laid by their ancestors that they accept as true and good. It is a high and noble work. Only the young can do it.

Index